THE PRONUNCIATION

OF

10,000 PROPER NAMES

GIVING

FAMOUS GEOGRAPHICAL AND BIOGRAPHICAL
NAMES, NAMES OF BOOKS, WORKS OF ART,
CHARACTERS IN FICTION,
FOREIGN TITLES, Etc.

BY

MARY STUART MACKEY

AND

MARYETTE GOODWIN MACKEY, B. A

NEW YORK

DODD, MEAD AND COMPANY

1909

UNIVERSITY PRESS · JOHN WILSON
AND SON · CAMBRIDGE, U. S. A.

Printing Statement:

Due to the very old age and scarcity of this book, many of the pages may be hard to read due to the blurring of the original text, possible missing pages, missing text, dark backgrounds and other issues beyond our control.

Because this is such an important and rare work, we believe it is best to reproduce this book regardless of its original condition.

Thank you for your understanding.

To the Memory

OF

JOHN ROSEBERY MACKEY,

THIS LITTLE BOOK IS DEDICATED.

PREFACE

It is hoped that this little book may be found useful by those who have not access to the large works in which alone the pronunciation of proper names has been given, or who find the large volumes inconvenient to handle. We have been able to include many names of recent interest which are not to be found in any other work, since they have come into prominence within the last two years.

We acknowledge our indebtedness to the standard works, but for words never included in these we take pleasure in expressing our obligations to Rev. Edward A. Steiner for help on Slavic names; to the officials of the War Department for assistance on Philippine names and geography; to Mrs. Alice Gordon Gulick for advice in regard to Spanish words; and to

Mrs. L. J. Ormsbee for help on the Samoan names. We also gladly take this opportunity to make known our appreciation of the assistance given us by Mr. E. E. Treffry, formerly of the staffs of the Century and Standard Dictionaries, who carefully examined the manuscript and made many valuable suggestions which we have adopted.

THE AUTHORS.

SANDUSKY, OHIO,
    March 9, 1901.

TABLE OF SIGNS, MARKS, AND ABBREVIATIONS.

ā as in fāte, āte.
ă " făt, ăt.
ä " fäther, mámmä.
â " fâre, câre.
à " sodà, àsk.

ē " mēte, wē.
ĕ " mĕt, bĕd.
ẽ " hẽr, fathẽr.

ī " fīle, sīte.
ĭ " fĭll, sĭt.

ō as in nōte, ōpen.
ŏ " nŏt, bŏx.
ô " ôr, fôr.
ŏ̄ " whŏlly.
ōō " fōol, sōoth.
ŏŏ as in lŏok, bŏok.

ū " ūse, attenūated.
ŭ " ŭs, flŭsh.
ü " *Fr.* sur, *Ger.* über.

adj.	for	adjective.	Lat.	for	Latin.
Am.	"	American.	loc.	"	local.
Arab.	"	Arabic.	L.	"	Lake.
Bib.	"	Bible, Biblical.	mod.	"	modern.
Boh.	"	Bohemian.	n.	"	noun.
class.	"	classical.	Nor.	"	Norwegian.
D.	"	Dutch.	Pers.	"	Persian.
Dan.	"	Danish.	pop.	"	popularly.
Eng.	"	English, England.	Port.	"	Portuguese.
Fl.	"	Flemish.	R.	"	River.
Fr.	"	French.	Russ.	"	Russian.
Ger.	"	German.	Sc.	"	Scotch.
Gr.	"	Greek.	Shak.	"	Shakespeare.
Heb.	"	Hebrew.	Sp.	"	Spanish.
Hind.	"	Hindu.	Sw.	"	Swedish.
Hung.	"	Hungarian.	St.	"	Saint.
I.	"	Island.	Turk.	"	Turkish.
Ice.	"	Icelandic.			

SOUNDS AND MARKS USED IN GIVING PRONUNCIATION.

ch is pronounced as in **choose**.

ċh   "   "   *Sc.* lo**ċh**, *Ger.* a**ċh**.

g is always hard in the pronunciation, as in **get**.

h   "   an aspirated sound.

·h is strongly aspirated, as in ·**hither**, ·**horrid**.

ng is pronounced as in **ring**.

ṅ   "   "   "   *Fr.* bo**ṅ**-bo**ṅ**.

oi   "   "   "   **oil**.

ow   "   "   "   **now**.

sh   "   "   "   **show**.

th   "   "   "   **thin**.

ťh   "   "   "   **thither**.

y   "   "   "   a consonant, as in **you**.

zh   "   "   "   **s** in **treasure**.

⌣ indicates a rapid pronunciation or running together of two syllables : as **Mercier**, mârs-ẹ̄-ā′, almost mârs-yā′.

′ indicates the principal accent.

″   "   "   secondary, or weaker accent.

NOTES ON SOUNDS IN FOREIGN LANGUAGES.

In all cases foreign sounds should be learned from a native, if possible. In many cases they can be indicated only approximately by English sounds. Some have *no* equivalent in English.

French.

1. **e** and **eu** are both sounded peculiarly in French. They have been indicated in most cases by ĕ as in **hĕr**. It should be remembered that this is *not the exact* sound.

xi

2. e at the end of a French word, and sometimes between two syllables, is pronounced very lightly. At the end of a word this has been indicated by the syllable **yu,** with the tie ⌣. Example, **Allemagne, äl-män′-yŭ.** This slight sound is lost in rapid speech, but should be indicated, rather than pronounced, when the word is spoken deliberately.

3. u is pronounced like the German ü. These sounds are not heard in English, but are between ū in flūte, and **w**ee in sweet. They are indicated by ü.

4. n in French has no equivalent in English. It is like a smothered **ng**, and is sometimes so indicated in dictionaries. But it is a worse fault to give it the full **ng** sound than to keep it a simple English **n.** It is indicated by ṅ.

5. **r** is rolled in the throat in a way difficult for an English-speaking person to acquire.

German.

1. **ch** is a strongly aspirated sound, and has no equivalent in English. If it is impossible to acquire this sound, it is perhaps best to use hard **c** or **k** instead. It is indicated by ċh. Ex. **Berchem, bĕr′-ċhĕm, — bĕr′-kĕm.**

2. **g** at the end of a word has nearly the same sound as **ch**, and has been indicated in the same way. In this case, however, one who cannot pronounce ċh, should use hard **g.** Ex. **Altenburg, äl′-tĕn-bōōrċh, — äl′-tĕn-bōōrg.**

3. ö is different from any English sound, and resembles eu in French. It has been indicated by ĕ as in hĕr, but this is *not the exact* sound.

4. ü has no equivalent in English, but is like u in French and in Dutch. It is a sound between ū in flute, and **w**ee in sweet, and is indicated by ü.

Spanish.

1. Spanish vowels are all pronounced, though sometimes syllables are run together rapidly. Ex. **Caimanera, kä-ē-mä-nā'-rä.** But the first two syllables are so rapidly spoken that they have the effect of **kī**, and the pronunciation is so given in some dictionaries. But here it has seemed best to keep the value of the vowels in most cases, according to Spanish rules. Sometimes this practice has appeared misleading ; accordingly, **Aranjuez, ä-räng-ċhōō-ĕth'**, has been given ä-räng-hwĕth', as less likely to be confusing.

2. **b** and **v** are often interchangeable, and have a sound between **b** and **v**, but as this is difficult for a foreigner, it has been given as a simple **b**, and may be pronounced **b** or **v** according to the letter employed in the Spanish word.

3. **d** is often softened or almost lost in Spanish, and in most dictionaries has been given as **ŧh**. But it has seemed better to indicate it here as a simple **d**.

4. **j** and **x** are interchangeable in Spanish, and have an aspirated sound much like the German **ċh**. If this is not to be acquired, it is better to use an aspirated ꞌh as in ꞌhither, and the sound is indicated by both ċh and ꞌh.

5. **r** is rolled with the tip of the tongue.

10,000 PROPER NAMES

A

Aachen	ä'-chĕn.
Aar	är.
Aare	är'-ŭ.
Aaron	ăr'-ŭn, âr'-ŭn, ā'-rŭn.
Ab	äb.
Abaco	ä'-bä-kō.
Abaddon	ă-băd'-ŭn, ă-băd'-ŏn.
Abana	ăb'-à-ná.
Abassides, *see* Abbassides	ă-băs'-īdz, ăb'-à-sīdz.
Abate, *see* Abbate	ä-bä'-tĕ.
Abbas	äb'-bäs.
Abbassides, *see* Abassides	ă-băs'-īdz, ăb'-à-sīdz.
Abbate, *see* Abate	ä-bä'-tĕ.
Abbaye	ä-bā'.
Abbeokuta, *see* Abeokuta	ăb-ĕ''-ō-kōō'-tà.
Abbotsford	ăb'-ŏts-fŭrd.
Abdallah, *see* Abdullah	äbd-äl'-äh.
Abd-el-aziz, *see* Abdul-Aziz	äbd''-ĕl-ä-zēz'.
Abd-el-Kader, *or* Kadir	äbd-ĕl-kä'-dĕr.
Abd-el-Wahab	äbd''-ĕl-wä-häb'.
Abd-er-Rahman	äbd-ĕr-rä'-män.
Abdiel	ăb'-dĭ-ĕl.
Abdul-Aziz, *see* Abd-el-aziz	äbd''-ōōl-ä-zēz'.
Abdullah, *see* Abdallah	äbd-ōōl'-äh.
Abdul-Medjid, *or* Mejid	äbd''-ōōl-mĕ-jēd'.
À Becket	á-bĕk'-ĕt.
Abednego	ă-bĕd'-nē-gō.
Abel	ā'-bel. *Nor.* ä'-bĕl.

Abelard, *Fr.* Abélard .   ăb'-ē-lärd.   *Fr.* ä-bā-lär'.
Abelian . . . . . .   ā-bĕl'-ĭ-ăn.
Abencerrages . . .   { ăb-ĕn'-sĕ-rāj-ĕz.
                { *Sp.* ä''-bĕn-thä-rä'-ċhĕs.
Abeokuta, *see* Abbeokuta   ăb-ē''-ō-kōō'-tä.
Abercrombie . . . . .   ăb'-ĕr-krŭm-bĭ.
Aberdeen . . . . . .   ăb-ĕr-dēn'.   [vĕn'ĭ.
Abergavenny . . .   ăb-ĕr-gā'-nĭ,   ăb''-ĕr-gă-
Abernethy . . . . .   ăb'-ĕr-nĕth-ĭ,   ăb'-ĕr-nē-
Abia, *or* Abiah . . .   á-bĭ'-á.   [thĭ
Abiathar . . . . . .   á-bĭ'-á-thär.
Abib . . . .   ā'-bĭb.
Abiezar, *or* Abiezer . .   ā-bĭ-ē'-zĕr.
Abigail . . . . . .   ăb'-ĭ-gāl.
Abihu . . . .   á-bĭ'-hū.
Abijah . . . .   á-bĭ'-jä.
Abila, *see* Abyla . . .   ăb'-ĭ-lä.
Abimelech . . . . .   á-bĭm'-ĕ-lĕk.
Abo . . . .   ä'-bō.   *Sw.* ô'-bō.
Abomey . . . . . .   ăb-ō'-mĭ, ä-bō-mä'.
Abonita . . . . . .   ä-bō-nē'-tä.
Abookeer, *see* Aboukir, }   ä-bōō-kēr'.
    Abukir . . . . . }
Abou-ben-Adhem . . .   ä'-bōō-bĕn-ä'-dĕm.
Aboukir, *see* Abookeer, }   ä-bōō-kēr'.
    Abukir . . . . . }
About, Edmond . . .   ĕd-môṅd' ä-bōō'.
Abra . . . .   ăb'-rá.
Abrantès, (Duc) d' . .   dä-brän'-tās.
Abruzzo . . . . . .   ä-brŏŏt'-sō.
Absalom . . . . . .   ăb'-sá-lŭm.
Abt . . . .   äpt.
Abu-Bekr . . . . . .   ä''-bōō-bĕk'-r.
Abukir, *see* Abookeer, }   ä-bōō-kēr'.
    Aboukir . . . . }
Abu-l-Hassan . . . .   ä'-bōōl-häs'-än, häs-än'.

Abul-Kasim-Mansur . . .	{ ä'-bōōl-kä-sēm' (*or* kä'-sēm) män-sōōr'.
Abydos	ă-bī'-dŏs, ā-bī'dŏs.
Abyla, *see* Abila	ăb'-ĭ-lä.
Abyssinia	ăb-ĭ-sĭn'-ĭ-ȧ.
Academus	ăk-ā-dē'-mŭs.
Acadia	ȧ-kā'-dĭ-ȧ.
Acadie	ä-kä-dē'.
Acapulco	ä-kä-pōōl'-kō.
Acbar, *see* Akbar . . .	äk'-bēr. *Hind.* ŭk'-bĕr.
Accademia della Crusca .	{ äk-kä-dā'-mē-ȧ dĕl'-lä krōōs'-kä.
Acciajoli, *or*	ä-chä-yō'-lē.
Acciajuoli	ä-chä-yōō-ō'-lē.
Accoramboni	äk-kō"-räm-bō'-nē.
Aceldama	ȧ-sĕl'dā-mä.
Acemetae, Acemeti, *see* Acoemitae	} ä-sĕm'-ē-tē, ä-sĕm'-ē-tī.
Acemetic	ăs-ē-mĕt'-ĭk.
Achaea, *see* Achaia . .	ā-kē'-yȧ, ă-kē'-yȧ.
Achaean, *see* Achean .	ā-kē'-ȧn, ă-kē'-ȧn.
Achaia, *see* Achaea . .	ā-kā'-yä, ă-kā'-yȧ.
Achaian, *see* Achean .	ā-kā'-yȧn, ă-kā'-yȧn.
Achan	ā'-kăn.
Achates	ă-kā'-tēz.
Achean, *see* Achacan .	ā-kē'-ȧn, ă-kē-ȧn.
Acheloös, *or* Achelous .	äk-ē-lō'-ŏs, äk-ē-lō'-ŭs.
Acheron	äk'-ĕ-rŏn.
Achillean	ăk-ĭl-ē'-ȧn.
Achilles	ă-kĭl'-ēz.
Achitophel, *see* Ahithophel	ā-kĭt'-ō-fĕl.
Achmet, *see* Ahmed . . .	äch'-mĕt.
Achray (Loch)	ăk'-rā.
Acis	ā'-sĭs.
Ackbar, *see* Akbar . . .	äk'-bēr. *Hind.* ŭk'-bĕr.
Acoemitae, *see* Acemetae .	ăs-ē-mī'-tō, *or* ă-sĕm'-ĭ-tē

Acre	ā'-ker'l, ä'-ker'l
Acropolis	ă-krŏp'-ō-lĭs.
Actaeon	ăk-tē'-ŏn.
Actian	ăk'-shĭ-ȧn.
Actium	ăk'-shĭ-ŭm, ăk'-tĭ-ŭm.
Adalbert	ăd'-ăl-bĕrt.
Adam (Mme.)	ä-däṅ'.
Adamawa	ä-dä-mô'-wä.
Adamic	ä-dăm'-ĭk.
Adamowski	ä-dä-mŏf'-skĭ.
Adar	ā'-där.
Adela	ăd'-ē-lȧ.
Adelaide	ăd'-ĕ-lād.
Adélaïde (Princess)	Fr. ä-dā-lä-ĕd'.
Adelaïde (Beethoven)	Ger. ä-dā-lä-ē'-dŭ.
Adelheid	ä'-dĕl-hīt.
Adelphi, or Adelphoe	ä-dĕl'-fī, ä-dĕl'-fē.
Aden	ä'-dĕn, ā'-dĕn.
Adeona	ăd-ē-ō'nȧ
Adige	ăd'-ĭj-ē. It. ä'-dē-jĕ.
Adjanta, Adjunta, see ⎫ Ajuntah ⎭	ä-jŭn'-tȧ.
Adjuntas	äd-'hōōn'-täs.
Adlai	ăd'-lī, ăd'-lē-ī.
Adler	äd'-lĕr.
Admetos, or Admetus	ăd-mē'-tŏs, ăd-mē'-tŭs.
Adonai	ăd-ō-nā'-ī, ä-dō-nī'.
Adonais	ăd-ō-nā'-ĭs.
Adonic	ȧ-dŏn'-ĭk.
Adonijah	ăd-ō-nī'-jȧ.
Adoniram	ăd-ō-nī'-răm.
Adonis	ä-dō'nĭs, ā-dō'-nĭs.
Adoni-zedec	ȧ-dō'-nī-zē'-dĕk.
Adraste	ä-dräst'.
Adrian	ā'-drĭ-ȧn.
Adriana	ā-drĭ-ā'-nȧ.

Adriatic	ā-drĭ-ăt′-ĭk, ăd-rĭ-ăt′-ĭk.
Adrienne Lecouvreur . .	ä-drē-ĕn′ lē-kōōv-rĕr′.
Adullam	á-dŭl′-ám.
Aeacides . . . . . , . .	ē-ăs′-ĭ-dēz.
Aeacus	ē′-á-kŭs.
Aegadian (Is.)	ē-gā′-dĭ-án.
Aegates	ē-gā′-tēz.
Aegean, see Egean . . .	ē-jē′-án.
Aegeria, see Egeria . . .	ē-jē′-rĭ-á.
Aegina, see Aigina . . .	ē-jĭ′-ná.
Aeginetan	ē-jĭ-nē′-tán.
Aeginetic	ē-jĭ-nĕt′-ĭk.
Aégis	ē′-jĭs.
Aeneas, see Eneas . . .	ē-nē′-ás.
Aeneid	ē-nē′-ĭd.
Aeolian, see Aiolian . . .	ē-ō′-lĭ-án.
Aeolic, see Eolic	ē-ŏl′-ĭk.
Aeolis, see Eolis	ē′-ō-lĭs.
Aeolus	ē′-ō-lŭs.
Aeschines	ĕs′-kĭ-nēz.
Aeschylean	ĕs-kĭ-lē′-án.
Aeschylus	ĕs′-kĭ-lŭs.
Aesculapius, see Asklepios	ĕs-kū-lā′-pĭ-ŭs. [ĭ-sĕr.
Aesir	ā′-sĕr, mod. ē′-sĭr. Ice.
Aesop, see Esop	ē′-sŏp.
Aethelberht, see Ethelbert	ăth′-ĕl-bĕrht.
Aethelwulf, see Ethelwulf	ăth′-ĕl-wōōlf.
Aether	ē′-thĕr.
Aëtion	ā-ē′-shĭ-ŏn.
Aetna, see Etna	ĕt′-ná.
Aetolian	ē-tō′-lĭ-án.
Afer	ā′-fĕr.
Afghan	ăf′-găn. [tän′.
Afghanistan	ăf-găn-ĭs-tän′, ăf-găn-ĭs-
Afium-Kara-Hissar . . .	ä-fē-ōōm′-kä-rä′-hĭs-sär′.
Africaine, L'	läf-rē-kān′.

Africander, *see* Afrikander	ăf-rĭ-kăn-dẽr.
Africanus	ăf-rĭ-kā'-nŭs.
Afridis	ä-frē'-dĭz.
Afrikander, *see* Africander	ăf-rĭ-kăn-dẽr.
Agades, Agadez, *see* Agdas	ä'-gă-dĕz.
Agag	ā'-găg.
Agamemnon	ăg-ā-mĕm'-nŏn.
Agaña	ä-gän'-yä. [ä-gä-sē'
Agassiz	ăg'-ăs-sĭ, ăg'-ăs-ē. *Fr.*
Agdas, *see* Agades . . .	ăg'-dás.
Agen	ä-zhŏń'.
Agenor	ă-jē'-nôr.
Agésilas	*Fr.* ä-zhä-sē-läs'.
Agesilaos, *or*	ă-jĕ-sĭ-lā'-ŏs.
Agesilaus	ă-jĕ-sĭ-lā'-ŭs.
Aghrim, *see* Aughrim . .	ôg'-rĭm. [kōōr'.
Agincourt, *see* Azincourt .	ăj'-ĭn-kōrt. *Fr.* äzh-ăṅ-
Aglaia	ăg-lā'-yä.
Agnolo	än'-yō-lō.
Agnus Dei	ăg'-nŭs dē'-ĭ.
Agoncillo, Felipe	fä-lē'-pä ä-gōn-thēl'-yō.
Agonistes	ăg-ŏn-ĭs'-tēz.
Agora	ăg'-ō-rá.
Agoult (Comtesse d') . .	dä-gōō'.
Agra	ä'-grá.
Agram	ä'-gräm.
Agricola	ă-grĭk'-ō-lä.
Agrigentum	ăg-rĭ-jĕn'-tŭm.
Agrippina	ăg-rĭ-pĭ'ná.
Aguadilla	ä-gwä-dĕl'-yä.
Aguado	ä-gwä'-dō.
Aguadores	ä-gwä-dō'-räs.
Aguas Buenas	ä'-gwäs bōō-ā'-näs.
Aguas Calientes	ä'-gwäs kä-lē-ĕn'-tĕs.
Aguinaldo	ä-gē-näl'-dō.
Agulhas (Cape)	ä-gōōl'-yäs.

Ahab	ā'-hăb.
Ahasuerus	ă-hăz-ū-ē'-rŭs.
Ahaz	ā'-hăz.
Ahimelech	ă-hĭm'-ĕ-lĕk. [fĕl.
Ahithophel, see Achitophel	ă-hĭth'-ō-fĕl, ā-hĭth'-ō-
Ahmed, see Achmet . . .	äh'-mĕd.
Ahmedabad	ä-mĕd-ä-bäd'.
Ahmednuggur	ä-mĕd-nŭg'-ẽr.
Ahriman	ä'-rĭ-män.
Aï, see Ay	ä'-ē, ī. Bib. ā'-ī.
Aibonito, see Aybonito . .	ä-ē-bō-nē'-tō.
Aïda	ä-ē'-dä.
Aïdé	ä-ē-dä'.
Aidenn	ā'-dĕn.
Aigina, see Aegina . . .	ī'-gĭ-nä.
Aiglon, L'	lä-glôn'.
Aiguille du Midi	ä-gē'-yŭ dü mē-dē'.
Aiguillon (Duc) d' . . .	dä-gē-yôn'.
Aijalon, see Ajalon . . .	ăj'-à-lŏn.
Aintab	ĭn-täb'.
Aiolian, see Aeolian . . .	ā-ō'-lĭ-án.
Aix	island, ā. city, āks, ās.
Aix-la-Chapelle	{ āks-lä-shä-pĕl', ās-lä- shä-pĕl'.
Aix-les-Bains	āks-lā-băn', ās-lā-băn'.
Ajaccio	ä-yä'-chō.
Ajalon, see Aijalon . . .	ăj'-à-lŏn.
Ajax	ā'-jăks.
Ajmere, or Ajmir . . .	äj-mẽr'.
Ajuntah, see Adjanta . .	ă-jŭn'-tà.
Akbar, or	} äk'-bẽr. Hind. ŭk'-bẽr
Akber. See Ekber . . .	}
Akiba (Rabbi)	ä-kē'-bä.
Akra	äk-rä'.
Aksakoff, or Aksakov . .	äk-sä'-kŏf.
Akyab	äk-yäb'.

Al Aaraaf, see Al Araf . .	al ar' af.
Alabama	ăl-á-bä′-má.
Alabamian	ăl-á-bä′-mĭ-án.
Alacoque	ä-lä-kŏk′.
Aladdin, or Ala-ed-Din .	á-lăd′-ĭn, ä-lä′-ĕd-dēn′.
Alamanni, see Alemanni .	ăl-á-măn′-ī.
Alamannic, see Alemannic	ăl-á-măn′-ĭk.
Alameda	á-lä-mä′-dä.
Alamo	ä′-lä-mō.
Al Araf, see Al Aaraaf . .	äl är′-äf.
Alarcon y Mendoza . . .	ä-lär-kōn′ē män-dō′-thä.
Alaric	ăl′-ăr-ĭk.
Alastor	ä-lăs′-tôr.
Alba (Duke of), see Alva .	ăl′-bá. Sp. äl′-bä.
Alba Longa	ăl′-bá lŏng′-gá.
Alban, St.	ăl′-băn, ôl′-bán.
Albani (Mme.)	äl-bä′-nē.
Albania	äl-bā′-nĭ-á.
Albano	äl-bä′-nō.
Albai, or Albay	äl-bä′-ē.
Alberic	ăl′-bĕr-ĭk.
Albert, D'	däl-bâr′.
Albertinelli	äl-bâr-tĕ-nĕl′-lō.
Albertini	äl-bâr-tē′-nē.
Albert Nyanza	ăl′-bért nyăn′-zá.
Albi, see Alby	äl-bē′.
Albigenses	ăl-bĭ-jĕn′-sēz.
Albion	ăl′-bĭ-ŏn.
Alboin	ăl′-boin.
Alboni (Mme.)	äl-bō′-nē.
Albrecht	äl′-brĕcht.
Albret, Jeanne d'	zhän däl-brä′.
Albuera	äl-bōō-ā′-rä.
Albuquerque	Sp. äl-bōō-kâr′-kä.
Alby, see Albi	äl-bē′.
Alcaeus	ăl-sē′-ŭs.

Alcalá de Henares . . .	äl-kä-lä' dä ā-nä'-rās.
Alcamenes	ăl-kăm'-ĕ-nēz.
Alcantara	äl-kän'-tä-rä.
Alcázar	äl-kä'-thär.
Alceste	ăl-sĕst'.
Alcibiades	ăl-sĭ-bī'-á-dēz.
Alcinous	ăl-sĭn'-ō-ŭs.
Alcmaeon	ălk-mē'-ŏn.
Alcmaeonidae	ălk-mē-ŏn'-ĭ-dē.
Alcmene	ălk-mē'-nē.
Alcoran, *see* Alkoran . .	äl'-kō-răn, ăl-kō-răn'.
Alcott, (Bronson) . . .	ôl'-kŭt.
Alcuin	ăl'-kwĭn.
Alcyone, *see* Halcyone . .	ăl-sī'-ō-nē. [rän'.
Aldebaran	äl-dĕb'-á-rán, äl-dĕ-bä-
Aldershot	ôl-dĕr-shŏt.
Aldine	äl'-dĭn, ôl'-dĭn.
Aldobrandini	äl-dō-brän-dē'-nē.
Aldus Manutius	ăl'-dŭs mă-nū'-shĭ-ŭs.
Alecto	ă-lĕk'-tō.
Alemanni, *see* Alamanni .	ăl-ē-măn'-ī.
Alemannic, *see* Alamannic	ăl-ē-măn'-ĭk.
Alembert, D'	dä-lŏṅ-bâr'. [sôṅ'.
Alençon	ä-lĕn'-sŭn. *Fr.* ä-lŏṅ-
Aleutian	ā-lū'-shĭ-ăn, ăl-ē-ū'-shĭ-
Aleuts	ăl'-ē-ūts. [ăn.
Alfadir	äl-fä'-dĭr.
Alfieri, Vittorio . . .	vēt-tō'-rē-ō äl-fē-ā'-rē.
Alfonso, *see* Alphonso . .	ăl-fŏn'-sō, ăl-fŏn'zō. *Sp.*
Alford	ôl'-fŭrd. [äl-fōn'-sō.
Alger	ăl'-jĕr, ôl'-gĕr.
Algerian	ăl-jē'-rĭ-án.
Algerine	ăl'-jĕ-rēn.
Algoa (Bay)	ăl-gō'-á. [kwĭn.
Algonkin, *or* Algonquin .	ăl-gŏn'-kĭn, ăl-gŏn'-
Alhambra	ăl-hăm'-brá.

Ali Baba	ä' 10 bä' bä.
Alighieri	ä-lē-gē-ä'-rē.
Aliwal	äl-ē-wäl'.
Alkmaar	älk-mär'.
Alkoran, see Alcoran . .	ăl'-kō-rán, ăl-kō-rán'.
Allah	ăl'-ä.
Allahabad	äl-ä-hä-bäd'.
Alleghany, or Allegheny .	ăl'-ē-gā-nĭ, ăl'-ē-gĕn-ĭ.
Allegri	äl-lä'-grē.
Allemagne	äl-män'-yŭ.
Aller	äl'-lĕr.
Allobroges	ăl-ŏb'-rō-jēz.
Almacks	ôl'-măks.
Almagest	ăl'-ma-jĕst.
Almahide	äl-mä-ēd'.
Almansa, see Almanza . .	äl-män'-sä.
Al Mansour, Al Mansur . .	äl män-sōōr'.
Almanza, see Almansa . .	äl-män'-thä.
Alma-Tadema	äl'-mä tä'-dĕ-mä.
Almeida	äl-mā'-ē-dä.
Almeyda (Bay)	äl-mā'-dä.
Almirante Oquendo . . .	äl-mē-rän'-tä ō-kĕn'-dō.
Almohades	ăl'-mō-hädz.
Alnwick	ăn'-ĭk.
Aloiadae, or Aloidae . . .	ă-lō-ĭ'-a-dē, ă-lō-ĭ'-dē.
Aloysius	ăl-ō-ĭsh'-ĭ-ŭs.
Alpes-Maritimes	älp-mär-ē-tēm'.
Alph	älf.
Alpheius, or Alpheus . .	äl-fī'-ŭs, äl-fē'-ŭs.
Alphonse	ăl-fôns'. [äl-fŏn'-sō.
Alphonso, see Alfonso . .	äl-fŏn'-sō, ăl-fŏn'-zō. _Sp._
Alpujarras, or Alpuxaras .	äl-pōō-ċhär'-räs.
Alsace-Lorraine	äl-zäs' lōr-rān'.
Al Sirat	äl sē-rät'.
Altai	äl-tī'.
Altaic	ăl-tā'-ĭk.

Alter Fritz	äl'-tĕr frĭts.
Althaea	ăl-thē'á.
Althing	äl'-tĭng.
Alton Locke	ôl'-tŭn lŏk.
Alva, Duke of, *see* Alba .	äl'-vá. *Sp.* äl'-bä.
Alvarado	äl-bä-rä'-dō.
Alvares	äl'-bä-rĕs. [bä-rĕth.
Alvarez	*Port.* äl'-vä-rĕz. *Sp.* äl'-
Alvary	äl-vä'-rĭ.
Alvinczy, *or* Alvinzi . . .	ôl'-vĭn-tsē.
Alwar, *see* Ulwar	äl'-wär.
Amadeo	ä-mä-dä'-ō.
Amadeus	ăm-á-dē'-ŭs.
Amadis of Gaul	ăm'-á-dĭs ŭv gôl.
Amalfi	ä-mäl'-fē.
Amalia, Anna	än'-ä ä-mä'-lē-ä.
Amants Magnifiques, Les .	lā zä-män' män-yē-fēk'.
Amaryllis	ăm-á-rĭl'-ĭs.
Amasa	ăm'-á-sá.
Amati	ä-mä'-tē.
Amaury	ă-mô'-rĭ. *Fr.* ä-mō-rē'.
Amazulu	ä-mä-zōō'-lōō.
Ambois	äṅ-bwä'.
Amboise	äṅ-bwäz'.
Ambrogio, San	sän äm-brō'-jō.
Ambrosius, (St.) . . .	ăm-brō'-zhĭ-ŭs.
Amenhotep	ä-mĕn-hō'-tĕp.
Amerigo Vespucci . . .	ä-mĕr-ē'-gō vĕs-pōō'-chē.
Amicis, De	dā ä-mē'-chēs.
Amiel	ā'-mĭ-ĕl. [ĕl'.
Amiel, Henri Frédéric . .	ŏṅ-rē' frä-dä-rĕk' ä-mē-
Amiens	ä-mē-äṅ'.
Amistad	*Sp.* ä-mēs-täd'.
Amlwch	ăm'-lōōk. [ăm'-ŏn.
Amon	*Bib. & Fr.* ā'-mŏn. *St.*
Amoor, *see* Amur	ä-mōōr'.

Amor	ā'-môr.
Amoret	ăm'-ō-rĕt.
Amorites	ăm'-ō-rīts.
Amory (Blanche)	ā'-mō-rĭ.
Amoskeag	ăm-ŏs-kĕg'.
Amoy	ä-moi'.
Ampère	än-pâr'.
Amphictyonic	ăm-fĭk-tĭ-ŏn'-ĭk.
Amphictyony	ăm-fĭk'-tĭ-ŏn-ĭ.
Amphion	ăm-fī'-ŏn.
Amphipolis	ăm-fĭp'-ō-lĭs.
Amphitrite	ăm-fĭ-trī'-tē.
Amphitryon	ăm-fĭt'-rĭ-ŏn.
Amritsar, see Umritsir . .	ăm-rĭt'-sär.
Amur, see Amoor	ä-mōōr'.
Amurath	ä-mōō-rät'.
Amyot	ä-mē-ō'.
Anabasis	å-năb'-å-sĭs.
Anacreon, see Anakreon .	ă-năk'-rē-ŏn.
Anadyomene	ăn-å-dĭ-ŏm'-ĕ-nē.
Anagni	än-än'-yē.
Anahuac	ä-nä'-wäk.
Anak	ā'-năk.
Anakim	ăn'-å-kĭm.
Anakreon, see Anacreon	ă-năk'-rē-ŏn.
Anam, see Annam . .	ăn-äm', än-äm'.
Ananias	ăn-å-nī'-ås.
Añasco	än-yäs'-kō.
Anastasius	ăn-ăs-tā'-shĭ-ŭs.
Anathoth	ăn'-å-thŏth.
Anatolian	ăn-å-tō'-lĭ-án.
Anaxagoras	ăn-ăks-ăg'-ō-rás.
Anaximenes	ăn-ăks-ĭm'-ĕ-nēz.
Anchises	ăn-kī'-sēz.
Ancillon	än-sē-yôṅ'.
Anckarström	äng'-kär-strĕm.

Ancona	än-kō'-nä.
Ancre (Marquis) d' . . .	dän'-kr.
Ancus Marcius	ăng'-kŭs mär'-shĭ-ŭs.
Andalucia	*Sp.* än-dä-lōō-thē'-ä.
Andalusia	ăn-dà-lū'-shĭ-à, ăn-dà-
Andaman	ăn'-dá-màn. [lōō'-zĭ-à
Andelys, Les	lä zän̄-dŭ-lē'.
Andermatt	än'-dĕr-mät.
Andernach	än'-dĕr-nàċh.
Andersen, Hans	häns än'-dĕr-sĕn.
Andes	ăn'-dēz.
Andorra	än-dŏr'-rä.
Andrássy	ŏn'-drä-shē. [drā'.
André	än'-drä, ăn'-drĭ. *Fr.* än̄-
Andrea del Sarto	än-drā'-ä dĕl sär'-tō.
Andrea Ferrara	ăn'-drē-à fĕr-rä'-rä.
Andrée	än'-drā.
Androclus	ăn'-drō-klŭs.
Andromache	ăn-drŏm'-ä-kē.
Andromaque	*Fr.* än̄-drō-mäk'.
Andromeda	ăn-drŏm'-ĕ-dà.
Andromède	än-drō-mād'.
Andronicus	{ ăn-drō-nī'-kŭs. { *Shak.* ăn-drŏn'-ĭ-kŭs.
Anelida	ă-nĕl'-ĭ-dà.
Angara (R.)	än-gä-rä'.
Angelico, Fra	frä än-jĕl'-ē-kō.
Angélique	än̄-zhä-lēk'.
Angelo	ăn'-jĕ-lō. *It.* än'-jä-lō.
Angelus	ăn'-jĕ-lŭs.
Angers	ăn'-jērs. *Fr.* än̄-zhā'.
Angevin, *or* Angevine . .	ăn'-jē-vĭn, ăn'-jē-vīn.
Anghiari	än-gē-ä'-rē.
Angleterre	än̄-gl-târ'.
Angola	än-gō'-là.
Angolalla	än-gō-läl'-lä.

Angora	ăn-gō'-rȧ
Angoulême	äṅ-gōō-lăm'.
Angra Pequena	äng'-grä pā-kän'-yä.
Anguila, *or* Anguilla . .	äng-gwĭl'-lä. *Sp.* än-gē'-
Anhalt	än'-hält. [lä.
Anhwei, *see* Ngan-hui .	än-hwā'-ē.
Anio	ä'-nē-ō.
Anjou	ăn'-jōō. *Fr.* äṅ-zhōō'.
Anna Comnena	än'-nȧ kŏm-nē'-nä.
Anna Ivanovna	än'-nä ē-vä'-nŏv-nä.
Anna Karénina	än'-nä kä-rä'-nē-nä.
Anna Leopoldovna . . .	än'-nä lä-ō-pōl'-dŏv-nä.
Annam, *see* Anam . . .	ăn-năm', än-näm'.
Anna Petrovna	än'-nä pĕ-trŏv'-nä.
Anne de Beaujeu	än dŭ bō-zhē'.
Anne of Geierstein . . .	gī'-ĕr-stīn.
Annesley	ănz'-lĭ.
Anno Domini	ăn'-nō dŏm'-ĭ-nĭ. [dzē-ō̱.
Annunzio, Gabriele d' . .	gä-brē-ä'-lä dä-nōōn'-
Annus Mirabilis	ăn'-ŭs mĭ-răb'-ĭ-lĭs.
Anoobis, *see* Anubis . . .	ă-nōō'-bĭs.
Anquetil	äṅk-tēl'.
Ansbach, *see* Anspach . .	äns'-bäċh.
Anse du Diamante, Grande	gräṅd äṅs dü dē-ä-mäṅt'.
Anspach, *see* Ansbach . .	äns'-päċh. [stĕr,
Anstruther	ăn'-strŭth-ĕr, *pop.* ăn'-
Antaeus	ăn-tē'-ŭs.
Antenor	ăn-tē'-nôr.
Anteros	ăn'-tĕ-rŏs.
Anthony, *or* Antony . . .	ăn'-tō-nĭ.
Antibes	äṅ-tēb'.
Anticyra	ăn-tĭs'-ĭ-rȧ.
Antietam	ăn-tē'-tăm.
Antigone	ăn-tĭg'-ō-nē.
Antigonus	ăn-tĭg'-ō-nŭs.
Antigua	än-tē'-gwä.

Antilles	än-tĭl'-lēz. *Fr.* äṅ-tēl'.
Antilochus	ăn-tĭl'-ō-kŭs.
Anti-Macchiavel . . .	ăn-tĭ-măk'-ĭ-á-vĕl.
Antin (Duc d')	däṅ-täṅ'.
Antinous	ăn-tĭn'-ō-ŭs.
Antioch	ăn'-tĭ-ŏk.
Antiochus	ăn-tĭ'-ō-kŭs.
Antiope	ăn-tī'-ō-pē.
Antipas, Herod	hĕr'-ŏd ăn'-tĭ-păs.
Antipater	ăn-tĭp'-á-tĕr.
Antiphanes	ăn-tĭf'-á-nēz.
Antiphon	ăn'-tĭ-fŏn.
Antipodes	ăn-tĭp'-ō-dēz, ăn'-tĭ-
Antipolo	än-tē-pō'-lō. [pŏds.
Antistates	ăn-tĭs'-tă-tēz.
Antium	ăn'-shĭ-ŭm.
Antivari	än-tē'-vä-rē.
Antoine de Bourbon . . .	äṅ-twän' dŭ bōōr-bôṅ'.
Anton Ulrich	än'-tōn ōōl'-rĭch.
Antonelli Giacomo (Cardinal)	jä'-kō-mō än-tō-nĕl'-lē.
Antonello da Messina . .	än-tō-nĕl'-lō dä mĕs-sē'-
Antonina	ăn-tō-nī'-nä. [nä.
Antoninus Pius	ăn-tō-nī'-nŭs pī'-ŭs.
Antonio	än-tō'-nē-ō.
Antraigues, *see* Entraigues	äṅ-trāg'.
Antwerp	ănt'-wĕrp.
Anubis, *see* Anoobis . . .	á-nū'-bĭs.
Anvers	äṅ-vâr'.
Aosta	ä-ōs'-tä.
Apache, *or*	ä-pä'-chä.
Apaches	*pop.* ä-păch'-ēz.
Apari, *or* Aparri . . .	ä-pär-rē'.
Apelles	á-pĕl'-ēz.
Apemantus	ăp-ĕ-măn'-tŭs.
Apennines	ăp'-ĕ-nīnz.
Aphrodite	ăf-rō-dī'-tē.

Apia	ä′ pō ä.
Apicius	ă-pĭsh′-ĭ-ŭs.
Apocalypse	á-pŏk′-á-lĭps.
Apocrypha	á-pŏk′-rĭ-fá.
Apollinare in Classe . . .	ä-pŏl-lē-nä′-rĕ ĭn kläs′-sĕ.
Apollino	ă-pŏl-lē′-nō.
Apollo Belvedere	{ á-pŏl′-ō bĕl-vē-dēr′. *It.* ä-pŏl′-lō bāl-vā-dā′-rĕ.
Apollo Chresterios . . .	á-pŏl′-ō krĕs-tē′-rĭ-ŏs.
Apollo Citharoedus . . .	á-pŏl′-ō sĭth-á-rē′-dŭs.
Apollo Sauroktonos . . .	á-pŏl′-ō sôr-ŏk′-tō-nŏs.
Apollodorus	á-pŏl″-ō-dō′-rŭs.
Apollonius	ăp-ŏl-ō′-nĭ-ŭs.
Apollyon	ă-pŏl′-yŏn, ā-pŏl′-ĭ-ŏn.
Apoxyomenos	ăp″-ŏks-ĭ-ŏm′-ĕ-nŏs.
Appalachian	ăp-á-lăch′-ĭ-ăn, ăp-á-lā′-
Appii Forum	ăp′-ĭ-ī fō′-rŭm. [chĭ-ăn.
Apponyi	ŏp′-pōn-yē.
Appuleius, *see* Apuleius .	ăp-ū-lē′-ŭs.
Apraxin	ä-präk′-sĭn.
Apries	ā′-prē-ēz.
Apuleius, *see* Appuleius	ăp-ū-lē′-ŭs.
Apulia. *It.* Puglia . .	á-pū′-lĭ-á.
Aquae Sextiae	ā′-kwē sĕk′-stĭ-ē.
Aquambo	ä-kwäm-bō′.
Aquapim	ä-kwä-pēm′.
Aquarius	á-kwā′-rĭ-ŭs.
Aquednek, *or*	ă-kwĕd′-nĕk.
Aquidneck	á-kwĭd′-nĕk.
Aquila	ä′-kwē-lä.
Aquinas	á-kwī′-nás.
Aquitaine	ăk-wĭ-tān′. *Fr.* ä - kē -
Arab	ăr′-áb. [tān′.
Arabia Petraea	á-rā′-bĭ-ä pē-trē′-ä.
Arabic	ăr′-á-bĭk. [*or* päsh′-á.
Arabi Pasha	ä-rä′-bē păsh-ô′, pá-shä′,

Ara Celi, *or* Coeli	ä'-rä sē'-lī.
Arachne	à-räk'-nē.
Araf, Al, *see* Al Aaraaf . .	äl ä'-ráf.
Arafat	ä-rä-fät'.
Arago	är'-à-gō. *Fr.* ä-rä-gō'.
Aragon	är'-à-gŏn. *Sp.* ä-rä-gōn'.
Araktcheyeff	ä-räk-chä'-yĕf.
Aral (Sea)	är'-ál.
Aram (Eugene)	ā'-rám.
Aramaic	är-á-mā'-ĭk.
Aramis	ä-rä-mēs'.
Aranjuez	ä-räng-'hwĕth'.
Arany János	ŏr-ŏn-yē' yä'-nōsh.
Arapaho, *or* Arapahoe . .	à-răp'-á-hō.
Ararat	är'-á-răt.
Arayat	ä-rä'-ē̠-ät.
Arbaces	är'-bă-sēz, är-bā'-sēz.
Arbate	är-bät'.
Arbela	är-bē'-lä.
Arblay (Mme.) d'	där-blä'.
Arbois	är-bwä'. [bŭth'-nŏt.
Arbuthnot	är'-bŭth-nŏt. *Sc.* är-
Arcades	är'-ká-dēz.
Arcady	är'-ká-dĬ. [twäl'.
Arc de Triomphe de L'Étoile	ärk dü trē-ôṅf' dü lä-
Arc de Triomphe du Car- ⎰	ärk dü trē-ôṅf' dü kä-
rousel . . . . . . ⎱	rōō-zĕl'.
Archangel	ärk-ān'-jĕl.
Archangelsk	är-chäng'-gĕlsk.
Archelaus	är-kē-lā'-ŭs.
Archias	är'-kĬ-ás.
Archidamus	är-kĬ-dä'-mŭs.
Archilochus	är-kĬl'-ō-kŭs.
Archimage	är'-kĬ-māj.
Archimago	är-kĬ-mä'-gō.
Archimedes	är-kĬ-mē'-dēz.

2

Arcis-sur-Aube	är-sē'-sür-ōb'.
Arcite	ar'-sĭt.
Arco dei Leoni	är'kō dā'-ē lā-ō'-nē.
Arco della Pace	är'-kō dĕl'-lä pä'-chĕ.
Arcola, *or* Arcole	är'kō-lä, är'-kō-lĕ.
Arcot	är-kŏt'.
Arcturus	ärk-tū'-rŭs.
Arcueil	är-kē̂'-yŭ.
Ardahan	är-dä-hän'.
Ardennais	är-dĕn-nā'.
Ardennes	är-dĕn'.
Arditi, Luigi	lōō-ē'-jē är-dē'-tē.
Ardres	ärdr.
Ardrossan	är-drŏs'-án.
Arduin	ärd'-wĭn.
Are, *see* Ari	ä'-rĕ.
Arecibo	ä-rā-sē'-bō.
Areopagite	ăr-ē-ŏp'-á-jīt.
Areopagitica	ăr''-ē-ō-pă-jĭt'-ĭ-kä.
Areopagus	ā-rē-ŏp'-ă-gŭs.
Ares	ā'rēz.
Arethusa	ăr-ē-thū'-sä.
Aretine	ăr'-ĕ-tĭn.
Aretino, Guido	gwē'-dō ä-rā-tē'-nō.
Arezzo	ä-rĕt'-sō.
Argam, *see* Argaum . . .	är-gäm'.
Argan	är-gäṅ'.
Argante (Spenser) . . .	är-găn'tĕ.
Argante (Molière) . . .	är-gäṅt'.
Argantes	är-găn'-tĕs.
Argaum *see* Argam . . .	är-gôm'.
Argenis	är'-jĕ-nĭs.
Argenson, d'	där-zhŏṅ-sôṅ'.
Argenteuil	är-zhŏṅ-tē'-yŭ. [tē'-nä.
Argentina	är-jĕn-tē'-nä. *Sp.*är-ċhĕn
Argentine	är'-jĕn-tĭn, är'-jĕn-tēn.

Argives	är'-jīvz.
Argolis	är'-gō-lĭs.
Argonauts	är'-gō-nôtz.
Argüelles	är-gwĕl'-yĕs.
Argyle, *or* Argyll	är-gīl'.
Ari, *see* Are	ä'-rē.
Ariadne	är-ĭ-ăd'-nē. ä-rĭ-ăd'-nē.
Arian	ā'-rĭ-ȧn.
Ariane	ä-rē-än'.
Arians	ā'-rĭ-ȧnz, ȧ'-rĭ-ȧnz.
Ariège	ä-rē-ĕzh'.
Ariel	ā'-rĭ-ĕl.
Aries	ā'-rĭ-ēz.
Ariete	ä-rē-ĕ'-tā.
Ariguanabo	ä-rē-gwä-nä'-bō.
Arimathaea, *or* Arimathea	är-ĭ-mā-thē'-ä.
Arion	ä-rī'-ŏn.
Ariosto	är-ĭ-ŏs'-tō. *It.* ä-rē-ŏs'-tō.
Arista (Gen.)	ä-rēs'-tä.
Aristagoras	är-ĭs-tăg'-ō-rȧs.
Aristarchus	är-ĭs-tär'-kŭs.
Ariste	ä-rēst'.
Aristeides, *or* Aristides . .	är-ĭs-tī'-dēz.
Aristippus	är-ĭs-tĭp'-ŭs.
Aristobulus	är''-ĭs-tō-bū'-lŭs.
Aristodemus	är''-ĭs-tō-dē'-mŭs.
Aristogeiton, *or* Aristogiton	är''-ĭs-tō-jī'-tŏn.
Aristophanes	är-ĭs-tŏf'-ȧ-nēz.
Aristotle	är'-ĭs-tŏtl.
Arius	är'-ĭ-ŭs, ā'-rĭ-ŭs.
Arkansas	är'-kăn-sô, är-kăn'-zȧs.
Arles	ärlz. *Fr.* ärl.
Arline	är'-lēn.
Armada	är-mä'-dä.
Armado, Don	dŏn är-mä'-dō.
Armageddon	är-mȧ-gĕd'-ŏn.

Armagh	är-mä'.
Armagnac	ȧr-mȧn-yȧk'.
Armande Béjart	är-mänd' bā-zhär'.
Armentières.	är-mŏṅ-tē̄-ȧr'.
Armida	är-mē'-dä.
Armide et Renaud . . .	är-mēd' ä rẽ-nō'.
Armorel of Lyonesse . .	är'-mō-rĕl ŭv lĭ'-ŏn-ĕs.
Armorica	är-mŏr'-ĭ-kä.
Armorican	är-mŏr'ĭ-kȧn.
Arnauld	är-nō'.
Arnaut	är'-nôt.
Arnim, Bettina von . . .	bĕt-tē'-nä fŏn är'-nĭm.
Arno	är'-nō.
Arnolfo di Cambio . . .	är-nōl'-fō dē̄ käm'-bē̄-ō.
Arnolfo di Lapo	är-nōl'-fō dē̄ lä'-pō.
Arnolphe.	är-nŏlf'.
Arondight	ā'-rŏn-dĭt.
Aroostook	ȧ-rō͞os'-tō͝ok.
Arouet	ȧ-rō͞o-ā'.
Arpachshad, see Arphaxad	är-păk-shăd'.
Árpád	är'-päd.
Arphaxad, see Arpachshad	är-făk'-săd.
Arquâ	är-kwä'.
Arques	ärk.
Arras	är-räs'.
Arrhidaeus	är-ĭ-dē'-ŭs.
Arrivabene	är-rē-vä-bā'-nĕ.
Arroyo Molinos	är-rō'yō mō-lē'nōs.
Arsaces	är'-sȧ-sēz, är-sā'-sēz.
Arsacidae	är-săs'-ĭ-dē̄.
Arsames	är'-sä-mēz.
Arsinoë	är-sĭn'-ō-ē̄.
Ars Poetica	ärz pō-ĕt'-ĭ-kȧ.
Artachshast	är-tăk-shăst'.
Artagnan, D'	där-tän-yäṅ'.
Artamène	är-tä-mān'.

Artaphernes	är-tȧ-fẽr'-nēz
Artaxerxes	är-tăks-ẽrks'-ēz.
Artegal	är'-tē-gȧl.
Artemas	är'tē-mȧs.
Artemidorus	är-tē-mǐ-dō'-rǔs.
Artemis	är'-tē-mǐs.
Artemisia	är-tē-mǐsh'-ǐ-ȧ.
Artemisium	är-tē-mǐsh'-ǐ-ǔm.
Artevelde, Van	văn är'-tě-věl-dě.
Artiago	är-tē-ä'-gō.
Artichofsky	är-tē-shõv'-skē.
Artois	är-twä'.
Aruba	ä-rōō'-bä.
Arundel	ăr'ŭn-děl.
Aruwimi	är-ōō-wē'-mē.
Arviragus	är-vǐr'-ȧ-gǔs.
Aryan	är'yȧn, är'-ǐ-ȧn.
Asaph	ā'-sȧf.
Asben	äs-běn'.
Asboth	ăs'-bŏth. *Hung.* ŏsh'-bōt.
Ascagne	äs-kän'-yǔ.
Ascalon, *see* Askelon . .	ăs'-kȧ-lŏn.
Ascanio	äs-kä'-nē-ō.
Aschaffenburg	ä-shäf'-ěn-bōōrĊh.
Ascham	ăs'-kăm.
Asdrubal, *see* Hasdrubal .	ăs'-drǔ-bȧl.
Asenath	ăs'ē-năth, ā-sē'-năth.
Aserraderos	ä-sȧr-rä-dä'-rōs.
Asgard	ăs'-gärd.
Ashango	ä-shän'-gō.
Ashantee *or* Ashanti . .	ä-shän'-tē, ă-shăn'-tē.
Ashby-de-la-Zouch . . .	ăsh'bǐ-děl-ȧ-zōōch'.
Ashestiel	ăsh'-ěs-tēl.
Ashtaroth, Ashteroth .	ăsh'-tȧ-rŏth.
Ashtoreth, *see* Ashtaroth .	ăsh'tō-rěth.
Asia	ā'shǐ-ȧ, ā'-zhǐ-ȧ.

Asiatic . . . . ȧ-shi ăt'-ĭk, ȧ-shi-ăt'-ĭk.
Asisi, *see* Assisi . . . . ä-zē'-zē.
Askabad . . . . äs-kä-bäd'.
Askelon, *see* Ascalon . . ăs'-kĕ-lŏn.
Askew (Anne) . . . . . ăs'-kū.
Asklepios, *see* Aesculapius ăs-klē'pĭ-ŏs.   [ŭs.
Asmodeus . . . . . . ăs-mō-dē'-ŭs, ăs-mō'-dē-
Asnières . . . . ä-nē̱-âr'.
Asola . . . . ä-zō'lä.
Asolando . . . . . . ̆ ăs-ō-lăn'-dō.
Asolo . . . . ä'-zō-lō.
Aspasia . . . . ăs-pā'-shĭ-ȧ.
Aspromonte . . . . . . äs-prō-mōn'-tĕ.
Assam . . . . ăs-săm'.
Assaye, *see* Assye . . . . äs-sī'.
Assen . . . . äs'-ĕn.
Assini . . . . äs-sē'-nē.
Assiniboia . . . . . . ăs"-ĭn-ĭ-boi'-ä.
Assisi, *see* Asisi . . . . ä-sē'-zē.
Assommoir, L' . . . . . lä-sŏm-mwär'.
Assouan, Assuan, *or* Asswan äs-swän'.
Assuay, *see* Azuay . . . äs-sōō-ī'.
Assye, *see* Assaye . . . . äs-sī'.
Astarte . . . . ăs-tär'tē.
Asterabad, *see* Astrabad . äs-tĕr-ä-bäd'.
Asti . . . . äs'tē.
Astolat . . . . ăs'-tō-lăt.
Astolfo, *or* Astolpho . . ăs-tŏl'fō.
Astorga . . . . äs-tŏr'-gä.
Astrabad, *see* Asterabad . äs-trä-bäd'.
Astraea, *or* Astrea Redux . ăs-trē'ä rē'dŭks.
Astrakhan . . . . . . äs-trä-ċhän'.
Astrée . . . . äs-trā'.
Astrolabe . . . . . . ăs'-trō-lāb.
Astrophel . . . . . . ăs'-trō-fĕl.
Asturias . . . . äs-tōō'-rē-äs.

Astyages	ăs-tī'ă jēr
Astyanax	ăs-tī'-á-năks.
Asuncion	ä-sōōn-thē-ōn'.
Asurbanipal	ä-sōōr-bä'-nĭ-pál.
Atahualpa	ä-tä-wäl'pä.
Atak, see Attock	ăt-ăk'.
Atala	ä-tä-lä'.
Atalanta in Calydon . .	ăt-á-lăn'-tä ĭn kăl'-ĭ-dŏn.
Ataliba	ăt-ă-lē'-bä.
Atalide	ät-ä-lēd'.
Atbara	ät-bä'-rä.
Ate	ā'-tē.
Aterno	ä-tĕr'-nō.
Athalaric, see Athalric .	ăth-ăl'-á-rĭk.
Athaliah	ăth-á-lī'-ä.
Athalie	ä-tä-lē'.
Athalric, see Athalaric .	ăth-ăl'-rĭk.
Athanasian	ăth-á-nā'-zhĭ-án.
Athanasius	ăth-á-nā'-shĭ-ŭs.
Atharvaveda	ät-här-vä-vā'-dä.
Athena	ă-thē'-nä.
Athenaeum, see Atheneum	ăth-ĕ-nē'-ŭm.
Athene	ă-thē'-nē.
Athene Parthenos . . .	ă-thē'-nē pär'-thĕ-nŏs.
Athene Polias	ă-thē'-nē pŏl'-ĭ-ăs.
Atheneum, see Athenaeum	ăth-ĕ-nē'-ŭm.
Athol	ăth'-ŏl.
Athos (Mt.)	ăth'ŏs.
Athos (Dumas)	ä-tōs'.
Atlantean	ăt-lăn-tē'-án.
Atlantides	ăt-lăn'-tĭ-dēz.
Atreus	ā'-trūs, ā'-trē-ŭs.
Atri	ä'-trē.
Atria	ä'-trē-ä.
Atridae	ă-trī'dē.
Atropos	ăt'-rō-pŏs.

Attalia	ăt-ā-ī′ā.
Attalus	ăt′-ā-lŭs.
Attar	ät-tär′.
Atticus	ăt′-Ĭ-kŭs.
Attila	ăt′-Ĭ-lä.
Attis, *see* Atys	ăt′-Ĭs.
Attock, *see* Atak	ăt-tŏk′.
Atys, *see* Attis	ăt′-Ĭs.
Aubanel	ō-bä-nĕl′.
Aubé, Jean Paul	zhŏń pōl ō-bā′.
Auber (D. F. E.)	ō-bâr′.
Auberge Rouge	ō-bârzh′ rōōzh′.
Aubigné, D'	dō-bēn-yā′.
Aucassin et Nicolette . .	ō-kă-săń′nā nē-kō-lĕt′.
Auch	ōsh.
Aude	ōd.
Audefroy le Bastard . . .	ōd-frwä′ lĕ bás-tär′.
Audenarde, *see* Oudenarde	ōd-närd′.
Audh, *see* Oudh, Oude . .	owd.
Audouin	ō-dōō-ăń′.
Audran	ō-dräń′.
Audrey	ôd′-rĭ.
Aue, Hartmann von . . .	härt′män fŏn ow′-ŭ.
Audubon	ô′-dū-bŏn.
Auerbach	ow′-ĕr-bäċh.
Auersperg	ow′-ĕrs-pĕrċh.
Auerstädt *or* Auerstedt . .	ow′ĕr-stĕt.
Auf der Höhe	owf dĕr hē′-yŭ.
Augarten	ow′-gär-tĕn.
Augean	ô-jē′-ăn.
Augeas	ô′-jē-ăs, ô-jē′-ăs.
Augereau	ōzh-rō′.
Aughrim, *see* Aghrim . .	ôg′-rĭm.
Augier, Émile	ā-mēl′ ō-zhē̱-ā′.
Augsburg	{ ôgz′-bĕrg. *Ger.* owgs′-bōōrċh.

Augusta Victoria . . . . { ô-gôs'tä vīlₑₜô'ₑrīₑä *Ger.*
ow-gŏŏs'-tä, fēk-tō'-rē-ä.

Augustenburg . . . . . ow-gŏŏs'tĕn-bōōrċh.

Augustine . . . . . . ô-gŭs'-tĭn, ô'-gŭs-tĭn.

Augusti y Davila . . . . ä-ōō-gŏŏs'-tē ĕ dä'-bĕ-lä.

Augustulus . . . . . . ô-gŭst'-yū-lŭs.

August Wilhelm . . . . *Ger.* ow'-gŏŏst vĭl'-hĕlm.

Aulis . . . . ô'-lĭs.

Aulnoy, *or* Aunoy . . . ō-nwä'.

Aumale, Duc 'd' . . . . dük dō-mäl'.

Aurangabad, *see* Auren- } ow-rŭng-gá-bäd'.
gabad . . . . {

Aurelle de Paladines . . ō-rĕl'dŭ pä-lä-dēn'.

Aurengabad, *or* Aurungabad ow-rŭng-gá-bäd'.

Aureng-zebe, *or* Aurung-zeb ô'-rŭng-zĕb'.

Aus der Ohe . . . . . ows dĕr-ō'-ŭ.

Aussa . . . . ow'-sä.

Austerlitz . . . . . . ows'-tĕr-lĭts.   [zhĭ-á.

Austrasia . . . . . . ôs-trä'-shĭ-á,   ôs-trä'-

Austria-Hungary . . . . ôs'-trĭ-ä-hŭng'-gä-rĭ.

Auteuil . . . . ō-tĕ'-yŭ.

Autolycus . . . . . . ô-tŏl'-ĭ-kŭs.

Automedon . . . . . . ô-tŏm'-ĕ-dŏn.

Autriche . . . . ō-trēsh.'

Auvergnat . . . . . . ō-vârn-yä'.

Auvergne . . . . . . ō-vârn'-yŭ.

Aux Cayes, *see* Cayes . . ō kä.

Auxerre . . . . ō-sâr'. ōks-âr'.

Auxerrois . . . . . . ō-sâr-wä', ōks-âr-wä'.

Avalon *or* Avallon . . . ăv'-ä-lŏn.

Avalos, D' . . . . . . dä-vä'-lŏs.

Avare, L' . . . . lä-vär'.   [mä-rē'-ä.

Ave Maria . . . . . . ā'-vē má-rī'-á. *It.* ä'-vä

Avenel . . . . āv'-nĕl.

Aventine . . . . ăv'-ĕn-tĭn.

Avenue de l'Opéra . . . ăv-nü' dŭ lō-pä-rä'.

Ave Roma Immortalis . .	ā' vō rō' má ĭm ôr tā' lĭs.
Averrhoës *or* Averroës . .	ă-vĕr'-ō-ĕz.
Avicenna	ăv-ĭ-sĕn'-ä.
Avignon	ä-vēn-yôṅ'.
Avila	ä'-vē-lä.
Avilion, *see* Avalon . . .	ă-vĭl'yŏn.
Aviz	*Port.* ä-vēz'; *Sp* ä'-vĭth.
Avogadro	ä-vō-gä'-drō.
Avon	ā'-vŏn, *local Am.* ăv'-ŏn.
Avondale (Ohio)	ăv'-ŏn-dāl.
Axayacatl, *or*	ă-tchä-yä-kä'-tl.
Axayacatzlin	ä-tchä-yä-kătz-lēn'.
Axim	äks'-ĭm, ä-shēng'.
Axminster	ăks'-mĭn-stĕr.
Ay, *see* Aï	ä'-ē.
Ayacucho	ä-ē-ä-kōō'-chō.
Ayala	ä-yä'-lä.
Aybonito, *see* Aibonito . .	ä-ē-bō-nē'-tō.
Ayesha	ä-yĕ'-shä.
Aymon	ā'-mōn.
Ayoub Khan, *see* Ayub Khan	ä-yōōb' khän.
Ayr	âr.
Ayscue	ās'-kū.
Aytoun	ā'-tōōn.
Ayub Khan, *see* Ayoub Khan	ä-yōōb' khän.
Azarael, *or* Azareel . . .	ăz'-á-rā-ĕl, äz'-á-rĕ-ĕl.
Azarias	ăz-á-rī'-ás.
Azazel	ă-zä'-zĕl.
Azaziel	ă-zā'-zĭ-ĕl.
Azeglio, D'	däd-zāl'-yō.
Azerbaijan	äz-ĕr-bī-jän'.
Azimgarh	ă-zĭm-gŭr'. [kōōr'.
Azincourt, *see* Agincourt .	ăz'-ĭn-kōrt. *Fr.* äzh-ăṅ-
Azof, *or* Azoff, *see* Azov. .	ä'-zŏf.
Azor	*Sp.* ä-thōr'.
Azores	ă-zōrz'.

Azov, *see* Azof . . . . . ä'-zŏf.
Azrael, *or* Azrail . . . . ăz'-rā-ĕl, ăz'-rā-ĭl.
Aztecas . . . . ăz'-tĕk-àz.
Azuay, *see* Assuay . . . ä-thōō-ī'.
Azucena . . . . äd-zōō-chā'-nä.

B

Baal . . . . bā'-àl.
Baalbac, *or* Baalbak . . bäl'-băk, bäl-băk'.
Baalbec, *or* Baalbek . . bäl'-bĕk, bäl-bĕk'.
Baalim . . . . bā'-à-lĭm.
Bab . . . . bäb.
Baba, Ali . . . . . . ä'-lē bä'-bä.
Bab-el-Mandeb . . . . bäb-ĕl-män'-dĕb.
Baber, *see* Babur . . . . bä'-bēr.
Babieca, *see* Bavieca . . bä-bē-ā'-kä.
Babington . . . . . . băb'-ĭng-tŏn.
Babist . . . . bäb'-ĭst.
Babur, *see* Baber . . . . bä'-bēr.
Babúyan (Is.) . . . . . bä-bōō'-yän.
Babylonic . . . . . . băb-ĭ-lŏn'-ĭk.
Bacchae . . . . băk'-ē.
Bacchante . . . . . . băk-kăn'-tē.
Bacchus . . . . băk'-ŭs.
Bacchylides . . . . . . bä-kĭl'-ĭ-dēz.
Bacciochi . . . . bä-chŏk'-kē.
Baccio della Porta . . . bä'-chō dĕl'-lä pōr'-tä.
Bach . . . . bäċh.
Bache . . . . bāch.
Backergunge, *see* Baker-
ganj . . . . } bäk'-ĕr-gŭnj.
Backhuysen . . . . . . bäk'-hoi-zĕn.
Bacolod . . . . bä-kō-lŏd'.
Bacolor . . . . bä-kō-lōr'.

Bacoor, see Bakoor . . . bă-kōōr′,
Bacsányi . . . . bä′-chän-yē.
Bactriana . . . . . . băk-trĭ-ā′-nä.
Badagry . . . . bä-dä-grē′. [hōth,
Badajos, or Badajoz . . . bäd-ä-hōs′. Sp. bä-dä-
Badebec . . . . bäd-běk′.
Baden . . . . bä′-děn.
Baden-Powell . . . . . bă-děn-powl′.
Badinguet-Radot . . . . bä-dăṅ-gä′ rä-dō′.
Badon (Mt.) . . . . . bā′-dŏn.
Badoura . . . . bă-dōō′-rä. [ĕr.
Baedeker . . . . . . bā′-děk-ĕr. Ger. bâ′-děk-
Baena . . . . Sp. bä-ā′-nä ; Port. bä-
Baer, Von . . . . . . fŏn bâr. [yā′-nä.
Baez . . . . bä′-āth.
Bafing, Ba-Fing . . . . bä-fēng′.
Bagalor . . . . bä-gä-lōr′.
Bagamoyo . . . . . . bä-gä-mō′-yō. [dăd.
Bagdad or Baghdad . . . bäg-däd′, commonly băg′-
Bagehot . . . . băj′-ŏt. [dăd.
Baghdad or Bagdad . . bäg-däd′, commonly băg′-
Bagnacavallo . . . . . bän″-yä-kä-väl′-lō.
Bagni di Lucca . . . . bän′-yē dē lōōk′-kä.
Bagration . . . . . . bä-grä-tsē-ōn′, bȧ-grä′-
Bahamas . . . . bä-hä′-mȧz. [shŭn.
Bahar, see Behar, Bihar . bă-här′.
Bahari . . . . bä-hä-rē′.
Bahawalpur . . . . . bä-hä-wäl-pōōr′.
Bahia . . . . bä-ē̯′-ä.
Bahia Honda . . . . . bä-ē̯′-ä ōn′-dä.
Baiae . . . . bā′-yē.
Baikal . . . . bī′-käl, bī-käl′.
Baillie . . . . bā′-lē.
Baillot . . . . bä-ē̯-yō′.
Bailly . . . . bā′-lē. Fr. bä-yē′.
Baiquiri . . . . bä-ē̯-kē′-rē.

Bairam, *see* Beiram . . . bī-räm'.
Baireuth, *see* Bayreuth . bī'rūth. *Ger.* bī-roit'.
Bairut, *see* Beirut, *or* Bey-
rout . . . . } bā-rōōt'.
Baja . . . . bä'-yä.
Bajazet, *see* Bayazid . . băj'-ā-zĕt, băj-ā-zĕt'.
Bajza . . . . bŏy'-zä.
Bakerganj, *see* Backergunge băk'-ĕr-gánj.
Bakhuyzen . . . . . băk'-hoi-zĕn.
Bakoor, *or* Bakor, *see* Bacoor bă-kōōr'.
Balaam . . . . . . bā'-lăm.
Balábac . . . . . . bä-lä'-bäk.
Balaclava, *or* Balaklava . bä-lä-klä'-vä.
Balafré, Le . . . . . lŭ bä-lä-frā'.
Balaguer . . . . . . bä-lä-gâr'.
Balaklava, *or* Balaclava . bä-lä-klä'-vä.
Balasore, Balasur . . . băl-á-sōōr'.
Balaustion . . . . . bă-lôs'-chŏn.
Balbek, *see* Baalbec . . bäl'-bĕk, bäl-bĕk'.
Balbo . . . . bäl'-bō.
Balboa, De . . . . . dā bäl-bō'-ä.
Balchen (Admiral) . . bôl'-chĕn.
Baldassare . . . . . bäl-däs-sä'-rä.
Balder, Baldur . . . bôl'-dĕr.
Bâle, *see* Basle . . . . bäl.
Baleares . . . . . . bā-lē-ā'-rēz.
Balearic . . . . . . băl-ē-ăr'-ĭk.
Baléchou . . . . . . bä-lä-shōō'.
Baler . . . . bä-lâr'.
Balestier . . . . . . băl-ĕs-tēr'.
Balfe . . . . bălf.
Balfour . . . . . . băl'-fōōr, băl'-fĕr.
Balimghem . . . . . bä-lăṅ-găṅ'.
Balin and Balan . . . bā'-lĭn, ănd bā'-lăn.
Baliol, *see* Balliol . . . bā'-lĭ-ŏl. *Fr.* bäl-yōl'.
Baliuag . . . . bäl-ē'-wäg.

Balize	bä-lēz'.
Ballran	bȯl' krln, bȧl krln'.
Ballarat	băl-á-răt'.
Ballari	bäl-lä'-rē.
Ballesteros	bäl-yĕs-tä'-rōs.
Balliol, see Baliol . . .	bā'-lĭ-ŏl. Fr. bäl-yōl'.
Balliol (College) . . .	bāl'-yĕl.
Balmaceda	bäl-mä-thā'-dä.
Balmoral	băl-mŏr'-ăl, băl-mō'-răl.
Balmung	bäl'-mōŏng. [mō'.
Balsamo	băl-sā'-mō. Fr. bäl-sä-
Balthasar, or Balthazar	băl-thā'-zär, bäl'-tä-zär.
Baluchistan, see Beluchistan, or Beloochistan . .	băl-ōō-chĭs-tän'.
Balwhidder	băl-whĭth'-ĕr. [zăk.
Balzac	bäl-zäk', commonly băl'-
Bamberg	bäm'-bĕrċh.
Banana	bä-nä'-nä.
Banaras, see Benares .	bă-nä'-räs.
Bancroft	băn'-krŏft.
Banér, see Banner . . .	bä-nâr'.
Bangkok	băng-kŏk'.
Bangor (Me.)	băn'-gŏr.
Bangor (Wales) . . .	băng'-gĕr.
Bangweolo	băng-wē-ō'-lō.
Banner, see Banér . . .	bä-nâr'.
Banquo	băn'-kwō, băng'-kwō.
Bantam	bän-täm'.
Bantu	băn'-tōō.
Banville (Théodore de) .	bäṅ-vēl'.
Banyoro	bä-nyō'-rō.
Bara Banki	bä'-rä bän'-kē.
Barabas, or Barabbas .	bā-răb'-ás.
Barabra, see Berabra .	bä-rä'-brä.
Baracoa	bä-rä-kō'-ä.
Baraguay d'Hilliers . .	bä-rä-gä' dĕ-yä'.

Barataria	băr-a̤-tā'-rĭ-ȧ. *Sp.* bä-rä-
Barbadoes, *or* Barbados	băr-bā'-dōz. [tä-rē'-ȧ.
Barbarelli	bär-bä-rĕl'-lē.
Barbarossa	bär-bȧ-rŏs'-ä.
Barbaroux	bär-bä-rōō'.
Barbary	bär'-bȧ-rĭ.
Barbauld	bär'-bôld. *Fr.* bär-bō'.
Barbazon, *see* Barbison	bär-bä-zôn'.
Barberini	bär-bā-rē'-nē.
Barbey d'Aurevilly . . .	bär-bā' dō̲-r̲ĕ-vē-yē'.
Barbier de Séville, Le . .	lŭ bär-bē̲-ä̲' dŭ sä-vēl'.
Barbiere de Seviglia, Il .	ēl bär-bē̲-ä̲'-rĕ dä sä-
Barbison, *see* Barbazon	bär-bē-zôn'. [vēl'-yä.
Barcellona	bär-chĕl-lō'-nä.
Barcelona . . . . . {	bär-sĕ-lō'-nä. *Sp.* bär- thä-lō'-nä.
Barclay de Tolly	bär-klā' dŭ tō-lē'.
Bardi, Bardo de'	bär'-dō dä bär'-dē.
Bardolph	bär'-dŏlf.
Bardwan, *see* Burdwan	bärd-wän'.
Bareja	bä-rā'-ċhä.
Barère de Vieuzac . . .	bä-râr' dŭ vē̲-ē̲-zä'.
Barfleur	bär-flĕr'.
Bargello	bär-jĕl'-lō.
Bargiel	bär'-gēl.
Bariatinski	bär-yä-tēn'-skē.
Baring	bā'-rĭng, bâr'-ĭng.
Baring-Gould	bâr'-ĭng-gōōld'.
Barlaymont	bär-lä-môn'.
Bar-le-Duc	bär-lĕ-dük'.
Barmecides	bär'-mē-sīdz.
Barnabas	bär'-nȧ-bȧs.
Barnato	bär-nä'-tō.
Barnay	*Ger.* bär'-nĭ.
Barnett	bär'-nĕt.
Barneveld	bär'-nĕ-vĕlt.

Baroccio, *see* Barozzio . . bä-rŏch'-ō.

Baroda . . . . bä-rō' ää.   [rŏṅ'.

Baron . . . . *Fr.* bä-rôṅ'.   *Ger.* bä-

Baronin . . . . bä-rō'-nēn.

Baronne . . . . bä-rŏn'.

Baroque . . . . bä-rōk'.

Barozzi . . . . bä-rŏt'-sē.

Barozzio, *see* Baroccio . . bä-rŏt'-sē-ō.

Barrackpur . . . . . . bär-äk-pōōr'.

Barradas . . . . bär-rä'-däs.

Barragan . . . . bär-rä-gän'.

Barranquilla . . . . bär-rän-kēl'-yä.

Barranquitas . . . . bär-rän-kē'-täs.

Barras . . . . bä-räs'.   *Fr.* bä-rä'.

Barré . . . . bä-rä'.

Barrès, Maurice . . . mō-rēs' bär-rĕs'.

Barrili . . . . bär-rē'-lē.

Barrot . . . . bä-rō'.

Barrundia . . . . . . bä-rōōn'-dē-ä.

Barry, Mme. du . . . . mä-däm' dü bär-rē'.

Bar-sur-Aube . . . . . bär-sür-ōb'.

Bartas . . . . bär-tä'.

Barth . . . . bärt.

Barthélemy-Saint-Hilaire . bär-tāl-mē'-săṅ-tē-lâr'.

Bartholdi . . . . . . bär-tŏl-dē'.

Bartholo . . . . bär-tō-lŏ'.

Bartimeus . . . . . . bär-tĭm-ē'-ŭs.

Bartol . . . . bär-tŏl'.

Bartoli . . . . bär'-tō-lē.

Bartolommeo . . . . . bär-tō-lŏm-mā'-ō.

Bartolozzi . . . . . . bär-tō-lŏt'-sē.

Baruch . . . . bā'-rŭk.

Bärwalde . . . . . . bâr'-väl-dŭ.

Barye . . . . bä-rē'.

Barzillai . . . . bär-zĭl'-ā-ī, bär'-zĭl-ā.

Baseelan, *see* Basilan . . bä-sē'-län.

Basel . . . .   bä'-zĕl.
Bashan . . . .   bā'-shăn.
Bashee, *or* Bashi (I.)   . .   bä-shē'.
Bashi-Bazouk . . . . .   băsh'-ĭ-bă-zōōk'.
Bashkirtseff, Marie . . .   mä-rē' bäsh-kĕrt'-sĕf.
Basil . . . .   bā-'zĭl, băz'-ĭl.
Basilan, *see* Baseelan . .   bä-sē'-län.
Basilicon Doron . . . .   bă-sĭl'-ĭ-kŏn dō'-rŏn.
Basque . . . . . .   bàsk.
Basra, *see* Bussora . . .   bäs'-rä.
Bassanio . . . .   bä-sä'-nĭ-ō.
Bassano (Duke of) . . .   bäs-sä'-nō.
Basses-Alpes . . . . .   bäs-zälp'.
Basses-Pyrénées . . . .   bäs-pē-rā-nā'.
Basse-Terre . . . . . .   bäs-târ'.
Bassi . . . .   bäs'-sē.
Bassompierre . . . . .   bä-sôn-pē-âr'.
Bastian . . . .   bäs'-tē-än.
Bastiat . . . .   bäs-tē-ä'.
Bastien-Lepage . . . .   bäs-tē-ĕn' lĕ-päzh'.
Bastile, *or* Bastille . . .   bäs'-tēl.   *Fr.* bäs-tē'-yŭ.
Basundi . . . .   bä-sōōn'-dē.
Basutoland . . . . . .   bä-sōō'-tō-länd.
Bataan . . . .   bä-tä-än'.
Batabano . . . . . .   bä-tä-bä'-nō.
Batalha . . . .   bä-täl'-yä.
Batan (I.) . . . . . .   bä-tän'.
Batanes . . . .   bä-tä'-nĕs.
Batangas . . . .   bä-tän'-gäs.
Báthori, *see* Batory . . .   bä'-tō-rē.   [bà.
Bathsheba . . . . . .   băth-shē'-bä, băth'-shĕ-
Baton Rouge . . . . .   { băt'-ŭn rōōzh. *Fr.* bä-
{ tôn' rōōzh.
Batory, *see* Báthori . . .   bä'-tō-rē.
Battenberg . . . . . .   { băt'-tĕn-bĕrg. *Ger.* bät'-
{ tĕn-bĕrċh.

Battersea . . . . băt' ẽr sŭ.
Batthyányi . . . . . . bŏt'-yän-yē.
Batum, *or* Batoum . . . bä-tōōm'.
Baucis . . . . bô'-sĭs.
Baudelaire . . . . . . bōd-lâr'.
Baudissin . . . . . . bow'-dĭs-sēn.
Baudricourt . . . . . bō-drē-kōōr'.
Baudry . . . . bō-drē'.
Bautista . . . . bä-ōō-tēs'-tä.
Bautzen . . . . bowt'-sĕn.
Bavieca, *see* Babieca . . bä-bē-ā'-kä.
Bayamo . . . . bä-yä'-mō.
Bayamon . . . . . . bä-yä-mōn'.
Bayard (Chevalier) . . . bā'-ärd. *Fr.* bä-yär'.
Bayard (James A.) . . . bī'-ärd.
Bayazid, *see* Bajazet . . bä-yä-zēd'.
Bayeux . . . . bä-yẽ'.
Bayle . . . . bāl.
Bayombong . . . . . bä-ē-ŏm-bōng'. [yŏn'.
Bayonne . . . . . . bā-yŏn', bī'-yŭn. *Fr.* bä-
Bayreuth, *see* Baireuth . bī'-rūth. *Ger.* bī-roit'.
Bazaine . . . . bä-zān'.
Bazan, Don Cesar de . dôṅ sä-zär' dŭ bä-zän'.
Bazán, Emilia . . . . . ä-mēl'-ē-ä bä-thän'.
Bazarof . . . . bä-zär'-ŏf.
Bazin . . . . bä-zäṅ'. [fēld.
Beaconsfield . . . . . bē'-kŏnz-fēld, bĕk'-ŏnz-
Béarn . . . . bā-är'.
Béarnais, Le . . . . . lŭ bā-är-nā'.
Beata Beatrix . . . . . bē-ä'-tä bē'-ä-trĭks.
Beaton . . . . bē'-tŏn. *Sc.* bā'-tŏn.
Beatrice . . . . { bē'-ä-trĭs. *Fr.* bā-ä-trēs' *It.* bä-ä-trē'-chĕ.
Beatrice Cenci . . . . . bä-ä-trē'-chĕ chĕn'-chē.
Beatrice Portinari . . . bä-ä-trē'-chĕ pōr-tē-nä'-
Beatrix . . . . bē'-ä-trĭks. [rē.

Béatrix	{ bē'-å-trĭks. *Fr.* bā-ä-trēks'.
Beattie	bē'-tĭ. *Sc.* bā'-tĭ.
Beau Brummel . . .	bō brŭm'-ĕl.
Beaucaire	bō-kâr'.
Beauchamp (Alphonse de)	*Fr.* bō-shän'
Beauchamp (Philip) . . .	*Eng.* bē'-chăm.
Beauclerc, *or* Beauclerk	bō-klärk', bō'-klärk.
Beaufort	*Eng.* bō'-fŭrt. *Fr.* bō-
Beaufort-en-Vallée . . .	bō-fōr'-tôṅ-väl-lā'. [fōr'.
Beaufort (Sir Francis) . .	bū'-fŭrt.
Beaugency	bō-zhŏṅ-sē'.
Beauharnais, Eugène de .	ē-zhän' dŭ bō-är-nā'.
Beauharnais, Joséphine de	zhō-zā-fēn' dŭ bō-är-nā'.
Beauharnais, Hortense de	ōr-tŏṅs' dŭ bō-är-nā'.
Beaulieu	bō-lē-ȩ̄'.
Beaumanoir	bō-mä-nwär'.
Beaumarchais	bō-mär-shā'.
Beaumont	{ *Eng.* bō'-mŏnt, *or* bū'-mŏnt. *Fr.* bō-môṅ'.
Beaumont-sur-Oise . . .	bō-môṅ'-sür-wäz'.
Beaune	bōn.
Beaune-la-Rolande . . .	bōn-lä-rō-läṅd'. [gär'.
Beauregard	bō'-rĕ-gärd. *Fr.* bō-rĕ-
Beaurepaire	bō-rĕ-pâr'.
Beauvais	bō-vā'.
Beaux	bō.
Bebel	bā'-bĕl.
Beccafumi	bĕk-kä-fōō'-mē.
Beccari	bĕk'-kä-rē.
Beccaria	bĕk-kä-rē'-ä.
Becher	bĕċh'-ĕr.
Bechuanaland	bĕt-chōō-ä'-nä-lănd.
Bechuanas	bĕt-chōō-ä'-näs.
Becket (Thomas) à . . .	å bĕk'-ĕt.
Becquerel	bĕk-rĕl'.

Bedaween, see Bedouin . .	bĕd′ à wŭn.
Bedel (Timothy)	bē′-dĕl.
Bedivere	bĕd′-ĭ-vēr.
Bedouin, see Bedaween	bĕd′-ōō-ĭn.
Bedreddin Hassan . . .	bĕd-rĕd-dēn′ häs′-sän.
Beelzebub, see Belzebub .	bē-ĕl′-zē-bŭb.
Beersheba	bē-ēr-shē′-bà, bē-ēr′-
Beethoven, Van	vän bā′-tō-vĕn. [shĕ-bà.
Befana	bā-fä′-nä.
Béguinage	bā-gē-näzh′.
Beguins, or Beguines . .	bĕg′-ĭnz.
Behaim	bā′-hīm.
Behar, see Bahar, Bihar .	bĕ-här′.
Behechio	bā-ā′-chē̤-ō̤, bā-ĕ-chē′-ō.
Behn (Mrs. Aphra) . . .	bän.
Behring, see Bering . . .	bē′-rĭng. Dan. bā′-rĭng.
Beira	bā′-rä.
Beiram, see Bairam . . .	bī-räm′.
Beirut, see Bairut and Beyrout . . . . }	bā-rōōt′.
Béjart, Armande	är-mänd′ bā-zhär′.
Bejol	bā-ċhōl′.
Bejucal	bā-ċhōō-käl′
Belarius	bĕ-lā′-rĭ-ŭs.
Belaspoor, see Bilaspoor .	bē-läs-pōōr′.
Belchite	bĕl-chē′-tā.
Beleek	bĕl-ēk′.
Belfagor, see Belphegor .	bĕl′-fá-gôr.
Belfast (Ireland)	bĕl-fäst′, bĕl-făst′.
Belfast (Maine)	bĕl′-fäst, bĕl-făst.
Belfort	Fr. bĕl-fōr′.
Belgian	bĕl′-jĭ-ăn.
Belgiojoso	bĕl-jō-yō′-zō.
Belgique	bĕl-zhēk′.
Belgium	bĕl′-jĭ-ŭm, pop. bĕl′-jŭm.
Belgrad	bĕl-gräd′.

Belgrade . . . . bĕl-grād'.
Belial . . . . bē'-lĭ-ăl.
Belianis (of Greece) . . . bā-lē-ä'-nēs.
Belisario . . . . bā-lē-zä'-rē-ō.
Belisarius . . . . . . bĕl-ĭ-sā'-rĭ-ŭs.
Bélise . . . . bā-lēz'.
Beliza . . . . bĕ-lē'-zä.
Bellagio . . . . bĕl-lä'-jō.
Bellario . . . . bĕl-lä'-rĭ-ō.
Bellarmine . . . . . . bĕl-lär-mēn'.
Bellatrix . . . . bĕl'-à-trĭks, bĕl-lā'-trĭks.
Bellay . . . . bĕ-lā'.
Belle Alliance, La . . . lä bĕl äl-lē-äns'.
Belleau . . . . bĕl-lō'.
Belle Île, *or* Belle Isle, en ⎱ bĕl ēl' ôn mâr'.
Mer . . . . ⎰
Belle-Isle (Newfoundland) bĕl-īl'.
Belle Jardinière, La . . . lä bĕl zhär-dēn-ē-âr'.
Belle Laitière, La . . . . lä bĕl lâ-tē-âr'.
Bellerophon . . . . . . bĕ-lĕr'-ō-fŏn.
Belliard . . . . bĕl-yär'.
Bellingham . . . . . . bĕl'-ĭng-àm.
Bellini . . . . . . bĕl-lē'-nē.   [bāl'-yō.
Bello, Andres . . . . bĕl'-yō. *Sp.* än-drās'
Belloc, Hilaire . . . . . ē-lâr' bĕl-ōk'.
Bellona . . . . bĕl-ō'-nà.
Belon . . . . bĕ-lôn', blôn.
Beloochistan, *see* Beluchis-⎱ bĕl-ōō-chĭs-tän'.
tan, Baluchistan . . . ⎰
Belphegor, *see* Belfagor . bĕl'-fĕ-gôr.
Belphoebe . . . . . . bĕl-fē'-bē.
Belshazzar . . . . . . bĕl-shăz'-är.
Beluchistan, *see* Baluchis-⎱ bĕl-ōō-chĭs-tän'.
tan, Beloochistan . . . ⎰
Belvedere . . . . . . bĕl-vĕ-dēr'. *It.* bāl-vă-
Belvoir . . . . *Eng.* bē'-vĕr. [dā'-rĕ.

Belzebub, *see* Beelzebub .   bĕl'-zē-bŭb.
Belzoni . . . . . . bĕl-tso'-ne.
Bemba (L.) . . . . . bĕm'-bä.
Bembesi . . . . . . bĕm-bā'-zē.
Benaiah . . . . . . bĕ-nā'-yä.
Benalcazar, *see* Velalcazar bā-näl-kä'-thär.
Benares, *see* Banaras . . bĕ-nä'-rĕz.
Benbow (Admiral) . . . bĕn'-bō.
Bendavid . . . . . . bĕn-dä'-fĭd.
Bender-Abbas, *or* . . . bĕn'-dĕr-äb'-bäs.
   Bender Abbasi . . . bĕn'-dĕr-äb-bä-sē'. [nō.
Benedetto da Majano . . bā-nā-dĕt'-tō dä mä-yä'-
Benedicite . . . . . bĕn-ĕ-dĭs'-ĭ-tē.
Beneke . . . . . . bĕ'-nĕ-kŭ.
Benevento . . . . . bĕn-ĕ-vĕn'-tō. *It.* bā-
Bengal . . . . . . bĕn-gôl'. [nā-vän'-tō.
Bengali . . . . . . bĕn-gô-lē'.
Benguela . . . . . . bĕng-gā'-lä.
Ben-hadad . . . . . bĕn-hā'-dăd.
Benicia . . . . . . bē-nĭsh'-ĭ-á.
Benin . . . . bĕ-nēn'.
Ben Ledi . . . . . . bĕn lĕd'-ĭ.
Ben Nevis . . . . . bĕn nĕv'-ĭs.
Bennigsen . . . . . bĕn'-nĭg-sĕn.
Benoit . . . . . . bĕ-nwä'.
Ben-oni . . . . . . bĕn-ō'-nĭ.
Bentham . . . . . . bĕn'-thám, bĕn'-tám.
Bentinck . . . . . . bĕn'-tĭngk.
Bentivoglio . . . . bĕn-tē-vōl'-yō.
Bentzon, Théodore . . . tā-ō-dōr' bôṅt-zôṅ'.
Benue, *see* Binue . . . . bĕn-wē'.   [nē.
Benvenuto Cellini . . . bān-vā-nōō'-tō chĕl-lē'-
Beowulf . . . . . . bā'-ō-wŏŏlf, bē'-ō-wŏŏlf.
Berabra, *see* Barabra . . bĕ-rä'-brä.
Béranger, de . . . . . dŭ bā-räṅ-zhä'.
Berar . . . . bā-rär'.

Berber . . . . běr'-běr.

Berbera . . . . bûl-bû-rä.

Berchem, *see* Berghem . . běrċh'-hěm.

Berea . . . . bě-rē'-à.　　　[gä'-rē-ä.

Berengaria . . . . . běr-ěn-gâr'-ĭ-à,　bā-rěn-

Berengarius . . . . . . běr-ěn-gâr'-ĭ-ŭs.

Bérenger . . . . bā-rŏṅ-zhā'.

Berenice . . . . běr-ě-nī'-sē.

Bérénice . . . . bā-rā-nēs'.

Beresford . . . . . . běr'-ěs-fŭrd.

Beresina, *or* Berezìna . . běr-ě-zē'-nä.　　[mē.

Bergami, Bartolomeo . . bär''-tō-lō-mā'-ō bâr'-gä-

Bergamo . . . . bâr'-gä-mō.

Bergen-op-Zoom . . . . běr'-ċhěn-ŏp-zōm'.

Bergerac, Cyrano de . . sĭr-ä-nō' dŭ běrzh-räk'.

Berghem, *see* Berchem . . běrċh'-hěm.

Bergsöe . . . . běrg'-sě.　　[bā'-rĭng.

Bering, *see* Behring . . . bā'-rĭng, *or* bē'-rĭng. *Dan.*

Bériot . . . . bā-rē-ō'.

Berkeley . . . . běrk'-lĭ, bärk'-lĭ.

Berlichingen, Götz von . . gēts fŏn běr'-lĭċh-ĭng-ěn.

Berlin . . . . běr-lĭn'. *Ger.* běr-lēn'.

Berlioz . . . . běr-lē-yōz'.

Bermoothes . . . . . . běr-mōō'-thěs.

Bermudas . . . . . . běr-mū'-dàz.

Bern, *see* Berne . . . běrn. *Ger.* běrn.　[dŏt'.

Bernadotte . . . . . . běr'-nà-dŏt. *Fr.* běr-nä-

Bernard . . ○ . . . . { běr'-närd, běr-närd'. *Fr.*
　　　　　　　　　　　{ 　bâr-när'.　　　[pē-âr'.

Bernardin de St. Pierre . běr-när-dăṅ'　dŭ　săṅ

Bernardine . . . . . . běr'-när-dĭn.　　[pē-ō.

Bernardo del Carpio . . . běr-när'-dō　děl　kär'-

Berne, *see* Bern . . . . běrn. *Fr.* běrn.

Bernese . . . . běr-nēs', běr-nēz'.

Bernhardt, Sarah . . . . { sā'-rä běrn'-härt.　*Fr.*
　　　　　　　　　　　{ sä-rä' bâr-när'.

Bernice	bẽr-nĭ'-sē.
Bernini	bẽr-ne'-ne.
Bernoulli, or Bernouilli	bẽr-nōō'-yē.
Berri, or Berry	bĕr'-Ĭ, Fr. bĕr-rē'.
Berthelot	bĕr-tĕ-lō'.
Berthier	bĕr-tĕ-ā'.
Berthollet	bĕr-tō-lä'.
Bertin	bĕr-tăṅ'.
Bertrand	bĕr-träṅ'.
Bertuccio	bâr-tŏŏch'-ō.
Berwick	bĕr'-Ĭk. [zĭl'-Ĭ-ŏŏs.
Berzelius	bẽr-zē'-lĭ-ŭs. Sw. bĕr-
Besançon	bĕ-zäṅ-sôṅ'.
Besant (Walter)	bĕs'-ȧnt.
Besant (Annie)	bĕz'-ȧnt.
Bessaraba	bĕs-sä'-rä-bä.
Bessières	bĕs-ē-ȧr'.
Betelgeux, or	bĕt-ĕl-gẽ'.
Betelgeuze	bĕt-ĕl-gẽz'. [or -gēs.
Betelguese	bĕt-ĕl-gēz', bĕt'-ĕl-gēz,
Bethabara	bĕth-ăb'-ȧ-rȧ.
Bethesda	bĕ-thĕz'-dȧ, bĕ-thĕs'-dȧ.
Bethlehem	bĕth'-lē-ĕm, bĕth'-lē-
Bethpeor	bĕth-pē'-ôr. [hĕm.
Bethphage	bĕth'-fā-jē, bĕth'-fāj.
Bethsaida	bĕth-sā'-Ĭ-dȧ, bĕth-sā'-
Bethuel	bĕ-thū'-ĕl. [dȧ.
Bethune	bĕ-thūn'.
Béthune	bā-tün'.
Bettina von Arnim . . .	bĕt-tē'-nä fŏn är'-nĭm.
Bettws-y-Coed	bĕt''-ŭs-ē-kō'-ĕd.
Beulah	bū'-lä, bĕ-ū'-lä.
Beust, von	fŏn boist.
Bevis	bē'-vĭs.
Bewick	bū'-Ĭk.
Bey	bā.

Beyle . . . . bāl.

Beyme, von . . . . . fŏn bī'-mŭ.

Beyrout, *see* Bairut, Beirut bā'-rōot. *Turk.* bī'-rōot.

Beza . . . . bē'-zȧ.

Bezaleel . . . . . . bĕ-zāl'-ē-ĕl.

Bèze, *or* Besze . . . . bāz.

Béziers . . . . bā-zē̱-ā̱'.

Bhagalpur, *see* Boglipoor bhä-gäl-pōōr', bŏg-ŭl-pōōr'.

Bhagavadgita . . . . bhă''-gă-văd-gē'-tä.

Bhagavatapurana . . . bhä''-gȧ-vă-tȧ-pōō-rä'-nä.

Bhartpur, *see* Bhurtpore bhŭrt-pōor'.

Bhawalpur . . . . . bhä'-wäl-pōor.

Bheel, *or* Bhil . . . . bēl.

Bhopal . . . . bhō-pôl'.

Bhurtpore, *see* Bhartpur bhĕrt-pōr'.

Biafra . . . . bē-ä'-frä.

Biagrassa . . . . . . bē-ä-gräs'-sä.

Bianca Capello . . . . bē-än'-kä kä-pĕl'-lō.

Bianchi . . . . . . bē-än'-kē.

Biarritz . . . . . . bē-är-rēts'.

Bias . . . . bī'-ȧs.

Bibbiena . . . . . . bēb-bē-ā'-nä.

Bibliothèque Nationale . bēb''-lē-ō-tĕk' näs-ē-ō̱-näl'.

Bichat . . . . bē-shä'.

Bicor . . . . bē-kŏr'.

Bidassoa . . . . . . bē-däs-sō'-ä.

Biddeford (Me.) . . . bĭd'-ĕ-fōrd.

Bideford (Eng.) . . . bĭd'-ĕ-fŭrd.

Bierstadt . . . . . . bēr'-stät.

Bigod . . . . bĭg'-ŏd.

Bihar, *see* Bahar, Behar bĭ-här'.

Bilaspoor, *see* Belaspoor bē-läs-pōor'.

Billardière . . . . . bē-yär-dē̱-ȧr'.

Billot (Gen.) . . . . bē-yō'.

Bimani, *or* . . . . . bē-mä-nē'.

Bimini . . . . bē-mē-nē'.

Binondo	bē-nŏn'-dō.
Binue, *see* Benue	bĭn'-wē.
Biot	bē-ō'.
Birmingham	bĕr'-mĭng-ȧm.
Birnam	bĕr'-nȧm.
Biron	bĭr'-ŏn. *Fr.* bē-rôṅ'.
Bisayas	bē-sä'-yäs.
Bismarck, *or* . . . . }	bĭz'-märk shĕn'-how-
Bismark-Schönhausen . . }	zĕn.
Bithynia	bĭ-thĭn'-ị-ȧ.
Biton	bĭ'-tŏn.
Bivar, Rodrigo de . . .	rōd-rē'-gō dä bē-bär'.
Bizet	bē-zā'.
Björnson, Björnstjerne . . {	bē̜-ĕrn'-stē̜-ĕrn-nĕ bē̜-ĕrn'-sŏn.
Blaise	blāz.
Blanc	bläṅ.
Blanchard	bläṅ-shär'.
Blanche	blănch. *Fr.* bläṅsh.
Blanco	blän'-kō.
Blandamour	blän'-dä-mōōr.
Blanqui	bläṅ-kē'.
Blasius	blä'-zĭ-ŭs.
Blavatsky	blä-vät'-skĭ.
Blaze de Bury	bläz dŭ bü-rē'.
Bléneau	blā-nō'.
Blenheim, *see* Blindheim .	blĕn'-ĭm.
Blifil	blĭ'-fĭl.
Blindheim, *see* Blenheim .	*Ger.* blĭnt'-hīm.
Bloemaert	blōō'-märt.
Bloemen	blōō'-mĕn.
Bloemfontein	blōōm'-fŏn-tīn.
Blois	blwä.
Bloomfield-Zeisler . . .	blōōm'-fēld-tsīs'-lĕr.
Blouet	blōō-ā'.
Blowitz	blō'-vĭts.

Blücher	bloo'-kĕr. *Ger.* blü'-ċhĕr.
Blum	bloom.
Blumenbach	bloo'-mĕn-bäċh.
Blumenthal	bloo'-mĕn-täl.
Boabdelin	bō-äb'-dĕ-lĭn.
Boabdil	bō-äb-dēl'.
Boadicea	bō-á-dĭ-sē'-á.
Boanerges	bō-á-nĕr'-jēz.
Boaz	bō'-ăz.
Bobadil	bŏb'-á-dĭl.
Bobadilla	bō-bä-dēl'-yä.
Boboli	bō'-bō-lē.
Boca del Drago . . .	bō'-kä dĕl drä'-gō.
Boca del Sierpe . . .	bō'-kä dĕl sē-ĕr'-pä.
Boccaccio	bŏk-käch'-ō.
Boccardo	bŏk-kär'-dō.
Boccherini	bŏk-kā-rē'-nē.
Böckh	bĕk.
Böcking	bĕk'-ĭng.
Bode	bō'-dŭ.
Bodin	bō-dăṅ'.
Bodleian	bŏd-lē'-án, bŏd'-lē-án.
Boece	bō-ēs', bois.
Boehm	bĕm.
Boeotia	bē-ō'-shĭ-á.
Boer	boor.
Boerhaave	bōr'-häv. *D.* boor'-hä-vĕ,
Boethius	bō-ē'-thĭ-ŭs.
Bogdanovitch	bŏg-dä-nō'-vĭch.
Boglipoor, *see* Bhagalpur	bŏg-lĭ-poor'.
Bogotá	bō-gō-tä'.
Bogra	bŏg-rä'.
Bohemond, Bohemund .	bō'-hē-mŭnd.
Bohio	bō-yō'.
Böhme	bĕ'-mŭ.
Bohol, *see Sp.* Bojol . .	bō-hŏl'.

Bohun	bō'-hŭn.
Boiardo, *or* Bojardo . . .	bŏ-yär'-dŏ.
Boieldieu	bwäl-dē-ē', bō-yĕl-dē-ē'
Boii	bō'-ĭ-ĭ.
Boileau-Despréaux . . .	bwä-lō'-dā-prā-ō'.
Bois de Boulogne	bwä dŭ bōō-lōn'-yŭ.
Boisdeffre	bwä-dĕfr'.
Bois de Vincennes . . .	bwä dŭ văṅ-sĕn'.
Bois Guilbert	bwä gēl-bâr'.
Boisrobert	bwä-rō-bâr'.
Boito	bō-ē'-tō.
Bojador (Cape) . . .	bŏj-ȧ-dōr'.
Bojol, *see* Bohol	bō-hŏl'.
Bokhara, *see* Bukhara, Bucharia	bōk-hä'-rä, bō-ċhä'-rä.
Boldini	bŏl-dē'-nē.
Boleyn, *or* Bellen . . .	bŏŏl'-ĕn.
Bolingbroke	bŏl'-ĭng-brŏŏk.
Bolivar	bŏl'-ĭ-vär. *Sp.* bō-lē'-vär.
Bologna	bō-lōn'-yä.
Bolognese.	bō-lōn-yēs', bō-lōn-yēz'.
Bolsena	bŏl-sā'-nä.
Bolsover (Castle)	bŏl'-sō-vẽr, bow'-zẽr.
Bombastes Furioso . . .	bŏm-băs'-tēz fū-rĭ-ō'-sō.
Bonaca, *or* Bonacca . . .	bŏn-ăk'-kä.
Bonacieux	bō-nä-sē-ē'. [pär'-tĕ.
Bonaparte, *see* Buonaparte	bō'-nȧ-pärt. *It.* bō-nȧ-
Bonapartist	bō'-nȧ-pärt''-ĭst.
Bonaventura	bō''-nä-vän-tōō'-rä.
Bonheur	bŏn-ẽr'.
Bonhomme Richard . . .	bŏn-ŏm' rē-shär'.
Boniface	bŏn'-ĭ-fās.
Bonn	bŏn. *Ger.* bŏn.
Bonnat	bŏn-nä'.
Bonnivard	bō-nē-vär'.
Bonnivet	bō-nē-vā'.

Bononcini, see Buononcini bŏn-ŏn-chē' nē.
Bonpland . . . . . . bôn-plän'.
Bon Silène . . . . . . bôn sē-lān'.
Bontemps . . . . . . bôn-tŏn'.
Boomplaats . . . . . . bōm'-pläts.
Boötes . . . . bō-ō'-tēz.
Booth . . . . bōōth.
Borachio . . . . bō-rä'-chē-ō, bō-rä'-chō.
Bordeaux . . . . . . bōr-dō'.
Bordereau (The) . . . . bōr-dē-rō'.
Bordone . . . . bōr-dō'-nĕ.
Boreas . . . . bō'-rē-ás.
Borghese . . . . bōr-gā'-zĕ.
Borgia . . . . bōr'-jä.
Borgo . . . . bōr'-gō.
Borneo . . . . bôr'-nē-ō.
Borodino . . . . bōr-ō-dē'-nō.
Borrioboola-gha . . . . bŏr"-ĭ-ō-bōō'-lä-gä'.
Borromean (Is.) . . . . bŏr-ō-mē'-án.
Borromée . . . . . . bŏr-rō-mā'.
Borromeo . . . . . . bōr-rō-mā'-ō.
Borromini . . . . . . bōr-rō-mē'-nē.
Bosanquet . . . . . . bō'-zăn-kĕt.
Bosboom . . . . bŏs'-bōm.
Boscawen (Admiral) . . bŏs'-kȧ-wĕn.
Boscobel . . . . bŏs'-kō-bĕl.
Boshof . . . . bŏs'-hŏf.
Bosna-Serai . . . . . . bŏs"-nä-sĕ-rī'.
Bosnia . . . . bŏz'-nĭ-ä.
Bosphorus, or . . . . . bŏs'-fō-rŭs.
Bosporus . . . . bŏs'-pō-rŭs.
Bossuet . . . . bō-sü-ā'.
Boston . . . . bŏs'-tŭn, bôs'-tŭn.
Boswell . . . . bŏz'-wĕl.
Botetourt . . . . . . bŏt'-ĕ-tōōrt.
Botha (Gen.) . . . . . bō'-tă.

Bothwell	bŏth'-wĕl, bŏth'-wĕl.
Botolph (St.)	bō-tŏlf', bō'-tŏlf.
Botticelli	bŏt-tē-chĕl'-lē. [chē.
Boturini Benaduci . .	bō-tōō-rē'-nē bä-nä-dōō'-
Botzaris, *see* Bozzaris .	bōt'-sä-rēs, *pop.* bŏ-zär'-ĭs.
Boucher de Perthes . .	bōō-shä' dŭ pârt'.
Boucicault	bōō'-sē-kō.
Boudinot	bōō'-dĭ-nŏt.
Boufflers	bōō-flâr'.
Bougainville	bōō-găn-vēl'.
Bouguereau	bōōg-rō', bōō-gĕr-ō'.
Bouillé	bōō-yä'.
Bouillon	bōō-yôn', bōōl-yôn'.
Boulainvilliers . . .	bōō-lăn-vē-yä'.
Boulak, *see* Bulak . .	bōō-läk'.
Boulanger	bōō-län-zhä'.
Boulevard des Italiens .	bōōl-vär' dä zē-täl-ē̠-ĕn'.
Boulogne, *or*	bōō-lōn'. *Fr.* bōō-lōn'-yŭ.
Boulogne-sur-Mer . . .	bōō-lōn'-sür-mâr'.
Bourbon	bōōr'-bŭn. *Fr.* bōōr-bôn'.
Bourbon (Kentucky) . .	*pop.* bĕr'-bŭn.
Bourdaloue	bōōr-dä-lōō'.
Bourdon	bōōr-dôn'.
Bourgeois (Sir Francis) .	bŭr-jois'.
Bourgeois (François) .	bōōr-zhwä'.
Bourges	bōōrzh.
Bourget, Paul	pōl bōōr-zhä'.
Bourgogne	bōōr-gōn'-yŭ.
Bourrienne, de	dŭ bōō-rē-ĕn'.
Bourse, La	lä bōōrs.
Boutet de Monvel . . .	bōō-tä' dŭ môn-vĕl'.
Bouvier	bōō-vēr'. *Fr.* bōō-vē̠-ä'.
Bouvines, *see* Bovines .	bōō-vēn'.
Bovary, Madame . . .	mä-dăm' bō-vä-rē'.
Bovines, *see* Bouvines .	bō-vēn'.
Bowditch	bow'-dĭch.

Bowdoin	bō'-dn.
Bowring	bow'-rĭng.
Boyacá	bō-yä-kä'.
Boyesen	boi'-ĕ-sĕn.
Boz	bŏz. [ĭs.
Bozzaris, *see* Botzaris . .	bŏt'-sä-rēs, *pop.* bŏ-zär'-
Brabançonne, La	lä brä-bän-sŏn'.
Brabant	{ brä - bănt', brä' - bant. *Fr.* brä-bän'.
Brabant (Gen.)	brä'-bănt.
Brabantio	brä-băn'-shĭ-ọ̄.
Braccio da Montone . . .	bräch'-ō dä mŏn-tō'-nĕ.
Bradwardine	brăd'-wär-dĭn.
Bragança	brä-gän'-sä.
Braganza	brä-gän'-zä.
Bragelonne	bräzh-ĕ-lŏn'.
Braham	brä'-am. [brä'-ĕ.
Brahe, Tycho	tī'-kō brä *or* brä. *Dan.*
Brahma	brä'-mä.
Brahman	brä'-man.
Brahmaputra	brä-má-pōō'-trá.
Brahmasamaj, *see* Brah-} mosomaj . . . . . }	brä"-mä-sä-mäj'.
Brahmin	brä'-mĭn.
Brahminism	brä'-mĭn-ĭzm.
Brahmosomaj, *see* Brah-} masamaj . . . . . }	brä"-mō-sō-mäj'.
Brahms	brämz.
Bramante	brä-män'-tĕ.
Brandenburg	{ brän'-dĕn-bĕrg. *Ger.* brän'-dĕn-bōōrċh.
Brandes	brän'-dĕs.
Branicki	brän-yĭt'-skē.
Brantôme	brän-tōm'.
Brassington	brás'-n.
Brauwer, *see* Brouwer . .	brow'-ĕr.

Bravo	brä'-vō.
Brazil. *Sp.* Brasil . . .	brä-zĭl'. *Port.* brä-zēl'.
Brazos	brä'-zōs.
Brazza	brät'-sä.
Brébeuf	brä-bĕf'.
Breda	*D.* brä-dä'.
Brederode	brä'-dä-rō''-dĕ.
Breisgau	brīs'-gow.
Breitenfeld	brī'-tĕn-fĕlt.
Breitmann, Hans	hänts brīt'-män.
Brema, Marie	mä-rē' brä'-mä.
Bremen	brĕm'-ĕn. *Ger.* brä'-mĕn.
Bremer (Frederika) . . .	bräm'-ĕr. *Sw.* brĭm'-ĕr.
Bremerhafen, *or*	brä'-mĕr-hä''-fĕn.
Bremerhaven	brĕm'-ĕr-hä''-vĕn.
Brentano	brĕn-tä'-nō.
Brera	brä'-rä.
Brescia	brĕ'-shä.
Breslau	brĕs'-low, brĕs'-lō.
Brest	brĕst.
Bretagne	brĕ-tän'-yŭ.
Breteuil	brĕ-tē'-yŭ.
Bretigny	brĕ-tĕn-yē'.
Breton (Cape)	brĭt'ŭn, brĕt'-ŭn.
Breton, Jules	zhül brĕ-tôṅ'.
Breughel	brĕ'-ċhĕl.
Brian Borohma, Boroihme, *or* Boru	brī'-än { bŏ-rō'-mä. bŏ-rōō'. }
Briançon	brē-äṅ-sôṅ'.
Briareus	brī-ā'-rē-ŭs, brī'-ā-rŭs.
Bridlington	bĕr'-lĭng-tŭn.
Brie	brē.
Briel	brēl.
Brighthelmstone, *or mod.* Brighton	brī'-tŭn.
Brihuega	brē-wä'-gä.

Bril	brēl.
Brilessus	brĭ-lĕs'-ŭs.
Brillant	brē-yäṅ'.
Brillat-Savarin	brē-yä' sä-vä-räṅ'.
Brindisi	brēn'-dē-zē.
Brinvilliers	brăṅ-vēl-yä'.
Briseis	brī-sē'-ĭs.
Brissot de Warville . . .	brē-sō' dŭ vär-vēl'.
Britomart, *or*	} brĭt'-ō-märt;
Britomartis	} brĭt-ō-mär'-tĭs.
Brobdingnag	brŏb'-dĭng-năg. [jĭ-ăn.
Brobdingnagian	brŏb-dĭng-năg'-ĭ-ăn, -nā'-
Broek	brōōk. `[lē'.
Broglie, de	dŭ brōg-lē'. *Fr.* dŭ brôg-
Broke (Sir Philip) . . .	brōōk.
Bromley	brŭm'-lĭ.
Brontë	brŏn'tē, brŏn'-tĕ.
Brough	brŭf.
Brougham	{ brōō'-ȧm, brōōm, brō'- ȧm. *Sc.* brōōċh'-ȧm.
Broughton (Hugh & Thos.)	brô'-tŭn.
Broughton (Rhoda) . . .	brow'-tŭn.
Brougniart	brōōn-ē-är'.
Brouwer, *see* Brauwer . .	brow'-ēr.
Brown-Séquard	brown-sā-kär'.
Bruch	brŏŏċh.
Brueys	brü-ā'.
Bruges	brōō'-jĕz. *Fr.* brüzh.
Brugsch Bey	brōōksh, *or* brōōsh bā.
Brühl	brül.
Bruis, *see* Bruys . . .	brü-ē'.
Brumaire	brü-mâr'.
Brummell	brŭm'-ĕl.
Brunehaut	brün-ṵ̆-ō'.
Brunehild	brōō'-nŭ-hĭlt.
Brunehilde, *see* Brunhild .	brōō''-nŭ-hĭl'-dŭ.

4

Brunelleschi	brōō''-něl-lěs'-kē
Brunetière	brün-tē-âr'.
Brunetto Latini . . .	brōō-nět'-tō lä-tē'-nē.
Brunhild, see Brunehilde .	brōōn'-hĭlt.
Brünig	brü'-nĭċh.
Brunn	brün.
Bruno	brōō'-nō. [büt''-těl.
Brunswick-Wolfenbüttel .	brŭnz'-wĭk-vŏl'-fěn-
Brut	brōōt.
Bruxelles	brüs-sěl', brüks-ěl'.
Bruys, see Bruis . . .	brü-ē'.
Brydges	brĭj'-ĕz.
Bryn Mawr (Pa.) . . .	*pop.* brĭn mär'.
Bryn Mawr (Wales) . .	brŭn-mowr'.
Bucentaur	bū-sěn'-tôr.
Bucephalus	bū-sěf'-à-lŭs.
Bucer, see Butzer . . .	bū'-sěr.
Buch, von	fŏn bōōċh.
Buchanan	bŭk-ăn'-ăn, bū-kăn'-ăn.
Bucharest, see Bukharest	bōō-kà-rěst', bū-kà-rěst'.
Bucharia, see Bokhara . .	bū-kā'-rĭ-à.
Büchner	büċh'-něr.
Buckingham	bŭk'-ĭng-àm. [dä-pěsht.
Buda Pesth	bū'-dá-pěst. *Hung.* bōō'-
Budaun	bōō-dä-ōōn'.
Buddha	bōŏd'-à, bōō'-dä, bŭd'-à.
Buddhist	{ bōŏd'-ĭst, bōōd'-ĭst, bŭd'-ĭst.
Buddism	{ bōŏd'-ĭzm, bōōd'-ĭzm, bŭd'-ĭzm. [nä vēs'-tä.
Buena Vista	bū'-ná vĭs'-tà. *Sp.* bwā'-
Buen Ayre	bwān ī'-rā.
Buencamino	bwän-kä-mē'-nō.
Buenos Aires	{ bō'-nŭs ā'-rĭz. *Sp.* bwā'- nōs ī'-rěs.
Buffon	bŭf'-ŭn. *Fr.* büf-ôṅ'.

Bugeaud de la Piconnerie	bü-zhō′ dŭ lä pē-kŏn-ē̆-
Bug Jargal	büg zhär-gäl′. [rē′.
Bukhara, see Bokhara, Bu- charia	bōō-chä′-rä.
Bukharest, see Bucharest .	bōō-kä-rĕst′, bū-kä-rĕst′.
Bukowina	bōō-kō-vē′-nä.
Bulacan	bōō-lä-kän′.
Bulak, see Boulak . . .	bōō-läk′.
Bulawayo, see Buluwayo .	bōō-lä-wä′-yō.
Bulgaria	bŏŏl-gā′rĭ-à.
Bullen, see Boleyn . . .	bŏŏl′-ĕn.
Buller (Gen.)	bŏŏl′-ĕr. [bü′-lŏ̆v′.
Bülow, Hans von	hänts fŏn bü′-lō. Ger.
Bultfontein	bŭlt′-fŏn-tīn.
Buluwayo, see Bulawayo .	bōō-lōō-wä′-yō. [känd′.
Bundelcund, Bundelkhand	bŭn-dĕl-kŭnd′, bŭn-dĕl-
Bundesrath	bŏŏn′-dĕs-rät. [zĕn.
Bunsen	bŭn′-sĕn. Ger. bŏŏn′-
Bunwool	bŭn′-wŏŏl.
Buonaparte, see Bonaparte	bōō-ōn-ä-pär′-tĕ.
Buonarroti	bōō-ōn-är-rō′-tē.
Buononcini, see Bononcini	bōō-ōn-ōn-chē′-nē.
Buonsignori	bōō-ōn-sēn-yō′-rē.
Burano	bōō-rä′-nō.
Burbon	bĕr′-bun.
Burdett-Coutts	bĕr-dĕt′-kōōts′.
Burdwan, see Bardwan .	bŭrd-wän′.
Bürger	bürg′-ĕr. [bōōrg.
Burgh, Hubert de . . .	hū′-bĕrt dĕ bĕrg or
Burghley, see Burleigh .	bŭr′-lĭ.
Burgkmair	bōōrk′-mīr.
Burgos	bōōr′-gōs.
Burgundy	bŭr′-gŭn-dĭ.
Burleigh, see Burghley . .	bŭr′-lĭ.
Burrhus, or Burrus . . .	bŭr′-ŭs.
Burschenschaft	bōōr′-shĕn-shäft.

Bury, Blaze de	blȧs dŭ bü rē'.
Busento	bōō-sĕn'-tō.
Bushiri bin Salim . . .	bōō-shē'-rē bĭn sä-lēm'.
Busiris	bū-sī'-rĭs.
Bussorah, *see* Basra . . .	bŭs'-sō-rä.
Bussy-Rabutin	büs-ē'-rä-bü-tăṅ'.
Bustamante	bōōs-tä-män'-tĕ.
Bustee	bŭs'-tē.
Buteshire	būt'-shĭr.
Butte	būt.
Buturlin	bōō-tōōr-lēn'.
Butzer, *see* Bucer . . .	bōōt'-zĕr.
Buxhöwden	bōōks-hĕv'-dĕn.
Bysshe	bĭsh.
Byzantian	bĭ-zăn'-shĭ-ȧn.
Byzantine	{ bĭ-zăn'-tĭn, bĭz'-ȧn-tĭn, bī-zăn'-tĭn.
Byzantium	bĭ-zăn'-shĭ-ŭm.

C

Caaba, *see* Kaaba	kä'-bȧ, kā'-ȧ-bȧ.
Cabal	kȧ-băl'.
Cabala, *see* Kabbala . . .	kăb'-ȧ-lä.
Caballero, Fernan . . .	fȧr-nän' kä-bäl-yā'-rō.
Caballos	kä-bäl'-yōs.
Cabanagem	kä-bä-nä'-zhäm.
Cabañas	kä-bän'-yäs.
Cabanel	kä-bä-nĕl'.
Cabanilla	kä-bä-nēl'-yä.
Cabanis	kä-bä-nēs'.
Cabanos	kä-bä'-nŏs.
Cabatuan	kä-bä-tōō-än'.
Cabazera	kä-bä-thā'-rä.

Cabeça de Vaca, *see* Cabeza	kä-bä′-thä dä bä′-kä.
Cabet	kä-bä′.
Cabeza de Vaca, *see* Cabeça	kä-bä′-thä dä bä′-kä.
Cabezas	kä-bä′-thäs.
Cabiao	kä-bē-ä′-ō̇.
Cabo Rojo	kä′-bō rō′chō̇.
Cabot	kăb′-ŏt.
Cabral	kä-bräl′.
Cabrera	kä-brä′-rä.
Cabul, *see* Kabul	kä-boōl′.
Cacama	kä′-kä-mä.
Cáceres	kä′-thä-rĕs.
Cadena	kä-dä′-nä.
Cadenus	kă-dē′-nŭs.
Caderousse	kăd-roōs′. [yäk′.
Cadillac	kăd′-ĭl-äk. *Fr.* kä-dĕl-
Cadiz	kä′-dĭz. *Sp.* kä′-dēth.
Cadmean	kăd-mē′-ȧn.
Cadoudal	kä-doō-däl′.
Caedmon	kăd′-mŏn, kĕd′-mŏn.
Caelian	sē′-lĭ-ȧn.
Caen	kän̂.
Caerleon	kär-lē′-ŏn.
Caernarvon, *see* Carnarvon	kär-när′-vŏn.
Caesalpinus	sĕs-ăl-pī′-nŭs.
Caesarea	sĕs-ā-rē′-ȧ, sĕz-ȧ-rē′-ä.
Caesarian, *see* Cesarian	sē-zā′-rĭ-ăn.
Caesarion	sē-zā′-rĭ-ŏn.
Caffarelli	käf-fä-rĕl′-lē.
Caffre, *see* Kaffir	kăf′-ēr.
Cagayan	kä-gä-yän′.
Cagliari	käl-yä′-rē.
Cagliostro	käl-yōs′-trō.
Caguas	kä′-gwäs.
Cahors	kä-ōr′.
Caiaphas	kā′-yȧ-fȧs, kī′-ȧ-fȧs.

Caibarien	kä-ē-bä′rē-ĕn.
Caicos, see Caycos . . .	kī′-kos. *Sp.* ku′se-kos.
Caimanera	kä-ē-mä-nä′-rä.
Caimanes	kä-ē-mä′-nĕs.
Ça ira	sä ē-rä′.
Cairo (Egypt)	kī′-rō.
Cairo (U. S.)	kā′-rō.
Caius Cestius	kā′-yūs sĕst′-ĭ-ŭs.
Caius (College)	kēz, kēs.
Cajetan, *or*	kăj′-ĕ-tăn.
Cajetano, *or*	*It.* kä-yä-tä′-nō.
Cajetanus	kăj-ĕ-tā′-nŭs.
Cajigal	kä-ċhē-gäl′.
Calabar	kăl-à-bär′, kä-lä-bär′.
Calabria	kä-lā′-brĭ-à.
Calais	kăl′-ĭs. *Fr.* kä-lā′.
Calajan	kä-lä-ʻhän′.
Calame	kä-läm′.
Calamianes	kä″-lä-mē-ä′-nĕs. [räs.
Calaveras	kăl-à-vā′-rás, kà-lä-vä′-
Calayan	kä-lä-yän′.
Calchas	kăl′-kás.
Calderari	kăl-dä-rä′-rē. [rōn′.
Calderon	kăl′-dĕr-ŏn. *Sp.* kăl-dä-
Calderon de la Barca . .	{ kăl′-dĕr-ŏn dŭ lä bär′-kà. *Sp.* kăl-dä-rōn′ dä lä bär′-kä.
Caldiero	kăl-dē-ā′-rō.
Calif, *see* Caliph, Khalif .	kā′-lĭf.
Caligula	kä-lĭg′-ū-là.
Caliph, *see* Calif, Khalif .	kā′-lĭf. [kăl-lä-o′.
Callao	kăl-lä′-ō, kăl-yä′-ō, *pop.*
Calle Obispo	kăl′-yĕ ō-bēs′-pō.
Callias	kăl′-ĭ-ăs.
Callicrates	kăl-lĭk′-rà-tēz.
Callimachus	kăl-lĭm′-à-kŭs.

Calliope	kăl-lī'-ō-pē.
Callirrhoë	kăl-līr'-ō-ē
Callisthenes	kăl-lĭs'-thĕ-nēz.
Callisto	kăl-lĭs'-tō.
Callistratus	kăl-lĭs'-trá-tŭs.
Callot	kä-lō'.
Calmar, see Kalmar . . .	käl'-mär.
Calne	kôn.
Calpurnia	kăl-pĕr'-nĭ-á.
Caltanissetta	käl''-tä-nē-sĕt'-tä.
Calumet	kăl'-ū-mĕt.
Calvados	käl-vä-dōs'.
Calvart, Calvaert	käl'-värt. Fr. käl-vär'.
Calvé	käl-vä'.
Calvo, Baldassare	bäl-dä-sä'-rĕ käl'-vō.
Calydon	kăl'-ĭ-dŏn.
Calypso	kă-lĭp'-sō.
Camacho	kä-mä'-chō.
Camaguey	kä-mä-gā'-ē.
Camanche, see Comanche .	kä-măn'-chē.
Cámara (Admiral) . . .	kä'-mä-rä.
Camaralzaman	kăm-á-răl'-zá-măn.
Cambacerès	käṅ-bä-sä-räs'.
Cambay	kăm-bā'.
Cambert	käṅ-bâr'.
Cambon, Jules	zhül käṅ-bôṅ'.
Cambray	kăm-brä'. Fr. käṅ-brä'.
Cambria	kăm'-brĭ-ā.
Canbronne	käṅ-brŏn'. [bŭs'-kán.
Cambuscan	kăm-bŭs-kăn', kăm-
Cambyses	kăm-bī'-sēz.
Camelot	kăm'-ĕ-lŏt.
Camerarius	kä-mä-rä'-rē-ōōs.
Cameroon, see Kamerun .	kăm-ĕr-ōōn', kä-mĕ-
Camille	kä-mēl'. [rōōn'.
Camillo	kă-mĭl'-lō.

Caminha	kä-mēn'-yä.
Camisards	kăm'-ĭ-zardz.
Camoens, or	kăm'-ō-ĕns.
Camões	Port. kä-môn'-ēsh.
Camorra	kä-mōr'-rä.
Campagna di Roma . . .	käm-pän'-yä dē rō'-mä
Campan	käṅ-pän'.
Campanini	käm-pä-nē'-nē.
Campaspe	kăm-păs'-pē.
Campbell	kăm'-bĕl. Sc. kăm'-ĕl.
Campeador, El	āl käm''-pä-ä-dōr'.
Campeachy, or Campeche .	kăm-pē'-chĭ, käm-pä'-
Campeggio	käm-pĕj'-ō. [chā.
Camperdown	kăm-pĕr-down'.
Campo Formido	käm'pō fōr-mē'-dō.
Campo Formio	käm'-pō fōr'-mē-ō.
Campos, Martínez . . .	mär-tē'-nĕth käm'-pōs.
Campo Santo	käm'-pō sän'-tō.
Campus Martius	kăm'-pŭs mär'-shĭ-ŭs.
Camtoos	käm-tōs', käm-tōōs'.
Canaan	kā'-năn, kā'-nä-ăn.
Canale, or Canaletto . .	kä-nä'-lĕ, kä-nä-lĕt'-tō.
Canalizo	kä-nä-lē'-thō.
Canaris, see Kanaris . .	kä-nä'-rĭs.
Cancao, see Kang-Kao . .	kän-kow'.
Cancelleria	kän''-chĕl-lä-rē'-ä.
Candace	kăn'-dȧ-sē. [här'.
Candahar, see Kandahar .	kän-dä-här', kăn-dȧ-
or Candehar	kän-dĕ-här', kăn-dĕ-
Candeish, see Khandesh .	khän-dāsh'. [här.'
Candide, ou l'Optimisme .	käṅ-dēd' ōō lŏp-tē-
Candolle	käṅ-dŏl'. [mēs'-mŭ.
Canea, see Khania . . .	kă-nē'-ä.
Caney, El	āl kä'-nä.
Can Grande	kän grän'-dā.
Canisius	kä-nē'-sē-ŭs.

Cannæ . . . . kăn'-ē.
Cannes . . . . kän.
Canon, Hans . . . . . hänts kä'-nōn.
Canossa . . . . kä-nŏs'-sä.
Canova . . . . kä-nō'-vä.   [yō.
Cánovas del Castillo . . . kä'-nō-väs däl käs-tēl'-
Canrobert . . . . käṅ-rō-bâr'.
Cantabrian (Mts.) . . . kăn-tā'-brĭ-án.
Cantacuzene . . . . . { kăn''-tȧ-kū-zēn'.
                       { Gr. kän-tä-kōō'-zĕ-nĕ.
Cantacuzenus . . . . . kăn''-tȧ-kū-zē'-nŭs.
Cantal . . . . käṅ-täl'.
Canto . . . . kän'-tŏ.
Canton (China) . . . . kăn-tŏn'.
Canton (Ohio) . . . . . kăn'-tŭn.
Cantú, Cesare . . . . . chä'-zä-rĕ kän-tōō'.
Canuck, see Kanuck . . . kă-nŭk'.
Canute, see Cnut . . . . kȧ-nūt'.
Cape Breton . . . . . . brĭt'-ŏn, brĕt'-ŏn.
Capel . . . . kăp'-ĕl.
Capella . . . . kă-pĕl'-lȧ.
Capello, see Cappello . . kä-pĕl'-lō.
Capernaum . . . . . . kă-pẽr'-nā-ŭm. [kä-pā'.
Capet . . . . kăp'-ā, or kä'-pĕt. Fr.
Cape Verd, or Verde . . . kāp vẽrd.
Cap Haitien . . . . . . kăp ä̇-ē-tē-ĕṅ'.
Capitoline . . . . . . kăp'-ĭ-tŏl-īn''.
Capiz . . . . kä-pēth'.
Capo d'Istria, or . . . . kä'-pō dēs'-trē-ä.
Capodistrias . . . . . . kä-pō-dēs'-trē-ȧs.
Cappadocia . . . . . . kăp-ȧ-dō'-shĭ-ȧ.
Cappello, see Capello . . kä-pĕl'-lō.
Capri . . . . kä'-prē.
Caprivi, von . . . . . . fŏn kä-prē'-vē.
Capua . . . . kăp'-ū-ȧ. It. kä'-pōō-ȧ.
Capuchins . . . . . . kăp'-ū-chĭnz.

Capulet . . . . kăp'-ū-lĕt.

Carabagh, see Kara-Bagh, } kä-rä-bäg'.
or Karabagh . . . . . }

Caracalla . . . . kăr-á-kăl'-á.

Caracallus . . . . . . kăr-á-kăl'-ŭs.

Caracas . . . . kä-rä'-käs.

Caractacus . . . . . . kăr-ăk'-tá-kŭs.

Cara-Mustafa, see Kara { kä'-rä or kä-rä' mŏŏs'-
Mustapha . . . . . . } tä-fä.

Caravaca . . . . kä-rä-vä'-kä.

Caravaggio . . . . . . kä-rä-väd'-jō.

Carbonari . . . . . . kär-bō-nä'-rē.

Cardenas . . . . kär'-dā-näs.

Cardonnel . . . . . . kär-dŏn'-ĕl.

Carducci . . . . kär-dŏŏch'-ē.

Carib . . . . kăr'-ĭb.

Caribbean . . . . . . kăr-ĭ-bē'-án.

Caribbees . . . . . . kăr'-ĭ-bēz.

Carignan . . . . kä-rēn-yäṅ'.

Carisbrooke . . . . . . kăr'-ĭs-brŏŏk.

Carlén (Madame) . . . . kär-lān'.

Carlier, Don Diego . . . dōn dē-ā'-gō kär-lḛ-âr'.

Carlovingian, see Karlovin- } kär-lō-vĭn'-jĭ-án.
gian . . . . }

Carlowitz, see Karlowitz . kär'-lō-vĭts.

Carlsbad, see Karlsbad . . kärlz'-bät.

Carlsruhe, see Karlsruhe . kärlz'-rŏŏ-ŭ.

Carmagnole, La . . . . lä kär-män-yōl'.

Carnarvon, see Caernarvon kär-när'-vŏn.

Carnaval de Venise . . . kär-nä-väl' dŭ vĕ-nēz'.

Carnegie . . . . } kär'-nĕ-gĭ,   kär-nā'-gĭ,
. . . . } kär-nĕg'-ē.

Carniola . . . . kär-nĭ-ō'-lä.

Carnot, Sadi- . . . . . sä-dē'-kär-nō'.

Carolina . . . . kăr-ō-lī'-ná.

Carolinian . . . . . . kăr-ō-lĭn'-ĭ-án.

Carolus Duran	kär-ō-lüs' dü-räṅ'.
Carpaccio . . . . , ,	kär-päch'-ō.
Carpeaux.	kär-pō'.
Carpio, Bernardo del . .	bĕr-när'dō dĕl kär'-pē-ō.
Carracci, Agostino . . .	ä-gōs-tē'-nō kär-räch'-ē.
Carracci, Annibale . . .	än-nē-bä'-lĕ kär-räch'-ē.
Carrara	kȧ-rä'-rȧ. _It._ kä-rä'-rä.
Carrière	kär-rē-âr'.
Carriès, Jean	zhäṅ kär-rē-äs'.
Carrousel	kär-ōō-zĕl'.
Cartagena, _see_ Carthagena {	kär-tȧ-jē'-nȧ. _Sp._ kär-tä-ċhä'-nä.
Cartesian	kär-tē'-zhĭ-ȧn.
Carthagena, _see_ Cartagena {	kär-thȧ-jē'-nȧ. _Sp._ kär-tä-ċhä'-nä·
Carthusian	kär-thū'-zhĭ-ȧn.
Cartier, Jacques . . .	zhäk kär-tē-ä'.
Caryatides	kă-rĭ-ăt'-ĭ-dēz.
Casabianca	kä″-zä-bē-än'-kä.
Casa Braccio	kä'-zä bräch'-ō.
Casa d'Oro	kä'-zä dō'-rō.
Casa Guidi	kä'-zä gwē'-dē.
Casas, Las	läs kä'-säs. [bôṅ'.
Casaubon.	kȧ-sô'-bŏn. _Fr._ kä-zō-
Caserta	kä-zâr'-tä.
Cases, Las	läs käz.
Cashmere, _see_ Kashmere, } Kashmir . . . . . }	kăsh-mēr'.
Casiguran (Bay) . . .	kä″-sē-gōō-rän'.
Casimir	kăs'-ĭ-mēr.
Casimir-Périer	käz-ē-mēr' pä-rē-ä'.
Cassagnac, Granier de . .	grä-nē-ä' dü käs-sän-
Cassibelaunus, _see_ Cassivel- } launus . . . . . . }	käs″-ĭ-bĕ-lô'-nŭs. [yäk'.
Cassiepeia, _or_	kăs″-ĭ-ĕ-pē'-yȧ.
Cassiopeia	kăs″-ĭ-ō-pē'-yȧ.

Cassivellaunus, *see* Cassi- } kăs″-ĭ-vĕ-lô′-nŭs.
lulaunus . . . . . . }

Castagno . . . . käs-tän′-yō.

Castaigne . . . . . . käs-tän′.

Castaños . . . . käs-tän′-yōs.

Castelar . . . . käs-tā-lär′.

Castelfranco . . . . . käs-tĕl-frän′-kō.

Castellon . . . . käs-tĕl-yōn′.

Castelnaudary . . . . . käs-tĕl″-nō-dä-rē′.

Castiglione . . . . . . käs-tēl-yō′-nĕ.

Castilla, *Sp. for* Castile . . käs-tēl′-yä.

Castillejo . . . . käs-tēl-yā′-ċhō.

Castillo . . . . käs-tēl′-yō.

Castro del Rio . . . . . käs′-trō dĕl-rē′-ō.

Catanduanes . . . . . kä″-tän-dōō-ä′-nĕs.

Catania . . . . kä-tä′-nē-ä.

Catarina Cornaro . . . . kä-tä-rē′-nä kōr-nä′-rō.

Cateau-Cambrésis . . . . kä-tō′ käṅ-brä-zē′.

Catiline . . . . kăt′-ĭ-lĭn.

Cattack, *see* Cuttack, Katak kŭt-tăk′, kŭt-täk′.

Cattegat, *see* Kattegat . . kăt′-ĕ-găt. [änz.

Caucasians . . . . . . kô-kā′-shánz, kô-kăsh′-

Caucasus (Mts.) . . . . kô′-kȧ-sŭs.

Cauldon . . . . kôl′-dŭn.

Caulincourt, de . . . . dŭ kō-lăṅ-kōōr′.

Cauterets . . . . . . kōt-rā′.

Cauto (River) . . . . . kä′-ōō-tō.

Cavaignac . . . . . . kä-vān-yăk′.

Cavalcanti, Guido . . . gwē′-dō kä-väl-kän′-tē.

Cavalleria Rusticana . . kä″-väl-lä-rē′-ä rōōs-tē-

Cavan . . . . kăv′-ȧn. [kä′-nä.

Cavendish . . . . . . käv′-ĕn-dĭsh, kăn′-dĭsh.

Cavey . . . . kä-bā′-ē.

Caviedes . . . . kä-bē̲-ĕd′-äs.

Cavité . . . . kä-bē-tä′.

Cavour . . . . kä-vōōr′.

Cawnpore, *or* Cawnpur . .	kôn-pōr′, kôn-pōōr′.
Cay	kä′-ē.
Caycos, *see* Caicos . . .	kī′-kŏs. *Sp.* kä′-ē-kōs.
Cayenne	kā-yĕn′, kī-ĕn′.
Cayes, *see* Aux Cayes . .	ō kā.
Cayister	kā-ĭs′-tēr.
Caylus	kā-lüs′. [mänz′.
Caymans	kī′-mȧnz. *Sp.* kä-ē-
Cayo Cocas	kī′-ō kō′-käs.
Cayor, *see* Kayor	kī-ōr′, *or* kī-ôr′.
Cay Smith	kī smĭth.
Cayster	kā-ĭs′-tēr.
Cazembe	kä-zĕm′-bĕ.
Cazin	kä-zȧṅ′.
Ceadda, *see* Chad	kĕ-ȧd′-dä.
Ceará	sē-ä-rä′.
Ceballos	thā-bäl′-yōs.
Cebú, *see* Zebú	sĕ-bōō′. *Sp.* thā-bōō′.
Cecil	sĕs′-ĭl, sĭs′-ĭl.
Cecrops, *see* Kekrops . .	sē′-krŏps.
Ced (St.), *or*	kĕd.
Cedda	kĕd′-dȧ.
Cedric of Rotherwood . .	{ kĕd′-rĭk } ŭv rŏth′-ēr-wŏŏd. / sĕd′-rĭk }
Cedron, *see* Kedron, Kidron	sē′-drŏn.
Celadon	sĕl′-ȧ-dŏn.
Celebes (Is.)	sĕl′-ĕ-bĕs, *or* sĕl′-ĕ-bēz.
Celia	sē′-lĭ-ä.
Célimène	sā-lē-mĕn′. [nĕ.
Cellini, Benvenuto . . .	bān-vā-nōō′-tō chĕl-lē′-
Celsius	sĕl′-sĭ-ŭs, sĕl′-shĭ-ŭs.
Celts, *see* Kelts	sĕlts, kĕlts.
Cenci	chĕn′-chē.
Cenis, Mont	môṅ sĕ-nē′.
Cephalonia	sĕf-ȧ-lō′-nĭ-ä.
Cephas	sē′-fȧs.

Cephisodotus	sĕf-ĭ-sŏd′-ō-tŭs.
Cerberian	sẽr-bē′-rē-ȧn.
Cerberus	sẽr′-bĕ-rŭs, sẽr′-bē-rŭs.
Cerdic	kẽr′-dĭk.
Ceres	sē′-rēz.
Ceri, di	dĕ chā′-rē.
Cerquozzi	châr-kwŏt′-zē.
Cerro (The)	thĕr′-rō.
Cerro Gordo	{ sẽr′-rō gôr′-dō. Sp. thẽr′-rō gōr′-dō.
Certosa, La	lä chĕr-tō′-zä.
Cervantes Saavedra	{ sẽr-văn′-tēz, sä-ä-vā′- drä. Sp. thâr-bän′-tĕs, sä-ä-bā′-drä.
Cervera	thâr-bā′-rä.
César Birotteau	sā-zär′ bē-rŏt-tō′.
Cesare	chā′-zä-rĕ.
Cesari	chā′-zä-rē.
Cesarian, see Caesarian	sē-zā′-rĭ-ȧn.
Cesario	sĕ-zä′-rĭ-ō.
Cesnola	chĕs-nō′-lä.
Céspedes, de	dā thĕs′-pā-dĕs.
Cetewayo, see Cettiwayo, Ketshwayo	sĕt-ĭ-wä′-yō.
Cetigne, or Cettinje, or Cettigno	tsĕt-tĭn′-yĕ, or chĕ-tēn′-yä. It. chĕt-tēn′-yō.
Cettiwayo, see Cetewayo, Ketshwayo	sĕt-ĭ-wä′-yō.
Ceuta	sū′-tä. Sp. thā′-o͝o-tä.
Cévennes	sā-vĕn′.
Ceylon	sē-lŏn′, sĕ-lŏn′.
Chabert, Le Colonel	lĕ kō-lō-nĕl′ shä-bâr′.
Chablis	shä-blē′.
Chabot	shä-bō′.
Chachapoyas	chä-chä-pō′-yäs.
Chacon y Castellon	chä-kōn′ ē käs-tāl-yōn′.

Chad (Lake), *see* Tchad, } chäd.
Tsad, Tschad . . . . }

Chad (St.), *see* Ceadde . . chăd.

Chaeronea, *or* . . . . . kĕr-ō-nē'-à.

Chaeroneia . . . . . . kĕr-ō-nē'-yà.

Chaillé-Long . . . . . shä-yā'-lôṅ'.

Chaillu, du . . . . . . dü shä-yü'.

Chalcis . . . . kăl'-sĭs.

Chaldea . . . . kăl-dē'-à.

Chaldean . . . . kăl-dē'-àn.

Chaldee . . . . kăl'-dē.

Chalgrin . . . . shäl-grăṅ'.

Challemel-Lacour . . . . shăl-mĕl'-lä-kōōr'.

Chalmers . . . . chăl'-mĕrz,   chä'-mĕrz.

Cham . . . . kăm.   [*Sc.* chô'-mĕrz.

Chamba . . . . chăm'-bá.

Chambertin . . . . . . shäṅ-bĕr-tăṅ'.

Chambéry . . . . . . shäṅ-bā-rē'.

Chambezi . . . . . . chăm-bē'-zĭ.

Chambord . . . . . . shäṅ-bōr'.

Chamisso . . . . shä-mĕs'-sō.

Chamonix, *or* . . . . . shä-mō-nē'.

Chamouni, *or* Chamouny . shä-mōō-nē'.   [păn'-yŭ.

Champagne . . . . . . shăm-pān'.   *Fr.* shäṅ-

Champaigne, de . . . . dŭ shäṅ-pān'-yŭ.

Champaran, *see* Chumparun chŭm-pä-rŭn'.

Champ-de-Mars . . . . shäṅ-dŭ-märs'.

Champfleury . . . . . shäṅ-flĕ-rē'.

Champigny . . . . . . shäṅ-pēn-yē'.   [plăṅ'.

Champlain . . . . . . shăm-plān'.   *Fr.* shäṅ-

Champollion . . . . . } shăm-pŏl'-ĭ-ŏn.
} *Fr.* shäṅ-pŏl-yôṅ'.

Champs-Élysées . . . . shäṅ-zā-lē-zā'.

Chanda . . . . chän'-dä.

Chang Chau . . . . . . chäng'-chow'.

Changsha . . . . chäng'-shä'.

Chanoine	shä nwăn'.
Chanson de Geste	shän-sôn' dŭ zhĕst'.
Chanson de Roland . . .	shän-sôn' dŭ rō-län'.
Chanson de Roncevaux .	shän-sôn' dŭ rôns-vō'.
Chantilly	shän-tĕ-yē'.
Chapelain	shăp-lăn'.
Chapu	chä-pōō', shä-pōō'.
Chapultepec	chä-pōōl''-tĕ-pĕk'.
Chardin	shär-dăn'.
Charente	shä-rŏnt'.
Chargé d'Affaires	chär-zhā' dăf-fâr'.
Charlemagne	shär'-lĕ-măn. *Fr.* shärl-
Charleroi	shär-lĕ-rwä'. [măn'-yŭ.
Charlevoix	shär-lĕ-vwä'.
Charmian	kär'-mĭ-ȧn.
Charon	kā'-rŏn.
Chartier, Alain	ä-län' shär-tē-ā'.
Chartism	chär'-tĭzm.
Chartres	shärtr.
Chartreuse	shär-trēz'.
Charybdis	kā-rĭb'-dĭs.
Chasles	shäl.
Chasseloup-Laubat . . .	shäs-lōō'-lō-bä'.
Chassepot	shäs-pō'.
Chastelard, de	dŭ shät-lär'.
Chasteler, du	dü shät-lā'.
Châtaigneric, La	lä shä-tän-yŭ-rē'.
Chateaubriand	shä-tō-brē-än'.
Château d'If	shä-tō' dēf'.
Châteauroux	shä-tō-rōō'.
Château-Thierry	shä-tō'-tē-âr-rē'.
Châtelet	shät-lā'.
Chatham	chăt'-ȧm.
Châtillon	shä-tē-yôn'.
Châtillon-sur-Seine . . .	shä-tē-yôn'-sür-sĕn'.
Chatrian	shä-trē-än'.

Chauvinism . . . . . . shō'-vĭn-ĭzm.

Chavannes, Puvis de . . . pü-vēs' dŭ shä-vän'.

Chedorlaomer . . . . . kē''-dôr-lā-ō'-mẽr, -lā'-ō-
[mẽr.

Che-kiang . . . . . . chē-kyäng'.

Chenab, Chenaub, *see* Chinab chē-nôb'.

Chénier . . . . shā-nē̤-ā̤'.

Cheops . . . . kē'-ŏps.

Cher . . . . shâr.
[bōōr'.

Cherbourg . . . . . shẽr'-bẽrg. *Fr.* shâr-

Cherbuliez . . . . . . shâr-bü-lē̤-ā̤'.

Chersonesus . . . . . kẽr-sō-nē'-sŭs.

Chertsey . . . . chĕs'-sĭ, chĕrt'-sĭ.

Cherubini . . . . . . kā-rōō-bē'-nē.

Chevalier . . . . shĕ-vä-lē̤-ā̤'.
[rōōzh.

Chevalier de Maison-Rouge shĕ-vä-lē̤-ā̤' dŭ mā-zôń'-

Chevalier de Saint George { shĕ-vä-lē̤-ā̤' dŭ sȧń
{ zhŏrzh'.
[täl'.

Chevalier d'Harmental . . shĕ-vä-lē̤-ā̤' där-mŏń-

Cheviot . . . . chĕv'-ĭ-ŭt, chĭv'-ĭ-ŭt.

Chevreuse . . . . . . shĕv-rẽz'.

Chevy Chase . . . . . chĕv'-ĭ chās.

Cheyne . . . . chān, chīn.

Chhatisgarh . . . . . . chŭt-tēs-gär'.

Chianti . . . . kē-än'-tē.

Chicago . . . . shĭ-kô'-gō.

Chicot . . . . shē-kō'.

Chienne . . . . shē-ĕn'.

Chieveley . . . . chĭv'-lĭ'.

Chih-li, *see* Chi-li . . . chē'-lē'.

Chihuahua . . . . . . chē-wä-wä.

Chi-li *see* Chih-li . . . . chē'-lē'.

Chile *or* Chili . . . . . chĭl'-ĕ, chĭl'-ĭ. *Sp.* chē'-lĭ.

Chillon . . . . shĭl'-ŏn. *Fr.* shē-yôń'.

Chilperic . . . . chĭl'-pĕ-rĭk.

Chimæra . . . . kī-mē'-rä.

Chimay . . . . shē-mā'.

Chinab, *see* Chenab . . .	chē-nôb'.
Chinese	chĭ-nēz', chĭ-nēs'.
Chingleput	chĭng-glĕ-pŭt'.
Chin-kiang	chĭn-kē-äng'.
Chinon	shē-nôṅ'.
Chioggia, *see* Chiozza . .	kē-ŏd'-jä.
Chios, *see* Scio	kĭ'-ŏs.
Chiozza, *see* Chioggia . .	kē-ŏt'-sä. [wä.
Chippewa	chĭp'-pē-wā, chĭp'-pē-
Chiron	kĭ'-rŏn.
Chisleu	kĭs'-lū.
Chiswick	chĭz'-ĭk.
Chitral	chĭt-räl', *or* chī'-tràl.
Chittagong	chĭt-tá-gŏng'.
Chittim, *see* Kittim . . .	kĭt'-ĭm.
Chivery	chĭv'-ĕ-rĭ.
Chloe	klō'-ē, *or* klō'-ĭ.
Chlopicki	ċhlō-pĭt'-skē.
Chlotar, *see* Clotaire . .	ċhlō'-tär.
Chmielnicki	ċhmē̦-ĕl-nĭt'-skē.
Choiseul	shwä-zēl'.
Choiseul-Praslin	shwä-zēl'-prä-lăṅ'.
Choisy	shwä-zē'.
Cholmondeley	chŭm'-lĭ.
Chopin	shō̄-păṅ'.
Chorazin	kō-rā'-zĭn.
Chosroes	kŏs'-rō-ēz, kŏs'-rō-ĕz.
Chota, *see* Chutia . . .	chō'-tä.
Chouans	shō̄ō'-ánz. *Fr.* shō̄ō-äṅ'.
Chrestien, *or* Chrétien de } Troyes . . . . . . }	krā-tē-ĕṅ' dŭ trwä'.
Chriemhild, *see* Kriemhild	krēm'-hĭlt.
Christe eleïson	krĭs'-tē ĕ-lā'-ĭ-sŏn.
Christian	krĭst'-yăn, *or* krĭst'-Ĭ-àn.
Christianity . . . . . {	krĭst-yăn'-Ĭ-tĭ, krĭst- ē̦-ăn'-Ĭ-tĭ.

Chrysostom . . . . . . krĭs'-ŏs-tŏm, krĭs-ŏs'-
Chumie . . . . cho͞o'-mē. [tŏm.
Chumparun, *see* Champaran chŭm-pȧ-rŭn'.
Chur, *see* Coire . . . . ko͞or.
Churubusco . . . . . . cho͞o-ro͞o-bo͞os'-kō.
Chusan . . . . cho͞o-sän'.
Chutia, *see* Chota . . . . cho͞o'-tē-ä.
Cialdini . . . . chäl-dē'-nē.
Cibo (Cardinal) . . . . thē'-bō.
Cibola, *see* Sibola . . . . sē'-bō-lä.
Cibrario . . . . chē-brä'-rē-ō.
Cicero . . . . sĭs'-ĕ-rō.
Cid, El . . . . ĕl sĭd. *Sp.* äl thĭd.
Cid, Le . . . . *Fr.* lĕ sēd.
Cienfuegos . . . . . . thē-än''-fo͞o-ä'-gŏs.
Ciergnon . . . . sē-ȧrn-yôn'.
Cifuentas . . . . thē-fo͞o-än'-täs.
Cimabue . . . . chē-mä-bo͞o'-ā. [nō.
Cima da Conegliano . . . chē'-mä dä kō-nāl-yä'-
Cimarosa . . . . chē-mä-rō'-zä.
Cimmeria . . . . sĭ-mē'-rĭ-ȧ.
Cimon . . . . sĭ'-mŏn.
Cincinnati . . . . . . sĭn-sĭn-nä'-tĭ.
Cincinnatus . . . . . . sĭn-sĭn-nā'-tŭs.
Cingalon . . . . thēn-gä-lōn'.
Cinq-Mars . . . . . . sän-mär'.
Cinque Ports . . . . . sĭngk pōrts.
Cipango . . . . sĭ-păng'-gō.
Circaean, *see* Circean . . sēr-sē'-ȧn.
Circe . . . . sĕr'-sē.
Circean, *see* Circaean . . sēr-sē'-ȧn. [nĭ-ä.
Cisleithania . . . . . . sĭs-lĭ-thä'-nĭ-ȧ, sĭs-lĭ-tä'-
Cisneros . . . . thēs-nā'-rŏs.
Cispadane . . . . . . sĭs-pā'-dän.
Cissey . . . . sē-sā'.
Città della Pieve . . . . chēt-tä' dĕl'-lä pē-ā'-vĕ.

Ciudad de Cuella . . . . Thḗ-ṓō-däd'-rā̇ h'-ä̇llllı

Ciudad Real . . . . thḗ-ōō-däd' rā-äl'.

Ciudad Rodrigo . . . . thḗ-ōō-däd' rōd-rḗ'-gō.

Cività Vecchia, Civitavecchia chḗ-vḗ-tä' vĕk'-kḗ-ä.

Claes . . . . kläz.

Clairault, _or_ Clairaut . . klā-rō'.

Clairvaux . . . . . . klâr-vō'.

Claretie . . . . klăr-tē'.   [lōr-rä̇n'.

Claude Lorrain . . . . . klôd lŏ-rän'. _Fr._ klōd

Cléante . . . . klā-ä̇nt'.

Cleishbotham . . . . . klēsh'-bŏfh-ȧm.

Cleisthenes, _see_ Clisthenes klĭs'-thĕ-nēz.

Clélie . . . . klā-lē'.

Clémenceau . . . . . . klā-mŏṅ-sō'.

Clément . . . . klā-môṅ'.

Clemente, San . . . . . sä̇n klā-mĕn'-tĕ.

Clementi . . . . klā-mĕn'-tē.

Clementine . . . . . . { klĕm'-ĕn-tĭn, klĕm'-ĕn-
{ tēn, _or_ klĕm-ĕn-tēn'.

Cleopas . . . . klē'-ō-păs.

Cleopatra . . . . klē-ō-pā'-trȧ.

Cléopâtre . . . . klā-ō-pätr'.

Cleves, _or_ . . . . klēvz.

Clèves . . . . _Fr._ klāv.

Clio . . . . klī'-ō.

Clisthenes, _see_ Cleisthenes . . klĭs'-thĕ-nēz.

Clitandre . . . . klē-tä̇ndr'.

Cloaca Maxima . . . . . klō-ā̇'-kȧ mȧk'-sĭ-mȧ.

Cloisonné . . . . klwä̇-zŏ̆n-nā'.

Clonmel . . . . klŏn-mĕl'.

Clotaire, _see_ Chlotar . . klō-târ'.

Clouet . . . . klōō-ā'.

Clough . . . . klŭf.

Cluseret (Gen.) . . . . klü-zẽ-rā'.

Clusium . . . . klū'-sĭ-ŭm, klū'-shĭ-ŭm.

Cnidian . . . . nĭd'-ĭ-ȧn.

Cnidus.	nĭ'-dŭs.
Cnut, *see* Canute	knōōt.
Coamo	kō-ä'-mō.
Coanza, *see* Kuanza, Quanza	kō-än'-zä.
Cobi, *see* Gobi	kō'-bē.
Coblenz, *or* Coblentz . .	kō'-blĕnts.
Cobre, El	ĕl kō'-brā.
Cochin China	kō'-chĭn chĭ'-ná.
Cockagne, *or* Cockaigne .	kŏk-än'.
Cockburn	kō'-bŭrn.
Cocytus	kō-sĭ'-tŭs.
Cœlebs	sē'-lĕbz.
Coelho, *or* Coello . . .	kō-ĕl'-yō.　[dŭ lē-ôṅ'.
Coeur de Lion	kêr dŭ lĭ'-ôn.　*Fr.* kêr
Cognac	kōn-yäk'.
Coimbatore, *see* Koimbatur	kō-ĭm''-bá-tōr'.
Coire, *see* Chur	kwär.
Coke	kōk, *originally* kōōk.
Colapur, *see* Kolhapur . .	kō-lä-pōōr'.
Colbert	*Fr.* kōl-bâr'.
Colenso	kō-lĕn'-sō.
Coleone, *see* Colleoni .	kō-lā-ō'-nā.
Colesberg	kōlz'-bêrg.
Colet . . . .　　　　　[yē'.	kŏl'-ĕt.
Coligni *or* Coligny . . .	kō-lēn'-yē.　*Fr.* kō-lēn-
Coliseum, *see* Colosseum .	kōl-ĭ-sē'-ŭm.
Colleoni, *see* Coleone . .	kōl-lā-ō'-nē.
Colletta	kōl-lĕt'-tä.
Colmar, *see* Kolmar . . .	kōl-mär'.
Cologne	kō-lōn'.　*Fr.* kō-lōn'-yŭ.
Colon	kō-lōn'.　*Sp.* kō-lōn'.
Colon Cristóbal	krēs-tō'-bäl kō-lōn'.
Colonel Chabert	kō-lō-nĕl' shä-bâr'.
Colonna	kō-lōn'-nä.
Coloocan	kŏl-ō'-kăn.
Colorado	kŏl-ō-rä'-dō.

Colosse	kŏ-lŏs'-se.
Colosseum, see Coliseum .	kŏl-ŏ-sē'-ŭm.
Colquhoun	kŏ-hōōn'.
Comacchio	kō-mäk'-kē̯-ọ̄.
Comanche, see Camanche .	kō-măn'-chē.
Combe	kōm, kōōm.
Comédie Française . . .	kō-mä-dē' fräṅ-sāz'.
Comédie Humaine . . .	kō-mä-dē' ü-män'.
Comeiro	kŏ-mā̯'-ē̯-rō.
Comines, or Commines . .	kŏ-mēn'.
Commodus	kŏm'-mō-dŭs.
Comnenl	kŏm-nē'-nī.
Comnenus	kŏm-nē'-nŭs.
Comorin	kŏm'-ō-rĭn.
Compagnie Général Trans-⎰	kŏṅ-pän-yē' zhä-nä-räl'
atlantique . . . . . .⎱	träṅz-ät-läṅ-tēk'.
Compiègne	kŏṅ-pē̱-äṅ'-yŭ.
Comte	kôṅt.
Comtesse de Rudolstadt .	kôṅ-tĕs' dŭ rü-dŏl-stät'.
Comus	kō'-mŭs.
Concas	kōng'-käs.
Concepcion	⎰ kŏn-sĕp'-shŏn. Sp. kŏn- ⎱ thäp''-thē-ōn'.
Concordat	kŏn-kôr'-dăt.
Condé	kôṅ-dä'.
Condé-sur-Noireau . . .	kôṅ-dä'-sür-nwä-rō'.
Condillac	kôṅ-dē-yäk'.
Condorcet, de	du kôṅ-dōr-sä'. [nō.
Conegliano, Cima da . . .	chē'-mä dä kō-nāl-yä'-
Confessio Amantis . . .	kŏn'-fĕsh'-ō ä-män'-tĭs.
Conflans	kôṅ-fläṅ'.
Coniston	kŏn'-ĭs-tŏn.
Connaught	kŏn'-nôt.
Conradin	kōn'-rä-dēn.
Consalvi	kōn-säl'-vē.
Constant de Rebecque . .	kôṅ-stäṅ' dŭ rē̆-bĕk'.

Constantine (Emperor) . .	kŏn'-stán-tīn.
Constantine (Algeria) . .	kŏn-stän-ten'. [sü-ā-lō'.
Consuelo	kŏn-sōō-ä-'lō. _Fr._ kôṅ-
Conte	_It._ kōn'-tā.
Contessa	kōn-tĕs'-sä.
Conti	kôṅ-tē'.
Contreras . . . ⸱. . .	kōn-trā'-räs.
Conybeare	kŭn'-ĭ-bĕr.
Coomassie, _see_ Kumassi .	kōō-mäs'-sē.
Coombe	kōōm.
Copenhagen	kō-pĕn-hä'-gĕn.
Copernicus	kō-pĕr'-nĭ-kŭs.
Cophetua	kō-fĕt'-ū-à.
Coppée François	fräṅ-swä' kŏp-pā'.
Coquelin	kŏk-lăṅ'.
Corday d'Armans	kôr-dä' där-mäṅ'.
Cordilleras	{ kôr-dĭl'-ĕr-àz. _Sp._ kōr- { dēl-yā'-räs. [bä.
Córdoba, _or_ Cordova . .	kôr'-dō-vä. _Sp._ kŏr'-dō-
Corea, _see_ Korea	kō-rē'-à.
Corean, _see_ Korean . . .	kō-rē'-àn.
Corfu	kŏr-fōō', kŏr-fū'.
Cori	kō'-rē.
Coriolanus	kō''-rĭ-ō-lā'-nŭs.
Corleone	kōr-lā-ō'-nā.
Cornaro	kôr-nä'-rō.
Corneille	kôr-nāl'. _Fr._ kōr-nā'-yŭ.
Cornelis	kŏr-nā'-lĭs.
Cornice, _or_	_It._ kōr'-nē-chä.
Corniche	_Fr._ kôr-nēsh'.
Corona Borealis	kō-rō'-nä bō-rē-ā'-lĭs.
Corot	kō-rō'.
Correa	kŏr-rā'-ä.
Correggio	kŏr-rĕd'-jō.
Corregidor	kŏr''-rāch-ē-dōr'.
Corrèze	kŏr-raz'.

Corrientes . . . . . . kŏr rḕ ŏn' tĕs.
Cortes (The) . . . . . kōr'-tĕs.
Cortés (Fernando) *or* . . kŏr-tās'.
Cortez . . . . kŏr'-tĕz.
Coruña, La . . . . . . lä kō-rōōn'-yä.
Corunna . . . . kō-rŭn'-à.
Corvisart-Desmarets . . . kōr-vĕ-zär' dä-mä-rä'.
Corydon . . . . . . kŏr'-ĭ-dŏn.
Cosette . . . . kō-zĕt'.
Cosimo . . . . . . kō'-zē-mō.
Cosmati . . . . . . kōs-mä'-tē.
Cosmo de Medici . . . . kōs'-mō dä mä'-dē-chē.
Cossack . . . . kŏs'-ăk.   [tä.
Costa Rica . . . . . kŏs'-tä rē'-kä. *Sp.* kŏs'-
Costis . . . . kŏs'-tĭs.
Côte d'Or . . . . . . kōt'-dōr'.
Côtes du Nord . . . . kōt'-dü-nōr'.
Cottin . . . . kŏt-tȧṅ'.
Coucy . . . . kōō-sē'.
Coulanges . . . . . . kōō-länzh'.
Courbet . . . . kōōr-bā'.
Courcelles . . . . . . kōōr-sĕl'.
Courland . . . . kōōr'-lănd.
Courtenay . . . . . . kĕrt'-nā, kŏŏrt'-nā.
Courtois . . . . kōōr-twä'.
Courtrai, *or* Courtray . . kōōr-trä'.
Cousin, Victor . . . . . vēk-tōr' kōō-zăṅ'.
Cousin Pons . . . . . . kōō-zăṅ' pôṅ.
Cousine Bette . . . . . kōō-zēn' bĕt.
Coutances . . . . . . kōō-täṅs'.
Coutras . . . . kōō-trä'.
Couture . . . . kōō-tür'.
Cowper . . . . kow'-pĕr, kōō'-pĕr.
Coysevox . . . . kwäs-vŏks'.
Cracovienne . . . . . . krä-kō''-vĭ-ĕn'.
Cracow, *see* Krakau . . . krä'-kō.

Craigenputtoch, *or* . . . *Sc.* krā-gĕn-pŭt′-ŏċh.
Craigenputtock . . . . krī-gĕn-pŭt′-ŏk.
Cramer . . . . *Ger.* krä′-mĕr.
Cranach (Lucas), *see* Kranach krăn′-àk, krä′-näċh.
Crapaud . . . . krä-pō′.
Crébillon . . . . krā-bē-yôṅ′.
Crécy, *see* Cressy . . . krĕs′-ĭ.   *Fr.* krā-sĕ′.
Credi . . . . krä′-dē.
Crédit Mobilier . . . . { krĕd′-ĭt mō-bē′-lĕ-ēr.
                         { *Fr.* krā-dĕ′ mō-bē-lē-ā′.
Crémieux . . . . krā-mē-ĕ′.   [nä.
Cremona . . . . krē-mō′-nä. *It.* krā-mō′-
Crespy, *or* Crêpy-en-Laonnais krā-pē′ ôṅ lä‿ō-nä′.
Cressida . . . . krĕs′-ĭ-dà.
Cressy, *see* Crécy . . . . krĕs′-ĭ.
Creusa . . . . krē-ū′-sà.
Creuse . . . . krĕz.
Creusot, *or* Creuzot . . . krĕ-zō′.
Crèvecœur . . . . . . kräv-kĕr′.
Crichton . . . . krī′tŏn.
Crillon . . . . krē-yôṅ′.
Crimea . . . . krĭ-mē′-à, krī-mē′-à.
Crispi . . . . krĭs′-pē.
Cristóbal Colón . . . . krĕs-tō′-bäl kō-lōn′.
Critias . . . . krĭt′-ĭ-às, krĭsh′-ĭ-às.
Crito . . . . krī′-tō.
Crivelli . . . . krē-vel′-lē.
Crna Gora, *see* Czernagora chĕr′-nä gō′-rä.
Croat . . . . krō′-ăt.
Croatia . . . . krō-ā′-shē-à.
Cromwell . . . . . . { krŏm′-wĕl, krŭm′-wĕl.
                       { *pop.* krŭm′-l.
Cronaca . . . . krŏn′-ä-kä.
Cronjé . . . . krŏn′-yĕ.   [stät.
Cronstadt, *see* Kronstadt . krŏn′-stät.   *Ger.* krŏn′-
Cronus,*or* Cronos,*see* Kronos krō′-nŭs.

Cruz . . . . . .   krōōth.

Ctesias . . . . tē'-shĭ-ás.

Cuba . . . . kū'-bä.   *Sp.* kōō'-bä.

Cuddalore . . . . . . kŭd-dȧ-lōr'.

Cuddapah, *see* Kadapa . . kŭd'-dȧ-pä.

Cuenca . . . . kōō-ĕn'-kä.

Culebra . . . . kōō-lā'-brä.

Culloden . . . . kŭl-lō'-dĕn.

Culmbach, *see* Kulmbach . kŏŏlm'-bäċh.

Cumae . . . . kū'-mē.

Cumaean . . . . kū-mē'-ȧn.

Cuneo . . . . kōō-nä'-ō.

Cupey . . . . kōō-pä'-ē.

Curaçao, *or* Curazao, *or* $\left\{\begin{array}{l} \text{kōō-rä-sä'-ō,} \quad \text{kū'-rȧ-sō,} \\ \text{kū'-rȧ-sō''-a, kōō-rä-sō'-ä,} \\ \text{kōō-rä-sō'.} \end{array}\right.$

Curaçoa . . . .

Curico . . . . kōō-rē-kō'. [kĕr'-shĭ-ŭs.

Curtius . . . . *Ger.* kōōr'-tse-ŏŏs.   *Lat.*

Cush . . . . kŭsh.

Custine . . . . küs-tēn'.

Custoza, *or* . . . . . . kŏŏs-tōd'-sä.

Custozza . . . . kŏŏs-tōt'-zä.

Cüstrin, *see* Küstrin . . . küs-trēn'.

Cuttack, *see* Cattack, Ku- $\left.\right\}$ kŭt-täk', kŭ-täk'.
tak . . . .

Cuvier . . . . kü-vē̮-ā'.

Cuxhaven . . . . . . $\left\{\begin{array}{l} \text{kŭks-hā'-vĕn.} \\ Ger. \text{ kōōks'-hä-fĕn.} \end{array}\right.$

Cuyo . . . . kōō'-yō.

Cuyos . . . . kōō'-yōs.

Cuyp, *see* Kuyp . . . . koip.

Cuzco . . . . kōōz'-kō.

Cwm . . . . kōōm.

Cyaxares . . . . sĭ-ăx'-ā-rēz.

Cybele . . . . sĭb-ē'-lē, sĭb'-ĕ-lĕ.

Cyclades . . . . sĭk'-lȧ-dēz.

Cymbeline . . . . sĭm'-bĕ-lĭn, *or* sĭm'-bĕ-
Cymry, *see* Kymry . . . kĭm'-rĭ. [lĭn.
Cynewulf . . . . . . kĭn'-ĕ-wŏŏlf.
Cyprian . . . . sĭp'-rĭ-àn.
Cyrano de Bergerac . . . sĭr-ä-nō' dŭ bår-zhĕ-räk'.
Cyrene . . . . sī-rē'-nē.
Cyril . . . . sĭr'-ĭl.
Cytherea . . . . sĭth-ĕ-rē'-à.
Cytherean . . . . . . sĭth-ĕ-rē'-àn.
Czajkowski, Czaykowski . chī-kŏv'-skē.
Czar . . . . zär, tsär.
Czardas . . . . chär'-däsh.
Czarevitch, *see* Tsarovitch . zär'-ĕ-vĭch, tsär'-ĕ-vĭch.
Czarevna, *see* Tsarevna . zär-ĕv'-nä, tsär-ĕv'-nä.
Czarina, *see* Tsarina . . . zär-ē'-nä, tsär-ē'-nä.
Czaritza . . . . zär-ĭt'-zä, tsär-ĭt'-zä.
Czarniecki . . . . . . chärn-yĕt'-skē.
Czarowitch . . . . . . zär'-ō-vĭch, tsär'-ō-vĭch.
Czarowitz, *see* Tsarowitz . zär'-ō-vĭtz, tsär'-ō-vĭtz.
Czartoryski . . . . . . chär-tō-rĭ'-skē.
Czaykowski, Czajkowski . chī-kŏv'-skē.
Czechs, *see* Tsech . . . . chĕchs, chĕks.
Czermak . . . . chĕr-mäk'.
Czernagora, *see* Crna Gora chĕr"-nä-gō'-rä.
Czernowitz . . . . . . chĕr'-nō-vĭts.
Czerny . . . . chĕr'-nē.

D

Dablon . . . . dä-blôṅ'.
Dacca, *see* Dhaka . . . dăk'-à.
Dacia . . . . dā'-shĭ-à.
Daedalus . . . . dē'-dà-lŭs, dĕd'-ā-lŭs,
Daghestan . . . . . . dä-gĕs-tän'.
Dagnan-Bouveret . . . . dän-yäṅ'-bōōv-rä'.

Dagobert . . . . dăg'-ō-bẽrt.   [bâr'.
Dagon . . . . dā'-gŏn.
Dagonet, or Daguenet . . dăg'-ō-nĕt, or dăg'-ĕ-nĕt.
Daguerre . . . . dä-gâr'.   [păn.
Dagupan or Dagúpan . . dä-gōō-păn', dä-gōō'-
Dahlgren . . . . dăl'-grĕn. Sw. dăl'-grĕn.
Dahn . . . . dän.
Dahomey . . . . dä-hō'-mĭ, dä-hō'-mā.
Daimio . . . . dī'-mē-ō.
Daiquiri . . . . dä-ē-kē'-rē.
D'Albert . . . . däl-bâr'.
D'Alembert . . . . . . dä-lŏn-bâr'.
Dalgetty . . . . dăl'-gĕt-ĭ.
Dalgleish . . . . dăl-glēsh'.
Dalhousie . . . . . . dăl-hōō'-zĭ, dăl-how'-zĭ.
Dalida . . . . dăl'-ĭ-dȧ.
Dalin . . . . dä'-lĭn.
Dalkeith . . . . dăl-kēth'.
Dalles . . . . dălz.
Dall' Ongaro . . . . . däl ŏng'-gä-rō.
Dalmatia . . . . däl-mā'-shĭ-ȧ.
Dalou, Jules . . . . . zhül dä-lōō'.
Dalrymple . . . . . . dăl-rĭm'-pl.
Daman, see Damaun . . dä-män'.
Damaraland . . . . . dä-mä'-rä-lånd.
Damaris . . . . dăm'-ȧ-rĭs.
Damascene . . . . . . dăm'-ȧ-sēn.
Damasus . . . . dăm'-ȧ-sŭs.
Damaun, see Daman . . dä-môn'.
Dame aux Camélias, La . lä däm ō kä-mā-lē-ä'.
Damiano . . . . dä-mē-ä'-nō.
Damien . . . . dä-mē-ĕn'.
Damis . . . . dä-mēs'.
Damnation de Faust . . . dăm-nä-sē-ŏn' dŭ fowst.
Damoclean . . . . . . dăm-ō-klē'-ȧn.
Damocles . . . . dăm'-ō-klēz.

Damon	dā'-mŏn.
Dampier	dăm'-pēr.
Damrosch	däm'-rŏsh.
Danaë	dăn'-ā-ē.
Danai	dăn'-ā-ī. [dēz.
Danaïdes	dă-nā'-ĭ-dēz, dā-nā'-ĭ-
Danaoi	dăn'-ā-oi.
Dandin, George	zhŏrzh dän-dăṅ'.
Dandolo	dän'-dō-lō.
Danegeld	dān'-gĕld.
Danelagh, Danelaw . . .	dān'-lô.
Dannecker	dän'-nĕk-ĕr.
Danse Macabre	däṅs mä-käbr'.
Dante Alighieri	{ dăn'-tĕ ăl"-ĭ-gĭ-â'-rĭ. It. dän'-tā ä"-lē-gē-ā'-rē.
Dantean	dăn'-tē-ȧn.
Dantès	däṅ-tās'.
Danton	dăn'-tŏn. Fr. däṅ-tôṅ'.
Dantsic, Dantzic, or Danzig	dänt'-sĭk. Ger. dänt'-
Daphne	dăf'-nē. [sĭch.
Daphnis	dăf'-nĭs.
Darbhangah, see Durbunga	dä-bän'-gä.
D'Arblay, Madame . . .	mä-dăm' där-blā'.
Darc, or D'Arc, Jeanne . .	zhän därk.
Dardanus	där'-dȧ-nŭs.
Dar-es-Salam	där"-ĕs-sä-läm'.
Darfor or Darfur . . .	där'-fŏr, där'-fōōr.
Darien	dā'-rĭ-ĕn. Sp. dä-rē-än'.
Darius	dă-rī'-ŭs.
Darwar, see Dharwar . .	där'-wär.
D'Aubigné, Merle	mĕrl dō-bēn-yā'.
Daubigny	dō-bēn-yē'.
Daudet, Alphonse . . .	äl-fôṅs' dō-dā'.
Daudet, Léon	lā-ôṅ' dō-dā'.
Daun	down.
Dauphin	dô'-fĭn. Fr. dō-fäṅ'.

Dauphiné	dō̇-fḗ-nā'.
Dauphiness	dô'-fĭ-něs.
Dauphiny	dô'-fĭ-nĭ.
Daur, *or* Dauria . . .	dä-ōōr', dä-ōō'-rē-ä.
Davalos	*Sp.* dä-bä'-lŏs.
David, Gheerardt . . .	gä-rärt' dä'-vĕt.
David (L. J.)	dä-vēd'.
Davila	dä'-vē-lä.
Da Vinci, Leonardo . . .	lä-ō-när'-dō dä vēn'-chē.
Davoust	dä-vōō'.
De Aar	dĕ är.
Deák	dā-äk'.
De Amicis	dā ä-mē'-chēs.
De Amicitia	dĕ ăm-ĭ-sĭsh'-ĭ-ạ.
Débonnaire, Louis le . . .	lōō-ē' lĕ dā-bŏn-är'.
Deborah	dĕb'-ō-rȧ. [sĭn.
Debreczin	dā-brĕt'-sĭn, *or* dā-brĕt'-
Decameron	dĕ-kăm'-ĕr-ŏn.
Decamps	dŭ-käṅ'.
Decazes	dŭ-käz'.
Decelean	dĕs-ē-lē'-ȧn.
Deffand, Marquise du . .	mär-kēz' dü dĕf-fäṅ'.
Defregger	dā-frĕg'-ĕr.
Degas	dĕ-gä'.
Dehli, *see* Delhi	dā'-lē.
Dehra Dun	dĕh'-rä dōōn.
Deianira, *see* Dejanira . .	dē-yȧ-nī'-rȧ. [krĭs'-tĭ.
De Imitatione Christi . .	dē Ĭm"-ĭ-tä-shĭ-ō'-nĕ
Dejanira, *see* Deianira . .	dĕj-ȧ-nī'-rȧ.
Dejean	dŭ-zhôṅ'.
Delacroix	dŭ-lä-krwä'.
Delagoa	dĕl-ȧ-gō'-ȧ.
Delambre	dŭ-läṅbr'.
De la Ramée	dŭ lä rä-mā'.
Delaroche	dŭ-lä-rōsh'.
Delavigne	dŭ lä-vēn'-yŭ.

Delegorgue	dḗ-lḗ-gōrg′.
Delft	dĕlft.
Delgado	dĕl-gä′-dō.
Delhi, *see* Dehli	dĕl′-hī.
Delian	dē′-lĭ-án.
Délibes	dā-lēb′.
Délila	*Fr.* dā-lē-lä′.
Delilah	dē-lĭ′-lä.
Della Cruscan	dĕl′-lá krŭs′-kán.
Delorme, Marion	mä-rē-ôṅ′ dŭ lôrm′.
Delos	dē′-lŏs.
Delphi	dĕl′-fī.
Delphic	dĕl′-fĭk.
Del Pino	dĕl pē′-nō.
Delsarte	dĕl-särt′.
De Lussan, Zélie	zā-lē′ dŭ lüs-säṅ′.
Delyannis	dĕl-ĭ-ăn′-ĭs.
Demange, Maître	mätr dŭ-mäṅzh′. [rĭ.
Demerara, *or* Demerary .	dĕm-ē-rä′-rá, dĕm-ēr-rä′-
Demeter	dĕ-mē′-tẽr.
Demetrius	dĕ-mē′-trĭ-ŭs.
Demidoff, Demidov . . .	dĕm′-ē-dŏf.
Democritus	dē-mŏk′-rĭ-tŭs.
Demogorgon	dē-mō-gôr′-gŏn.
Demos	dē′-mŏs.
Demosthenes	dē-mŏs′-thĕ-nēz.
Deneb	dē′-nĕb, dĕn′-ĕb.
Den Haag	dĕn häċh. [dŭ-nē′.
Denis, St., *see* Denys . .	sānt dĕn′-ĭs. *Fr.* säṅ
Dent du Midi	dŏṅ dü mē-dē′. [dŭ-nē′.
Denys, St., *see* Denis . .	sānt dĕn′-ĭs. *Fr.* säṅ
D'Épinay	dā-pē-nā′.
Dépit Amoureux, Le . . .	lḗ dā-pē′ tä-mōō-rḗ′.
De Prés, Josquin, *see* Desprez	zhŏs-kăṅ′ dŭ prā′.
De Quincey	dŭ kwĭn′-zĭ.
Derajat	dĕr-á-jăt′.

Derby	dĕr'-bĭ, där'-bĭ.
Dercetas	dĕr'-sĕ-tȧs.
Dernier Chouan, Le . . .	lŭ dĕr-nē-ā' shōō-äṅ'.
Déroulède	dā-rōō-lād'.
De Ruyter	dē rī'-tĕr. *D.* dŭ roi'-tĕr.
Dervis, Dervise, *or* **Dervish**	dĕr'-vĭs, dĕr'-vĭsh.
Desaix de Veygoux . . .	dŭ-sā' dŭ vā-gōō'.
Descartes	dā-kärt'.
Deschamps	dā-shäṅ'.
Desdemona	dĕz-dĕ-mō'-nä.
Desdichado	dĕs-dĭ-chä'-dō.
Deseada	dĕs-ĕ-ä'-dä.
Désirade	dā-zē-räd'.
Desmoulins	dā-mōō-läṅ'.
Despenser	dĕ-spĕn'-sĕr.
Desprez, Josquin, *see* De Prés	zhŏs-käṅ' dā-prā'.
Dessalines	dĕs-ä-lēn'.
Dessau	dĕs'-sow.
Dessauer	dĕs'-sow-ĕr.
De Staël-Holstein. . . .	{ dŭ stä'-ĕl-hŏl'-stĭn. *Fr.* dŭ stä-ĕl-ōl-stäṅ'.
D'Este	dās'-tĕ.
De Stendhal	dŭ stŏṅ-däl'.
Destouches	dā-tōōsh'.
Detaille	dŭ-tä'-yŭ. [vēl'.
De Tocqueville	dŭ tŏk'-vĭl. *Fr.* dŭ tŏk-
Deucalion	dū-kā'-lĭ-ŏn.
Deutsch	doich. [tōŏng.
Deutsche Tages-Zeitung .	doich'-ŭ tä'-gĕs tsī'-
Deux-Ponts	dē pôṅ.
Deux-Sèvres	dē sāvr.
Devereux	dĕv'-ĕr-ōō, dĕv'-ĕr-ŭ.
De Vigny	dŭ vēn-yē'.
Devizes	dē-vī'-zĕz.
D'Ewes	dūz.
De Wet	dā-vĕt'.

Dewetsdorp	dā-vĕts'-dŏrp.
De Wette	dĕ wĕt'-tĕ. *D.* dĕ vĕt'-tĕ.
De Witt	dĕ wĭt. *D.* de vĭt.
Dhaka, *see* Dacca . . .	dhä'-kä.
Dhar	dhär.
Dharwar, *see* Darwar . .	där'-wär.
Dhawalaghiri	dhá-wäl''-ă-ghĕr'-ē.
Dholpur	dhŏl-po͞or'.
Diabelli	dē-ä-bĕl'-lē.
Diable, Robert le . . .	rō-bâr' lē dē̠-äbl'.
Diadochi	dī-ăd'-ō-kī.
Diane de Poitiers . . .	dē-ăn' dŭ pwä-tē̠-ä'.
Diarbekir, *or* Diarbekr .	dē-är''-bĕ-kēr', dē-är-
Dias	dē'-äs. [bĕkr'.
Diavolo, Fra	frä dē-ä'-vō-lō.
Diaz	dē'-äth.
Diderot	dēd-rō'.
Didot	dē-dō'.
Didymus	dĭd'-ĭ-mŭs.
Diederichs, von . . .	fŏn dē'-dä-rĭks.
Diego	dē-ā'-gō.
Dieppe	dē-ĕp'.
Dies Irae	dī'-ēz ī'-rē.
Dieskau	dēs'-kow.
Dietrich von Bern . . .	dē'-trĭch fŏn bĕrn.
Dijon	dē-zhôṅ'.
Dilke	dĭlk.
Dimitri	dē-mē'-trē.
Dinan	dē-näṅ'.
Dinant	dē-nänt'. *Fr.* dē-näṅ'
Dingaan	dĭn-gän', *or* dĭng-gän'.
Diodorus Siculus . . .	dī-ō-dō'-rŭs sĭk'-ū-lŭs.
Diomedes	dī-ō-mē'-dēz.
Dionysia	dī-ō-nĭsh'-ĭ-à.
Dionysius	dī-ō-nĭsh'-ĭ-ŭs.
Dionysus	dī-ō-nī'-sŭs.

Dioscuri	dī-ŏs-kū'-rī.
Dippel	dĭp'-pĕl.
Dirce	dẽr'-sē.
Discobolus	dĭs-kŏb'-ō-lŭs.
Disraeli	dĭz-rā'-lĭ, dĭz-rĕ'-lĭ.
Dives	dī'-vēz.
Divina Commedia . . .	dē-vē'-nä kŏm-mä'-dē-ä.
Dnieper, or Dniepr . . .	nē'-pĕr. *Russ.* dnyĕp'-ĕr.
Dniester, or Dniestr . . .	nēs'-tĕr. *Russ.* dnyĕs'-tĕr.
Dodona	dō-dō'-nä.
Dogali	dō-gä'-lē.
Dolce	dŏl'-chĕ. *It.* dŏl'-chä.
Dolci	dŏl'-chĭ. *It.* dŏl'-chē.
Dolgorouki, or Dolgoruki .	dŏl-gŏ-rōō'-kē.
Döllinger	dĕl'-ĭng-ĕr.
Dolores	dō-lō'-rĕs.
Domenichino	dō''-mä-nē-kē'-nō.
Domingue	dŏ-mằng'.
Dominica	dŏm-ĭn-ē'-kȧ.
Dominique, La	lä dŏm-ē-nēk'.
Domitian	dō-mĭsh'-ȧn.
Domremy-la-Pucelle . . .	dôṅ-rä-mē'-lä-pü-sĕl'.
Doña	dŏn'-yä.
Donalbain	dŏn'-ăl-bān.
Donatello	dŏn-ä-tĕl'-lŏ.
Donati	dō-nä'-tē.
Donauwörth	dō'-now-vẽrt.
Don César de Bazan . . .	dôṅ sä-zär' dŭ bä
Don Giovanni	dŏn jō-vän'-nē.
Dongola	dŏng'-gō-lä.
Donizetti	dō-nē-dzĕt'-tē.
Don Juan	dŏn jū'-ȧn. *Sp.* dōn
Donna	dŏn'-nä. [·hōō-än'.
Donnay	dŏn-ā'.
Don Pasquale	dŏn päs-kwä'-lä. [tä-rä.
Don Pedro de Alcantara .	dŏn pā'-drŏ dä äl-kän'-

Don Quixote, *Sp.* Quijote { dŏn kwĭks′-ōt.
                      { *Sp.* dōn ке-chō′-tä.

Dorado, El . . . . ′. . āl dō-rä′-dō.   [dōn′-yŭ.
Dordogne . . . . . . dôr - dōn′.   *Fr.* d̄ōr -
Dordrecht . . . . . . dôr′-drĕcht.
Doré . . . . dō-rā′.
Doria . . . . dō′-rē-ä.
Dorian . . . . dō′-rĭ-án.
Doric . . . . dôr′-ĭk, dŏr′-ĭk.
D'Orléans . . . . . . dôr-lā-äṅ′.   [rō-tā′-ä.
Dorothea . . . . dŏr-ō-thē′-ȧ. *Ger.* dō-
Dorothée . . . . dō-rō-tā′.
D'Orsay, Quai . . . . . kā dôr-sā′.
Dort . . . . dôrt.
D'Orthez, *see* Orthez . . dŏr-tĕss′ *or* -tāz′.
Dossi, Dosso . . . . . . dŏs′-sō dŏs′-sē.
Dossier, The . . . . . . dŏs-sē-ā′.
Dostoievsky, *or* Dostoyevsky dŏs-tō-yĕf′-skĭ.
Dotheboys Hall . . . . dō′-thē-boiz hôl.
Douai, *or* Douay . . . . dōō-ā′.
Doubs . . . . dōō.
Doulton . . . . dōl′-tŏn.
Douw, *or* Dow . . . . . dow.   [chĕn-fĕlz.
Drachenfels . . . . . . drăk′-ĕn-fĕlz. *Ger.* drä′-
Draconic . . . . drā-kŏn′-ĭk.
Drakenberg (Mts.) . . . drä′-kĕn-bĕrch.
Dreux . . . . drĕ.
Dreyfus . . . . drā-füs′.
Drogheda . . . . . drŏch′-ĕ-dä, drŏ′-hĕd-ȧ.
Drouet . . . . drōō-ā′.
Droz . . . . drō.
Druses . . . . drōōz′-ĕz.
Dryope . . . . drī′-ō-pē.
Dry Tortugas . . . . . drī tôr-tōō′-gáz.
Dubois . . . . *Fr.* dü-bwä′.
Du Bois-Reymond . . . dü bwä-rā-môṅ′.

Duc	*Fr.* dük.
Duca	dōō'-kä.
Ducange, *or* Du Cange . .	dü-känzh'. [sän'-yä.
Duccio di Buoninsegua . .	dōōch'-ō dē bōō-ōn''-ēn-
Du Chaillu	dü shä-yü'.
Du Châtelet	dü shät-lä'.
Duchessa	*It.* dōō-kĕs'-sä.
Duchesse	*Fr.* dü-shĕs'.
Ducrot	dü-krō'.
Dudevant	düd-vän'.
Du Guesclin, *or* Duguesclin	dü gä-klän'.
Dulcinea del Toboso . . .	{ dŭl-sĭn'-ē-ä dĕl tō-bō'-sō *Sp.* dōōl-thē-nä'-ä däl tō-bō'-sō.
Dumas	dōō-mä'. *Fr.* dü-mä'.
Du Maurier	dü mō-rē-ā'.
Dumbarton	dŭm-bär'-tŏn.
Dumfries	dŭm-frēz'.
Dumouriez	dü-mōō-rē-ā'.
Dünaburg	dü'-nä-bōōrg.
Dunbar	dŭn-bär'.
Dunedin	'dŭn-ē'-dĭn, dŭn-ĕd'-ĭn.
Dunes (Battle of the) . .	dünz.
Dunkeld	dŭn-kĕld'.
Dunois	dü-nwä'.
Duomo	dōō-ō'-mō.
Dupaty	dü-pä-tē'.
Du Paty de Clam	dü pä-tē' dŭ klåm'.
Duplessis	dü-plĕ-sē'.
Duplessis-Mornay	dü-plĕ-sē'-mōr-nä'.
Duprat	dü-prä'.
Dupré	dü-prä'.
Duprétis	dōō-prä-tēs'.
Dupuy	dü-pwē'.
Duquesne	dü-kän'.
Duquesnoy	dü-kä-nwä'.

Duran, Carolus . . . . kä-rō-lüs' dü-räṅ'.
Durandarte . . . . . . dōō-rän-där'-tā.
Durango . . . . dōō-rän'-gō.
Durazzo . . . . dōō-rät'-sō.
Durban, *or* D'Urban . . . dẽr'-băn.
Durbunga, *see* Darbhangah dŭr-bŭn'-gä.
Dürer . . . . dü'-rẽr.
Durham . . . . dŭr'-ȧm.
Duroc . . . . dü-rŏk'.
Duruy . . . . dü-rü-e͟'.
Durward . . . . dẽr'-wård.   [dōō'-zĕ.
Duse . . . . dōō'-sĕ, dōō'-sā. *It.*
Düsseldorf . . . . . . düs'-sĕl-dŏrf.
Dvořák, Anton . . . . . än'-tōn dvōr'-zhäk.
Dyak . . . . dī'-ăk.
Dyea . . . . dī'-ā.

E

Eadred . . . . ĕd'-rĕd.
Eames (Emma) . . . . āmz.   [lōn'-yŭ
Eau de Cologne . . . . ō dŭ kō-lōn'. *Fr.* kō-
Ebal . . . . ē'-băl.
Eberhard . . . . ā'-bĕr-härt.
Ebers, Georg . . . . . gā-ōrċh' ā'-bĕrs.
Eblis, *see* Iblis . . . . . ĕb'-lĭs.
Eboli . . . . ā'-bō-lē.   [kŭm.
Eboracum, *see* Eburacum . ē-bŏr'-ȧ-kŭm, ĕb-ō-rā'-
Ebro . . . . ē'-brō. *Sp.* ā'-brō. [kŭm.
Eburacum, *see* Eboracum . ē-bŭr'-ȧ-kŭm, ĕb-ōō-rā'-
Ecbatana . . . . ĕk-băt'-ȧ-nȧ.
Eccelino da Romano, *see* ⎰ ĕch-ā-lē'-nō dä rō-mä'-
  Ezzelino . . . . . . ⎱ nō.
Ecclefechan . . . . . . ĕk-l-fĕċh'-ȧn, ĕk-l-fĕk'-
Ecclesiastes . . . . . . ĕk-klē''-zĭ-ăs'-tēz. [ȧn.

Echague	ĕchȧ-gu̇ĕ.
Echegaray	ā″-chä-gä-rä′-ē.
Echo	ĕk′-ō, ē′-kō.
École des Beaux Arts, L'	lä-kōl′ dā bō-zär′.
École des Femmes, L'	lä-kōl′ dā făm′.
École des Maris, L'	lä-kōl′ dā mă-rē′.
École Polytechnique	ā-kōl′ pō-lē-tăk-nĕk′.
Écorcheurs, Les	lā zā-kōr-shĕr′. [dōr′.
Ecuador	ĕk-wá-dōr′. *Sp.* ā-kwä-
Edam	ē′-dăm. *D.* ā-dăm′.
Eden	ē′-dn.
Edgecote	ĕdj′-kōt. [bŭr″-ŭ.
Edinburgh	ĕd′-ĭn-bŭr″-ō, ĕd′-ĭn-
Edmond	*Fr.* ĕd-môṅ′.
Edom	ē′-dŏm.
Édouard	ā-dōō-är′.
Edrei	ĕd′-rē-ĭ.
Eckhoud, Georges	zhŏrzh āk′-howt.
Égalité, Philippe	fē-lēp′ ā-gäl-ē-tā′.
Egean, *see* Aegean	ē-jē′-án.
Eger	ā′-gĕr.
Egeria, *see* Aegeria	ē-jē′-rĭ-á.
Egeus	ē-jē′-ŭs.
Eginhard, *see* Einhard	ā′-gĭn-härd.
Eglamour	ĕg′-lȧ-mōōr.
Eglantine	ĕg′-lȧn-tīn.
Ehrenbreitstein	ā-rĕn-brīt′-stīn.
Ehrenfels	ā-rĕn-fĕlz.
Eichberg	īċh′-bĕrċh.
Eiffel	ī′-fĕl. *Fr.* ā-fĕl′.
Eikon Basilike	ī′-kŏn bȧ-sĭl′-ĭ-kē.
Eikonoclastes	ī-kŏn″-ō-klăs′-tēz.
Eimbeck, or Einbeck	īm′-bĕk, īn′-bĕk.
Einhard, *see* Eginhard	īn′-härd.
Eisenach	ī′-zā-näċh.
Eisleben	īs′-lā-bĕn.

Eisteddfod . . . . . ī-stĕŧh'-vōd.

Ekaterinburg, *see* Yeka- } ĕ-kä''-tĕ-rēn-bōŏrg'.
terinburg . . . . . }

Ekber, *see* Akbar . . . ĕk'-bĕr. *Hind.* ŭk'-bĕr.

Elagabalus, *see* Helioga- } ē-lá-găb'-á-lŭs, ĕl''-á-găb'-
balus . . . . . . } á-lŭs, ĕl''-ā-gā-bā'-lŭs.

Elamite . . . . . . ē'-lám'-īt.

Elandslaagte . . . . ā-lănts-läċh'-tĕ.

Elbe . . . . ĕlb. *Ger.* ĕl'-bŭ.

Elberfeld . . . . . . ĕl'-bĕr-fĕlt.

Elbrooz, Elbruz . . . ĕl-brōōz'.

El Campeador . . . . āl käm''-pā-ä-dōr'.

El Caney . . . . . . āl kä-nā'-ē. [dō.

El Dorado . . . . . ĕl dō-rā'-dō. *Sp.* āl dō-rä'-

Eleanor . . . . . . ĕl'-ē-ā-nôr'', ĕl'-á-nĕr.

Eleanora d'Este . . . ā''-lā-ō-nō'-rä dās'-tĕ.

Eleatic . . . . . . ĕl-ē-ăt'-ĭk.

Eleazar . . . . . . ĕl-ē-ā'-zár, ē-lē'-ā-zär.

Eleusinia . . . . . . ĕl-ū-sĭn'-ĭ-á.

Eleusis . . . . . . ĕ-lū'-sĭs.

Eleuthera . . . . . ĕ-lū'-thĕ-rá.

Elgin . . . . ĕl'-gĭn.

Elia . . . . ē'-lĭ-á.

Eliab . . . . ē-lī'-ăb.

Eliakim . . . . . . ē-lī'-á-kĭm.

Elias . . . . ē-lī'-ás.

Elidure . . . . . . ĕl'-ĭ-dūr.

Élie de Beaumont . . ā-lē' dŭ bō-môǹ'.

Eliezer . . . . . . ĕl-ĭ-ē'-zĕr.

Elihu . . . . ĕ-lī'-hū.

Elimelech . . . . . ĕ-lĭm'-ĕ-lĕk.

Elío (Gen.) . . . . . ā-lē'-ō.

Eliodoro . . . . . . ā''-lē-ō-dō'-rō.

Eliphalet . . . . . . ĕ-lĭf'-á-lĕt.

Élise . . . . ā-lēz'. [bĕth'-án.

Elizabethan . . . . . ē-lĭz'-ā-bĕth''-án, *or* ē-lĭz''-ā-

Elkanah	ĕl-kā'-nä, ĕl'-kā-nä.
Ellichpur	ĕl-ĭch-pōōr'.
El Mahdi, *see* Mahdi .	āl mä'-dē.
Elmire	ĕl-mēr'.
El Obeid	ĕl ŏb-ād'.
Elohim	ē-lō'-hĭm, ĕl'-ō-hĭm.
El Puerto	āl pwâr'-tō, pōō-âr'-tō.
Elsass	āl'-zäs.
Elsass-Lothringen . .	āl'-zäs-lōt'-rĭng-ĕn.
Elsinore	ĕl-sĭ-nōr'.
Elssler	ĕls'-lēr.
Eltekeh	ĕl'-tĕ-kē.
Elul	ē'-lŭl.
Élysée	ā-lē-zā'. [ē-lĭzh'-ăn.
Elysian	ē-lĭz'-ĭ-ăn, ē-lĭzh'-ē-ăn,
Elysium	{ ē-lĭz'-ĭ-ŭm, ē-lĭzh'-ĭ-ŭm, / ē-lĭzh'-ŭm.
Elzevir	ĕl'-zĕ-vēr, ĕl'-zē-vēr.
Emeer, *see* Emir . .	ē-mēr'.
Émigrés, Les	lä zā-mē-grā'.
Emil	ā'-mēl.
Émile	ā-mēl'.
Emilian	ē-mĭl'-ĭ-ȧn.
Éminence Grise, L' . .	lä-mē-nŏńs' grēz.
Emin Pacha (*or* Bey) .	ā'-mēn pȧsh-ô' (bā), pä-shä',
Emir, *see* Emeer . .	ē'-mēr, ē-mēr'. [päsh'-ȧ.
Emmaus	ĕ-mā'-ŭs, ĕm'-mā-ŭs.
Empedocles	ĕm-pĕd'-ō-klēz.
Ems	ĕmz.
Énault (Louis) . . .	ā-nō'.
Enceladus	ĕn-sĕl'-ȧ-dŭs.
Encke	ĕng'-kŭ.
Encyclopédie	ŏń-sē-klō-pā-dē'.
Endymion	ĕn-dĭm'-ĭ-ŏn.
Eneas, *see* Aeneas . .	ē-nē'-ȧs.
Eneid	ē-nē'-ĭd, ē'-nē-ĭd.

Enemessar . . . . . . ĕn-ē-mĕs'-sȧr.

Engadine . . . . ĕn-gä-dēn'.

Engaño . . . . ĕn-gän'-yō.

Engedi . . . . ĕn-gē'-dī, ĕn'-gē-dī.

Enghien, Duc d' . . . . dük dȧn-gē-ăn', dȧn-

England . . . . ĭng'-glȧnd.　　　[gȧn'.

English . . . . ĭng'-glĭsh.

Enid . . . . ē'-nĭd.

Enobarbus . . . . . . ĕn-ō-bär'-bŭs.

Entraigues, Henriette d', } ŏn-rē-ĕt' dŏn-träg'.
　see Antraigues . . . . }

Eolian, *see* Aeolian . . . ē-ō'-lĭ-ȧn.

Eolic, *see* Aeolic . . . . ē-ŏl'-ĭk.

Eolis, *see* Aeolis . . . . ē'-ō-lĭs.

Epaminondas . . . . . ē-păm"-ĭn-ŏn'-dȧs.

Epaphroditus . . . . . ē-păf"-rō-dī'-tŭs.

Epeiros, *see* Epirus . . . ē-pī'-rŭs.

Épernay . . . . ā-pĕr-nā'.

Épernon, d' . . . . . . dā-pĕr-nôn'.

Epes . . . . ĕps.

Ephesians . . . . . . ē-fē'-zhȧnz.

Ephesus . . . . ĕf'-ĕ-sŭs.

Ephraim . . . . ē'-frā-ĭm.

Ephrata . . . . ĕf'-rā-tä, ĕf'-rȧ-tȧ.

Epicœne . . . . ĕp'-ĭ-sēn.

Epictetus . . . . ĕp-ĭk-tē'-tŭs.　　[rē-ȧn.

Epicurean . . . . . . ĕp"-ĭ-kū-rē'-ȧn, ĕp-ĭ-kū'-

Epicureanism . . . . . { ĕp"-ĭ-kū-rē'-ȧn-ĭzm, ĕp-
　　　　　　　　　　　　　{　ĭ-kū'-rē-ȧn-ĭzm".

Epicurus . . . . ĕp-ĭ-kū'-rŭs.

Épidaurus . . . . . . ĕp-ĭ-dôr'-ŭs.

Epinay, d' . . . . . . dā-pē-nā'.

Epipsychidion . . . . . ĕp"-ĭ-sī-kĭd'-ĭ-ŏn.

Epirot . . . . ē-pī'-rŏt.

Epirote . . . . ē-pī'-rōt.

Epirus, *see* Epeiros . . . ē-pī'-rŭs.

Epithalamium . . . . . ep″-ĭ-thā-lā′-mĭ-ŭm.
Érard . . . . ā-rär′.
Erasmus . . . . ē-răz′-mŭs.
Éraste . . . . ā-räst′.
Erastianism . . . . . . ē-răst′-yăn-ĭzm.
Erato . . . . ĕr′-ā-tō.
Eratosthenes . . . . . ĕr-ā-tŏs′-thē-nēz.
Erckmann-Chatrian . . . ĕrk′-män-shä-trē-äṅ′.
Erebus . . . . ĕr′-ē-bŭs. [thē′-ŭm.
Erechtheum . . . . . . ĕr-ĕk-thē′-ŭm, ē-rĕk-
Eretria . . . . ĕ-rē′-trĭ-à.
Eretrian . . . . ĕ-rē′-trĭ-àn.
Erfurt . . . . ĕr′-foͦrt.
Eric, see Erik . . . . . ĕr′-ĭk, ē′-rĭk.
Ericsson . . . . ĕr′-ĭk-sŏn. [ĭ-jē′-nà.
Erigena . . . . ē-rĭj′-ē-nä, ĕr-ĭj′-ĕ-nà, ĕr-
Erik, see Eric . . . . . ĕr′-ĭk, ē′-rĭk. Sw. ä′-rĭk.
Erin . . . . ē′-rĭn.
Erinnyes, or Erinyes, or ⎰ ĕr-ĭn′-ĭ-ēz, ē-rĭn′-ĭ-ēz,
  Erinnys . . . . . . ⎱ ĕr-ĭn′-ēz, ē-rĭn′-ēz.
Erivan . . . . ĕr-ĭ-vän′.
Erlangen . . . . ĕr′-läng-ĕn. [nĭ́ch.
Erl-King, or Ger. Erl-König ērl′-kĭng. Ger. ĕrl kē′-
Eroica . . . . ā-rō′-ē-kä.
Eros . . . . ē′-rŏs.
Erostratus . . . . . . ē-rŏs′-trā-tŭs.
Erskine . . . . ērs′-kĭn.
Erzerum . . . . ĕrz-roͦm′.
Esaias . . . . ē-zā′-yàs.
Escalus . . . . ĕs′-kà-lŭs. [bäch.
Eschenbach, Wolfram von . vŏ̆lf′-räm fŏn ĕsh′-ĕn-
Escorial, or . . . . . . ĕs-kō′-rĭ-ăl. Sp. ĕs-kō-
Escurial . . . . ĕs-kū′-rĭ-ăl. [rē-äl′.
Esdraelon . . . . . . ĕs-drắ-ē′-lŏn, ĕs-drā′-ē-
Eskimo, see Esquimaux . ĕs′-kĭ-mō. [lŏn.
Esop, see Aesop . . . . ē′-sŏp.

España	ās-pän′-yä.
Española	ās-pän-yō′-lä.
Espinasse, de l', *see* Lespinasse . . . . . . }	dŭ lä-pē-näs′.
Espiritu Santo	ās-pē′-rē-tōō sän′-tō.
Esprémesnil, *or* Éprémenil	ā-prā-mā-nēl′.
Esquiline	ĕs-kē-lēn′, ĕs′-kwĭ-lĭn.
Esquimaux, *or* Eskimo . .	ĕs-kē-mō′.
Esquirol	ĕs-kē-rōl′.
Essenes	ĕs-sēnz′, ĕs′-sē-nēz.
Essipoff	ĕs-ē-pŏf′.
Estaing, d'	dĕs-tăṅ′.
Estcourt	ĕst′-kōrt.
Este	ās′-tĕ.
Esterhazy, *see* Eszterházy . {	ĕs′-tĕr-hä-zĭ, ĕs-tĕr-hä′-zē.　　*Fr.* ās-târ-ä-zē′.
Esther	ĕs′-tĕr.
Esthonia	ĕs-thō′-nĭ-à.
Estienne, *see* Étienne . .	ā-tē̮-ĕn′.
Estrées, Gabrielle d' . . .	gä-brē-ĕl′ dās-trā′.
Estrella, La	lä ĕs-trāl′-yä.
Estremadura	ĕsh″-trä-mä-dōō′-rä.
Eszterházy, *see* Esterhazy . {	ĕs′-tĕr-hä-zĭ, ĕs-tĕr-hä′-zē.　　*Fr.* ās-târ-ä-zē′.
Etah	ē′-tà.
Etampes	ā-täṅp′.
Etesian	ē-tē′-zhĭ-àn, ē-tē′-zhàn.
Ethelbert, *see* Aethelberht	ĕth′-ĕl-bĕrt.
Ethiopic	ē-thĭ-ŏp′-ĭk, ē-thĭ-ō′-pĭk.
Étienne, *see* Estienne . .	ā-tē̮-ĕn′.
Eu	ĕ.
Eubœa	ū-bē′-ä.
Eudes	ĕd.
Eudoxia	ū-dŏk′-sĭ-à.
Euergetes	ū-ĕr′-jĕ-tēz.
Eugene.	ū-jēn′.

Eugène   Ĕŭ̇, ŏ̃ṅhā̇ṅ′,
Eugène de Beauharnais .   ē-zhän′ dŭ bō-är-nā′.
Eugénie de Montijo . . { ē-zhā-nē′ dŭ mŏṅ-tē-zhō′.
                         { Sp. dā mōn-tē′-ċhō.
Eugénie Grandet . . .   ē-zhā-nē′ gräṅ-dā′.
Eulalia . . . .   ā-o͞o-lä′-lē-ä.
Eulalie . . . . . .   ē-lä-lē′.
Eulate . . . .   ā-o͞o-lä′-tä.
Eulenspiegel . . . .   oi′-lĕn-spē″-gĕl.
Euler . . . .   oi′-lĕr.
Eumenes . . . . . .   ū′-mē-nēz.
Eumenidæ . . . . .   ū-mĕn′-ĭ-dē.
Eumenides . . . . .   ū-mĕn′-ĭ-dēz.
Eunice . . . .   ū′-nĭs, ū-nī′-sē.
Euphrates . . . . .   ū-frā′-tēz.
Euphrosyne . . . . .   ū-frŏs′-ĭn-ē.
Euphues . . . . . .   ū′-fū-ēz.
Eurasia . . . . . .   ū-rā′-shĭ-ȧ, ū-rā′-zhĭ-ȧ.
Eurasian . . . . . .   ū-rā′-shĭ-ȧn, ū-rā′-zhĭ-ȧn.
Eure . . . .   ēr.
Eure-et-Loire . . . .   ēr-ā-lwär′.   [dē-chē.
Euridice . . . . . .   Fr. ēr-ē-dēs′. It. ā-o͞o-rē′-
Euripides . . . . .   ū-rĭp′-ĭ-dēz.
Euroclydon . . . .   ū-rŏk′-lĭ-dŏn.
Europa, or . . . .   ū-rō′-pä.
Europe . . . . . .   ū′-rŏp, class. ū-rō′-pē.
European . . . . . .   ū-rō-pē′-ȧn.
Eurydice . . . . . .   ū-rĭd′-ĭs-ē.
Eusenada Honda . . .   ā″-o͞o-sā-nä′-dä ōn′-dä.
Eustache, St. . . . .   säṅ-tēs-täsh′.
Eustachian . . . .   ūs-tā′-kĭ-ȧn.
Eustachio . . . . .   ā-o͞os-tä′-kē-ō.
Eustachius . . . .   ūs-tā′-kĭ-ŭs.
Euterpe . . . . . .   ū-tĕr′-pē.
Euterpean . . . . .   ū-tĕr′-pē-ȧn.
Euxine . . . . . .   yūks′-ĭn.

Evangeline . . . . . ē-văn'-jĕ-lĭn, ē-văn'-jĕ-lēn.
Evelina . . . . . . ĕv-ĕ-lī'-na, ĕv-ĕ-lē'-na.
Evesham . . . . . . ēvz'-hăm, ēvz'-ăm, ĕv'-
Ewart . . . . ū'-ȧrt. [shăm.
Exeter . . . . ĕks'-ĕ-tĕr.
Eyck, van . . . . . văn īk.
Eylau . . . . ī'-low.
Eyre . . . . âr.
Eytinge . . . . . . ĕt'-tĭng.
Ezekias . . . . . . ĕz-ĕ-kī'-ȧs.
Ezekiel . . . . . . ē-zē'-kĭ-ĕl.
Ezra . . . . ĕz'-rä.
Ezzelino da Romano, *see* ⎱ ĕt-zä-lē'-nō dä rō-mä'-nŏ.
  Eccelino . . . . . ⎰

F

Fabian . . . . . . fā'-bĭ-ȧn.
Fabliau . . . . . . fä-blē-ō'.
Fabliaux . . . . . . fä-blē-ō'.
Fabre . . . . fäbr.
Fabriano . . . . . . fä-brē-ä'-nō.
Faenza . . . . . . fä-ĕn'-dzä.
Fahrenheit . . . . . fä'-rĕn-hīt.
Faidherbe . . . . . fä-dârb'.
Failly . . . . fä-yē'.
Fainéants, Les Rois . . lä rwä fä-nä-äṅ'.
Faizabad, *see* Fyzabad . fī-zä-bäd'.
Fajardo, *see* Faxardo . *Sp.* fä-ċhär'-dō.
Falaise . . . . . . fä-lāz'.
Falernian . . . . . fā-lĕr'-nĭ-ȧn.
Falieri . . . . . . fä-lē-ä'-rē.
Faneuil . . . . . . făn'-ĕl. *pop.* fŭn'-ĕl.
Fantine . . . . . . fäṅ-tēn'.
Faraday . . . . . . făr'-ȧ-dā.

Farallones	fä-räl-yō'-nĕs.
Faridpur, *see* Furidpur .	fŭr-ĕd-poor'.
Farnese	fär-nēz'. *It.* fär-nā'-zĕ.
Faro, *or* Faroe	fā'-rō, fā'-rōō-ĕ.
Farquhar	fär'-kwär, fär'-kär.
Farrakhabad, *see* Farruk-habad	fŭr-rŭk-ä-bäd'.
Farrar (Canon)	fär'-ȧr.
Farrukhabad, *see* Farrak-habad	fŭr-rŭk-ä-bäd'.
Fashoda	fä-shō'-dä.
Fata Morgana	fā'-tȧ môr-gä'-nȧ, fä'-tä môr-gä'-nä.
Fathipur, *see* Futtehpur .	fŭt-ē-poor'.
Fatima	fä'-tē-mä. *pop.* făt'-ĭ-mȧ.
Fatimites	făt'-ĭ-mīts.
Faubourg St. Antoine . .	fō-boor' săṅ-täṅ-twäṅ'.
Faubourg St. Germain . .	fō-boor' săṅ zhâr-măṅ'.
Faure, Félix	fä-lēks' fōr'.
Fauresmith	fôr'-smĭth.
Faust	fowst.
Favre	fävr.
Faxardo, *see* Fajardo . .	fä-ċhär'-dō.
Fayal	fī-ôl'. *Port.* fī-äl'.
Fayoum, Fayum	fī-ōōm'.
February	fĕb'-rōō-ā''-rĭ.
Fechter	fĕċh'-tĕr, fĕsh'-tĕr.
Fédora	fä-dō'-rä.
Feejee, *see* Fiji	fē'-jĕ.
Feejeean, *see* Fijian . . .	fē-jē'-ȧn.
Felice	*It.* fä-lē'-chä.
Félice	*Fr.* fä-lēs'.
Félicité	fä-lēs-ē-tā'.
Felipe	fä-lē'-pā.
Felix	fē'-lĭks.
Félix	*Fr.* fä-lēks'.

Femme de Trente Ans . .	făm dŭ trŏnt än. [lôn'.
Fénelon	fĕn'₌ĕ₌lŏn Fr fā₌nñ₌
Feodor	fā'-ō-dōr.
Ferichta, Ferishta, Fer- ischta, see Firishtah . .	} fĕr'-ĭsh-tä. [nän'-dĕth.
Fernandez	fĕr-năn'-dēz. Sp. fĕr-
Fernandina . . . . · ·	{ fĕr-nän-dē'-ná. { Sp. fĕr-nän-dē'-nä.
Fernando, San	sän fĕr-năn'-dō, sän fĕr-
Ferney or Fernex . . .	fâr-nā'. [nän'-dō.
Ferozepore, see Firozpur .	fē-rōz-pōr'.
Ferrand	fĕ-rän'.
Ferrara	fĕr-rä'-rä.
Ferrières	fĕr-ē-âr'.
Ferrol, El	äl fĕr-rōl'.
Ferronnière, La Belle . .	lä bĕl fĕr-rŏn-ē-âr'.
Ferry, Jules	zhül fĕ-rē'.
Fétis	fā-tēs'.
Feuerbach	foi'-ĕr-bäch.
Feuillet Octave	ōk-täv' fĕ-yā'.
Feydeau	fā-dō'. [grō.
Feyjoo y Montenegro . .	fā-ē-hō' ē mŏn-tā-nā'-
Fezzan	fĕz-zän'.
Fichte	fĭch'-tŭ.
Fidelio	fē-dā'-lē-ō.
Fierabras	fē-ā-rä-brä'.
Fiesole	fē-ā'-zō-lĕ.
Figaro	fē-gä-rō'.
Fiji, see Feejee	fē'-jē.
Fijian, see Feejeean . .	fē-jē'-ȧn.
Filarete	fē-lä-rā'-tĕ. [nä.
Filipina	fĭl-ĭ-pē'-ná, Sp. fē-lē-pē'-
Filipino	fĭl-ĭ-pē'-nō. Sp. fē-lē-
Filippo	fē-lēp'-pō. [pē'-nō.
Fille du Régiment, La . .	lä fē dü rā-zhē-mŏn'.
Filomena (St.)	fĭl-ō-mē'-nȧ.

Finistère, *or* Finisterre . . fĭn-ĭs-târ′.

Firishtah, *see* Ferishta . . fō′ rŏoh tä.

Firmin Didot . . . . . fĕr-măn′ dē-dō′.

Firozpur, *see* Ferozepore . fē-rōz-pōōr′.

Fiume . . . . fē-ōō′-mĕ.

Flameng . . . . . . flä-măng′.

Flammarion . . . . flä-mä-rē-ôn′.

Flandrin . . . . . . flän-drăn′.

Flaubert . . . . . . flō-bâr′.

Fleance . . . . . . flē′-ȧns.

Fleurus . . . . . . flē-rüs′.

Fleury . . . . flē-rē′.

Floréal . . . . . . flō-rä-ăl′.

Florentine . . . . . flŏr′-ĕn-tĭn, flŏr′-ĕn-tīn.

Flores . . . . flō′-rĕs.

Florizel . . . . . . flŏr′-ĭ-zĕl.

Flotow, von . . . . . fŏn flō′-tō, *Ger.* flō′-tōv.

Flourens . . . . . . flōō-rŏn′.

Foggia . . . . . . fŏd′-jä.

Foix . . . . fwä.

Fokien, *see* Fu-kien . . fō-kē-ĕn′.

Foligno, *see* Fuligno . . fō-lēn′-yō.

Folkething . . . . . fōl′-kĕ-tĭng.

Fomalhaut . . . . . fō-măl-ō′.

Fonseca . . . . . . fŏn-sä′-kä.

Fontainebleau . . . . fôn-tän-blō′.   [nwä′.

Fontenoy . . . . . . fŏnt′-ĕ-noi.   *Fr.* fônt-

Fontevrault . . . . . fôn-tĕ-vrō′.

Foochow, *see* Fu-chau . fōō-chow′.

Forlì . . . . fōr-lē′.

Formosa . . . . . . fôr-mō′-sä.

Formosan . . . . . fôr-mō′-sȧn.

Fornarina, La . . . . lä fôr-nä-rē′-nä.

Forres . . . . fŏr′-ĕs.

Fort de France . . . . fōr dŭ fräns.

Fortinbras . . . . . fôr′-tĭn-brȧs.

Fortunatus . . . . . . fôr-tū-nā'-tŭs.

Fortuny . . . . fōr-tōō'-nē.

Foscari . . . . fŏs'-kä-rē.

Foscarini . . . . . . fŏs-kä-rē'-nē.

Foscolo . . . . fŏs'-kō-lŏ.

Foucault . . . . fōō-kō'.

Fouché . . . . fōō-shā'.

Foucquet . . . . fōō-kā'.

Foulques . . . . fōōk.

Fouqué . . . . fōō-kā'.

Fourier . . . . fōō-rē-ā'.

Fourierism . . . . . . fōō'-rǐ-ěr-ĭzm".

Fracasse, Capitaine . . kä-pē-tān' frä-käs'.

Fra Diavolo . . . . . frä dē-ä'-vō-lō.

France . . . . frăns.   *Fr.* fräṅs.

France, Anatole . . . ä-nä-tōl' fräṅs.

France, Île de . . . . ēl dŭ fräṅs'.

Francesca da Rimini . ⎰ frăn-sĕs'-kȧ dä rē'-mē-nē.
⎨ *It.* frän-chĕs'-kä dä-rē'-
⎱ mē-nē.   [kō.

Francesco . . . . . . frän-sĕs'-kō. *It.* frän-chĕs'-

Franche-Comté . . . fräṅsh kôṅ-tä'.

Francia . . . . frän'-chä.   [kō.

Francisco . . . . . . frän-sĭs'-kō. *Sp.* frän-thēs'-

Francis de Sales . . . frän'-sĭs dŭ sālz. *Fr.* säl.

François . . . . fräṅ-swä'.

Françoise . . . . . . fräṅ-swäz'.

Franconian . . . . . frăng-kō'-nǐ-ȧn.   [pä'-nē.

Frangipani . . . . . frän-jǐ-pän'-ǐ. *It.* frän-jē-

Franz . . . . fränts.

Franz-Josef . . . . . fränts'-yō'-zĕf.

Frari . . . . frä'-rē.

Frascati . . . . fräs-kä'-tē.

Fraunhofer . . . . . frown'-hō-fĕr.

Freiberg . . . . frī'-bĕrċh.

Freiburg, *see* Fribourg . frī'-bōōrċh.

7

Freiligrath	frī'-lĭg-rät.
Freischütz, Der	dĕr frī'-shüts.
Freitag, see Freytag . . .	frī'-täċh.
Frelinghuysen	frē'-lĭng-hī''-zĕn.
Frémiet	frä-mē-ā'.
Fréminet	frä-mē-nä'.
Frémont (Gen.)	frä-mŏnt'. pop. frē'-mŏnt.
Fremont (Ohio)	frē-mŏnt', frē'-mŏnt.
Freneau	frĕ-nō'.
Frere	frĕr.
Frère	frâr.
Frescobaldi	frĕs-kō-bäl'-dē.
Frey	frī.
Freya	frī'-ä.
Freycinet.	frä-sē-nä'.
Freytag, see Freitag . . .	frī'-täċh.
Fribourg, see Freiburg . .	frē-bōōr'.
Fridthiof, see Frithjof . .	frēt'-yŏf.
Friedland	frēd'-länt.
Friedrichsbau	frēd'-rĭċhs-bow.
Friesian, see Frisian . . .	frēz'-yȧn, frēzh'-yȧn.
Frimaire	frē-mâr'.
Frisian, see Friesian . .	frĭz'-ị-ȧn, frĭzh'-yȧn.
Frithjof, see Fridthiof . .	frēt'-yŏf.
Fritz, Der Alte	dĕr äl'-tŭ frĭts.
Fritz, Unser	ŏŏn'-zĕr frĭts.
Friuli	frē'-ōō-lē.
Fröbel, or Froebel . . .	frē'-bĕl.
Froissart	froi'-särt. Fr. frwä-sär'.
Frollo, Claude	clōd frŏ-lō'.
Fromentin	frō-mŏṅ-tăṅ'.
Fronde	frŏnd. Fr. frôṅd.
Front de Bœuf	frôṅ dŭ bĕf.
Frontenac	frôṅt-näk'.
Frossard	frŏs-sär'.
Froude	frōōd.

Frou-Frou . . . . . . frōō'-frōō'.
Fructidor . . . . . . frük-tĕ-dōr'.
Fu-chau, *see* Foochow . . fōō-chow'.
Fuji-san, *or* . . . . . . fōō'-jē-sän'.
Fuji-yama . . . . . . fōō'-jē-yä'-mä.
Fu-kien, *see* Fokien . . . fōō-kē-ĕn'.
Fulc, *see* Fulk . . . . . fōōlk.
Fulda . . . . fōōl'-dä.
Fulham . . . . fŭl'-ȧm.
Fuligno, *see* Foligno . . . fōō-lēn'-yō.
Fulk, *see* Fulc . . . . . fōōlk.
Furidpur, *see* Faridpur . . fŭr-ēd-pōōr'.
Furness . . . . fêr'-nĕs.
Furor . . . . fū'-rôr'.   *Sp.* fōō-rōr'.
Fürst . . . . fürst.
Fürstin . . . . fürst'-ĭn.
Fusan . . . . fōō-sän'.
Fust . . . . fōōst.
Futtehpur, *see* Fathipur . fŭt-tĕ-pōōr'.
Fyne, Loch . . . . . . lŏċh fīn.
Fyt, Jan . . . . yän fīt.
Fyzabad, *see* Faizabad . . fī-zä-bäd'.

G

Gabael . . . . găb'-ā-ĕl, gā'-bā-ĕl.
Gaberones . . . . . . găb-ĕ-rō'-nĕs.
Gaboriau, Émile . . . . ā-mēl' gä-bō-rē̤-ō'.
Gabriel . . . . gā'-brĭ-ĕl.
Gabriele . . . . gä-brē-ā'-lĕ.
Gabrielle . . . . *Fr.* gä-brē-ĕl'.
Gabrielli . . . . gä-brē-ĕl'-lē.
Gadarenes . . . . . . găd-ä-rēnz'.
Gaddi, Gaddo . . . . . gäd'dō gäd'-dē.
Gade . . . . gä'-dĕ.

Gadeira, or   gä-dī'-rä

Gades . . . . gā'-dēz.

Gadhelic . . . . găd-ĕl'-ĭk, găd'-ĕl-ĭk.

Gadite . . . . gā'-dīt.

Gæa, see Ge . . . . . jē'-à.

Gaekwar, see Gaikwar . . gīk'-wär.

Gael . . . . gāl.

Gaelic . . . . gā'-lĭk.

Gaeta . . . . gä-ā'-tä.

Gaikwar, see Gaekwar . gīk'-wär.   [gānz'-brō.

Gainsborough . . . . . gānz'-bŭr-ŭ, gānz'-bŭr-ō,

Gaiseric . . . . gī'-zĕr-ĭk.   [pä-gōs.

Galapagos (Is.) . . . . găl-à-pā'-gōs. *Sp.* gä-lä'-

Galashiels . . . . găl-à-shēlz'.

Galatea . . . . găl-à-tē'-à.

Galatians . . . . gà-lā'-shĭ-àns.

Galdos, Pérez . . . . . pā'-rĕth găl'-dōs.

Galen . . . . gā'-lĕn.

Galignani . . . . . . gä-lēn-yä'-nē.

Galilean . . . . găl-ĭ-lē'-ăn.

Galilee . . . . găl'-ĭ-lē.

Galilei, Galileo . . . . gä-lē-lā'-ō gä-lē-lā'-ē.

Galitzin, see Gallitzin . . gä-lēts'-ēn.

Gallait . . . . găl-lä'.

Gallaudet . . . . . . găl-ô-dĕt'.

Gallicism . . . . găl'-ĭ-sĭzm.

Gallienus . . . . găl-ĭ-ē'-nŭs.

Gallifet, de . . . . . . dŭ găl-ē-fā'.   [ō-lē.

Gallipoli . . . . . . găl-lĭp'-ō-lĭ. *It.* gäl-lēp'-

Gallitzin, see Galitzin . . gä-lēts'-ēn.

Galuppi . . . . gä-lŏŏp'-pē.

Galvani . . . . gäl-vä'-nē.

Galveston . . . . . găl'-vĕs-tŭn.

Gama, da . . . . dä gä'-mä.

Gamaliel . . . . . . gă-mā'-lĭ-ĕl.   [bĕt-tä'.

Gambetta . . . . . . găm-bĕt'-tä.   *Fr.* gäṅ-

Gambia . . . . găm'-bĭ-ä.
Gananoque . . . . . . gä-nä-nōk'.
Gand, see Ghent . . . . gäṅ.
Gandercleugh . . . . . găn'-dĕr-klŭċh.
Gando . . . . găn'-dō.
Ganga, or . . . . . . Hind. gŭng'-gä.
Ganges . . . . găn'-jēz.
Ganjam . . . . gän-jäm'.
Ganymede . . . . . . găn'-ĭ-mēd. [ä-gäṅ-tü-ä'.
Garagantua, see Gargantua gär-à-găn'-tü-ä. Fr. gär-
Garay . . . . gä-rä'-ē.
Garbieh, see Gharbieh . . gär-bē'-yĕ.
Garcia, or . . . . . . gär'-shĭ-à. Sp. gär-thē'-ä·
Garcias, see Garzia . . . gär-thē'-äs.
Gard . . . . gär.
Gardafui, see Guardafui . gär-dä-fwē'. [gäṅ-tü-ä'.
Gargantua, see Garagantua gär-găn'tü-ä. Fr. gär-
Garguille . . . . gär-gē'-yŭ.
Garhwal, see Gurhwal . . gŭr-wäl'. [bäl'-dē.
Garibaldi . . . . gär-ĭ-băl'-dĭ. It. gä-rē-
Garigliano . . . . . . gä-rēl-yä'-nō.
Garnier . . . . gär-nē-ā'.
Garnier-Pagés . . . . . gär-nē-ā'-pä-zhäs'.
Garofalo . . . . gä-rŏ'-fä-lō.
Garonne . . . . gä-rŏn'. Fr. gä-rōn'.
Garzia, see Garcia . . . gär-thē'-ä.
Gascogne . . . . gäs-kōn'-yŭ.
Gascony . . . . găs'-kō-nĭ.
Gassend . . . . gäs-sŏṅ'. [dē'.
Gassendi . . . . gäs-sĕn'-dē. Fr. gä-säṅ·
Gastein . . . . gäs'-tīn.
Gaston de Foix . . . . gäs-tôṅ' dŭ fwä.
Gaston d'Orléans . . . . gäs-tôṅ' dōr-lä-äṅ'.
Gatacre . . . . găt'-à-kêr.
Gatshina . . . . gä'-chē-nä.
Gaudenzio . . . . . . gow-dĕn'-dzē-ō.

Gaudissart   gō-dē-sär'   [tä-mä

Gautama, *see* Gotama . .   gô'-tà-mà.   *Hind.* gow'-

Gautier, Théophile . . .   tä-ō-fēl' gō-tē̳-ā̳'.

Gavan . . . .   găv'-àn.

Gavin . . . .   găv'-ĭn.   [tôn'.

Gaveston . . . .   găv'-ĕs-tŭn.   *Fr.* gä-vĕs-

Gavroche . . . . . .   gä-vrōsh'.

Gawain, *or* Gawayne . .   gä'-wān.

Gay-Lussac . . . . . .   gä-lüs-säk'.

Gaza . . . .   gä'-zà.

Gazaland . . . .   gä'-zä-länd.

Ge, *see* Gæa . . . . . .   gē.

Geber . . . .   gä'-bĕr.

Gebir . . . .   gä'-bĕr.

Geddes . . . . . .   gĕd'-ĕs.

Gefleborg . . . . . .   yäf'-lĕ-bōrg.

Gehenna . . . . . .   gē-hĕn'-ä.

Geierstein . . . . .   gī'-ĕr-stīn.

Geikie . . . .   gē'-kī.

Gelée, Claude . . . . .   klōd zhē-lä'.

Gellert . . . . . .   gĕl'-lĕrt.

Gemini . . . . . .   jĕm'-ĭ-nī.

Geminiani . . . . .   jäm"-ē-nē-ä'-nē.

Genesareth, *see* Gennesaret   gĕ-nĕs'-à-rĕth.

Genesis . . . .   jĕn'-ĕ-sĭs.

Geneva . . . . . .   jĕ-nē'-vä.

Geneviève, Ste. . . . .   säṅt zhĕn-vē̳-ĕv'.

Genghis Khan, *see* Jenghiz   jĕn'-gĭs khän

Genlis, de . . . . . .   dŭ zhŏṅ-lēs'.   [rĕt.

Gennesaret, *see* Genesareth   gĕn-nĕs'-à-rĕt, jŏ-nĕs'-à-

Genoa . . . .   jĕn'-ō-ä.

Genoese . . . . . .   jĕn-ō-ēz', jĕn-ō-ēs'.

Genovefa . . . . . .   gä-nō-fä'-fä.

Genseric . . . . . .   jĕn'-sĕr-ĭk.

Gentiles . . . . . .   jĕn'-tīlz.

Geoffrey . . . . . .   jĕf'-rĭ.

Geoffrin	zhō-frăn'.
Geoffroy	zhō-frwä'.
Georg	*Ger.* gā-ōrċh'.
Georges	zhŏrzh.
Geraint	gĕ-rānt'.
Gérard	*Fr.* zhā-rär'.
Gerardy (Jean) . . .	zhē-rär-dē'.
Gergesenes	gĕr-gē-sēnz'. [härt.
Gerhardt	*Fr.* zhā-rär'. *Ger.* gâr-
Géricault	zhā-rē-kō'.
Gerizim	gĕr'-ĭz-ĭm.
Germain . , ...	jĕr-mān'. *Fr.* zhär-măn'.
Germinal	zhär-mē-năl'.
Gernszheim	gĕrns'-hĭm.
Gérôme	zhā-rōm'.
Gerona, *see* Jerona, Xerona	*Sp.* ḣā-rō'-nä.
Geronimo, Chief	{ jĕ-rŏn'-ĭ-mō. *Sp.* ḣā- { rŏn'-ē-mō.
Gerry	gĕr'-ĭ.
Gers	zhâr.
Gerster	gĕrs'-tĕr.
Gervais	zhĕr-vā'.
Gervaise	zhĕr-vāz'.
Gervase	jĕr'-vās, jĕr-vāz'.
Gervex	zhâr-vā'.
Geryon	jē'-rĭ-ŏn.
Geryones	jē-rĭ'-ō-nēz. [nē-ŏŏs.
Gesenius	gĕ-sē'-nĭ-ŭs. *Ger.* gā-zā'-
Gessart, *see* Gossaert .	gĕs'-ärt.
Gesta Romanorum . .	jĕs'-tä rō-mā-nō'-rŭm.
Gethsemane	gĕth-sĕm'-á-nē. [lănks'.
Geulincx	ċhē'-lĭnks. *Fr.* zhē-
Gezer	gē'-zĕr.
Gharbieh, *see* Garbieh .	gär-bē'-yĕ.
Ghats, Ghauts	gôts.
Ghazipur	gä-zē-pŏōr'

Ghent, *see* Gand . . . . gĕnt. [rär-dĕs'-kä.

Gherardesca, Ugolino della Jŏ-gŏ-lē'-no dĕl'-la ga-

Ghetto . . . . gĕt'-tō.

Ghibellines . . . . . . gĭb'-ĕ-lĭnz.

Ghiberti . . . . gē-bĕr'-tē.

Ghirlandajo . . . . . . gēr-län-dä'-yō.

Ghizeh, *see* Gizeh . . . gē'-zĕ.

Ghoorkas, *see* Goorkhas, *or* ⎫
Ghurkas . . . . ⎭ gōōr'-käz.

Giacomo . . . . jä'-kō-mō. [kŏn'-tē.

Gian Galeazzo Visconti . jän gä-lä-ätz'-ŏ vĭs-

Gibara . . . . ċhē-bä'-rä.

Gibeah . . . . gĭb'-ē-ä.

Gibra . . . . ċhē'-brä.

Giers . . . . gērs.

Gila . . . . hē'-lä. *Sp.* ċhē'-lä.

Gil Blas de Santillane . . zhēl bläs dŭ sän-tēl-än'.

Gilboa . . . . gĭl-bō'-ä, gĭl'-bō-ä.

Gilead . . . . gĭl'-ē-ăd.

Gilgal . . . . gĭl'-găl.

Ginevra . . . . gĭ-nĕv'-rä, jē-nĕv'-rá.

Gioconda, La . . . . . lä jō-kŏn'-dä.

Giocondo . . . . jō-kŏn'-dō.

Gioja del Colle, *or* Gioia . jō'-yä däl kŏl'-lĕ.

Giordano Bruno . . . . jŏr-dä'-nō brŏŏ'-nō.

Giorgio . . . . jŏr'-jō.

Giorgione . . . . . . jŏr-jō'-nĕ.

Giotto . . . . jŏt'-tō.

Giovanni . . . . jō-vän'-nē.

Girardin . . . . zhē-rär-dăṅ'.

Girgeh . . . . jēr'-jĕ.

Girgenti . . . . jēr-jĕn'-tē.

Girolamo . . . . jē-rō'-lä-mō.

Gironde . . . . jĭ-rŏnd'. *Fr.* zhē-rôṅd'.

Girondins . . . . . . ⎧ jĭ-rŏṅ'-dĭnz. *Fr.* zhē-
⎩ rôṅ-dăṅ'.

Girondists	jĭ-rŏn'-dĭsts.
Gisors	zhē-zŏr'.
Gittite	gĭt'-īt.
Giulia	jōōl'-yä.
Giuliano	jōō-lḙ̄-ä'-nō.
Giulio di Pietro di Filippo	{ jōō'-lḙ̄-ō dḗ pḙ̄-ä'-trō dḗ fē-lēp'-pō.
Giulio Romano	jōō'-lḙ̄-ō rō-mä'-nō.
Giuseppe	jōō-sĕp'-pĕ.
Giustiniani	jōōs''-tē-nē-ä'-nē.
Gizeh, see Ghizeh . . .	gē'-zŭ.
Gladstone	glăd'-stŭn, glăd'-stōn.
Glamis, or Glammis . . .	glämz.
Glamorgan	glă-môr'-găn.
Glasgow	glăs'-gō.
Glaucus	glô'-kŭs.
Glendower	glĕn-dow'-ẽr, glĕn'-dōōr.
Gloriana	glō-rĭ-ä'-nä.
Gloster, or Gloucester . .	glŏs'-tẽr.
Glück	glük.
Glumdalclitch	glŭm-dăl'-klĭch.
Glycera	glĭs'-ĕ-rä.
Glyptotheca	glĭp-tō-thē'-kȧ.
Glyptothek	glĭp-tō-tāk'.
Gneist	g̣-nīst.
Gnostics	nŏs'-tĭks.
Goa	gō'-ä.
Goajira, see Guajira . . .	gō-ä-·hē'rä, gwä-·hē'-rä.
Goalpara	gō-äl-pä'-rä.
Gobelin	gōb-lăṅ'.
Gobi, see Cobi	gō'-bē.
Gobseck	gŏb-sĕk'.
Godavari	gō-dä'-vä-rē. [yôṅ'.
Godefroy de Bouillon . .	Fr. gō-dŭ-frwä' dŭ bōō-
Godfrey of Bouillon . . .	gŏd'-frĭ ŏv bōō-yôṅ'.
Godiva	gō-dĭ'-vȧ.

Godolphin	gŏ-dŏl'-fĭn.
Godoy	go'-doi. *Sp.* go-do'-e.
Godunoff	gō-dōō-nŏf'.
Goebel (Wm.)	gō'-bĕl.
Goessler, *see* Gössler . . .	gĕs'-lĕr.
Goethe, *see* Göthe . . .	gē'-tŭ.
Goetz von Berlichingen, *see* ⎱ Götz . . . . ⎰	gētz fŏn bâr'-lĭċh-ĭng''-ĕn.
Gogol	gō'-gŏl.
Goldoni	gōl-dō'-nē.
Golgotha	gŏl'-gō-thȧ.
Goliath	gō-lī'-ăth.
Gomara	gō-mä'-rä.
Gomez	gō'-mĕz. *Sp.* gō'-mĕth.
Gomorrah	gŏ-mŏr'-ä.
Gonaive, La	lä gō-nä-ēv'.
Gonaives, Les	lā gō-nä-ēv'.
Goncourt, de	dŭ gôṅ-kōōr'.
Gonda	gŏn'-dä.
Goneril	gŏn'-ĕr-ĭl.
Gonfaloniere	gŏn''-fä-lō-nē-ä'-rĕ. [vä.
Gonsalvo de Cordova . .	gōn-säl'-vō dĕ kŏr'-dō-
Gonse	gōn'-sĕ.
Gonzaga	{ gŏn-zä'-gä. *Sp.* gŏn-thä'- gä. *It.* gŏn-dzä'-gä.
Gonzales	*Sp.* gŏn-thä'-lĕs.
Gonzalez	gŏn-thä'-lĕth. [bä.
Gonzalo de Córdoba . .	gŏn-thä'-lō dä kŏr'-dō-
Goorkhas, *see* Ghoorkas .	gōōr'-käz.
Gorakhpur, *see* Goruckpur	gŏ-rŭk-pōōr'.
Gorboduc	gôr'-bō-dŭk.
Gordian, *or* Gordianus .	gôr'-dĭ-ȧn, gôr-dĭ-ā'-nŭs.
Görgei, *or* Görgey . . .	gẽr'-gĕ-ĭ.
Gorgias	gôr'-jĭ-ȧs.
Goriot, Père	pâr gō-rē-ō'.
Görlitz	gẽr'-lĭts.

Gortchakoff, *or* kow, *or* kov gŏr-chä-kŏf'.
Goruckpur, *see* Gorakhpur gŏ-ruk-pŏŏr'.
Görz . . . . gĕrts.
Goshenland . . . . . gō'-shĕn-lănd.
Gossaert, *see* Gessart . . gŏs'-ärt.
Gossé, *or* Gossec . . . . gŏs-sā', gō-sĕk'.
Gössler, *see* Goessler . . gĕs'-lĕr.
Got . . . . gō.
Gotama, *see* Gautama . . gŏ'-tà-mà.
Göteborg, *see* Gothenburg . yĕ'-tĕ-bŏrċh.
Gotha (duchy) . . . . . gō'-thä. *Ger.* gō'-tä.
Gotha (canal) . . . . . gĕ'-tä. *Sw.* yĕ'-tä.
Gotham . . . . gō'-thâm.
Göthe, *see* Goethe . . . . gĕ'-tŭ.
Gothenburg, *see* Gotten- ⎫
burg, Göteborg . . . . ⎭ gōt'-ĕn-bŏŏrċh.
Gothland, *or* . . . . . gŏth'-lånd.
Gotland, *Sw.* . . . . . gŏt'-länd.
Gotland (I.) . . . . . . gŏt'-länd.
Gottenburg, *see* Gothenburg gŏt'-ĕn-bŏŏrċh.
Götterdämmerung, Die . . dē gĕt-tĕr-däm'-mĕ-
Göttingen . . . . . . gĕt'-tĭng-ĕn. [rŏŏng.
Gottschalk . . . . . . gŏt'-shälk.
Götz von Berlichingen, *see* ⎫ gĕts fŏn bâr'-lĭċh-ĭng''-ĕn.
Goetz . . . . ⎭
Gough . . . . gŏf.
Goujon . . . . gŏŏ-zhŏn'.
Gounod . . . . gŏŏ-nō'.
Gouvion-Saint-Cyr . . . gŏŏ-vĭ-ôn'-săn-sēr'.
Gower . . . . gow'-ĕr.
Goya y Lucientes . . . . gō'-yä ē lŏŏ-thē-ĕn'-tĕs.
Goyaz . . . . gō-yäz'.
Gozo, *or* Gozzo . . . . . gŏd'-zō, gŏt'-sō.
Gozzoli, Benozzo . . . . bā-nŏt'-sō gŏts'-ō-lē.
Graal, *see* Grail, Grael . . gräl.
Gracias á Dios . . . . . grä'-thē-äs ä dē-ōs'.

Gradiska	grä-dǐs'-kä.
Graefe, Gräfe, von . . .	fŏn grä'-fǔ.
Grael, *see* Grail, Graal . .	gräl.
Graeme	gräm.
Graf	gräf.
Gräfin	grä'-fǐn.
Graham	grä-àm, gräm.
Grail, *see* Grael, Graal . .	gräl.
Gramont	grä-môṅ'.
Granada	grä-nä'-dä. [mäṅt'.
Grande Anse du Diamante	gräṅ däṅs dü dē-ä·
Grande Mademoiselle, La .	lä gräṅd mäd-mwä-
Grande-Terre	gräṅd-târ'. [zĕl'-ǔ.
Grandet, Eugénie	ē-zhä-nē' gräṅ-dā'.
Grand Monarque, Le . . .	lẽ gräṅ mō-närk'.
Grandpré	gräṅ-prā'.
Grand Prix, Le	lẽ gräṅ prē. [yäk'.
Granier de Cassagnac . .	grä-nē̲-ā' dǔ käs-sän-
Gratiano	grä-shǐ-ä'-nō. *It.* grä-
Gratz, *see* Graz	gräts. [tē̲-ä'-nō.
Gravelines, *or*	gräv-lēn'.
Gravelingen, *or*	*Ger.* grä'-vĕ-lǐng''-ĕn.
Gravelinghe	*Fl.* grä'-vĕ-lǐng''-ĕ.
Gravelotte	gräv-lŏt'.
Graz, *see* Gratz	gräts.
Greenough	grēn'-ō.
Greenwich	*Eng.* grǐn'-ĭj.
Greig	grĕg.
Gremio	grē'-mǐ-ō.
Grenada	grĕn-ä'-dä.
Grenoble	grĕ-nō'-bl. [ćhĕn.
Gretchen	grĕch'-ĕn. *Ger.* grät'-
Gretel	grā'-tĕl.
Grétry	grä-trē'.
Greuze	grẽz.
Grève	grāv.

Greville	grĕv'-ĭl.
Gréville	*Fr.* grā-vēl'.
Grévy	grā-vē'.
Griboyédoff	grē-bō-yā'-dŏf.
Gridley	grĭd'-lĭ.
Grieg	grĕg.'
Grillparzer	grĭl'-pärt-zĕr.
Grindelwald	grĭn'-dĕl-vält.
Griqualand	grē'-kwȧ-lănd.
Grisi	grē'-zē.
Grisons	grē-zôṅ'.
Grodno	grŏd'-nō.
Grolier	grō'-lē̦-ā. *Fr.* grō-lē̦-ā'.
Groningen, *or*	*D.* ċhrō'-nĭng-ċhĕn.
Gröningen, *Ger.*	grē'-nĭng-ĕn.
Groot	grōt.
Groote Kerke	grō'-tĕ kĕr'-kĕ.
Gros	grō.
Grossi	grŏs'-sē.
Grosvenor	grŏv'-nēr, grō'-vĕ-nēr.
Grote	grōt.
Grotius	grō'-shĭ-ŭs.
Grouchy, de	dŭ grōō-shē'.
Grütli, *see* Rütli	grüt'-lĭ.
Gruyère, Gruyères	grü-yâr'.
Guadalajara	gwä''-dä-lä-ċhä'-rä.
Guadalquivir	{ gô-dăl-kwĭv'-ēr. *Sp.* gwä''-däl-kē-vēr'.
Guadalupe	{ gô-dä-lōōp'. *Sp.* gwä-dä-lōō'-pä.
Guadeloupe	gô-dĕ-lōōp'. *Fr.* gäd-
Guahan, *Sp.* Guajan	gwä-hän'. [lōōp'.
Guaira, La, *see* La Guayra	{ lä gwī'-rȧ, lä gī'-rȧ. *Sp.* lä gwä'-ē̦-rä.
Guajan, *see* Guahan	*Sp.* gwä-'hän'.
Guajira, *see* Goajira	gwä-'hē'-rä.

Gualfonda	gwäl-fŏn'-dä.
Guam	gwăm. *Sp.* gwäm.
Guanabacoa	gwä″-nä-bä-kō'-ä.
Guanahani	gwä-nä-ä-nē'.
Guanaja	gwä-nä'-'hä.
Guanajay	gwä-nä-ċhä'-ē.
Guanica	gwä-nē'-kä.
Guantanamo	gwän-tä-nä'-mō.
Guap, *see* Yap	gwäp.
Guardafui, *see* Gardafui	gwär-dä-foō-ē'.
Guarico	gwä'-rē-kō.
Guarneri, *or*	gwär-nä'-rĕ.
Guarnerius	gwär-nē'-rĭ-ŭs. [mä'-lä.
Guatemala	gô-tē-mä'-lä. *Sp.* gwä-tä-
Guayaquil	gī-ȧ-kēl'. *Sp.* gwī-ä-kēl'.
Guayra, La, *see* La Guaira	{ lä gwī'rä, lä gī'rä. { *Sp.* lä gwä'-ē-rä.
Gudrun	goō-droōn'.
Guébriant	gä-brē-äṅ'.
Guelfs, Guelphs	gwĕlfs.
Guendolen	gwĕn'-dō-lĕn.
Guenevere	gwĕn'-ĕ-vēr.
Guercino	gwĕr-chē'-nō.
Guérin	gä-răṅ'.
Guernsey	gĕrn'-zī.
Guerrière, La	lä gâr-rē-âr'.
Gueux	gē.
Guglielmo	goōl-ē-ĕl'-mō.
Gui, *see* Guy	*Fr.* gē.
Guiana, *see* Guyana	gē-ä'-nä.
Guicciardini	gwē-chär-dē'-nē.
Guiccioli	gwē-chō'-lē.
Guiderius	gwĭ-dē'-rĭ-ŭs.
Guidi, Casa	kä'-zä gwē'-dē.
Guido Aretino	gwē-dō ä-rä-tē'-nō.
Guido d'Arezzo	gwē'-dō dä-rĕt'-sō.

Guido of Lusignan, *see* Guy de gwē'-dŏ ŭv lü-zēn-yän'.

Guido Reni . . . . . .   gwē'-dŏ rä'-nē.

Guillaume . . . . . .   gē-yŏm'-ŭ.

Guillotin . . . .   gē-yō-tăn'.

Guimarás . . . .   gē-mä-räs'.

Guines . . . .   gēn.

Guinever, Guinevere . . .   gwĭn-ĕ-vēr'.

Guion . . . .   gī'-ŏn. *Fr.* gē-ôn'.

Guiscard . . . .   gēs-kär'.

Guise, de . . . .   dŭ gēz, dŭ gü-ēz'.

Guizot . . . .   gē-zō'.

Gujranwala . . . . . .   gŭzh-rán-wä'-lä.

Gujrat . . . .   gŭzh-rät'.

Gula . . . .   gōō'-lä.

Gulistan . . . .   gōō-lĭs-tän'.

Günther, Guenther . . .   gün'-tĕr.

Gurdaspur . . . . . .   gōōr-däs-pōōr'.

Gurhwal, *see* Garhwal . .   gŭr-wäl'.

Gurkhas, *see* Ghoorkas . .   gōōr'-käz.

Gustavus Adolphus . . .   { gŭs-tā'-vŭs ā-dŏl'-fŭs.
                            { *Ger.* gŏŏs-tä'-vōōs ä-dŏl-
                            { fŏŏs. [vōōs vä'-sä.

Gustavus Vasa . . . . .   gŭs-tā'-vŭs, gŏŏs-tä-

Gutenberg . . . .   gōō'-tĕn-bĕrg. *Ger.* gōō'-

Gutzkow . . . .   gōōts'-kō. [tĕn-bĕrch.

Guy, *see* Gui . . . . .   gī. *Fr.* gē.

Guyana, *see* Guiana . . .   gē-ä'-nä.

Guyandotte . . . . . .   gī-ăn-dŏt'.

Guy de Lusignan, *see* Guido ⎰
  of Lusignan . . . . . ⎱ gē dŭ lü-zēn-yän'.

Guyon . . . .   gī'-ŏn. *Fr.* gē-ôn'.

Guyot . . . .   gē-ō'.

Guzman . . . .   gōōth-män'.

Gwalior . . . .   gwä'-lē-ôr.

Gyges . . . .   gī'-jēz.

H

Haag, Den, *see* The Hague   děn häċh.

Haas . . . .   häs.

Habakkuk . . . . . .   hă-băk'-ŭk, hăb'-ȧ-kŭk.

Habana, *see* Havana . . .   ä-bä'-nä.

Habsburg, *see* Hapsburg .   häps'-bōōrċh.

Hadad . . . .   hā'-dăd.

Haden . . . .   hā'-dn.

Hades . . . .   hā'-dēz.

Hading (Jane) . . . . .   ä-dăṅ'.

Hadrian, *see* Adrian . . .   hā'-drĭ-ȧn.

Haeckel . . . .   hĕk'-l. *Ger.* hâk'ĕl.

Hafiz . . . .   *Pers.* hô-fíz'.

Hagar . . . .   hă'-gär.

Hagedorn, von . . . . .   fŏn hä'-gä-dôrn.

Hagen . . . .   *Ger.* hä'-gĕn.

Haggai, *or* Haggi . . . .   hăg'-ī.   [rȧ-fä.

Hagiographa . . . . .   hă-jĭ-ŏg'-rȧ-fä, hăg-ĭ-ŏg'-

Hague (The), *see* Den Haag, } hāg.
     La Haye . . . . . }

Hahnemann . . . . . .   hä'-nä-män.

Haidarabad, *see* Hyderabad   hī''-dä-rȧ-bäd'.

Haidar-Ali, *see* Hyder Ali .   hī'-där ä'-lē.

Haidee . . . .   hī-dē'.

Haiduks, *see* Hayduks . .   hī'-dōōks.

Hainan . . . .   hī-nän'.

Hainault, *or* Hainaut . .   hä-nō'. *Fr.* ā-nō'.

Haiti, *see* Hayti . . . .   hā'-tĭ. *Fr.* ä-ē-tē'.

Hakluyt . . . .   hăk'-lōōt.

Hakodate . . . .   hä-kō-dä'-tä.

Halberstadt . . . . . .   häl'-bĕr-stät.

Halcyone, *see* Alcyone . .   hăl-sī'-ō-nē.

Haldeman . . . . . .   hôl'-dĕ-män.

Halévy . . . .   ä-lā-vē'.

Halle . . . . häl'-lŭ.

Haller, von . . . . . . fōn häl'-lĕr.

Hals . . . . häls.

Hamah, or Hamath . . . hä'-mä, hā'-măth.

Hamburg . . . . . . { hăm'-bĕrg.
{ Ger. häm'-boorċh.

Hamelin, or Hameln . . . hä'-mŭ-lĭn, hä'-mĕln.

Hamerling . . . . . . hä'-mĕr-lĭng.

Hamerton . . . . . . hăm'-ĕr-tŭn.

Hamilcar Barca . . . . hä-mĭl'-kär bär'-kä.

Hamitic . . . . hăm-ĭt'-ĭk.

Hanau . . . . hä'-now.

Händel, Handel . . . . hän'-dĕl.   Ger. hân'-dĕl.

Hang-chau, or Hangchow . häng'-chow.

Hangshan . . . . . . häng'-shän.

Han Hok . . . . hän' hōk.

Han-Kow, or Hankow, or } hän-kow'.
Han-kau . . . . . . }

Hannover, see Hanover . hän-nō'-vĕr.

Hanoi . . . . hä-nō'-ĭ.

Hanover, see Hannover . hän'-ō-vĕr.

Hanotaux . . . . . . än-ō-tō'.

Hans . . . . hänts.

Hansa . . . . hän'-sä.

Hanseatic . . . . . . hăn-sē-ăt'-ĭk.

Hanyang . . . . hän-yäng'.

Hapsburg, see Habsburg . { hăps'-bĕrg.
{ Ger. häps'-boorċh.

Hardanger Fjord . . . . här'-däng-ĕr fyôrd.

Harderwijk . . . . . . här'-dĕr-wīk.

Hardicanute . . . . . här"-dĭ-kä-nūt'.

Hardoi . . . . hŭr'-dō-ē.

Harfleur . . . . är-flĕr'.

Harleian . . . . här'-lē-ȧn.

Harlequin . . . . . . { här'-lē-kwĭn, här'-lĕ-
{ kĭn.

8

Haro, Luis de . . . . . . lōō-ēs' dä ä'-rō.

Haroun al Raschid, *see* { hä-rōōn' äl räsh'-ĭd, hä-
Harun . . . . { rōōn' äl rä-shēd'.

Harpagon . . . . . . är-pä-gôṅ'.

Harpagus . . . . . . här'-pä-gŭs.

Harpignies . . . . . . är-pēn-yē'.

Hartmann von Aue . . . härt'-män fŏn ow'-ŭ.

Harun al Rashid, *see* Haroun { hä-rōōn' äl räsh'-ĭd, *or* { rä-shēd'.

Harwich . . . . här'-ĭch, här'-ĭj.

Harz . . . . härts.

Hasan, *see* Hassan . . . hä'-sán.

Hasdrubal, *see* Asdrubal . häs'-drōō-băl.

Hassan, *see* Hasan . . . häs'-sán.

Hauch (J. C.) von . . . fŏn howċh.

Hauck (Minnie) . . . . hôk.

Haupt . . . . howpt.

Hauptmann, Gerhart . . gâr'-härt howpt'-män.

Hauser, Caspar . . . . käs'-pär how'-zĕr.

Haussman (Baron) . . . ōs-män'.

Haute-Garonne . . . . ōt-gä-rŏn'.

Haute-Loire . . . . . . ōt-lwär'.

Haute-Marne . . . . . ōt-märn'.

Hautes-Alpes . . . . . ōt-zälp'.

Haute-Saône . . . . . ōt-sōn'.

Haute-Savoie . . . . . ōt-sä-vwä'.

Hautes-Pyrénées . . . . ōt-pē-rä-nä'.

Haute-Vienne . . . . . ōt-vē-ĕn'.

Haüy, Abbé . . . . . . äb-ä' ä-wē', ä-ü-ē'.

Havana, *see* Habana . . hä-văn'-á.

Havel . . . . hä'-fĕl.

Haverhill . . . . . . { *Am.* hä'-vĕr-ĭl. { *Eng.* hăv'ĕr-ĭl.

Havilah . . . . hăv'-ĭl-á.

Havre-de-Grace . . . . ä'-vr-dŭ-gräs'.

Hawaii . . . . hä-wĭ'-ē.

Hawaiian	hä-wī'-yán.
Hawarden	Lôr'-dn, háu'-děn.
Haweis	hois.
Haydée	ā-dā'.
Haydn	hā'-dn. *Ger.* hī'-dn.
Hayduks, *see* Haiduks	hī'-dōoks.
Haye, La, *see* The Hague, Den Haag	} lä ā.
Hayti, *see* Haiti	hā'-tĭ. *Fr.* ä-ē-tē'.
Hazael	hăz'-ā-ĕl, hā'-zā-ĕl.
Hazaribagh	hä-zä-rē-bô'.
Hazlitt	hăz'-lĭt.
Hebe	hē'-bē.
Hébert	ā-bâr'.
Hebraist	hē'-brā-ĭst.
Hebrides	hĕb'-rĭ-dēz.
Hebron	hē'-brŏn.
Hecate	hĕk'-ā-tē, hĕk'-āt.
Hecuba	hĕk'-yū-bà.
Hedin, Sven	svĭn hĭ-dēn'.
Hedone	hĕd'-ō-nē.
Hédouin	ā-dōo-ăṅ'.
Hegel	hā'-gĕl.
Hegelian	hē-gē'-lĭ-àn.
Hegira, *see* Hejira	hē-jī'-rà, hĕj'-ĭ-rà.
Heidelberg	{ hī'-dĕl-bērg. *Ger.* hī'-dĕl-bĕrċh.
Heidenmauer	hī'-dĕn-mow''-ĕr.
Heijn (Admiral)	hĭn.
Heilbronn	hīl'-brŏn.
Heimskringla	hĭms'-krĭng-lä.
Heine	hī'-nŭ.
Heinrich	hĭn'-rĭċh.
Hejira, *see* Hegira	hē-jī'-rà, hĕj'-ĭr-à.
Helen	hĕl'-ĕn.
Helena	hĕl'-ĕ-nà.

Helena (Montana) . . .	hĕl'-ĕ-ná,
Helena, St. (I.)	sĕnt hĕl-ē'-ná.
Helgoland, *see* Heligoland	hĕl'-gō-länd.
Helicanus	hĕl-ĭ-kā'-nŭs.
Helicon	hĕl'-ĭ-kŏn.
Heligoland, *see* Helgoland	hĕl'-ĭ-gō-länd".
Heliodorus	hē"-lĭ-ō-dō'-rŭs.
Heliogabalus, *see* Elagaba- ⎧	hē"-lĭ-ō-găb'-ā-lŭs, hē"-
lus . . . . ⎩	lĭ-ō-gā-bā'-lŭs.
Heliopolis	hē-lĭ-ŏp'-ō-lĭs.
Helios	hē'-lĭ-ŏs.
Hellenes	hĕl-lē'-nēz, hĕl'-ēnz.
Hellenic	hĕl-lē'-nĭk, hĕl-lĕn'-ĭk.
Hellespont	hĕl'-lĕs-pŏnt.
Hellevoetsluis, *see* Helvoet- ⎫	hĕl-lĕ-vōōt-slois'.
sluis . . . . ⎭	
Héloïse	ā-lō-ēz'.
Helots	hĕl'-ŏts, hē'-lŏts.
Helsingfors	hĕl'-sĭng-fŏrs.
Helsinki	hĕl'-sĭng-kĭ.
Helvetia	hĕl-vē'-shĭ-á. [sĕ-üs'.
Helvétius	hĕl-vĕ'-shĭ-ŭs. *Fr.* āl-vā-
Helvoetsluis	hĕl-vōōt-slois'.
Hemans (Mrs.)	hĕm'-ánz. *pop.* hē'-mánz.
Hengist	hĕng'-gĭst.
Hengstenberg	hĕng'-stĕn-bĕrċh.
Henlopen	hĕn-lō'-pĕn.
Hennepin	hĕn'-ĕ-pĭn. *Fr.* ĕn-păṅ'.
Hennequin	hĕn'-nĕ-kwĭn. *Fr.* ĕn-
Henri	ŏṅ-rē'. [kăṅ'.
Henriade	ŏṅ-rē-yăd'.
Henrici	hān-rēt'-sē.
Henri de Bourbon . . .	ŏṅ-rē' dŭ bōōr-bôṅ'.
Henriette	hĕn-rĭ-ĕt'. *Fr.* ôṅ-rē-ĕt'.
Henri Quatre	ŏṅ-rē' kätr'.
Henriquez	ān-rē'-kĕth.

Henry (Col.)	ŏ̇n̆₋rē′
Hephæstion	hē-fĕs′-tĭ-ŏn.
Hephæstus	hē-fĕs′-tŭs.
Heptameron	hĕp-tăm′-ĕ-rŏn.
Heptarchy	hĕp′-tär-kĭ.
Heptateuch	hĕp′-tȧ-tūk.
Hera	hē′-rä.
Heraclean	hĕr-ȧ-klē′-ȧn.
Heracles	hĕr′-ȧ-klēz.
Heraclidæ	hĕr-ā-klĭ′-dē.
Heraclitus	hĕr-ā-klĭ′-tŭs.
Herat	hĕr-ät′.
Hérault	ā-rō′.
Herculaneum	hĕr-kū-lā′-nē-ŭm.
Hercules	hĕr′-kū-lēz.
Here	hē′-rē.
Heredia	Sp. ā-rā′-dē-ä.
Hérédia	Fr. ā-rā-dē-ä′.
Hereford	hĕr′-ĕ-fŭrd.
Hereward	hĕr′-ĕ-wȧrd.
Héricourt	ā-rē-kōōr′.
Heristal, or Heristall, see ⎫ Herstal . . . . . ⎭	hĕr′-ĭs-täl.
Hermann	hĕr′-män.
Hermant	âr-mäṅ′.
Hermaphroditus	hĕr-măf″-rō-dĭ′-tŭs.
Hermes	hĕr′-mēz.
Hermione	hĕr-mĭ′-ō-nē.
Hermogenes	hĕr-mŏj′-ĕ-nēz.
Hernandez	är-nän′-dĕth.
Hernani	är-nä′-nē.
Herod	hĕr′-ŏd.
Herodian	hē-rō′-dĭ-ȧn.
Herodias	hē-rō′-dĭ-ȧs.
Herodotus	hē-rŏd′-ō-tŭs.
Hérold	ā-rŏld′.

Horrora	är rä´ rä.
Herreros	är-rä´-rōs.
Herschel	hĕr´-shĕl.
Herstal, *see* Heristal . . .	hĕr´-stäl.
Hertford	hĕrt´-fôrd, här´-fôrd.
Heruli	hĕr´-ōō-lī.
Hervé Riel	är-vä´ rē-ĕl´.
Hervieu, Paul	pōl är-vē-ē̦´.
Herzegovina	hĕrt´´-sĕ-gō-vē´-nä.
Herzog	hĕrt´-zōċh.
Herzogin	hĕrt´-zō-gĭn.
Heshvan, *see* Hesvan . .	hĕsh´-vän.
Hesiod	hē´-sĭ-ŏd, hē´-shĭ-ŏd.
Hesiodus	hē-sĭ´-ō-dŭs.
Hesperides	hĕs-pĕr´-ĭ-dēz.
Hesse	hĕs.
Hesse-Cassel	hĕs-kăs´-ĕl.
Hessen	hĕs´-sĕn.
Hesse-Nassau	hĕs-năs´-ô.
Hessian	hĕsh´-ĭ-ȧn.
Hesvan, *see* Heshvan . .	hĕs´-vän.
Heureaux, Ulisse	ü-lēs´ ĕr-ō´.
Heyne	hī´-nŭ.
Heyse	hī´-zŭ.
Hiawatha	hĭ-ȧ-wô´-thȧ, hĭ-ȧ-wô´-tȧ.
Hibernia	hĭ-bĕr´-nĭ-ȧ.
Hidalgo	ē-däl´-gō.
Hiero	hī´-ĕ-rō.
Hieron	hī´-ĕ-rŏn.
Hieronymus	hi-ē-rŏn´-ĭ-mŭs.
Hilary	hĭl´-ȧ-rĭ.
Hildebrandslied	hĭl´-dä-bränts-lēt.
Hilo	hē´-lō. lȧ´-yä.
Himalaya	hĭm-ä´-lä-yȧ, hĭm-ä-
Himilco	hĭ-mĭl´-kō.
Hindoo, *see* Hindu . . .	hĭn´-dōō, hĭn-dōō´.

Hindoostan, *see* Hindustan   hĭn-dōō-stän'.

Hindoostanee, *see* Hindu-   } hĭn-dōō-stän'-ē.
stani . . . . . . }

Hindostan, *see* Hindoostan, { hĭn-dō-stän',   hĭn-dō-
Hindustan . . . . (stän'.

Hindu, *see* Hindoo . . .   hĭn'-dōō, hĭn-dōō'.

Hindu Kush . . . . . .   hĭn'-dōō kōōsh.

Hindustan, *see* Hindoostan   hĭn-dōō-stän'.

Hindustani, *see* Hindoo- } hĭn-dōō-stän'-ē.
stanee . . . . . .)

Hiogo . . . .   hē-ō'-gō.

Hippocrates . . . . .   hĭp-pŏk'-rā-tēz.   [nē.

Hippocrene . . . . . .   hĭp'-ō-krēn, hĭp-ō-krē'-

Hippolita, *or* Hippolyta .   hĭ-pŏl'-ĭ-tä.

Hippolyte . . . . .   hĭ-pŏl'-ĭ-tē. *Fr.* ē-pō-lēt'.

Hippolytus . . . . .   hĭ-pŏl'-ĭ-tŭs.

Hiren . . . .   hī'-rĕn.

Hiroshima . . . . .   hē-rō-shē'-mä.

Hirsch . . . .   hērsh.

Hispania . . . . . .   hĭs-pā'-nĭ-ạ.

Hispaniola . . . . . { hĭs''-păn-ĭ-ō'-lạ.
(*Sp.* ēs''-pä-nē-ọ'-lä.

Hissar . . . .   hĭs-sär'.

Hittite . . . .   hĭt'-īt.

Hivite . . . .   hī'-vīt.

Hlangwane (Hill) . . .   hlăng-wä'-nŭ.

Hoang-ho, *see* Hwang-ho .   hwăng'-hō.

Hobbema . . . . . .   hŏb'-bĕ-mä.

Hobbes . . . . . .   hŏbz.

Hobbesian . . . . .   hŏb'-zĭ-ạn.

Hobbididence . . . .   hŏb'-ĭ-dĭ''-dĕns.

Hoboken . . . . . .   hō'-bō-kĕn, hō-bō'-kĕn.

Hoche (Gen.) . . . . .   ōsh.

Hochkirch . . . . .   hōċh'-kērċh.

Höchst . . . .   hĕċhst.

Höchstädt . . . . . .   hĕċh'-stĕt.

Hogolen, or Hogolin	hṓ-gō-lĕn, hṓ-gō-lĭn.
Hogolu, or Hogolou	hṓ-gō-lōō.
Hohenlinden	hō-ĕn-lĭn'-dĕn.
Hohenlohe	hō-ĕn-lō'-ŭ.
Hohenlohe-Schillingsfürst	hō-ĕn-lō'-ŭ shĭl'-lĭngs-fürst.
Hohenstaufen, or stauffen	hō'-ĕn-stow-fĕn.
Hohenzollern	hō'-ĕn-tsŏl-lĕrn.
Hohenzollern-Sigmaringen	hō'-ĕn-tsŏl-lĕrn zēg'-mä-rĭng"-ĕn.
Hokkaido	hŏk-kī'-dō.
Holbein	hōl'-bīn, hŏl'-bīn.
Holberg	hŏl'-bĕrċh.
Holborn	hō'-bŭrn.
Holger Danske	hŏl'-gĕr däns'-kĕ.
Holguin	hŏl-gēn', ŏl-gēn'.
Holinshed	hŏl'-ĭnz-hĕd.
Holofernes	hŏl-ō-fĕr'-nĕz.
Holstein	hōl'-stīn.
Holyhead	hŏl-ĭ-hĕd', hŏl'-ĭ-hĕd.
Holyoke	hōl'-yōk.
Holyrood	hŏl'-ĭ-rōōd, hōl'-ĭ-rōōd.
Homildon Hill	hŏm'-l-dŏn hĭl.
Houdekoeter	hŏn'-dĕ-kōō"-tĕr.
Honduras	hŏn-dōō'-räs.
Hong-Kong	hŏng'-kŏng'.
Honiton	hŭn'-ĭ-tŭn.
Honolulu	hō-nō-lōō'-lōō.
Honoré	ō-nō-rā'.
Hooghly, see Hugli	hōōg'-lē.
Hoogvliet	hōċh'-vlēt.
Hoopstad	hōp'-stät.
Hoorn (Count), see Horn	hōrn.
Horæ	hō'-rē.
Horatii	hō-rā'-shĭ-ī.
Horatio	hō-rā'-shĭ-ō.

Horatius Cocles	hō-rā'-shǐ-ǔs kō'-klēz.
Horn (Count), *see* Hoorn .	hŏrn.
Hortense	ôr-täṅs'.
Hortensio	hôr-tĕn'-shǐ-ō.
Hortensius	hôr-tĕn'-shǐ-ǔs.
Hortus Inclusus	hôr'-tǔs ǐn-klū'-sǔs.
Hosea, *see* Hoshea . . .	hō-zē'-à.
Hoshangabad, *see* Hu- shangabad . . . . . }	hō-shǔng'-ä-bäd.
Hoshea, *see* Hosea . . .	hō-shē'-à.
Hôtel de Cluny	ō-tĕl' dǔ klü-nē'.
Hôtel de Rambouillet . .	ō-tĕl' dǔ räṅ-bōō-ē-ā'.
Hôtel des Invalides . . .	ō-tĕl' dā zăṅ-vä-lēd'.
Hôtel de Ville	ō-tĕl' dǔ vēl.
Houdin	ōō-dăṅ'.
Houdon	ōō-dôṅ'.
Houssain, *see* Hussain, *and* } Hussein . . . . . . }	'hōō'-sīn, 'hōō-sīn', 'hōō'- sān.
Houssaye, Arsène	är-sĕn' ōō-sā'.
Houston (Tex.)	hūs'-tŏn.
Houyhnhnms	hōō'-ǐn-ǐn-mz.
Hubert de Burgh	hū'-bĕrt dǔ bĕrg, bōōrg.
Hudibras	hū'-dǐ-brăs.
Hué, *or*	hōō-ā', hwā.
Hué-fu	hōō-ā'-fōō'. [pā'.
Hugh Capet	hū kā'-pĕt. *Fr.* üg kä-
Hugli, *see* Hooghly . . .	hōōg'-lē.
Hugo, Victor	hū'-gō. *Fr.* ü-gō'.
Huguenots	hū'-gĕ-nŏts.
Huguenots, Les	lā üg-ǔ-nō'.
Huis ten Bosch	hois tĕn bŏsċh'.
Humacao	ōō-mä-kä'-ō. [bōlt.
Humboldt	hǔm'-bōlt. *Ger.* hōōm'-
Humphrey	hǔm'-frǐ.
Hungarian	hǔng-gā'-rǐ-àn.
Hungary	hǔng'-gä-rǐ.

Hunyady János . . . . hōōn'-yä-dē yä'-nōsh.
Hus, *see* Huss . . . . . hŭs. *Ger.* hōōs.
Hushangabad, *see* Ho- } hŭsh-ŭng'-ä-bäd.
  shangabad . . . . . }
Huss, *see* Hus . . . . . hŭs. *Ger.* hōōs.
Hussain, *see* Houssain, *or* } 'hōō'-sĭn, 'hōō-sĭn', 'hōō'-
  Hussein . . . . . . } sän.
Hussan . . . . 'hōō'-sän.
Huygens, *or* Huyghens . . hī'-gĕnz. *D.* hoi'-ċhĕns.
Huysmans . . . . . . hois'-mäns.
Huysum, Jan van . . . . yăn văn hoi'-sŭm.
Hwang-ho, *see* Hoang-ho . hwän'-hō.
Hyacinthe, Père . . . . pâr ē-ä-săṅt'.
Hyades . . . . hī'-ä-dēz.
Hybla . . . . hī'-blä.
Hyderabad, *see* Haidarabad hī''-dĕr-ä-bäd'.
Hyder Ali, *see* Haidar Ali . hī'-dĕr ä'-lē.
Hyères . . . . ē-âr'.
Hygeia . . . . hī-jē'-ȧ.
Hyksos . . . . hĭk'-sŏs, hĭk'-sōz.
Hypatia . . . . hī-pā'-shĭ-ạ.
Hyperboreans . . . . . hī-pĕr-bō'-rē-ȧnz.
Hypereides, Hyperides . . hī-pĕr-ī'-dēz.
Hyperion . . . . hī-pē'-rĭ-ŏn, hī-pĕr-ī'-ŏn.
Hyppolite . . . . . . ē-pō-lēt'.

I

Iachimo . . . . yăk'-ĭm-ō, ĭ-ăk'-ĭ-mō.
Iago . . . . ē-ạ̈'-gō.
Ian . . . . ī'-ȧn *or* ē'-ȧn.
Ibea . . . . ī-bē'-ȧ.
Ibiza, *see* Iviça . . . . ē'-bē-thä.
Iblis, *see* Eblis . . . . . ĭb'-lĭs.
Ibo, *see* Igbo . . . . . ē'-bō. *Port.* ē'-bōō.

Ibrahim Pasha	Ĭb-rä-hēm′ păsh-ô′, pȧ-
Ibsen	Ĭb′-sĕn. [shä′, päsh′-ȧ.
Icarian	i-kā′-rĭ-ȧn.
Icarus	Ĭk′-ȧ-rŭs, Ĭk′-ā-rŭs.
Ichabod	Ĭk′-ȧ-bŏd.
Ichang	ē-chäng′.
Icolmkill	ĭ-kōm-kĭl′.
Ictinus	ĭk-tī′-nŭs.
Ides	īdz.
Idumæa, Idumea . . .	ĭ-dū-mē′-ȧ, Ĭd-ū-mē′-ȧ.
Idumæan, Idumean . . .	ĭ-dū-mē′-ȧn.
Idzo	ēd′-zō.
If, Château d′	shä-tō′ dĕf′.
Igbo, see Ibo	ēg′-bō.
Igdrasil, see Yggdrasil .	Ĭg′-drȧ-sĭl.
Igerna, or	ĭ-gĕr′-nȧ.
Igerne, see Yguerne . . .	ĭ-gĕrn′.
Ignatieff	Ĭg-nät′-yĕf.
Ignatius	Ĭg-nā′-shĭ-ŭs.
Igorrote	ē-gōr-rō′-tā.
Ik Marvel	ik mär′-vĕl.
Ile-de-France	ēl-dŭ-fräns′.
Ile de la Tortue . . .	ēl dŭ lä tôr-tü′.
Il Flauto Magico . . .	ēl flä′-ōͅo-tō mä′-jē-kō.
Illinois	ĭl-ĭ-noi′, ĭl-ĭ-noiz′.
Illusions Perdues, Les .	lä zē-lü-zē-ôn′ pȧr-dü′.
Ilocos	ē-lō′-kōs.
Iloilo	ĭ′-lō-ĭ′-lō. Sp. ē-lō-ē′-lō.
Ilori, or Ilorin	ē-lō′-rē, ē-lō′-rēn.
Il Penseroso	Ĭl pĕn-sĕ-rō′-sō.
Il Pensiero	ēl pān-sē-ā′-rō.
Imber	ăṅ-bâr′.
Imbert de Saint-Amand .	ăṅ-bâr′ dŭ săṅ-tä-mäṅ′.
Imola	ē′-mō-lä.
Imus	ē′-mo͞os.
Inca	Ĭng′-kä.

Indore	ĭn′-dōr.
Indre-et-Loire	ăṅdr-ā-lwär′.
Ines	ē-nĕs′.
Inez	ĭ′-nĕz. *Port.* ē-nĕs′.
Infanta	ĭn-fän′-tȧ. *Sp.* ēn-fän′-tä.
Infante	ĭn-fän′-tĕ. *Sp.* ēn-fän′-tā.
Inferno	ĭn-fĕr′-nō. *It.* ēn-fĕr′-nō.
Ingelow, Jean	jĕn ĭn′-jĕ-lō.
Ingres	ăṅg′-r.
Inigo	ĭn′-ĭ-gō. [Ingk-ĕr-män′.
Inkerman	ĭnk′ - ĕr - mȧn. *Russ.*
In Montibus Sanctis . . .	ĭn mŏn′-tĭ-bŭs sănk′-tĭs.
Innsbruck, *or* Innspruck .	ĭns′-brŏŏk, ĭns′-prŏŏk.
Interlachen, *or*	ĭn′-tĕr-läċh-ĕn.
Interlaken	ĭn′-tĕr-lä-kĕn.
Intombi	ĭn-tŏm′-bĭ.
Invalides, Hôtel des . . .	ō-tĕl′ dä-zăṅ-văl-ēd′.
Inverness	ĭn-vĕr-nĕs′.
Io	ĭ′-ō.
Ion	ĭ′-ŏn.
Iona	ī-ō′-nä.
Ionia	ī-ō′-nĭ-ȧ.
Ionian	ī-ō′-nĭ-ȧn.
Ionic	ī-ŏn′-ĭk.
Iowa	ĭ′-ō-wä.
I Pagliacci	ē päl-yä′-chē.
Iphigeneia, *or* Iphigenia	ĭf″-ĭ-jē-nī′-ȧ. [rĭs.
Iphigenie auf Tauris . . .	ĭf-ē-gā′-nē-ŭ owf tow′-
Iphigénie en Aulide . . .	ĭf-ē-zhā-nē′ ŏṅ-nō-lēd′.
Ipswich	ĭps′-wĭch.
Iquique	ē-kē′-kā.
Iran	ē-rän′.
Iras	ĭ′-rȧs.
Irawadi, *see* Irrawaddy	ĭr-ȧ-wăd′-ĭ.
Irenæus	ī-rē-nē′-ŭs.
Irene	ī-rē′-nē. *pop.* ī-rēn′.

Irène . . . . *Fr.* ē-rān'.
Iriarte, *see* Yriarte . . . ē-rē-är'-tā.
Iris . . . . ĭ'-rĭs.
Irkutsk, Irkootsk, Irkoutsk ĭr-kōōtsk'.   [kwä'.
Iroquois . . . . . . ĭr-ō-kwoĭ'. *Fr.* ĭr-o-
Irrawaddy, *see* Irawadi . ĭr-à-wăd'-ĭ.
Isaacs, Jorge . . . . . ċhŏr'-ċhā ē-zäk'.
Isabela . . . . ēs-ä-bā'-lä.
Isabey . . . . ēz-ä-bā'.
Isaiah . . . . ī-zā'-yä, ī-zä'-ĭ-à.
Isandlana, *or* Isandula . . ē-sänd-lä'-nä,   ē-sän-
Isar (R.) . . . . ē'-zär.   [dōō'-lä
Ischia . . . . ēs'-kē-ä.
Isengrim . . . . ĭs'-ĕn-grĭm.
Iser . . . . ĕ'-zēr.
Iseult, *see* Isolde, Yseult . ĭ-sōōlt', ē-sēlt'.
Isfahan, *see* Ispahan . . ĭs-fá-hän'.
Isham . . . . ĭ'-shăm.
Ishbosheth . . . . . . ĭsh-bō'-shĕth.
Ishmael . . . . ĭsh'-mā-ĕl.
Ishmaelite . . . . . . ĭsh'-mā-ĕl-īt''.
Isis . . . . ī'-sĭs.
Isla, *see* Islay . . . . *Sp.* ēs'-lä. *Sc.* ī'-lä.
Isla de Pinos . . . . . ēs'-lä dä pē'-nōs.
Islam . . . . ĭs'-lăm.
Islamite . . . . ĭs'lâm-īt.
Islas Filipinas . . . . ēs'-läs fē-lē-pē'-näs.
Islay, *see* Isla . . . . . ī'-lä.
Islip . . . . ĭs'-lĭp.   [päsh'-ä.
Ismail Pasha . . . . . ĭs-mä-ēl' päsh-ô', pá-shä',
Ismailia . . . . { ĭs-mā'-lĭ-à.
                  { *Turk.* ĭs-mä-ē'-lē-ä.
Isocrates . . . . ī-sŏk'-rà-tēz.
Isola Bella . . . . . . ē'-zō-lä bĕl'-lä.
Isolde, *see* Iseult, Yseult . ĭ-sōld'. *Ger.* ē-zōl'-dŭ.
Isoude, *see* Ysoude . . . ē-sōōd'.

Ispahan, *see* Isfahan . . .	Ĭs-pȧ-hän'.
Israel	Ĭz'-rȧ-ĕl.
Israelitic	Ĭz''-rä-ĕl-ĭt'-ĭk.
Israelitish	Ĭz''-rä-ĕl-ĭt'-ĭsh. [rä-äls'.
Israels, Josef	yō'-sĕf Ĭz'-rä-ĕls. *D.* ēz-
Israfil, Israfel, Israfeel . .	{ Ĭz-rä-fĕl', Ĭs'-rä-fĕl, Ĭz'-rä-fĕl.
Istamboul, *or* Istambul . .	ēs-täm-bōōl'.
Isthmian	Ĭs'-mĭ-ȧn.
Italian	Ĭ-tăl'-yȧn.
Italiens, Boulevard des . .	bōōl-vär' dä zē-täl-yĕṅ'.
Ithaca	Ĭth'-ȧ-kȧ.
Ithuriel	Ĭ-thōō'-rĭ-ĕl.
Ito	ē'-tō.
Ituræa	Ĭ-tū-rē'-ä.
Iturbide	ē-tōōr-bē'-dä.
Iulus	Ĭ-ū'-lŭs.
Ivan	ī'-văn. *Russ.* ē-vän'.
Ivan Ivanovitch	ē-vän' ē-vän'-ō-vĭch.
Iviça, *or* Iviza, *see* Ibiza .	ē'-bē-thä.
Ivry-la-Bataille	ēv-rē'-lä-bä-tä'-yŭ.
Ivry-sur-Seine	ēv-rē'-sür-sĕn'.
Ixion	Ĭks-ī'-ŏn.
Ixtaccihuatl, *see* Iztacci-huatl	{ ēs-täk-sē'-hwätl.
Iyar	ē'-är.
Izdubar	Ĭz-dōō-bär'.
Iztaccihuatl, *see* Ixtacci-huatl	} ēs-täk-sē'-hwätl.

J

Jabalpur, *see* Jubbulpore .	jŭb-ăl-pōōr'.
Jablunka (Pass)	yäb-lōōn'-kä.
Jacmel	zhäk-mĕl'.

Jacob . . . . { jā'-kŏb.
{ *Ger.* yä'-kŏp. [án.

Jacobean, Jacobian . . . jăk-ō-bē'-án, já-kō'-bē-
Jacobi . . . . já-kŏ'-bĭ. *Ger.* yä-kō'-bē.
Jacobins . . . . . . jăk'-ō-bĭnz.
Jacobites . . . . . . jăk'-ō-bīts.
Jacòbo . . . . . . ʰä-kō'-bō.
Jacobsdal . . . . . . yä'-kŏps-dăl.
Jacopo . . . . yä'-kō-pō.
Jacquard . . . . . . jăk'-ärd. *Fr.* zhä-kär'.
Jacqueline . . . . . zhäk-lēn'.
Jacquerie . . . . . . zhäk-rē', zhäk-ĕr-ē'.
Jacques . . . . zhäk.
Jael . . . . jā'-ĕl.
Jaëll . . . . yä'-ĕl.
Jaen . . . . ʰä-ĕn'.
Jaffa, *see* Yafa, Japho, *Heb.* jăf'-fä, yäf'-fä.
Jagellons . . . . . . yä-gĕl'-ŏnz.
Jagua . . . . ḥä'-gwä.
Jah . . . . yä.
Jahveh . . . . yä'-vä, yä'-vĕ.
Jaime (Don) . . . . . ʰä-ē'-mä.
Jain . . . . jīn.
Jaipur, *see* Jeypore . . . jī-pōōr'.
Jairus . . . . { jī'-rus *in New Testament.*
{ jā'-ĭr-ŭs *in Apocrypha.*
Jakobäa . . . . . . yä-kō-bā'-ä.
Jakutsk, *see* Yakutsk . . yä-kōōtsk'.
Jalabert . . . . . . zhä-lä-bâr'.
Jalalabad, *see* Jelalabad . jăl-á-lä-băd'.
Jalandhar, *see* Jullunder . jŭl'-án-dhär.
Jalapa, *see* Xalapa . . . ḥä-lä'-pä.
Jalisco, *see* Xalisco . . . ḥä-lēs'-kō.
Jamaica . . . . . . já-mā'-ká.
Jamblichus . . . . . jăm'-blĭk-ŭs.
Jameson . . . . . . jā'-mĕ-sŭn.

Jammersberg	yăm'-ĕrs-bĕrċh.
Jamont	zha-mon'.
Jan	*D.* yăn.
Janauschek	yä'-now-shĕk.
Jane Eyre	jān âr.
Janet, Paul	pōl zhä-nā'.
Janiculum	jăn-ĭk'-yū-lŭm.
Janin, Jules	zhül zhä-năn'.
Janina, *see* Yanina . .	yä'-nē-nä.
Jansen	jăn'-sĕn. *D.* yän'-sĕn.
Jansenist	jăn'-sĕn-ĭst.
Jansenius	jăn-sē'-nĭ-ŭs.
January	jăn'-ū-ä-rĭ.
Janus	jā'-nŭs.
Japanese	jăp-ăn-ēz' *or* -ēs'.
Japheth *or* Japhet . . .	jā'-fĕth, jā'-fĕt.
Japho, *Heb., see* Jaffa, Yafa	jä'-fō.
Jaquenetta	jăk-ĕ-nĕt'-tä.
Jaques.	{ jāks, jäks. *Shakspere,* jā'-kwēz. *Fr.* zhäk.
Jardin des Plantes . . .	zhär-dăn' dā plänt.
Jardine	jär-dēn'.
Jardines	*Sp.* 'här-dē'-nĕs.
Jardinière, La Belle . .	lä bĕl zhär-dēn-ē-âr'.
Jardinillos	'här-dē-nēl'-yōs.
Jarnac	zhär-näk'.
Jarndyce	järn'-dĭs.
Jaroslaff, *see* Yaroslaff .	yä-rō-släf'.
Jaruco	'hä-rōō'-kō.
Jasher	jā'-shĕr.
Jaudenes	'hä-ōō-dā'-nĕs.
Jauja, *see* Xauxa . . .	'how'-ċhä.
Jaunpur, *see* Jounpoor .	jown-pōōr'.
Java	jä'-vä.
Javan	*adj.* jä'-vȧn. *Bib.* jā'-văn.
Javert	zhȧ-vâr'.

Jean de Meun	zhŏṅ dŭ mŭṅ'.
Jean Jacques Rousseau . .	zhŏṅ zhäk rōō-sō'.
Jeanne d'Albret	zhän däl-brā'.
Jeanne d'Arc, or Darc . .	zhän därk'.
Jean Paul	zhŏṅ pŏl.
Jebusite	jĕb'-ū-zīt.
Jedburgh	jĕd'-bŭr-ŭ.
Jeddo, see Yeddo . . .	yĕd'-dō.
Jehoahaz	jē-hō'-á-hăz.
Jehoiachin	jē-hoi'-á-kĭn.
Jehoiada	jē-hoi'-á-dä.
Jehoiakim	jē-hoi'-á-kĭm.
Jehoram, see Joram . . .	jĕ-hō'-rám.
Jehoshaphat	jē-hŏsh'-á-făt.
Jeisk, see Yeisk	yā'-ĭsk.
Jekyll	jĕ'-kĭl.
Jelalabad, see Jalalabad .	jĕl''-á-lä-bäd'.
Jellyby	jĕl'-ĭ-bĭ.
Jemappes, see Jemmapes .	zhĕ-mäp'.
Jemima	{ jē-mĭ'-má. *Bib.* jē-mī'-má, jĕm'-ĭm-á.
Jemmapes, see Jemappes .	zhĕ-mäp'.
Jena	jĕn'-á. *Ger.* yā'-nä.
Jenghiz Khan, see Genghis Khan, or Jinghis Khan	{ jĕn'-gĭs khän.
Jenner	jĕn'-ẽr.
Jephthah	jĕf'-thä.
Jeremiah	jĕr-ĕ-mī'-á.
Jeres, see Xeres, or . . .	'hā'-rĕs.
Jerez de la Frontera, see Xerez de la Frontera . .	{ 'hā-rĕth' dä lä frŏn-tā'-rä.
Jerome	jĕ-rōm', jĕr'-ōm.
Jérôme Bonaparte . . .	zhā-rōm' bō-nä-pärt'.
Jerona, see Gerona, Xerona	'hā-rō'-nä.
Jerrold	jĕr'-ŏld.
Jerusalem	jĕ-rōō'-sá-lĕm.

Jesso, *see* Yesso . . . . yĕs'-sō.
Jessur, *or* Jessure . . . . jĕs-sur'.
Jesuit . . . . jĕz'-yū-ĭt.
Jethro . . . . jĕth'-rō, jē'-thrŏ.
Jeunesse Dorée . . . . zhē-nĕs' dō-rā'.
Jevons . . . . jĕv'-ŏnz.
Jeypore, *see* Jaipur . . . jĭ-pōr'.
Jezebel . . . . jĕz'-ĕ-bĕl.
Jezreel . . . . jĕz'-rē-ĕl.
Jhansi . . . . jän'-sē.
Jiguani . . . . 'hē-gwä'-nē.
Jimena, *see* Ximena . . . ċhē-mĕn'-ä.
Jimenez, *see* Ximenez . . ċhē-mĕn'-ĕth.
Jinghis Khan, *see* Jenghiz } jĭn'-gĭs khän.
 Khan, Genghis Khan . . {
Jitomir, *see* Zhitomir . . zhĭt-ōm'-ēr. [äċh-ĭm.
Joachim . . . . jō'-à-kĭm. *Ger.* yō'-
Joan of Arc . . . . . { jōn, *or* jō-ăn', *or* jō'-àn
                       { ŏv ärk.
João . . . . *Port.* zhō-owṅ'.
Joaquin . . . . 'hō-ä-kēn'.
Jodhpur . . . . jōd-pōōr'.
Johann . . . . yō'-hän. [nĕs.
Johannes . . . . jō-hăn'-ēz. *Ger.* yō-hän'-
Johannisberg . . . . { jō-hăn'-nĭs-bĕrg.
                     { *D.* yō-hăn'-nĭs-bĕrċh.
John o' Groat's . . . . jŏn ō grôts.
Joinville . . . . zhwăṅ-vēl'.
Jókai . . . . yō'-kä-ĭ.
Joló, *see* Sooloo . . . . ċhō-lō'.
Jomelli, *see* Jommelli . . yō-mĕl'-lē.
Jomini . . . . zhō-mē-nē'.
Jommelli, *see* Jomelli . . yŏm-mĕl'-lē.
Jongleur . . . . zhôṅ-glĕr'.
Joram, *see* Jehoram . . jō'-räm.
Jordaens . . . . yŏr'-däns.

Jordanes, *or*	jôr-dä'-nĕz.
Jordanis, *see* Jornandes .	jôr-dä'-nĭs.
Jorge	*Sp.* ċhōr'-ċhä.
Jorilla	ċhō-rēl'-yä.
Jornandes, *see* Jordanes	jôr-năn'-dēz.
Jorullo, see Xorullo . .	ċhō-rōōl'-yŏ.
José	'hō-sā'.
Joseffy	yŏ-sĕf'-ĭ.
Josephus	jō-sē'-fŭs.
Josiah . . . . · . . .	jō-sī'-ä.
Josquin Desprez . . .	zhŏs-kăṅ' dä-prä'.
Jost	yōst.
Jotham	jō'-thảm.
Jötunheim	yĕ'-tōōn-hīm.
Jouaust	zhōō-ō'.
Joubert, *Fr.*	zhōō-bâr'.
Joubert, *D.*	yow'-bĕrt.
Joule	jōōl.
Jounpoor, *see* Jaunpur .	jown-pōōr',
Jourdain	zhōōr-dăṅ'.
Jourdan	zhōōr-däṅ'.
Journal des Débats . .	zhōōr-năl' dä dä-bä'.
Jouvenet, Jean	zhäṅ zhōōv-nä'.
Jowett	jow'-ĕt.
Joyeuse Garde, La . . .	lä zhwä-yĕz' gärd.
Juan	'hōō-än'.
Juana, *see* Juanna . . .	'hōō-ä'-nä.
Juan Diaz	'hōō-än' dē'-äth.
Juan Fernandez . . . {	jōō'-ȧn fĕr-năn'-dēz. *Sp.* 'hōō-än' fĕr-năn'-dĕth.
Juanna, *see* Juana . .	'hōō-än'-nä.
Juarez	'hōō-ä'-rĕth.
Juba	jōō'-bä.
Jubbulpore, *see* Jabalpur	jŭb-bŭl-pōr'.
Jubilate	jū-bĭl-ä'-tē, jū-bĭl-ä'-tē.
Júcar, *see* Xúcar . . .	'hōō'-kär.

Júcaro . . . . 'hŏō'-kä-rō.
Judaic . . . . jū-dā'-ĭk.
Judas Maccabeus . . . . jŏō'-dás măk-á-bē'-ŭs.
Judic . . . . zhü-dēk'.
Juggernaut . . . . . . jŭg'-ĕr-nôt.
Jugurtha . . . . jŏō-gĕr'-thä.
Juif Errant, Le . . . . lẽ zhü-ēf' ĕr-räṅ'.
Jules . . . . zhül.
Jülich, see Juliers . . . yü'-lĭćh.
Julie . . . . Fr. zhü-lē'.
Julien . . . . Fr. zhü-lē-äṅ'.
Juliers, see Jülich . . . Fr. zhü-lē-ā'.
Juliet . . . . jū'-lĭ-ĕt.
Julliot . . . . zhü-lĭ-ō'.
Jullunder, see Jalandhar . jŭl'-lŭn-dĕr.
Jumel . . . . zhü-mĕl'.
Jumièges . . . . zhü-mē-āzh'.
Jungfrau . . . . yŏōng'-frow.
Juniata (R.) . . . . . jŏō-nĭ-ăt'-ä.
Junkers . . . . yŏōng'-kĕrz.
Junot . . . . zhü-nō'.
Junta . . . . jŭn'-tä.
Jupiter . . . . jŏō'-pĭ-tĕr.
Jura (I. and Mts.) . . . jŏō'-rä.
Jura . . . . Fr. zhü-rä'.
Jurgensen . . . . . . yŏōr'-gĕn-sĕn.   [sē-ē'.
Jussieu, de . . . . . . dŭ jŭs-sū'. Fr. dŭ zhü-
Jutes . . . . jŏōts.
Juvenal . . . . jŏō'-vĕ-nál.

K

Kaaba, see Caaba . . . kä'-bä, kā'-á-bá.
Kaaterskill . . . . . . kä'-tĕrs-kĭl.
Kabail, see Kabyle . . . ká-bīl'.

Kabbala, *see* Cabala . . . kăb'-à-lä.
Kabul, *see* Cabul. . . . . kä-bōōl'.
Kabyle, *see* Kabail . . . . kà-bīl'.
Kadapa, *see* Cuddapah . . kŭd'-ä-pä.
Kadesh Barnea . . . . . kā'-dĕsh bär'-nē-ä.
Kaffa . . . . kăf'-fä.
Kaflir, *see* Kafir, Caffre, ⎫ kăf'-ēr.
Kaffre . . . . ⎭
Kaffraria . . . . kăf-frâr'-ĭ-à.
Kaffre, *see* Kafir, Caffre . . kăf'-ēr.
Kafir, *see* Kaflir, Caffre, ⎫ kăf'-ēr.
Kaffre . . . . ⎭
Kaifeng, *or* . . . . . . kī-fĕng'.
Kai-fung . . . . kī-fŭng'.
Kaiser . . . . kī'-zĕr.
Kaiser Friedrich . . . . . kī'-zĕr frēd'-rĭċh.
Kaiserin . . . . kī'-zĕr-ĭn. [tä.
Kaiserin Augusta . . . kī'-zĕr-ĭn ow-gŏŏs'-
Kaiser Wilhelm . . . . . kī'-zĕr vĭl'-hĕlm.
Kalakaua . . . . kăl-à-kow'-ä.
Kalevala, *or* Kalewala . . kä-lĕ-vä'-lä.
Kalidasa . . . . kä-lĭ-dä'-sà.
Kalmar, *see* Calmar . . . käl'-mär.
Kálnoky. . . . . käl'-nŏ-kĭ.
Kaluga . . . . kä-lōō'-gä.
Kamchatka, *see* Kamtchatka käm-chät'-kä.
Kamehameha . . . . . . kä-mä''-hä-mä'-hä.
Kamerun, *see* Cameroon . . kä-mĕ-rōōn'.
Kamtchatka, *Fr.*, *see* Kam- ⎫ käm-chät'-kä.
chatka . . . . . . ⎭
Kanakas . . . . kä-năk'-àz.
Kanaris, *see* Canaris . . . kä-nä'-rĭs.
Kanawha . . . . kà-nô'-wà.
Kanazawa . . . . kä-nä-zä'-wä.
Kanchanjanga, *see* Kunchain- ⎫ kän-chän-jäng'-gä.
Junga, Kinchinjinga . . ⎭

Kandahar, *see* Candahar, *or*   kän-dä-här′, kăn-dà-här′.

Kandehar . . . . . .   kän-dĕ-här′, kăn-dĕ-här′.

Kang-Kao, *see* Cancao . .   käng-kow′.

Kang-Wu-Wei . . . . .   käng′-wōō-wā′.

Kansas . . . .   kăn′-zás.

Kan-su . . . .   kän-sōō′.

Kant . . . .   känt.

Kantian . . . .   kăn′-tĭ-àn.

Kanuck, *see* Canuck . .   kă-nŭk′.

Kara Bagh, *or* . . . .   ⎫
Karabagh, *see* Carabagh . ⎭ kä-rä-bäg′.

Kara-Hissar . . . . . .   kä″-rä-hĭs-sär′.

Kara Mustapha, *see* Cara ⎫ kä′-rä mŏŏs′-tä-fä, kä-rä′
   Mustafa . . . . . . ⎭   mŏŏs′-tä-fä.

Karénina, Anna . . . .   än′-nä kä-rä′-nē-nä.

Karlovingian, *see* Carlo- ⎫ kär-lō-vĭn′-jĭ-àn.
   vingian . . . . . . ⎭

Karlowitz, *see* Carlowitz .   kär′-lō-vĭts.

Karlsbad, *see* Carlsbad .   kärlz′-bät.

Karlsruhe, *see* Carlsruhe .   kärlz′-rōō-ŭ.

Kartoum, Kartum, *see* ⎫ kär-tōōm′, ċhär-tōōm′.
   Khartoum . . . . . ⎭

Kasan, *see* Kazan . . .   kä-zän′.   [gär′.

Kashgar . . . .   kăsh′-gär.   *Turk.* käsh-

Kashmere, Kashmir, *see* ⎫ kăsh-mēr′.
   Cashmere . . . . . ⎭

Kassai, (R.) . . . . . .   kä-sī′.

Katahdin, *see* Ktaadn . .   kà-tä′-dĭn.

Katak, *see* Cattack, Cuttack   kà-täk′.

Kathiawar, *see* Kattywar .   kät″-ē-ä-wär′.

Kathlamba, *see* Quath- ⎫ kät-läm′-bä.
   lamba . . . . . . ⎭

Katrine, Loch . . . . .   lŏċh kăt′-rĭn.

Kattegat, *see* Cattegat . .   kăt′-ĕ-gät.

Kattywar, *see* Kathiawar .   kät-ē-wär′.

Kauai (I.) . . . .   kow-ī′.

Kauffman	kowf'-män.
Kaulbach	kowl'-bäċh.
Kaunitz	kow'-nĭts.
Kavanagh	kăv'-ă-nä.
Kay	kā. *Ger.* kī·
Kayor, *see* Cayor	kī-ōr'.
Kazak	kä-zäk'.
Kazan, *see* Kasan . . .	kä-zän'.
Keang-Se, *see* Kiang-sĭ . .	kē-äng'-sē'.
Keang-Soo, *see* Kiang-su .	kē-äng'-sōō'.
Kearney	kär'-nĭ.
Kearsarge	kēr'-särj.
Keble	kē'-bl.
Kedron, *see* Cedron, Kidron	kē'-drŏn.
Kehama	kē-hä'-mä.
Kei (R.)	kā.
Keighley, *or* Keithley . .	kēth'-lĭ.
Kekrops, *see* Cecrops . .	kē'-krŏps.
Kelat, *see* Khelat	kĕ-lät'.
Kelts, *see* Celts	kĕlts.
Kempis, (Thomas) á . . .	ä kĕm'-pĭs.
Kenelm Chillingly . . .	kĕn'-ĕlm chĭl'-ĭng-lĭ.
Kenilworth	kĕn'-l-wĕrth.
Kennebec	kĕn-ē-bĕk'.
Kensington	kĕn'-zĭng-tŭn.
Keokuk	kē'-ō-kŭk. [lôṅ'.
Kerguelen	kĕr'-gĕl-ĕn. *Fr.* kĕr-gā·
Kerman, *see* Kirman . .	kĕr-män'.
Kéroualle, *see* Quérouaille	kā-rōō-äl'.
Keshab Chandra Sen . .	kĕ-shŭb' chăn'-drȧ sän.
Kesho	kĕsh'-ō.
Ketshwayo, *see* Cettiwayo	kāch-wä'-yō.
Khafra	khăf'-rä.
Khalif, *see* Calif, Caliph .	kä-lēf', kā'-lĭf.
Khalifa, *or*	kä-lē'-fä.
Khaliff	kä-lēf'.

Khan	kôn, kän, kăn.
Khandesh, see Candeish .	khän-desh'.
Khania, see Canea . . .	kä-nē'-ä.
Khartoum, or Khartum, see Kartoum	} kär-tōōm', chär-tōōm´.
Khedive	{ kä-dēv', kē'-dĭv, kĕ-dēv', kä-dē'-vä.
Khelat, see Kelat	kĕ-lät'.
Kherson	chĕr-sōn'.
Khiva	kē'-vä, chē'-vä.
Khorasan, or Khorassan .	chō-rä-sän'.
Khorsabad	khōr-sä-bäd'.
Khosru, or	kŏs-rōō'.
Khusrau	khŭs-row'.
Kiang-si, see Keang-Se . .	kē-äng'-sē'.
Kiang-su, see Keang-Soo .	kē-äng'-sōō'.
Kiao-chau.	kĭ-ä'-ō-chow'.
Kichinef, Kichenev, see Kishineff	} kĭsh-ĭ-nĕf'.
Kidron, see Cedron . . .	kĭd'-rŏn.
Kieff, see Kiev	kē'-ĕf, kē-ĕf'.
Kiel	kēl.
Kiev, or Kiew, see Kieff	kē'-ĕv, kē-ĕf'.
Kilauea	kē-low-ā'-ä.
Kilimane, see Quilimane .	kē-lē-mä'-nä.
Kimry, Kymry, see Cymry .	kĭm'-rĭ.
Kincardine	kĭn-kär'-dĭn.
Kinchinjinga, see Kanchan-janga, Kunchain-Junga	} kĭn-chĭn-jĭng'-gä.
King-te-chen	kĭng-tĕ-chĕn'.
Kioto, see Kyoto	kē-ō'-tō.
Kirchhoff	kērch'-hŏf.
Kirchner	kērch'-nĕr.
Kirghiz	kĭr-gēz'.
Kirkcaldy.	kēr-kô'-dĭ.
Kirkcudbright	kēr-kōō'-brĭ.

Kirman, see Kerman . . . Kĕr-man'.

Kishineff, Kichenev, Kisch-enew, see Kichinef . . } kĕsh-ē-nĕf'.

Kishlangov, or . . . . . kĕsh-län-gŏv'.

Kishlanou . . . . . . kĕsh-lä-nō'.

Kiskelim . . . . kĭs-kē'-lĭm.

Kissingen . . . . . . kĭs'-sĭng-ĕn.

Kittim, see Chittim . . . kĭt'-ĭm.

Kiung-chau . . . . . . kē-ōōng'-chow.

Kiusiu . . . . kyōō'-syōō'.

Kizil-Irmak (R.) . . . . kĭz'-ĭl-ĭr-mäk'.

Klamath . . . . klä'-măt.

Klaus . . . . klows.

Kléber . . . . { klē'-bĕr, klā'-bâr.
{ Fr. klä-bâr'.

Klephts . . . . klĕfts.

Klindworth . . . . . . klĭnt'-vŏrt.

Knaus . . . . k-nows'.

Knecht Ruprecht . . . . k-nĕċht rōō'-prĕċht.

Kneisel . . . . k-nī'-zĕl.

Kneller . . . . nĕl'-ĕr.

Knollys . . . . nōlz.

Knut, see Canute . . . . k-nōōt.

Kobe . . . . kō'-bĕ.

Koedoesberg, see Koodoes-berg . . . . } kōō-dōōs'-bĕrċh.

Koedoes Rand, see Koodoos Rand . . . . . . } kōō-dōōs' rănt.

Koerner, see Körner . . . kĕr'-nĕr.

Koffyfontein . . . . . kŏf''-fī-fŏn'-tīn.

Koh-i-nur, Kohinoor . . . kō-ē-nōōr'.

Köhler . . . . kē'-lĕr.

Koimbatur, see Coimbatore kō-ĭm''-bȧ-tōōr'.

Kokstadt . . . . kŏk'-stăt.

Kolapoor, Kolapur, Kol-hapur, see Colapur . . } kō-lä-pōōr'.

Kolmar, *see* Colmar . . . kŏl-mär'.
Köln . . . . kĕln.
Kolokol . . . . kŏl-ō-kŏl'.
Komorn . . . . kō'-mŏrn.
Koniah, *or* . . . . . . kō'-nē-ä.
Konieh . . . . kō'-nē-ĕ.
König . . . . kĕ'-nĭċh.
Königgrätz . . . . . . kĕ'-nēg-grâtz.
Königin . . . . kĕ'-nē-gĭn.
Königsberg . . . . . . { kĕn'-ĭgz-bērg.
{ *Ger.* kĕ'-nĭċhs-bĕrċh.
Koodoesberg, *see* Koedoes-
berg . . . . } kōō-dōōs'-bĕrċh.
Koodoes Rand, *see* Koedoes
Rand . . . . } kōō-dōōs' rănt.
Koordistan, *see* Kurdistan kōōr-dĭs-tän'.
Koords, *see* Kurds . . . kōōrdz.
Koorll, *see* Kurile . . . kōō'-rĭl.
Koran . . . . kō'-răn, kō-rän'.
Kordofan . . . . . . kŏr-dō-fän'.
Korea, *see* Corea . . . . kō-rē'-ä.
Korean, *see* Corean . . . kō-rē'-án.
Körner, *see* Koerner . . . kĕr'-nĕr.
Korn Spruit . . . . . . kŏrn sproit.
Kosciusko, *or* . . . . . kŏs-sĭ-ŭs'-kō.
Kosciuszko . . . . . . kōsh-chōō'-skō.
Kossuth . . . . { kŏs-sōōth'.
{ *Hung.* kŏsh'-ōot.
Kotzebue (von) . . . . kŏt'-sĕ-bōō, kŏt'-sē-bōō.
Koutouzof, *see* Kutusoff . kōō-tōō'-zŏf.
Kouyunjik . . . . . . kōō'-ŭn-jĭk.
Kraaft, *or* Krafft, *or* Kraft kräft.
Krag-Jorgensen . . . . kräg'-yŏr'-gĕn-sĕn.
Krakau, *or* . . . . . . krä'-kō, krä'-kow, *or*
Krakow, *see* Cracow . . *Pol.* krä'-kŏf.
Kranach, *see* Cranach . . krăn'-âk. *Ger.* krä'-näċh.

Krapf . . . . kräpf.
Krapotkin . . . . . . krä-pŏt'-kĭn.
Krasnoi, *or* . . . . . . kräs-noi',
Krasnyi Jar . . . . . . kräs-noi' yär.
Krause . . . . krow'-zŭ.
Kremlin . . . . krĕm'-lĭn.
Kreutzer, Kreuzer . . . kroit'-zĕr.
Kriemhild, *see* Chriemhild krĕm'-hĭlt.
Kronos, *see* Cronus . . . krŏn'-ŏs. [stät.
Kronstadt, *see* Cronstadt . krŏn'-stät. *Russ.* krōn'-
Kroonstad . . . . . . krōn'-stät.
Kruger . . . . krü'-gĕr.
Krugersdorp . . . . . krü'-gĕrs-dŏrp.
Krupp . . . . krŏŏp.
Ktaadn, *see* Katahdin . . ḵ-tä'-dn.
Kuanza, *see* Coanza, Quanza kwän'-zä.
Kubla Khan, *or* . . . . kōōb'-lä khän.
Kublai Khan . . . . . kōōb'-lī khän.
Ku-Klux-Klan . . . . . kū'-klŭks-klän.
Kuku-Khoto . . . . . kōō'-kōō-kō'-tō.
Kuli Khan . . . . . . kōō'-lē khän.
Kulmbach, *see* Culmbach . kŏŏlm'-bäċh.
Kumassi, *see* Coomassie . kōō-mäs'-sē.
Kunchain-Junga, *or* . . . kŭn-chīn-jŭng'-gȧ.
Kunchin-Ginga, *or* . . . kōōn-chĭn-jĭng'-gȧ.
Kunchin-Junga, *see* Kanchanjanga . . . . . } kōōn-chĭn-jŭng'-gȧ.
Kunersdorf . . . . . . kōō'-nĕrs-dŏrf.
Kurdistan, *see* Koordistan kōōr-dĭs-tän'.
Kurds, *see* Koords . . . kōōrdz.
Kurfürst . . . . kōōr'-fürst.
Kurile, *see* Kooril . . . kōō'-rĭl.
Kursk . . . . kōōrsk.
Kurukshetra . . . . . kōō-rōōk-shä'-trȧ.
Küstrin, *see* Cüstrin . . . küs-trēn'.
Kutais . . . . kōō-tīs'.

Kutusoff, *or* Kutuzoff, *see* { kōō-tōō'-zŏf
Koutouzof . . . . (

Kuychau, *see* Kweichow . kwī-chow'.

Kuyp, *see* Cuyp . . . . koip.

Kwangsi, *see* Quangsi . . kwäng-sē'.

Kwang Su . . . . . . kwäng-sōō'.

Kwangtung, *see* Quangtong kwäng-tōōng'.

Kweichow, *see* Kuy-chau . kwī-chow'.

Kwhichpak . . . . . . kwĭk-päk'.

Kymry, *see* Cymry . . . kĭm'-rĭ.

Kyoto, *see* Kioto . . . kē-ō'-tō.

Kyrie eleïson . . . . . kĭr'-ĭ-ĕ ĕ-lā'-ĭ-sŏn.

L

La Antigua . . . . . . lä än-tē'-gwä.

Labanoff de Rostoff . . . lä-bä'-nŏf dŭ rŏs'-tŏf.

Labienus . . . . lä-bĭ-ē-nŭs.

Lablache, Luigi . . . . lōō-ē'-jē lä-bläsh'.

Labori, Maître . . . . . mätr lä-bō-rē'.

Labouchere . . . . . . lä-bōō-shâr'.

Laboulaye . . . . . . lä-bōō-lä'.

Labrador . . . . lăb-rȧ-dôr'.

La Bruyère . . . . . . lä brü-yâr'.

Labuan . . . . lä-bōō-än'.

La Cabaña . . . . . . lä-kä-bän'-yä.

La Caille, *or* Lacaille . . lä kä'-yŭ.

La Caimanera . . . . . lä kä''-ē-mä-nä'-rä.

Laccadive, *see* Lakkadiv . lăk'-ȧ-dīv.

Lacedaemon . . . . . . lăs-ē-dē'-mŏn.

Lacépède . . . . lä-sā-pād'.

Lachaise, *or* La Chaise . . lä shāz'.

Lachesis . . . . lăk'-ē-sĭs.

Lachine . . . . lä-shēn'.

Lachme, *see* Lakme . . . lăk'-mĕ.

Laconia . . . . lă-kō′-nĭ-à.
Lacroix . . . . la-krwa′.
Ladikieh, see Latakia . . lä-dē-kē′-ĕ.
Ladislaus . . . . lăd′-ĭs-lôs.
Ladoga . . . . lä′-dō-gä.
Ladrone (Is.) . . . . . lä-drōn′.   [nĕs.
Ladrones . . . . lä-drōnz′. Sp. lä-drō′-
Ladybrand . . . . . . lā′-dĭ-brănd.
Laennec . . . . lĕn-nĕk′.
Laertes . . . . lä-ĕr′-tēz.
La Estrella . . . . . . lä ĕs-trāl′-yä.
La Farge . . . . lä färj. Fr. färzh.
Lafayette, De . . . . . dŭ lä-fā-ĕt′.
La Ferrière . . . . . . lä fĕr-rē-âr′.
Lafeu . . . . lä-fĕ′.
Lafitte . . . . lä-fēt′.
La Fontaine, de . . . . { dŭ lä fŏn′-tān.
{ Fr. dŭ lä fôn-tän′.
La Fourche . . . . . . lä fōōrsh′.
L'Africaine . . . . . . lä-frē-kän′.
Lagado . . . . lä-gä′-dō.
La Gazza Ladra . . . . lä gät′-zä lä′-drä.
La Gloire . . . . lä glwär′.   [gōōs.
Lagos . . . . Af. lä′-gŏs. Port. lä′-
Lagrange, de . . . . . dŭ lä gräṅzh′.
La Granja . . . . . . lä grän′-ċhä.
Lagthing . . . . läg′-tĭng.
La Guaira, or La Guayra . { lä gwī′-rä or gī′-rà.
{ Sp. lä gwä′-ē-rä.
Laguna de Bay . . . . lä-gōō′-nä dä bä′-ē.
La Haye, see The Hague . lä ā′.
Lahor, or Lahore . . . . lä-hōr′.
Laibach, see Laybach . . lī′-bäċh.
L'Aiglon . . . . lä-glôṅ′.
Laing's Nek . . . . . . längz nĕk.
Lajeunesse . . . . . . lä-zhĕn-ĕs′.

Lakhimpur, *see* Luckimpur	lŭk-ĭm-pōōr'.
Lalthnau, *see* Lucknow . .	luk·now. *pop.* lŭk'·no.
Lakkadiv, *see* Laccadive .	lăk'-ȧ-dīv.
Lakme, *see* Lachmi . . .	lăk'-mē.
Lakshmi, *or* Lakchmi . .	lăksh'-mē.
Lalage	lăl'-ā-jē.
La Liberté	lä lē-bĕr-tā'.
Lalitpur, *see* Lullitpur . .	lŭl-lĭt-pōōr'.
Lalla Rookh	lä'-lä-rōōk.
L'Allegro	lä-lä'-grō.
Lamartine	lä-mär-tēn'.
Lamballe, Princesse du . .	prăṅ-sĕs' dŭ läṅ-bäl'.
Lambert, Louis	lōō-ē' läṅ-bâr'.
Lamech	lā'-mĕk.
Lamennais	lä-mĕ-nā'.
Lamia	lā'-mĭ-ȧ.
La Miranao	lä mē-rä-nä'-ō.
Lammermoor, *or*	lăm-mĕr-mōōr'.
Lammermuir	lăm-mĕr-mūr'.
Lamoricière	lä-mō-rē-sḝ-âr'.
La Motte-Fouqué	lä mŏt'-fōō-kā'.
Lamoureux	lä-mōō-rē'.
Lanark	lăn'-ärk.
La Navidad	lä nä-vē-däd'.
Lancaster	lăng'-kăs-tẽr.
Lancelot du Lac	lăn'-sē-lŏt dū lăk.
Lan-chau	län-chow'.
Lanciani	län-chä'-nē.
Landes (The)	länd.
Landgraf	länt'-gräf.
Landgravine	länt'-grä-vēn.
Landsthing	läns'-tĭng.
Landtag	länt'-täċh.
Landwehr	länt'-vâr. [fräṅ'.
Lanfranc	lăn'-frăngk. *Fr.* läṅ-
Lange	läng'-ŭ.

Langres	längr.
Languedoc, *or* Langue d'Oc	{ lăng'-gwē-dŏk. *Fr.* län-gŭ-dŏk'.
Langue d'Oil	län dwē'.
Lanier	lă-nēr'.
Lanjuinais	län-zhwē-nā'.
Lannes	lăn. *Fr.* län.
La Noue	lä nōō'.
Laocoön	lā-ŏk'-ō-ŏn.
Laodameia, *or* Laodamia .	lā''-ŏd-ā-mī'-á.
Laodicea	lā''-ŏd-ĭs-ē'-á.
Laomedon	lā-ŏm'-ē-dŏn.
Laon	lŏn.
Laos	lä'-ōs.
Lao-tsze	lä'-ō-tsä'.
La Patrie	lä pä-trē'.
La Paz	lä päz. *Sp.* lä päth.
Lapithæ	lăp'-ĭ-thē.
La Place, de	dŭ lä pläs.
La Plata	lä plä'-tä.
La Princesse Lointaine . .	lä prăn-sĕs' lwăn-tān'.
Laputa	là-pū'-tà.
Lara	lä'-rä.
La Rábida	lä rä'-bē-dä.
Lares	lā'-rēz.
Larisa, *or* Larissa	lä-rēs'-á.
La Rochefoucault	lä rōsh-fōō-kō'.
La Rochejacquelein . . .	lä rōsh-zhäk-lăn'.
La Rochelle	lä rō-shĕl'.
Larrey	lä-rā'.
Larroumet	lär-rōō-mā'.
La Saisiaz	lä sä-zē-äss'.
La Salle	lä săl. *Fr.* lä säl.
Lascaris	läs'-kä-rĭs.
Las Casas, de	dā läs kä'-säs.
Las Cases, de	*Fr.* dŭ läs käz.

Las Guasimas . . . . . läs gwä-sē'-mäs.

La Scoupe . . . . . . lä ꜱꝏ kü'-pꞈ

La Sorbonne. . . . . . lä sōr-bŏn'.

Laspiñas . . . . läs-pēn'-yäs.

Lassalle . . . . lä-säl'.

Lassen . . . . läs'-sĕn.

Latakia, or Latakiyah, see } lä-tä-kē'-à.
   Ladikieh . . . . . .

Lateran . . . . lăt'-ēr-ăn.

Latour d'Auvergne . . . lä-tōōr' dō-vârn'-yŭ.

La Trappe . . . . . . lä träp.

Latreille . . . . lä-trā'-yŭ.

Laud . . . . lôd.

Laudon, see Loudon . . . low'-dŏn.

Lauenburg . . . . . . low'-ĕn-bōōrċh.

Laura . . . . lô'-rá.   It. lä'-ōō-rä.

Laurent . . . . lō-rŏṅ'.

Laurier . . . . lō'-rẹ-ạ.

Lausanne. . . . . . . lō-zän'.

La Vallière . . . . . . lä väl-lẹ-âr'.

Lavater . . . . { lä'-vä-tĕr.   Ger. lä-fä'-
                  tĕr.   Fr. lä-vä-târ'.

Lavedan . . . . lä-vŭ-dän'.

Laveleye . . . . läv-lā'.

La Vendée . . . . . . lä vŏṅ-dā'.

Lavengro . . . . lăv-en'-grō.

Lavigerie . . . . lä-vēzh-rē'.

Lavoisier . . . . lä-vwä-zẹ-ā'.

Laweman, or . . . . . lô'-măn.

Layamon . . . . lä'-yà-mŏn.

Layard . . . . lā'-àrd.

Laybach, see Laibach . . lī'-bäċh.

Leah . . . . lē'-ä.

Leamington Spa . . . . lĕm'-ĭng-tŏn spä.

Leander . . . . lē-ăn'-dĕr.

Léandre . . . . lā-äṅdr'.

Lebbaeus, *or* Lebbeus . . lĕb-bē'-ŭs.
Leboeuf . . . . . . lē-bĕf'.
Lebrun, *see* Vigée-Lebrun . lē-brŭn'.
Lecce . . . . lĕch'-ĕ.
Leclerc, *or* Le Clerc . . . lē-klâr'.
Leconte de Lisle . . . . lē-kônt' dŭ lēl'.
Lecouvreur, Adrienne . . ä-drē-ĕn' lē-kōōv-rēr'.
Ledru-Rollin . . . . . lē-drü'-rōl-lăn'.
Leeds . . . . lēdz.
Leeuwarden . . . . . . lā'-vär-dĕn.
Leeuwenhoek, *see* Leuwen- } lā'-vĕn-hōōk.
hoek . . . . . . }
Leeward . . . . lē'-wȧrd, lē'-ärd, lū'-ärd.
Lefebre, *or* Lefèvre . . . lē-fāvr'.
Legaré (H. S.) . . . . . lŭ-grē'.
Legaspi, *or* . . . . . . lā-gäs'-pē.
Legazpe . . . . lā-gäth'-pā.
Legendre . . . . lē-zhŏndr'.
Leghorn . . . . lĕg'-hôrn, lĕg-hôrn'.
Legnago . . . . län-yä'-gō.
Legouvé . . . . lē-gōō-vā'.
Le Grand Monarque . . . lē grän mō-närk'.
Leibnitz, *or* Leibniz . . . līb'-nĭtz.
Leicester . . . . lĕs'-tĕr.
Leiden, *see* Leyden . . . lī'-dĕn.
Leigh . . . . lē.
Leighton . . . . lā'-tŭn.
Leila . . . . lē'-lá.
Leinster . . . . lēn'-stĕr, lĭn'-stĕr.
Leipsic, *or* . . . . . . līp'-sĭk.
Leipzig . . . . līp'-tsĭch.
Leith . . . . lēth.
Le Journal des Débats . . lē zhōōr-näl' dä dā-bä'.
Lely (Sir Peter) . . . . lē'-lĭ.
Lemaître . . . . lē-mātr'.
Léman . . . . lā-män'.

Le Mans	lĕ mäṅ.
Lemercier	lĕ-mar-se͟-a'.
Lemerre	lĕ-mĕr'.
Lemonnier, Camille . . .	kä-mēl' lĕ-mŏn-ē-ä'.
Le Moyne	lĕ moin'. *Fr.* lĕ mwăn'.
Lemprière	{ lĕm-prēr', lĕm'-prē-ĕr. *Fr.* lŏṅ-prē-âr'.
Lenape	lĕn'-ă-pē.
Lenbach	lĕn'-bäċh.
Lenclos, Ninon de, *or* L'Enclos	} nē-nôṅ' dŭ lôṅ-klō'.
Lenni-Lenape	lĕn'-nĭ-lĕn'-ă-pē.
Lenore	lĕ-nōr'.
Lenôtre	lĕ-nōtr'.
Leo	lē'-ō. *It.* lā'-ō.
Leofric	lĕ-ŏf'-rĭk.
Leofwine	lĕ-ŏf'-wĭn-ĕ.
Leominster	lĕm'-ĭn-stĕr.
Leon	lē'-ŏn. *Sp.* lā-ŏn'.
Léon	*Fr.* lā-ôṅ'.
Leonardo da Vinci . . .	lā-ō-när'-dō dä vēn'-chē.
Leonato	lē-ō-nä'-tō.
Leonidas	lē-ŏn'-ĭ-dăs.
Léonore	lā-ō-nōr'.
Leontes	lē-ŏn'-tēz.
Leopardi	lā-ō-pär'-dē.
Lepage, Bastien	bäs-tē-ĕṅ'-lĕ-päzh'.
Lepando	lā-pän'-dō.
Lepanto	lĕ-păn'-tō, lā-pän'-tō.
Lérida	lĕr'-ē-dä.
Lérius, Îles de	ēl dŭ lā-rän'.
Lermontoff, Lermontov . .	lĕr'-mŏn-tŏf.
Leroux	lĕ-rōō'.
Leroy-Beaulieu	lĕ-rwä'-bō-lē-ē͟'.
Le Sage, *or* Lesage . . .	lĕ-säzh'.
Lesdiguières	lā-dē-gē-âr'.

Les Italiens . . . . . . lä zē-tä-lē-äṅ'.

Lespinasse, de, *see* Espinasse dŭ lä-pē-näs'.

Les Rougon-Macquart . . lä rōō-gôṅ'-mäk-är'.

Lesseps, de . . . . . . { dŭ lĕs'-ĕps.
{ *Fr.* dŭ lē-sĕps'.

Lessing . . . . lĕs'-sĭng.

Le Sueur, *or* Lesueur . . lē-sü-ẽr'.   [skē.

Leszczynski, Stanislaus . . stän'-ĭs-läs   lĕsh-chĭn'-

Le Temps . . . . . . lē tôṅ.

Lethe . . . . lē'-thē.

Lethean . . . . lē-thē'-án.

L'Étoile . . . . lä-twäl'.

Leucophryne . . . . . lū-kō-frī'-nē.

Leucothea . . . . . . lū-kō'-thē-ä.

Leuctra . . . . lūk'-trä.

Leuk . . . . loik.

Leuthen . . . . loi'-tĕn.

Leutze . . . . loit'-zŭ.

Leuwenhoek, *see* Leeuwen- } lē'-vĕn-hōōk.
hoek . . . . }

Lévan . . . . lä-väṅ'.

Levant . . . . lĕ-vänt', lē-vänt'.

Lever . . . . lē'-vẽr.   [rē-ä'.

Leverrier, *or* Le Verrier . lŭ-vẽr'-ĭ-ẽr.   *Fr.* lē-vĕ-

Leveson-Gower . . . . lū'-sŭn-gōr'.

Levite . . . . lē'-vīt.

Levitic . . . . lē-vĭt'-ĭk.

Leviticus . . . . . . lē-vĭt'-ĭ-kŭs.

Lévy (Émile) . . . . . lä-vē'.

Lewes . . . . lū'-ĕs.

Leyden, *see* Leiden . . . lī'-dĕn.

Leyds . . . . lits.

Leyra (Antonio), de . . . dä lä'-ē-rä.

Leys . . . . līs, lä.

Leyte . . . . lä'-tä, *Sp.* lä'-ē-tä.

L'hermitte . . . . . . lĕr-mēt'.

L'Hôpital, *or* L'Hospital . lō-pē-täl'.
Liautung . . . . lō-ow-tōŏng'.
Libanius . . . . lĭ-bā'-nĭ-ŭs.
Libanus . . . . lĭb'-ā-nŭs.
Libau . . . . lē'-bow.
Liber . . . . lĭ'-bĕr.
Liberi . . . . lē'-bā-rē.
Liberia . . . . . . lĭ-bē'-rĭ-à.
Libra . . . . lĭ'-brä.
Lichas . . . . lĭ'-kás.
Lichtenstein . . . . . lĭċh'-tĕn-stīn.
Liddell . . . . lĭd'-ĕl.
Lie (Jonas) . . . . . lē.
Lieber . . . . lē'-bĕr.
Liebig . . . . lē'-bĭċh.
Liège . . . . *Fr.* lē-ĕzh'.
Liegnitz . . . . lēg'-nĭtz. *Ger.* lēċh'-nĭtz.
Ligea, *or* Ligeia . . . . lĭ-jē'-ä.
Ligne, de . . . . . . dŭ lēn'-yŭ.
Ligny . . . . lēn'-yĭ. *Fr.* lēn-yē'.
Ligonier . . . . lĭg-ō-nēr'.
Liguori . . . . lē-gwō'-rē.
Li Hung Chang . . . . lē hōōng chông.
Lilis . . . . lĭ'-lĭs.
Lilith . . . . lĭ'-lĭth, lĭl'-ĭth.
Liliuokalani . . . . . lē''-lē-wō-kä-lä'-nē.
Lille . . . . lēl.
Lillibullero . . . . . . lĭl''-lĭ-bŏŏl-lâ'-rō.
Lima . . . . lĭ'-mà. *Sp.* lē'-mä.
Limerick . . . . lĭm'-ĕ-rĭk.
Limoges, *see* Lymoges . . lē-mōzh'.
Limousin . . . . lē-mōō-zăṅ'.
Limpopo . . . . lĭm-pō'-pō.
Linares . . . . lē-nä'-rĕs.
Lincoln . . . . lĭng'-kŭn.
Lingayen . . . . lēn-gä-yĕn'.

Linlithgow	lĭn-lĭth'-gō.
Linnæan, *see* Linnean . .	lĭn-nē'-ản.
Linnæus	lĭn-nē'-ŭs.
Linnean, *see* Linnæan . .	lĭn-nē'-ản.
Linz	lĭnts.
Liotard	lē-ọ̄-tär'.
Lipari	lĭp'-ä-rē.
Lippe	lĭp'-pŭ.
Lippi, Lippo	lēp'-pō lēp'-pē.
Lisboa, *or*	*Port. and Sp.* lēs-bō'-ä.
Lisbon	lĭz'-bŏn.
Lisieux	lē-zẹ̄-ẹ̄'.
Lisle, Leconte de	lē-kŏnt' dŭ lēl'.
L'Isle, Rouget de	rōō-zhä' dŭ lēl'.
Liszt	lĭst.
Littorale	lēt-tō-rä'-lä.
Littré	lē-trä'.
Liu Kiu, *see* Loo Choo, Lieou Khieou, *and* . .	lē-ōō' kē-ōō'.
Liu Tchou	lē-ōō' chōō.
Liutprand, *see* Luitprand .	lĭ-ōōt'-prånd.
Livonia	lĭ-vō'-nĭ-ả.
Llanberis	ċhlăn-bĕr'-ĭs.
Llandaff	ċhlăn-dăf'.
Llangollen	ċhlăn-gŏċh'-lĕn.
Llanos	*Sp.* l-yä'-nŏs.
Llewelyn ap Gruffydd, *or* Llywelyn ap Gruffydd . .	ċhlōō-ĕl'-ĭn ăp grü'-fĕth.
Loanda	lō-än'-dä. [dä.
Loanda, São Paulo de . .	säṅ pow'-lōō dĕ lō-än'-
Loango	lō-äng'-gō.
Loangwa	lō-ăng'-wä.
Lobengula	lō-bĕng-gōō'-lä.
Lochaber	lŏċh-ä'-bĕr.
Lochiel	lŏċh-ēl'.
Lochinvar	lŏċh-ĭn-vär'.

Loch Katrine	lŏċh krăt'-rĭn.
Lochleven	lŏċh-lĕv'-n, lŏċh-lē'-vn.
Lockroy	*Fr.* lōk-rwä'.
Lodi	lō'-dē.
Lodovico	lō-dō-vē'-kō.
Lódz	lŏdz.
Loew	lĕv.
Loffoden, *or* Lofoden, *or*	lŏf-fō'-dĕn.
Lofoten	lō-fō'-tĕn.
Loggia dei Lanzi	lōj'-jä dā'-ē länd'-zē.
Logroño	lō-grōn'-yō.
Lohardaga, *or*	lō-här-dä'-gä.
Lohardugga	lō-här-dŭg'-gä.
Lohengrin	lō'-ĕn-grĭn.
Loire	lwär.
Loire, Haute	ōt-lwär'.
Loire-Inférieure	lwär'-ăṅ-fā-rē̱-ȇr'.
Loiret	lwä-rä'.
Loir-et-Cher	lwär'-ā-shâr'.
Lokal-Anzeiger	lō-käl'-än'-tsī-gĕr.
Loke, *or* Loki	lō'-kĕ.
Loki	lō'-kē.
Lola Montez	lō'-lä mŏn'-tĕz.
Lombard's Kop	lŏm'-bärts kŏp.
Lombardy	lŏm'-bär-dĭ.
Lombroso	lŏm-brō'-zō.
Lome	lō'-mā.
Lomonosoff	lō-mō-nō'-sŏf.
Lomza	lŏm'-zhä.
Longchamp	lôṅ-shäṅ'.
Longimanus	lŏn-jĭm'-ā-nŭs.
Longinus	lŏn-jī'-nŭs.
Longjumeau	lôṅ-zhü-mō'.
Longueville, de	dŭ lôṅg-vēl'.
Loo Choo, Liu Tchou, *see* Liu Kiu, *and* Lieou Khieou	lōō chōō.

Lope de Vega	lō'-pā dā vā'-gä.
Lopez	lō'-pāth.
Lopez (C. A., Pres. Paraguay)	lō'-pāth, *locally* lō'-pāz.
Lorbrulgrud	lôr-brŭl'-grŭd.
Lorelei, *or* Loreley, *see* Lurlei	lō'-rā-lī.
Lorenzetti	lō-rĕnd-zĕt'-tē.
Lorenzo	lō-rĕn'-zō. *It.* lō-rĕnd'-zō. *Sp.* lō-rĕn'-thō.
Lorenzo de' Medici	lō-rĕnd'-zō dā mā'-dē-chē.
Lorenzo Marques, *see* Lourenço Marques	lō-ren'-sō mär'-kĕs. *Port.* lō-răñ'-sŏō mär'-kĕs.
Loreto, *or*	lō-rā'-tō.
Loretto	lō-rĕt'-tō.
Lorraine	lŏr-rān'. *Fr.* lō-rān'.
Los Angeles	lŏs ăn'-jĕl-ĕs. *Sp.* lōs äng'-ċhā-lās.
Lot-et-Garonne	lō-tā-gä-rŏn'.
Lothario	lō-thā'-rē-ō.
Loti, Pierre	pē-âr' lō-tē'.
Lotophagi	lō-tŏf-ā-jī.
Lotto, Lorenzo	lō-rĕnd'-zō lŏt'-tō.
Lotze	lōt'-sŭ.
Loubet	lōō-bā'.
Loudon, *see* Laudon	low'-dŏn.
Loudun	lōō-dŭñ'.
Louis	lōō'-ĭs. *Fr.* lōō-ē'.
Louisiana	lōō''-ē-zē-ä'-nä, lōō''-ē-zē-ăn'-ä.
Louis Lambert	lōō-ē' läñ-bâr'.
Louis Philippe	lōō-ē' fē-lēp'.
Louis Quatorze	lōō-ē' kă-tôrz'.
Louis Quinze	lōō-ē' kăñz.
Louis Seize	lōō-ē' sĕz.
Louis Treize	lōō-ē' trĕz.
Louisville	lōō'-ĭ-vĭl, lōō'-ĭs-vĭl.

Lourdes . . . . lōōrd.

Lourenço Marques, *see* Lo- ⎱ lō-rĕn'-sō mär'-kĕs.
renzo Marques . . . . ⎰ *Port.* lōō-räṅ'-sōō mär'

Louvain . . . . lōō-väṅ'. [kĕs.

Louverture, Toussaint, *or* ⎱ tōō-säṅ' lōō-vĕr-tür'.
L'Ouverture . . . . . ⎰

Louvre . . . . lōōvr.

Louys, Pierre . . . . . pē-âr' lōō-ē'.

Lowestoft . . . . . . lō'-stŏft, lō'-ĕ-stŏft.

Loyola . . . . loi-ō'-lä. *Sp.* lō-yō'-lä.

Lozère . . . . lō-zâr'.

Lo Zingaro . . . . . . lō dzĕn'-gä-rō.

Lualaba . . . . lōō-ä-lä'-bä.

Luapula . . . . lōō-ä-pōō'-lä.

Lübeck . . . . lü'-bĕk.

Lübke . . . . lüb'-kŭ.

Lublin . . . . lōō'-blĭn.

Lucania . . . . lū-kā'-nĭ-ạ̇.

Lucaya . . . . lōō-kī'-ä.

Lucayos . . . . lōō-kī'-ōs.

Lucca, Bagni di . . . . bän'-yē dē lōōk'-ä.

Lucchese . . . . lŭk-ēz', lŭk-ēs'.

Lucerne . . . . lū-sĕrn'. *Fr.* lü-sârn'.

Lucia di Lammermoor . . lōō-chē'-ä dē läm-mĕr-

Lucian . . . . lū'-shĭ-ăn. [mōōr'.

Luciana . . . . lōō-shĭ-ä'-nä.

Lucina . . . . lū-sī'-nä.

Lucinda . . . . lū-sĭn'-dȧ.

Lucinde . . . . lü-säṅd'.

Luckimpur, *see* Lakhimpur lŭk-ĭm-pōōr'.

Lucknow, *see* Lakhnau . . lŭk'-now. *pop.* lŭk-nō.

Luçon, *see* Luzon . . . . lōō-zōn'. *Sp.* lōō-thōn'.

Lucrece . . . . lū'-krēs, lū-krēs'.

Lucretius . . . . lū-krē'-shĭ-ŭs.

Lucrezia Borgia . . . . lōō-kräd'-zē-ä bŏr'-jä.

Lucullus . . . . lū-kŭl'-ŭs.

Ludhiana	lōō-dē-ä'-nä.
Ludovisi Ares	lōō-dō-vē'-zē ä'-rēz.
Ludwig	lōōd'-vĭċh.
Lugano	lōō-gä'-nō.
Lugo	lōō'-gō.
Luigi	lōō-ē'-jē.
Luini	lōō-ē'-nē.
Luis	lōō-ēs'.
Luitpold	lōō'-ĭt-pōlt.
Luitprand, see Liutprand .	lōō-ĭt'-pränd.
Luiz	Port. lōō-ēth'.
Lulli	lŏŏl'-lē.
Lullitpur, see Lalitpur . .	lŭl-lĭt-pōōr'.
Lüneburg	lü'-nĕ-bōōrċh.
Lunéville	lü-nä-vēl'.
Lupercal	lū'-pĕr-kăl, lū-pĕr'-kăl.
Lupercalia	lū-pĕr-kä'-lĭ-à.
Luria	lōō'-rē-ä.
Luristan	lōō-rĭs-tän'.
Lurlei, see Lorelei . . .	lōōr'-lī.
Lusiad	lū'-sĭ-ăd.
Lusignan	lü-zēn-yäṅ'.
Luther	lū'-thĕr. Ger. lōō'-tĕr.
Lützen	lüt'-zĕn.
Luxembourg	lüks-äṅ-bōōr'.
Luxemburg	{ lŭk'-sĕm-bĕrg. D. lük'-sĕm-bŭrċh.
Luxor	lŭks'-ôr, lŏŏks'-ôr.
Luynes, de	dŭ lü̱-ēn'.
Luzon, see Luçon . . .	lōō-zōn'. Sp. lōō-thōn'.
Lvoff	l-vŏf'.
Lycaon	lī-kā'-ŏn.
Lycaonia	lĭk-à-ō'-nĭ-à.
Lyceum	lī-sē'-ŭm.
Lycidas	lĭs'-ĭ-dàs.
Lydenburg	lī'-dĕn-bŭrċh.

Lyell	lī'-ĕl
Lyly (John)	lĭl'-ĭ.
Lymoges, *see* Limoges . .	lē-mōzh'.
Lyonesse	lī-ŏn-ĕs'.
Lyonnais	lē-ŏn-ā'.
Lyons	lī'-ŏnz. *Fr.* lē-ôn'.
Lys dans la Vallée, Le . .	lē lēs dän lä väl-ā'.
Lysias	lĭs'-ĭ-ăs.
Lysimachus	lī-sĭm'-à-kŭs.
Lysippus	lī-sĭp'-ŭs.
Lystra	lĭs'-trà.
Lytton	lĭt'-ŭn.

M

Maartens, Maarten . . .	mär'-tĕn mär'-tĕnz.
Maas, *see* Meuse	mäs.
Maastricht, *see* Maestricht, Mastricht	mäs'-trĭċht.
Mabillon	mä-bē-yôn'.
Mabinogion (The) . . .	măb-ĭ-nō'-gĭ-ŏn.
Mabuse, *see* Maubeuge . .	mä-büz'.
Macao	mä-kä'-ō, mä-kow'.
Macbeth	măk-bĕth'.
Maccabaeus	măk-à-bē'-ŭs.
Maccabean	măk-à-bē'-àn.
Maccabees	măk'-à-bēz.
Macchiavelli, *see* Machiavelli	{ măk''-ĭ-à-vĕl'-lĭ. *It.* mä''-kē-ä-vĕl'-lē.
Macedonia	mäs-ē-dō'-nĭ-à.
Maceo	mä-thā'-ō.
Macerata	mä-chā-rä'-tä.
Machiavel	măk'-ĭ-à-vĕl''.
Machiavelian	{ măk''-ĭ-à-vēl'-yán, măk''-ĭ-à-vē'-lĭ-án.

rălĕ'-ĭ-ā-rĕ'-lĭ
mă"-lĕ-ā-ĕ'-lĭ
ăk-pē'-lă
n̄ā-thē'-ĭs
măc-ĕ'-vôr
măk-ĭ', măk-ā', măk-ĭ
ĭ'-ăn, ĭ'-ăn mă-dā-rĕ
măk-ā'-zăn
mā-klĕs, măk-ĕ
măk-mă'-ŏn
Fr. măk-nā-ôn
Fr. mā-kŏn
mā-kŏn.
mā-krē'-dĭ, măk-rē'-dĭ
măk-tān'
mā-dăm' bō-vā-rē'
mā-dā'-ā-rĭ, mā-ē'-r
mā-dē'-rā   Por. mā-
măd-lĕn'   [păr
măd-mwā-zĕl' du mō-
lā grănd măd-mwā-zĕl'
mā-dŏn'-ā
It. mā-dŏn-nā
mā-drăs, măd-răs"
mĭl-drā'-thĕ

Maffei	mäf-fā'-ṝ
Maffla, *or* Mafia	mä-fē'-ä.
Magalhães, *see* Magellan .	*Port.* mä-gäl-yä'‿ĕṅs.
Magaliesberg	măg'-ă-lēs-bĕrċh.
Magallanes, *see* Magellan .	mä-gäl-yä'-nĕs.
Magdala	{ (*Abyssinia*) măg-dä'-lȧ. *Bib.* măg'-dȧ-lä.
Magdalen	{ măg'-dȧ-lĕn. Eng. col- lege, môd'-lĭn.
Magdalene	măg-dä-lē'-nĕ, măg'-dä-
Magdeburg	{ măg'-dĕ-bŭrg. [lĕn. *Ger.* mäċh'-dä-bōōrċh.
Magellan, *see* Magalhães,	} mȧ-jĕl'-ȧn.
Maghellanes	} *Sp.* mä-gĕl-yän'.
Magellanic	măj-ĕl-lăn'-ĭk. [dē'.
Magendie.	mȧ-jĕn'-dĭ. *Fr.* mä-zhŏṅ-
Magenta	mä-jĕn'-tä.
Magersfontein	mä''-ċhĕrs-fŏn'-tīn.
Maggiore	mäd-jō'-rĕ.
Maghellanes, *see* Magellan	mä-gĕl-lä'-näs.
Magi	mä'-jī.
Magian	mä'-jĭ-ȧn.
Magna Carta, *or* Magna	} măg'-nä kär'-tä.
Charta	} *pop.* ċhär'-tȧ.
Magnusson	mäg'-nōōs-sŏn.
Maguindanao, *see* Mindanao	mä-gēn''-dä-nä'-ō.
Magyar	môd'-yŏr, mä-jär'.
Mahabarata, *or* Mahabha-rata	} mä''-hä-bä'-rä-tä.
Mahableshwur	mä''-hä-blĕsh-wŭr'.
Mahalaleel	mȧ-hā'-lȧ-lē''-ĕl, mȧ-hăl'-
Mahan	mȧ-hăn'. ȧ-lē''-ĕl.
Maharajah	mä-hä-rä'-jä.
Mahdi, *see* El Mahdi · ·	mä'-dē.
Mahican, *see* Mohican . .	mä-hĭk'-ȧn.
Mahmud	mä-mōōd'.

Mahomet, *see* Mohammed . { mā-hŏm'-ĕt, mā'-hō-mĕt, mä'-hō-mĕt.

Mahon . . . . má-hōn'.

Mahony . . . . . . má-hō'-nĭ, mä'-hŏ-nĭ.

Mahopac . . . . . . mā'-ō-păk.

Mahound . . . . . . mă-hownd', mä'-hownd.

Mahrattas, *see* Marhattas . mă-răt'-äz, mä-rä'-táz.

Mahu . . . . mä'-hoō, má-hoō'.

Maia . . . . mā'-yá.

Mailand, *Ger.* for Milan . mī'-länt.

Maimansinh, *see* Mymensing mĭ-mán-sĭn'.

Maimonides . . . . . mĭ-mŏn'-ĭ-dēz.

Main (R.) . . . . . . mān. *Ger.* mīn.

Maindron . . . . . . mä̇n-drôǹ'.

Maine-et-Loire . . . . mān'-ā-lwär'.

Mainpuri, *see* Mynpuri . . mĭn-poō'-rē.

Maintenon, de . . . . . dŭ mäṅ-tŭ-nôǹ'.

Mainz, *see* Mayence . . . mĭnts.

Maison Vauquer . . . . mā-zôǹ' vō-kā',

Maistre, Xavier de . . . { zăv'-ĭ-êr. *Fr.* ksăv-ē-ā' dŭ mĕt'-r, mā'-tr.

Maisur, *see* Mysore . . . mĭ-soōr'.

Maiwand . . . . . . mī-wänd'.

Majano . . . . . . mä-yä'-nō.

Majorca, *see* Mallorca . . má-jôr'-kä.

Majuba . . . . . . mä-joō'-bä.

Makart . . . . . . mäk'-ärt, mä-kärt'.

Makua . . . . mä-koō'-ä.

Malabar . . . . . . mǎl-á-bär'.

Malacca . . . . . . má-lǎk'-ä.

Malaga . . . . . . mǎl'-á-gá. *Sp.* mä'-lä-gä.

Malate . . . . . . mä-lä'-tā.

Malay . . . . mā-lā'.

Malayan . . . . . . mā-lā'-án.

Malaysia . . . . . . { mā-lā'-shĭ-á, mā-lā'-zhĭ-á.

Malbrook, *or*	măl-brŏŏk'.
Mallbrough	măl-brŏŏk'.
Maldive	măl'-dīv.
Male-bolge	mä-lĕ-bōl'-jĕ.
Malebranche	mäl-bränsh'.
Malesherbes, de	dŭ mäl-zârb'.
Malet, Lucas	lū'-kȧs măl-ā'.
Malherbe	mäl-ârb'.
Malibon	mä-lē-bōn'.
Malibran	mä-lē-bräṅ'.
Malignants	mȧ-lĭg'-nȧnts.
Malines, *see* Mechlin . .	mä-lēn'.
Mallarmé, Stéphane . . .	stā-fän' mäl-är-mā'.
Mallorca, *see* Majorca . .	mäl-yŏr'-kä.
Mallory, *see* Malory . . .	măl'-lŏ-rĭ.
Malmaison	mäl-mä-zôṅ'.
Malmesbury	mämz'-bĕr-ĭ.
Malmö	mäl'-mĕ.
Malmsey	mäm'-zĭ.
Malolos	mä-lō'-lōs.
Malory, *see* Mallory . .	măl'-ŏ-rĭ.
Malot, Hector	ĕk-tōr' mä-lō'.
Malpighi	mäl-pē'-gē. [ȧn.
Malpighian	mäl-pē'-gĭ-ȧn, măl-pĭg'-ĭ-
Malplaquet	mäl-plä-kä'.
Malta, *or*	môl'-tȧ. *It.* mäl'-tä.
Malte, *Fr.*	mält-'ŭ.
Maltese	môl-tēz', môl-tēs'.
Malthus	măl'-thŭs.
Malthusianism	{ măl-thū'-sĭ-ăn-ĭzm", *or* {măl-thū'-zhăn-ĭzm.
Malvern (Ark.)	măl'-vĕrn.
Malvern (Eng.)	mô'-vĕrn.
Malvolio	măl-vō'-lĭ-ō.
Mambrino	măm-brē'-nō.
Mambrinus	măm-brī'-nŭs.

Mambulao	mäm-bōō-lä′-ō.
Mamelukes	măm′-ĕ-lūks. [tēn.
Mamertine	măm′-ĕr-tīn, măm′-ĕr-
Mamertines, or	măm-ēr-tīnz.
Mamertini	măm-ĕr-tī′-nĭ.
Mamiani della Rovere . .	mä-mē-ä′-nē dĕl′-lä rō′-
Mamre	măm′-rē. [vä-rä.
Manbhoom, Manbhum . .	män′-bhōōm.
Mancha, La	lä män′-chä.
Manchester	măn′-chĕs-tēr.
Manchoos, see Manchus .	măn-chōōz′.
Manchuria, see Mantchuria	măn-chōō′-rĭ-à.
Manchus, see Manchoos .	măn-chōōz′.
Mancinelli	män-chē-nĕl′-lē.
Mancini	män-chē′-nē.
Mandalay, or	măn′-dà-lä.
Mandelay	măn′-dĕ-lä.
Manet	mä-nä′.
Manetho	măn′-ĕ-thō.
Mangalore, or	măng-gà-lōr′.
Mangalur	măng-gà-lōōr′.
Manichæans, or Manicheans	măn-ĭ-kē′-ànz.
Manichee	măn′-ĭ-kē.
Manila, Manilla	mà-nĭl′-à. Sp. mä-nē′-lä.
Manin	mä-nēn′.
Manipur, see Mannipur .	măn-ĭ-pōōr′.
Manito, see Manitou . . .	măn′-ĭ-tō. [bà.
Manitoba	măn-ĭ-tō-bä′, măn-ĭ-tō′-
Manitou, see Manito . . .	măn′-ĭ-tōō.
Mannheim	män′-hīm.
Mannipur, see Manipur .	măn-ĭ-pōōr′.
Manoah	mà-nō′-ä.
Manon Lescaut	mä-nôṅ′ lĕs-kō′.
Mans, Le	lẽ män.
Mansard, or Mansart . .	{ män-sär′.
	{ Anglicized, măn′-särd.

Mansfeld	mäns'-fĕlt.
Mansour, *or* Mansur, Al .	al män-sōōr'.
Mantalini	măn-tà-lē'-nē.
Mantchuria, *see* Manchuria	măn-chōō'-rĭ-à.
Mantegna	măn-tān'-yä.
Mantelli	măn-tĕl'-lē.
Manteuffel	män'-toif-fĕl.
Mantinea, *or* . . .	măn-tĭ-nē'-à.
Mantineia	măn-tĭ-nī'-ä.
Mantova, *or*	*It.* män'-tŏ-vä.
Mantua	măn'-tū-à.
Mantuan	măn'-tū-àn.
Manutius	mă-nū'-shĭ-ŭs.
Manzanares	män-thä-nä'-rĕs.
Manzanilla	män-thä-nēl'-yä.
Manzanillo	män-thä-nēl'-yō.
Manzoni	män-dzō'-nē.
Maori	mä'-ō-rĭ, mow'-rĭ.
Maoris	mä'-ō-rĭz, mow'-rĭz.
Map (Walter), *or* . . .	măp.
Mapes (Walter)	māps.
Maracaibo, *or* Maracaybo .	mä-rä-kī'-bō.
Marah	mā'-rä.
Marais, Le	lĕ mä-rā'.
Marat	mä-rä'.
Marathon	măr'-à-thŏn.
Maratta, *or*	mä-rät'-tä.
Maratti	mä-rät'-tē.
Marceau	mär-sō'.
Marchesa	mär-kä'-zä.
Marchese	mär-kä'-zĕ.
Marchesi	mär-kä'-zē.
Marcke, von	fŏn mär'-kŭ.
Marcus Aurelius Antoninus {	mär'-kŭs ô-rē'-lĭ-ŭs ăn-tō-nī'-nŭs.
Mardi Gras	mär'-dē grä'.

Marengo	mä-rĕng'-gō [tĬs
Mareotis	mä-rĕ-ō'-tĬs, mä-rĕ-ō'-
Mareuil, Villebois- . . .	vēl-bwä'-mä-rĕ'-yŭ.
Margarethe	mär-gä-rä'-tŭ.
Margot, La Reine	lä rĕn mär-gō'.
Margrave	mär'-grāv.
Margravine	mär'-grä-vēn.
Marguérite	mär-gä-rēt'.
Marhattas, see Mahrattas .	mä-rä'-tȧz, mȧ-răt'-äz.
Maria de' Medici, see Marie de Médicis . . . . . }	mä-rĕ'-ä dä mä'-dĕ-chē.
Maria Feodorovna . . .	mä-rĕ'-ä fä-ō-dōr'-ŏv-nä.
Maria-Hérédia, José de . .	ċhō-sä' dä mä-rĕ'-ä ā-rā-
Mariamne	mä-rĬ-ăm'-nē. [dĕ-ä'.
Marian (Maid)	mȧr'-Ĭ-ȧn.
Mariana (Is.)	mä-rĕ-ä'-nä.
Mariana (Mason's) . . .	mä-rĬ-ā'-nȧ.
Mariana (Shak.)	mä-rĬ-ăn'-ȧ, mȧ-rĕ-ä'-nä.
Marianao	mä''-rē-ä-nä'-ō.
Marianne, La	lä mär-ē-än'.
Maria Theresa	{ mä-rĬ'-ȧ tē-rĕ'-sȧ. Ger. mä-rĕ'-ä tä-rā'-zä.
Mariazell	mä-rĕ''-ä-tsĕl'.
Marie Amélie	mä-rĕ' ä-mä-lē'.
Marie Antoinette	{ mȧr'-Ĭ ăn-toi-nĕt'. Fr. mä-rē' äṅ-twä-nĕt'.
Marie de Médicis, see Maria de' Medici . . . . . . }	mä-rē' dŭ mä-dē-sēs'.
Marie Galante	mä-rē' gä-länt'.
Marienburg	mä'-rĕ-ĕn-bŏŏrċh''.
Marignano, see Melegnano	mä-rēn-yä'-nō.
Marilhat	mär-ē-lä'. [rĕ'-nä.
Marina	Shak. mȧ-rĬ'-nȧ. Sp. mä-
Marinduque	mä-rēn-dŏŏ'-kä.
Marini, or	mä-rē'-nē.
Marino	mä-rē'-nō.

11

Marino Faliero	mä-rē'-nō fä-lē̞-ā'-rō.
Mario	mä'-rē-ō.
Mariolatry	mår'-ĭ-ŏl'-á-trĭ.
Marion Delorme . . .	mä-rē-ôṅ' dŭ-lôrm'.
Mariotte	mä-rē-ŏt'.
Maris	mär'-ēs.
Maritzburg	mär'-ĭts-bōōrċh.
Marius	mā'-rĭ-ŭs.
Marivaux	mä-rē-vō'.
Mariveles . . . : .	mä-rē-vā'-lĕs.
Marjoribanks	märsh'-bănks.
Markgraf	märk'-gräf.
Marlboro, or Marlborough	{ *Am.* märl'-bŭr-ō, môl'-brō.
Marlborough (Duke) . .	môl'-brō, môl'-bŭr-ŭ.
Mármaros-Sziget . . .	mär'-mŏ-rŏsh-sĭg'-ĕt.
Marmont	mär-môṅ'.
Marmontel	mär-môṅ-tĕl'.
Marmora (Sea)	mär'-mō-rá.
Marne	märn.
Marni	mär-nē'.
Marochetti	mä-rō-kĕt'-tē.
Maronite	mär'-ō-nīt.
Marot, Clément . . .	klä-mŏṅ' mä-rō'.
Marquesas (Is.)	mär-kā'-säs.
Marquis	{ mär'-kwĭs. *orig.* mär'-kĭs. *Fr.* mär-kē'.
Marquise	mär-kēz'.
Marryat	mär'-ĭ-ăt. [mär-sā-yāz'.
Marseillaise, La . . .	lä mär-sĕl-āz'. *Fr.* lä
Marseille, *Fr. or* . . .	mär-sā'-yŭ.
Marseilles	mär-sālz'.
Marshalsea	mar'-shăl-sē.
Mars-la-Tour	märs-lä-tōōr'.
Marsyas	mär'-sĭ-ás.
Martel de Janville . . .	mär-tĕl' dŭ zhŏṅ-vĕl'.

Martin, Henri	ôṅ-rē' mär-tăṅ'.
Martineau	mär'-tĭ-nō.
Martinez Campos . . .	mär-tē'-nĕth käm'-pōs.
Martini-Henry	mär-tē'-nē-hĕn'-rĭ.
Martini, Simone	sē-mō'-nä mär-tē'-nē.
Martinique	mär-tĭ-nēk'.
Martinist	mär'-tĭn-ĭst.
Martius	mär'-shĭ-ŭs.
Marullus	mä-rŭl'-ŭs.
Marylebone	mā'-rĭ-lĕ-bōn'', mär'-lĕ-bŭn, mär'-ĭ-bŭn.
Masaccio	mä-zät'-chō.
Masaniello	mä-zä-nē-ĕl'-lō.
Masbate	mäs-bä'-tä.
Mascagni	mäs-kän'-yē.
Mascarene	mäs-kȧ-rēn'.
Mascarille	mäs-kä-rēl'.
Mashonaland	mä-shō'-nä-lănd, mä-shō'-nä-länd.
Maskelyne	mäs'-kĕ-lĭn, mäs'-kĕ-līn.
Masolino da Panicale . .	mä-zō-lē'-nō dä pä-nē-kä'-lĕ.
Massada	mäs-sä'-dä.
Massasoit	mäs'-ȧ-soit.
Masséna	mä-sä'-nä. Fr. mä-sā-nä'.
Massenet	mäs-nā'.
Massillon	U. S. mäs'-ĭl-ŏn. Fr. mä-sē-yôṅ'.
Massimo	mäs'-ē-mō.
Massinger	mäs'-ĭn-jĕr.
Masso	mäs'-sō.
Massuccio, see Masuccio .	mä-sŏŏt'-chō.
Massys, see Matsys and Metsys	mäs-sīs'.
Mastricht, see Maastricht and Maestricht	mäs'-trĭċht.

Masuccio di Salerno, *see* { mä n̈ŏŏt' ohō dō nä lŏr'
Massuccio . . . . . { nō.

Mataafa . . . . má-tä'-fá.

Matabele, *see* Matabeli *and* } mä-tä-bā'-lĕ.
Matebeli . . . . . }

Matabeleland . . . . . mä-tä-bā'-lĕ-länd.

Matabeli, *see* Matabele *and* } mä-tä-bā'-lē.
Matebele . . . . . . }

Matanzas . . . . { mă-tăn'-zás.
{ *Sp.* mä-tän'-thäs.

Matapan (Cape) . . . . mä-tä-pän'. *pop.* măt-á-

Matebele, *see* Matabele . . mä-tĕ-bā'-lĕ. [păn'.

Mater Dolorosa . . . { mā'-tĕr dŏl-ō-rō'-sä, mä'‑
{ tĕr dō-lō-rō'-zä.

Materna . . . . má-tĕr'-nä. *Ger.* mä-tĕr'-

Mather (Cotton) . . . . măth'-ĕr. [nä.

Mathieu . . . . mä-tē̱-ē̱'.

Mathilde . . . . mä-tēld'.

Matsys, Quentin, *see* Massys } kwĕn'-tĭn mät-sīs'.
and Metsys . . . . . }

Mattei, Tito . . . . . . tē'-tō mät-tā'-ē. [äs.

Matthias . . . . má-thī'-ás. *Ger.* mät-tē'-

Matthias Corvinus . . . má-thī'-ás kôr-vī'-nŭs.

Maturin . . . . măt'-ū-rĭn.

Maubeuge, *see* Mabuse . . mō-bĕzh'.

Mauch Chunk . . . . . môk chŭngk'.

Maui (I.) . . . . mow'-ē.

Mauna Kea . . . . . . mow'-nä kā'-ä.

Mauna Loa . . . . . . mow'-nä lō'-ä.

Maupassant . . . . . . mō-pä-säṅ'.

Maupertuis . . . . . . mō-pâr-twē'. [păṅ'.

Maupin, Mlle. de . . . . mäd-mwä-zĕl' dŭ mō-

Mauprat . . . . mō-prä'.

Maurel . . . . mō-rĕl'.

Maurepas . . . . mō-r̆ĕ-pä'.

Maurice . . . . *Fr.* mō-rēs'.

Mauritius . . . . mô-rĭsh'-ĭ-ŭs.

Maurocordatos, *see* Mavro- } mäv''-rō-kŏr-dä'-tŏs.
cordatos . . . . . }

Mauser . . . . mow'-zĕr.

Mausolus . . . . mô-sō'-lŭs.

Mauve . . . . mōv.

Mavrocordatos, *see* Mauro- } mäv''-rō-kŏr-dä'-tŏs.
cordatos . . . . . }

Maximilian . . . . . . { mäks-ĭ-mĭl'-yán.
{ *Ger.* mäks-ē-mē'-lē-än.

Maximin . . . . mäks'-ĭ-mĭn.

Maya . . . . mä'-yä, mī'-ä.

Mayaguez . . . . . . mī-ä-gwĕth'.

Maybun . . . . mä̤-ē-bōōn'.

Mayence, *see* Mainz . . . *Fr.* mä-yŏns'.

Mayenne . . . . mī-ĕn', mä-yĕn'.

Mayer . . . . mä'-ĕr. *Ger.* mī'-ĕr.

Maysi . . . . mä-ē'-sē.

Maytsouye . . . . . . māt-sōō'-yĕ.

Mazanderan . . . . . . mä''-zán-dĕ-rän'.

Mazarin . . . . { mäz'-á-rĭn, mäz-ăr-ēn'.
{ *Fr.* mä-zä-räṅ'.

Mazarini . . . . mäd-zär-ē'-nē.

Mazzini . . . . mät-sē'-nē.

Mazzuola . . . . mät-zōō-ō'-lä.

Meagher . . . .' . mä'-ċhĕr, mä'-'hĕr.

Meaux . . . . mō.

Mechlin, *see* Malines . . . mĕk'-lĭn. *D.* mĕċh'-lĭn.

Mechoacan, *see* Michoacan ma-chō''-ä-kän'.

Mecklenburg-Schwerin . . { mĕk-lĕn-bōōrċh-shvä-
{ rēn'.

Mecklenburg-Strelitz . . mĕk'-lĕn-bōōrċh-strä'-

Medea . . . . mē-dē'-ä. [lĭts.

Médée . . . . mā-dā'.

Medici, de' . . . . . . dā mä'-dē-chē.

Médicis, de . . . . . . dŭ mä-dē-sēs'.

Medina	{ *Sp.* mā-dē'-nä. { *U. S.* mē-dĭ'-nȧ.
Medina-Celi	mā-dē'-nä-thā'-lē.
Medina-Sidonia	mā-dē'-nä-sē-dō'-nē-ä.
Medjidi	mĕ-jēd'-ē.
Médoc	mā-dŏk'.
Medusa	mĕ-dū'-sä.
Meerkatsfontein	mâr'-kăts-fŏn'-tīn.
Meerut, *see* Mirat	mē'-rŭt.
Mefistofele	mā-fēs-tō'-fā-lā.
Megæra	mĕ-gē'-rȧ.
Megara	mĕg'-ȧ-rä.
Megiddo	mĕ-gĭd'-ō.
Mehemet Ali, *see* Moham- med Ali	mā'-hĕ-mĕt ä'-lē.
Méhul	mā-ül'.
Meilhac	mā-yäk'.
Meissen	mī'-sĕn.
Meissonier	mā-sō-nē̱-ā'.
Meistersinger von Nürnberg, Die	dē mīs'-tĕr-zĭng"-ĕr fŏn nürn'-bĕrċh.
Mekhong, *or* Mekong . .	mā-kŏng'.
Melanchthon, *or*	{ mē-lăngk'-thŏn. { *Ger.* mā-längċh'-tōn.
Melanthon	mĕ-lăn'-thŏn.
Melba	mĕl'-bä.
Melchisedec, *or* Melchizedek	mĕl-kĭz'-ĕ-dĕk.
Meleager	{ mĕl-ē-ā'-jĕr, mē-lē-ā'-jĕr, { mē-lē'-ā-jĕr.
Melegnano, *see* Marignano	mā-lān-yä'-nō.
Meliboeus	mĕl-ĭ-bē'-ŭs.
Méline	mā-lēn'.
Melita	mĕl'-ĭt-ȧ.
Mello (José de)	mā'-lōō.
Melozzo da Forlì	mā-lŏt'-zō dä fŏr-lē'.
Melpomene	mĕl-pŏm'-ĕ-nē.

Melton Mowbray	mĕl'-tŭn mō'-brā, mō'-
Melusina	mĕl-ōō-sī'-nä. [brĕ.
Mélusine, *Fr.*	mā-lü-zēn'.
Memling	mĕm'-lĭng.
Menabrea.	mā-nä-brä'-ä.
Menahem.	mĕn'-á-hĕm. [mĕn'-ĕ.
Menai	mĕn'-ī. *pop.* mĕn'-ā *or*
Mencayan	mān-kä-yän'.
Menchikoff, *see* Menshikoff	mĕn'-shē-kŏf.
Mencius	mĕn'-shĭ-ŭs.
Mendelssohn-Bartholdy .	mĕn'-dĕl-sōn-bär-tōl'-dē.
Mendès, Catulle	kä-tül' mŏn-däs'.
Mendocino	mĕn-dō-sē'-nō.
Mendoza	mĕn-dō'-thä.
Menelaus	mĕn-ĕ-lā'-ŭs. [läs.
Menendez de Aviles . . .	mā-nän'-däth dā ä-bē'-
Ménippée, Satire	sä-tēr' mā-nē-pā'.
Menorca, *Sp. for* Minorca .	mā-nōr'-kä.
Menshikoff, *see* Menchikoff	mĕn'-shē-kŏf.
Menton, *or*	mŏn-tôn'.
Mentone	mĕn-tō'-nĕ.
Menzel	mĕnt'-zĕl.
Mephibosheth	{ mĕ-fĭb'-ō-shĕth. { *Heb.* mĕf-ĭ-bō'-shĕth.
Mephistophelean	mĕf''-ĭs-tō-fē'-lē-án.
Mephistopheles	mĕf-ĭs-tŏf'-ĕ-lēz.
Mercator	{ mĕr-kā'-tēr. { *D.* mĕr-kä'-tŏr.
Mercedes	mĕr-thā'-dĕs.
Mercia	mĕr'-shĭ-á.
Mercier	mār-sē-ā'.
Mercurius	mĕr-kū'-rĭ-ŭs.
Mercutio	mĕr-kū'-shĭ-ō.
Mergui	mĕr-gē'.
Mérimée	mā-rē-mā'.
Merle (Maj.)	mĕrl.

Merle d'Aubigné	mĕrl dō-bēn-yā'.
Merodach	mer'-ō-dak.
Meroë	mĕr'-ō-ē.
Merom	mē'-rŏm.
Merope	mĕr'-ō-pē.
Merovingians	mĕr-ō-vĭn'-jĭ-ánz.
Merowig, see Merwig . .	mĕr'-ō-wĭg.
Merrilies	mĕr'-ĭ-lēz.
Mersey	mĕr'-zĭ.
Merwig, see Merowig . .	mĕr'-wĭg.
Méry	mā-rē'.
Mesa, or	mē'-zä.
Mesha	mē'-shä.
Meshach	mē'-shăk.
Mesmer	mĕs'-mĕr.
Mesolonghi, see Missolonghi	mā-sō-lŏng'-gē.
Mesolongion, mod. Gr. . .	mā-zō-lŏng'-gē-ŏn.
Messalina, or Messallina .	mĕs-ă-lī'-nä.
Messianic	mĕs-sĭ-ăn'-ĭk.
Messidor	mĕs-ē-dōr'. [nä.
Messina, Antonello da . .	än-tō-nĕl'-lō dä mĕs-sē'-
Mesurado (Cape)	mā-sōō-rä'-dō.
Metastasio	mā-täs-tä'-zē-ō.
Methuen (Gen.)	mĕth'-ŭ-ĕn.
Methuen (U. S.)	mĕ-thū'-ĕn.
Methuselah	mĕ-thū'-sĕ-lä.
Metsu, see Metzu	mĕt'-sü.
Metsys, see Massys and Matsys . . . . . . }	mĕt-sīs'.
Metternich-Winneburg . .	mĕt-tĕr-nĭċh-vĭn'-nĕ-bōōrċh.
Metzu, see Metsu	mĕt'-zü.
Meung, Jean de	zhäṅ dü mŭṅ.
Meurthe-et-Moselle . . .	mĕrt'-ā-mō-zĕl'.
Meuse, see D. Maas . . .	mūz. Fr. mēz.
Meyerbeer	mī'-ĕr-bār.

Meynell . . . . mā'-nĕl.

Meyrick . . . . mī'-rĭk.

Mézières . . . . mā-zē-âr'.

Mezzofanti . . . . . . mĕt-zō-fän'-tē.

Miako . . . . mē-ä'-kō.

Miami . . . . mĭ-äm'-ē, mī-äm'-Ĭ.

Miantonomoh . . . . mĭ-ăn''-tō-nō'-mō.

Micawber . . . . . . mĭ-kô'-bĕr.

Michael . . . . . mī'-kĕl, mī'-kā-ēl.

Michael Angelo . . . . mī'-kā-ĕl ăn'-jē-lō.

Michael Nicolaevitch (Grand Duke) . . . . } mī'-kĕl nē-kō-lā'-ĕ-vĭch.

Michaelmas . . . . . . mĭk'-ĕl-más.

Michal . . . . mī'-kăl.

Michel . . . . *Fr.* mé-shĕl'.

Michelagnolo, *or* . . . mē-kĕl-än'-yō-lō.

Michelangelo . . . . ∘ { mī-kĕl-än'-jĕ-lō. *It.* mē-kĕl-än'-jä-lō.

Michelet . . . . mēsh-lā', mē-shĕ̥-lā'.

Michelis . . . . mē-ċhā'-lĭs.   [lŏt'-zē.

Michelozzo Michelozzi . . mē-kĕ-lŏt'-zō   mē-kĕ-

Michoacan, *see* Mechoacan   mē-chō-ä-kän'.

Mickiewicz . . . . . . mĭts-kē-ĕv'-Ĭch.

Micronesia . . . . . . mĭ-krō-nē'-shĭ-à.

Micronesian . . . . . { mĭ-krō-nē'-shĭ-an, mĭk-rō-nē'-shĭ-an.

Midas . . . . mī'-dăs.

Midgard . . . . mĭd'-gärd.

Midianites . . . . . . mĭd'-Ĭ-ăn-īts''.

Midnapur. . . . . . . mĭd-ná-pōōr'.

Mierevelt. . . . . . . mē'-rĕ-vĕlt.

Mieris . . . . mē'-rĭs.

Mieroslawski . . . . mē-ā-rō-släv'-skĕ.

Mignet . . . . mēn-yā'.

Mignon . . . . mēn-yôn'.

Miguel . . . . mē-gĕl'.

Mikado	mǐ-kä'-dō.
Milan (City)	mǐl'-ăn, mǐ-lăn'.
Milan (King of Servia) . .	mǐl'-än.
Milanese	mǐl-ăn-ēz', *or* ēs'.
Milano, *see* Milan . . .	mē-lä'-nō. [zhán.
Milesian (Irish)	mǐ-lē'-shǐ-ạn, mǐ-lē'-
Millais	mǐl-lā'.
Millet	{ *Eng.* mǐl'-lĕt. *Fr.* mē-yā'. { *pop.* mē-lā'.
Millevoye	mēl-vwä'.
Millot	mē-yō'.
Milne-Edwards	{ mǐln-ĕd'-wȧrdz. { *Fr.* mēl-nä-dōō-är', *or* { mēl-nä-dōō-ärs'.
Milnes	mǐlnz.
Miloradovitch	mē-lō-rä'-dō-vǐch.
Miltiades	mǐl-tǐ'-ȧ-dēz.
Mimir	mē'-mǐr.
Mincio	mǐn'-chō.
Mindanao, *see* Maguinda- nao	{ mǐn-dä-nä'-ō. { *Sp.* mēn-dä-nä'-ō.
Mindoro	{ mǐn-dō'-rō. { *Sp.* mēn-dō'-rō.
Minerva	mǐn-ẽr'-vȧ.
Ming	mēng.
Minho, *Port., see* Miño .	mēn'-yōō.
Minié	mǐn'-ĕ. *Fr.* mē-nē-ā'.
Minna von Barnhelm . .	mǐn'-ä fŏn bärn'-hĕlm.
Minnewit, *see* Minnuit .	mǐn'-ĕ-wǐt.
Miño, *Sp., see* Minho . .	mēn'-yō.
Mino da Fiesole	mē'-nō-dä fē-ā'-zō-lä.
Minorca, *see* Menorca . .	mǐ-nôr'-kä.
Minos	mī'-nŏs.
Minotaur	mǐn'-ō-tôr.
Minnuit, *see* Minnewit . .	mǐn'-ū-ǐt.
Mirabeau	mǐr'-ȧ-bō. *Fr.* mē-rä-bō'.

Miragoane	{ mĭ-rȧ-gōn' { *Fr.* mē-rä-gwän'.
Miramon	mē-rä-mōn'.
Miranao, La	lä mē-rä-nä'-ō.
Miranda	{ *Shak.* mĭ-răn'-dȧ. { *Sp.* mē-rän'-dä. [dō-lä.
Mirandola, Pico della . .	pē'-kō dĕl'-lä mē-rän'-
Mirat, *or*	mē'-rȧt.
Mirath, *see* Meerut . . .	mē'-räth.
Mirbeau, Octave	ŏk-täv' mēr-bō'.
Mirbel	mēr-bĕl'.
Mirebalais	mē-rĕ-bä-lā'.
Mirecourt	mēr-kōōr'.
Mirouët, Ursule . . .	ür-sül' mē-rōō-ā'.
Mirs (Bay)	mērs.
Mirzapur	mēr-zä-pōōr'.
Mirza-Schaffy	mēr'-zä-shäf-fē'.
Misanthrope, Le	lĕ mē-zäṅ-trōp'.
Mise of Amiens	{ mīz ŏv ăm'-ĭ-ĕns. { *Fr.* äm-ē-äṅ'.
Misérables, Les	lä mē-zā-rä'-bl.
Misericordia	mē"-zä-rē-kōr'-dē-ä.
Missolonghi, *see* Mesolonghi, *mod. Gr.* Mesolongion .	mĭs-sō-lŏng'-gē.
Missouri	{ mĭs-sōō'-rĭ, mĭ-zōō'-rĭ. { *pop.* mĭz-ōō'-rȧ.
Misterosa	mēs-tā-rō'-sȧ.
Mistral	mēs-träl'.
Mithradates, *see* Mithridates	mĭth-rȧ-dā'-tēz.
Mithridate	*Fr.* mēt-rē-dät'.
Mithridates, *see* Mithradates	mĭth-rĭ-dā'-tēz.
Mithridatic	mĭth-rĭ-dăt'-ĭk.
Mitylene, *see* Mytilene . .	mĭt-ĭ-lē'-nē.
Mivart	mĭv'-ärt.
Mizraim	mĭz-rā'-ĭm, mĭz'-rā-ĭm.
Mnemosyne	nē-mŏs'-ĭn-ē.

Moa , . , ...	mō'-ä.
Moab	mō'-ăb.
Mobangi	mō-bäng'-gē.
Mobile	mō-bēl'.
Mocenigo	mō-chā-nē'-gō.
Mocha	mō'-kä. *Arab.* mō'ŗchä.
Modder	mŏd'-ĕr.
Modder's Spruit . . .	mŏd'-ĕrs sproit.
Modena	mō'-dĕ-nä. *It.* mō-dā'-nä.
Modeste Mignon	mō-dĕst' mēn-yôṅ'.
Modjeska	mŏd-jĕs'-kȧ.
Modred, *see* Mordred . .	mō'-dred, mŏd'-rĕd.
Moeris (L.)	mē'-rĭs.
Mogilef, *see* Mohileff . .	mō-gē-lĕf'.
Moguls, *see* Mughals . .	mō-gŭlz'.
Mohács	mō-häch'.
Mohammed, *see* Mahomet .	mō-hăm'-ĕd.
Mohammed Ali, *see* Mehemet Ali . . . . . }	mō-hăm'-ĕd ä'-lē.
Mohican, *see* Mahican . .	mŏ-hĭk'-án.
Mohileff, *see* Mogilef . .	mō-ċhē-lĕf'.
Mohun	mō'-hŭn.
Moivre	mwävr.
Mojave	mō-'hä'-vā.
Moldau	mŏl'-dow.
Molech, *see* Moloch . . .	mō'-lĕk.
Molenbeek-Saint-Jean . .	mō-lŏṅ-bāk'-sȧṅ-zhäṅ'.
Molière	mō-lē̱-ȧr'.
Molina	mō-lē'-nä.
Molinists	mō'-lĭ-nĭsts.
Molinos	mō-lē'-nōs.
Mollwitz, *see* Molwitz . .	mŏl'-vĭts.
Moloch, *see* Molech . . .	mō'-lŏk.
Molokai	mō-lō-kī'.
Moltke, von	{ fŏn mŏlt'-kĕ. *Ger.* mōlt'-kŭ.

Moluccas . . . . mō-lŭk'-ăz.
Molwitz, see Mollwitz . . mŏl-vĭts.
Mombas, or . . . . . . mŏm-bäs'.
Mombasa, or . . . . . mŏm-bä'-sä.
Mombaz . . . . mŏm-bäs'.
Mombuttu, see Monbuttu . mŏm-bōōt'-tōō.
Mommsen . . . . . . mŏm'-zĕn.
Momus . . . . mō'-mŭs.
Monaco . . . . mŏn'-ä-kō.
Mona Lisa . . . . . . mō'-nä lē'-zä.
Monarque, Le Grand . . . lĕ grän mō-närk'.
Monbuttu, see Mombuttu . mŏn-bōōt'-tōō.
Moncey . . . . mŏṅ-sä'.
Monet . . . . mō-nā'.
Monge . . . . mŏṅzh.
Monghir, or Monghyr, see ⎫
  Mungir . . . . ⎬ mŏn-gēr'.
Monmouth . . . . . . mŏn'-mŭth, mŭn'-mŭth.
Monreale . . . . mŏn-rā-ä'-lĕ.
Mons . . . . mŏṅs.
Monseigneur . . . . . mŏṅ-sān-yĕr'.
Mons-en-Pévèle . . . . mŏṅs'-ŏṅ-pā-vāl'.
Monserrat, see Montserrat mŏn-sĕr-rät'.
Monsieur . . . . mŏ̆-sē̠-ē̠'.
Monson . . . . mŭn'-sŭn.
Montagu, or Montague . . mŏnt'-à-gū.
Montaigne . . . . . . ⎰ mŏn-tän'.
                        ⎱ Fr. môṅ-tän'-yŭ.
Montalembert . . . . . môṅ-tä-lŏṅ-bâr'.
Montalvan . . . . . . mŏn-täl-bän'.
Montana . . . . mŏn-tä'-nä.
Montargis . . . . . . môṅt-är-zhē'.
Montauban . . . . . . môṅ-tō-bäṅ'.
Montauk (Point) . . . . mŏn-tôk'.
Mont Blanc, see Mount ⎫
  Blanc . . . . ⎬ Fr. môṅ bläṅ.

Montcalm Gozon de Saint-Véran	{ mŏnt-käm', Fr. môn-kälm' gō-zôn' dŭ săn-vā-rän'.
Mont Cenis	môn sĕ-nē'.
Montebello	mōn-tā-bĕl'-lō.
Monte Cristo	mŏn'-tĕ krĭs'-tō.
Montecucoli, or	mŏn-tĕ-kōō'-kō-lē.
Montecuculi	mŏn-tĕ-kōō'-kōō-lē.
Montefiore	mŏn-tĕ-fē̱-ō'-rĕ.
Montego (Bay)	mŏn-tē'-gō.
Montejo	mōn-tā'-ċhō.
Montenegro	{ pop. mŏn-tĕ-nē'-grō. It. mōn-tā-nā'-grō.
Montereau	môṅ̲-tĕ-rō'.
Monterey (Cal.)	mŏn-tĕ-rā'.
Monterey (Mexico)	mōn-tā-rā̲'-ē.
— Montero Rios	mōn-tā'-rō rē'-ōs.
Montes, Lola, see Montez	lō'-lä mōn'-tĕs.
Montespan	{ mŏn-tĕs-păn'. Fr. môn-tĕs-pän'.
Montesquieu	{ mŏn-tĕs-kū'. Fr. môn-tĕs-kē̱-ĕ'.
Monte Testaccio	mōn'-tĕ tĕs-tä'-chō.
Monteverde	{ It. mŏn-tĕ-vâr'-dĕ. Sp. mōn-tā-vĕr'-dā.
Montevideo	{ mŏn-tĕ-vĭd'-ē-ō. Sp. mŏn''-tā-vē-dā'-ō.
Montez, Lola, see Montes	lō'-lä mōn'-tĕs.
Montfleury	môn-flĕ-rē'.
Montfort	mŏnt'-fôrt. Fr. môn-fōr'.
Montgolfier	{ mŏnt-gŏl'-fĭ-ēr. Fr. môn-gōl-fē̱-ā'.
Montholon	môn-tō-lôn'.
Monti, Vincenzo	vēn-chĕnd'-zō mŏn'-tē.
Monticello	{ mŏn-tē-sĕl'-lō. It. mŏn-tē-chĕl'-lō.

Montijo . . . . *Sp.* mŏn-tē'-ċhō. [zhō'.

Montijo, Eugénie de . . . *Fr.* ē-zhā-nē' dŭ môṅ-tē.

Montijoie. . . . . . . môṅ-zhwä'.

Montluc . . . . môṅ-lük'.

Montmartre . . . . . . môṅ-mär'-tr.

Montmirail . . . . . . môṅ-mē-rä'-yŭ.

Montmorenci, *or* . . . . { mŏnt-mō-rĕn'-sē.

Montmorency . . . . . { *Fr.* môṅ-mō-rŏṅ-sē'.

Montojo . . . . mōnt-ō'-ċhō.

Montpelier . . . . . . mŏnt-pēl'-yĕr.

Montpellier . . . . . *Fr.* môṅ-pĕl-lē-ā'.

Montpensier . . . . . . môṅ-pŏṅ-sē-ā'.

Montreal . . . . { mŏn-trē-äl'.
{ *Fr.* môṅ-rä-äl'.

Montreuil-sous-Bois . . . môṅ-trē'-yŭ-sōō-bwä'.

Montserrat, *see* Monserrat   mŏnt-sĕr-rät', mŏnt-sĕ-

Montserrat (I.) . . . . mŏnt-sĕ-rät'. [rät'.

Monza . . . . mōn'-zä.

Moodkee, *see* Mudki . . . mōōd'-kē.

Mooi . . . . mō'-ē.

Mooltan, *see* Multan . . . mōōl-tän'.

Moore (Thomas) . . . . mōōr, mōr.

Moorshedabad, *see* Murshi- } mōōr''-shĕ-dä-bäd'.
dabad . . . . }

Moradabad, *see* Muradabad   mō''-räd-ä-bäd'.

Morales . . . . mō-rä'-lĕs.

Moran (Thomas) . . . . mō-răn'.

Moray . . . . mŭr'-ĭ, mŭr'-ā.

Mordecai . . . . môr'-dĕ-kī, môr'-dē-kā.

Mordred, *see* Modred . . môr'-drĕd.

Morea . . . . mō-rē'-ä.

Moreau . . . . mō-rō'.

Moren . . . . mō-rän'.

Morghen . . . . mŏr'-gĕn.

Morgue . . . . môrg. *Fr.* mōrg.

Moriah . . . . mō-rī'-ä.

Morillo	mō-rēl'-yṅ.
Moritz	mō'-rĭts.
Mornay, Duplessis . . .	dü-plä-sē' mōr-nä'.
Morny	mōr-nē'.
Moro (Castle), *see* Morro	mŏr'-rō. *Sp.* mōr'-rō.
Moroko	mō-rō'-kō.
Moron de la Frontera . .	mō-rōn' dä lä frōn-tä'-rä.
Morosini	mō-rō-zē'-nē.
Morpheus	môr'-fē-ŭs, môr'-fūs.
Morrisania	mŏr-rĭs-ā'-nĭ-à.
Morro (Castle), *see* Moro	mŏr'-rō. *Sp.* mōr'-rō.
Morte d'Arthur	môrt där-tür'.
Mortier	mōr-tē-ā'.
Moscheles	mōsh'-ĕ-lĕs.
Moscow	mŏs'-kō.
Mosel, *see* Moselle . . .	mō-zĕl'.
Moselle, *see* Mosel . . .	mō-zĕl'.
Mosenthal	mō'-zĕn-täl.
Mosheim	mōs'-hīm.
Moskva	mŏsk-vä'.
Moslem	mŏs'-lĕm.
Mosquitia, *or*	mōs-kē-tē'-ä.
Mosquito	mōs-kē'-tō.
Mossoul, Mosul, *see* Mousul	mō'-sŭl.
Moszkowski	mōs-kŏv'-skĭ.
Moukden, *see* Mukden . .	mōōk-dĕn'. [trĭ.
Moultrie	mōl'-trĭ, mōōl'-trĭ, mōō'-
Mounet Sully	mōō-nä' sü-lē'.
Mount Blanc, *see* Mont } Blanc . . . . . . }	mownt blăngk.
Mount Desert	mownt dĕ-zĕrt'.
Mousqueton	mōōsk-ŭ-tôṅ'.
Mousul, *see* Mossoul . . .	mōō'-sŭl.
Mouton	mōō-tôṅ'.
Mowbray	mō'-brā.
Mozambique	mō-zăm-bēk'.

Mozarab . . . . mōz-âr'-ăb, mō-zä'-răb.

Mozart . . . . mō'-zärt. *Ger.* mō'-tsärt.

Mozuffergurh, *see* Muzaffar- } mŭz-ŭf-ár-gōōr'.
garh . . . .

Mozuffernugger, *see* Muzaf- } mŏz-ŭf-ẽr-nŭg'-gẽr.
farnagar . . . . .

Mozufferpore, *see* Muzaffar- } mŏz-ŭf-ẽr-pōr'.
pur . . . .

Msta . . . . mstä.

Mtesa . . . . mtä'-sä.

Mudki, *see* Moodkee . . . mōōd'-kē.

Muette de Portici, La . . lä mü-ĕt' dŭ pōr'-tē-chē.

Mughals, *see* Moguls . . . mōō'-gálz.

Mühlbach . . . . . mül'-bäċh.

Mukden, *see* Moukden . . mōōk-dĕn'.

Müller (Max) . . . . . mül'-ẽr.

Multan, *see* Mooltan . . . mōōl-tän'.

Muncaczy, *see* Munkácsy . } mōōn-kä'-chē,   mōōn'-
kä-chē.

Münchausen, *see* Münch- } *Eng.* mŭn-chô'-zĕn.
hausen . . . . . . } *Ger.* münċh-how'-zĕn.

München, *see* Munich . . mün'-ċhĕn.

Münchhausen, *see* Mün- } *Eng.* mŭn-chô'-zĕn.
chausen . . . . . . } *Ger.* münċh-how'-zĕn.

Mungir, *see* Monghir . . . mŭn-gẽr'.

Munich, *see* München . . mū'-nĭk.   [kä-chē.

Munkácsy, *see* Muncaczy . mōōn-kä'-chē,   mōōn'-

Muñoz . . . . mōōn-yōth'.

Münster . . . . . . mün'-stĕr.

Murad . . . . mōō'-räd.

Muradabad, *see* Moradabad mōō''-räd-ä-bäd'.

Murano . . . . . . mōō-rä'-nō.

Murat . . . . mū-răt'. *Fr.* mü-rä'.

Muratori . . . . . . mōō-rä-tō'-rē.

Muravieff . . . . . . mōō-rä-vē-ĕf'.   [thē-ä.

Murcia . . . . mẽr'-shĭ-á. *Sp.* mōōr'-

Murfreesboro, *or* Murfrees-borough . . . . . . } mẽr'ₐfrēz₋bŭr"₋ō

Murger . . . . mür-zhâr'. [yō.

Murillo . . . . mū-rĭl'-ō. *Sp.* mōō-rēl'-

Muroy Salazar . . . . . mōō'-rō-ē sä-lä-thär'.

Murshidabad, *see* Moorshe-dabad . . . . . . } mōōr"-shĭ-dä-bäd'.

Musée des Thermes . . . mü-zā' dā-târm'.

Musée du Louvre . . . . mü-zā' dü lōōvr'.

Musée du Luxembourg . . mü-zā' dü lük-sŏṅ-bōōr'.

Muskingum . . . . . . mŭs-kĭng'-gŭm.

Musset . . . . müs-ā'.

Mussulman . . . . . . mŭs'-sŭl-mán.

Mustafa, *or* Mustapha . . mŏŏs'-tä-fä.

Mutra . . . . mŭt'-rä.

Mutsuhito . . . . . . mōōt'-sōōsh-tō.

Muzaffargarh, *see* Mozuffer-gurh . . . . } mŭz-ăf-ȧr-gär'.

Muzaffarnagar, *see* Mozuf-fernugger . . . . . } mŭz-ăf-ȧr-năg'-är.

Muzaffarpur, *see* Mozuffer-pore . . . . } mŭz-ăf-ȧr-pōōr'.

Muziano . . . . mōōd-zē-ä'-nō.

Mycale . . . . mĭk'-ä-lē.

Mycenæ . . . . mī-sē'-nē.

Mymensing, *see* Maimansinh mī-mĕn-sĭng'.

Mynpuri, *see* Mainpuri . . mĭn-pōō'-rē.

Myrmidons . . . . . . mẽr'-mĭ-dŏnz.

Myron . . . . mī'-rŏn.

Mysia . . . . mĭsh'-ĭ-ạ.

Mysore, *see* Maisur . . . mī-sōr'.

Mytilene, *see* Mitylene . . mĭt-ĭ-lē'-nē.

N

Naaman	nā'-à-màn.
Naauw Poort	nä'-üv-pōrt.
Nabonidus	năb-ō-nī'-dŭs.
Nadir Shah	nä'-dĕr shä.
Nadiya, see Nuddea . . .	nŭd'-ē-yä.
Nagasaki, see Nangasaki .	nä-gä-sä'-kē.
Nägeli	nä'-gĕ-lē.
Nagoya	nä-gō'-yä.
Nagpore, or	näg-pōr'.
Nagpur	näg-pōōr'.
Nahant	nà-hänt', nà-hănt'.
Naiad	nā'-yàd.
Nain	nā'-ĭn.
Nájara, or	nä'-ċhä-rä.
Nájera	nä'-ċhä-rä.
Namaqualand	nä-mä'-kwä-länd.
Namur	nā'-mōōr. *Fr.* nä-mür'.
Nana	nä-nä'.
Nana Sahib	nä'-nä sä'-hĭb.
Nan-chang	nän-chäng'.
Nancy (France) . . .	nän'-sĭ. *Fr.* näṅ-sē'.
Nangasaki, see Nagasaki .	nän-gä-sä'-kē.
Nanking	nän-kĭng'.
Nansen	nän'-sĕn.
Nantes	nănts. *Fr.* näṅt.
Naomi	nā-ō'-mī, nā'-ō-mī.
Naphtali	năf'-tà-lī, năf'-tä-lī.
Napier	nā'-pĭ-ĕr.
Napoleon	nà-pō'-lē-ŏn.
Napoléon	*Fr.* nä-pō-lä-ôṅ'.
Narbada, see Nerbudda .	när-bä'-dä.
Narciso Lopez	{ när-thē'-sō lō'-pĕs, *or* lō'-pĕth.

Narcissus . . . . när-sĭs'-ŭs.
Narvaez . . . . när-bä'-ĕth.
Naseby . . . . nāz'-bĭ.
Nasik, see Nassick . . . nä'-sĭk.
Nasmyth . . . . nā'-smĭth.
Nasr-ed-Din, see Nassr-ed-Din . . . . } näs'-r-ĕd-dēn'.
Nassau . . . . { năs'-ô.   Ger. näs'-sow. Fr. nä-sō'.
Nassau (Is.) . . . . . . năs'-ô.
Nassick, see Nasik . . . nä'-sĭk.
Nassr-ed-Din, see Nasr-ed-Din . . . . } näs'-r-ĕd-dēn'.
Natal . . . . ná-tăl'.   Port. nä-täl'.
Natalie, see Nathalie . . . năt'-á-lē.   Fr. nä-tä-lē'.
Natchitoches . . . . . { năk-ē-tŏsh', năch-ĭ-tŏch'-ĕs.
Nathalie, see Natalie . . . năth'-á-lē.
National Zeitung . . . . năt''-zē-ō-näl'tzī'-tŏŏng.
Naucydes . . . . nô-sĭ'-dēz.
Nauplia . . . . nô'-plĭ-á.
Nausicaa . . . . nô-sĭk'-ā-ä, nô-sĭ-kā'-ä.
Nautch . . . . nôch.
Navajo . . . . năv'-ă-ʰhō.
Navarete, see Navarrette . nä-vär-rā'-tā.
Navarino . . . . nä-vär-rē'-nō.
Navarra, Sp., or . . . nä-vär'-rä.
Navarre . . . . ná-vär'.   Fr. nä-vär'.
Navarrette, see Navarete . nä-vär-rā'-tā.
Navarro . . . . nä-vär'-rō.
Nazarene . . . . năz-á-rēn', năz'-á-rēn.
Nazarite . . . . năz'-á-rīt.
Naze . . . . Eng. nāz.   Norw. nä'-zĕ.
Nazianzen . . . . nä''-zĭ-än'-zĕn.
Nebuchadnezzar, or . . . nĕb''-ū-kăd-nĕz'-är.
Nebuchadrezzar . . . . nĕb''-ū-kăd-rĕz'-är.

Nebushazban	nĕb͵ū͵shăz′͵băn.
Neckar (R.)	nĕk′-kär.
Necker (Jacques)	nĕk′-ẽr. *Fr.* nā-kâr′.
Neerwinden	när′-vĭn-dĕn.
Négrier	nā-grē͵ā′. [tōs.
Negritos	nĕ-grē′-tŏs. *Sp.* nā-grē′-
Negropont	nĕg′-rō-pŏnt.
Negros (Philippine I.) . .	nā′-grōs.
Nekrasoff, *or* Nekrassoff .	nĕk-rä′-sŏf.
Nellore, *or*	nĕ-lōr′.
Nellur	nĕ-lōōr′.
Nemea (City)	nē′-mē-à, nĕ-mē′-à.
Nemea (Games)	{ nĕ - mē′ - à, nē′ - mē - à nĕm′-ē-à.
Nemean	nĕ-mē′-àn, nē′-mē-àn.
Nemesis	nĕm′-ĕ-sĭs.
Nemours	nē-mōōr′.
Neoptolemus	nē-ŏp-tŏl′-ē-mŭs.
Nepal, *or* Nepaul, *see* Nipal	nĕ-pôl′.
Nepissing, *see* Nipissing . .	nĕp′-ĭs-ĭng.
Nepomuk	nā′-pō-mōōk.
Nepos	nē′-pŏs.
Neptune	nĕp′-tūn.
Nerbudda, *or* Nerbuddah, *see* Narbada	} nẽr-bŭd′-dä.
Nereids	nē′-rē-ĭdz.
Nereus	nē′-rē-ŭs, nē′-rūs.
Nergalsharezer	nẽr″-gäl-shă-rē′-zẽr.
Neri	nā′-rē.
Nerissa	nē-rĭs′-sä.
Néron	nā-rôṅ′.
Neuchâtel	nē-shä-tĕl′.
Neuilly-sur-Seine	nē-yē″-sür-sĕn′.
Neumann	nū′-mȧn. *Ger.* noi′-män.
Neuss	nois.
Neuvillette, Christian de .	krĭs-tē͵äṅ′ dŭ nē-vēl-ĕt′.

Neuwied	noi'-vēt.
Nevada	nĕ-vä'-dä.
Nevers	nĕ-vâr'.
Nevis	nĕv'-ĭs.
Nevskii Prospekt	nĕf'-skĭ-ĭ prŏs-pĕkt'.
New-Chwang, see Niu- chuang	nū-chwäng'.
Newfoundland	*pop.* nū - fownd' - länd, *loc.* nū' - fŭnd - länd, nū-fŭnd-länd'.
Newnham	nūn'-ȧm. [lä-ȧṅ'.
New Orleans	nū ôr'-lē-ȧnz. *loc.* nū ōr-
Ney	nā.
Nez Percé	nā pĕr-sā'.
Ngan-hui, see Anhwei . .	n-gän-hwē'.
Niam-Niam, see Nyam-Nyam	nĭ-ȧm'-nĭ-ȧm'.
Niassa, see Nyassa. . . .	nē-äs'-sä.
Nibelungenlied, *or* Nibelun- gen Lied	nē'-bĕ-lŏŏng''-ĕn-lēt.
Nicæa	nĭ-sē'-ä. [rä'-gwä.
Nicaragua	nĭk-ȧ-rä'-gwä, nē-kä-
Niccola Pisano, see Nicola .	nēk'-ō-lä pē-zä'-nō.
Niccolini	nēk-kō-lē'-nē.
Niccolò, see Nicolò . . .	nē-kō-lō'.
Nice.	nēs.
Nicene	nĭ'-sēn.
Nicias	nĭs'-ĭ-ȧs, nĭsh'-ĭ-ȧs.
Nicola, see Niccola . . .	*It.* nē-kō'-lä.
Nicolai	nē'-kō-lĭ.
Nicolò de' Lapi, see Niccolò	nē-kō-lō' dā lä'-pē.
Nicot	nē-kō'.
Nictheroy, see Nitherohi .	nē-tä-rō'-ē.
Niebuhr	nē'-bōōr.
Niepce de St. Victor . . .	nē-ĕps' dŭ säṅ-vēk-tōr'.
Nietzsche	nēt'-shŭ.
Nieuport, see Nieuwport .	nē-ĕ-pōr'.

Nieuwe Kerke	nē-ĕv'-ĕ kĕrk'-ĕ.
Nieuwport, *see* Nieuport .	nē-ĕv'-pōrt.
Nieuwveld	nē-ĕv'-fĕlt.
Nièvre	nē-ĕvr'.
Niflheim	nĕf'-l-hĭm.
Nigel	nĭ'-jĕl.
Niger	nĭ'-jĕr.
Nigra	nē'-grä.
Niigata	nē-ē-gä'-tä.
Nijni-Novgorod, *or* Nijniy-Novgorod, *see* Nizhni-Novgorod	nēzh'-nĭ-nŏv'-gŏ-rŏd.
Nike Apteros	nĭ'-kē ăp'-tĕ-rŏs.
Nikisch	nē'-kĭsh.
Nikita	nē-kē'-tä.
Nikko	nēk'-kō.
Nikola	nē'-kō-lä.
Nilsson (Christine) . . .	nĭl'-sŏn.
Nimar	nē-mär'.
Nimeguen, *see* Nimwegen .	nĭm'-ā-gĕn.
Nîmes, *see* Nismes	nēm.
Nimwegen, *see* Nimeguen *and* Nymegen	nĭm'-wā-gĕn.
Niña, La	lä nēn'-yä.
Nineveh	nĭn'-ĕ-vŭ.
Ningpo, *or*	nĭng'-pō'.
Ningpo-fu	nĭng'-pō'-fōō'.
Niño	nēn'-yō.
Ninon de Lenclos, *or* L'Enclos	nē-nôn' dŭ lŏn-klō'.
Niobe	nĭ'-ō-bē.
Nipal, *see* Nepal . . .	nĭ-pôl'.
Niphon, *see* Nipon . .	nĭf-ŏn'.
Nipissing, *see* Nepissing .	nĭp'-ĭs-sĭng.
Nipon, *or*	nĭp-ŏn'.
Nippon, *see* Niphon . . .	nĭp-ŏn'.

Nirvana	nĭr-vä'-na,
Nisan	nĭ'-săn.
Nisard	nē-zär'.
Nisch, *or* Nish, *see* Nissa .	nēsh.
Nismes, *see* Nimes	nēm.
Nissa, *see* Nisch	nēs'-sä.
Nitherohi, *see* Nictheroy .	nē-tā-rō'-ē.
Nitocris	nĭ-tō'-krĭs.
Niu-chuang, *see* New-Chwang . . . . . }	nū-chwäng'.
Nivernais	nē-vĕr-nā'.
Nivôse	nē-vōz'.
Nizam	nĭ-zăm', nī'-zăm.
Nizhni-Novgorod, *see* Nijni-Novgorod . . . . . }	nēzh'-nĭ-nŏv'-gŏ-rŏd.
Noachian	nō-ā'-kĭ-án.
Noacolly, *see* Noakhali . .	nō-ă-kŏl'-ĭ.
Noailles	nō-ī', nō-ä'-yŭ.
Noakhali, *see* Noacolly . .	nō-äk-hä'-lē. [nē.
Noctes Ambrosianae . . .	nŏk'-tēz ăm-brō''-zĭ-ā'-
Nodier	nō-dē̱-ā'.
Noël	nō-ĕl'.
Noir Fainéant	nwär fā-nā-äṅ'.
Noli me tangere . . .	nō'-lī mē tăn'-jĕ-rē.
Nombre de Dios . . .	nŏm'-brä dä dē'-ōs.
Nome	nōm.
Nord	*Fr.* nōr.
Nordau	nōr'-dow.
Nordenskjöld	nôr'-dĕn-shĕld.
Nordica	nôr'-dĭ-kä.
Nördlingen	nĕrd'-lĭng-ĕn.
Norn	nôrn.
Northanger (Abbey) . .	nôrth'-ān-jĕr.
Norumbega	nō-rŭm-bē'-gä.
Norwich	*Eng.* nŏr'-ĭch, nŏr'-ĭj. *Am.* nôr'-wĭch.

Nôtre Dame	nō'-tr däm'.
Nourmahal	nōōr-mȧ-häl'.
Novalls	nō-vä'-lĭs.
Novara	nō-vä'-rä.
Nova Scotia	nō'-vȧ skō'-shĭ-ȧ.
Novaya Zemlya, *or* . . .	*Russ.* nō'-vä-yä zĕm-lĭ-ä'.
Nova Zembla	nō'-vȧ zĕm'-blȧ.
Novgorod	nŏv'-gŏ-rŏd.
Novikoff	nŏv'-ĭ-kŏf.
Nowanagar, *or* . . .	nō''-wä-nä-gär'.
Nowanuggur . . .	nō''-wä-nŭ-gŭr'.
Nozze di Figaro, Le . . .	lā nŏt'-sĕ dē fē'-gä-rō.
Nucingen, La Maison . .	lä mä-zôṅ' nü-säṅ-zhăṅ'.
Nuddea, *see* Nadiya . . .	nŭd'-ē-ä. [thē'-ä.
Nueva Andalucía . . .	nōō-ä'-vä än''-dä-lōō-
Nueva Ecija	nōō-ä'-vä ā'-thē-ċhä.
Nueva Galicia	nōō-ä'-vä gä-lē'-thē-ä.
Nueva Vizcaya	nōō-ä'-vä bēth-kī'-ä.
Nuevitas	nōō-ä''-vē-täs'.
Nuevo Leon	nōō-ä'-vō lā-ōn'.
Nuggur	nŭg'-ŭr.
Nundydroog	nŭn-dĭ-drōōg'.
Nuneaton	nŭn'-ē-tŭn.
Nuñez	nōōn'-yĕth.
Nuova Antologia . . .	nōō-ō'-vä än-tō-lō'-jä.
Nu-Pieds, Nu-pieds . . .	nü-pē-ä'.
Nyam-Nyam	n-yäm'-n-yäm'.
Nyanza	n-yăn'-zä.
Nyassa, *see* Niassa . .	nē-äs'-sä.
Nyassaland	nē-äs'-ä-lănd.
Nydia	nĭd'-ĭ-ä.
Nyland	nü'-länd.
Nymegen, *see* Nimwegen .	nĭm'-ā-gĕn.
Nyoro	n-yō'-rō.
Nystad	nü'-städ.

O

Oahu . . . . ō-ä'-hōō, wä'-hōō.
Ob, *see* Obi . . . . . . ōb.
Obeid, El . . . . ĕl ō-bād', ĕl ō-bā'-ēd.
Ober Ammergau . . . . ō'-bĕr äm'-mĕr-gow.
Oberland . . . . ō'-bĕr-länt.
Obermann . . . . . . ō-bĕr-män'.
Oberon . . . . ō'-bĕ-rŏn, ŏb'-ĕr-ŏn.
Oberpfalz . . . . . . ō'-bĕr-pfälts.
Obi, *see* Ob . . . . . . ō'-bē.
Obidicut . . . . ō-bĭd'-ĭ-cŭt.
Obispo, Calle . . . . . käl'-yä ō-bēs'-pō.
Obiter dicta . . . . . . ō'-bĭ-tĕr dĭk'-tä.
Obrenovitch . . . . . ō-brĕn'-ō-vĭch.
Ocaña . . . . ō-kän'-yä.
Oceana . . . . { ō-sē'-à-nä, ō-shē-ä'-nà,
ō-shē-ā'-nà. [nĭ-à.
Oceania, *or* . . . . . . ō-sē-ā'-nĭ-à, ō-shē-ä'-
Oceanica . . . . ō-sē-ăn'-ĭ-kà, ō-shē-ăn'-
Oceanides . . . . . . ō-sē-ăn'-ĭ-dēz. [ĭk-à.
Oceanus . . . . ō-sē'-à-nŭs.
Ochiltree . . . . ōċh'-l-trē.
Ocklawaha . . . . . . ŏk-lä-wä'-hä.
Oconomowoc . . . . . ō-kō-nŏm'-ō-wŏk.
Octavian . . . . ŏk-tā'-vĭ-àn.
Odelsthing . . . . . . ō'-dĕlz-tĭng.
Odéon . . . . ō-dē'-ŏn. *Fr.* ō-dā-ôṅ'.
Odessa . . . . ō-dĕs'-ä.
Odoacer, *see* Ottokar, *or* ō-dō-ā'-sĕr.
Odovaker . . . . . . ō-dō-vä'-kär.
Odysseus . . . . ō-dĭs'-ē-ŭs, ō-dĭs'-sūs.
Odyssey . . . . ŏd'-ĭs-ē.
Œdipe . . . . *Fr.* ē-dēp'.
Œdipus Coloneus . . . . ĕd'-ĭ-pŭs kō-lō-nē'-ŭs.

Œdipus Tyrannus .... ĕd'ĭ-pŭs tĭr-ăn'ŭs.

Oehlenschläger, see Öhlen- } ē'-lĕn-shlä''-gĕr.
schläger . . . . . . }

Oersted, see Örsted . . . ĕr'-stĕd.

Oesterreich, see Österreich ĕs'-tĕr-rīch.

Offenbach, Jacques . . . { zhäk ŏf-ĕn-bäk'.
{ Ger. ŏf-ĕn-bäch'.

Ofterdingen . . . . . . ŏf'-tĕr-dĭng''-ĕn.

Oggione, see Uggione . . ōj-jō'-nĕ.

Ogier . . . . ō'-jĭ-ĕr.

Ogier de Danemarcke . . ō-zhē-ā' dŭ dän-märk'.

Ogier le Danois . . . . ō-zhē-ā' lĕ dä-nwä'.

Ogoway, or Ogowé . . . ō-gō-wā'.

O'Higgins . . . . . . ō-hĭg'-ĭnz. Sp. ō-ē'-gēns.

Öhlenschläger, see Oehlen- } ē'-lĕn-shlä''-gĕr.
schläger . . . . . . }

Ohnet, Georges . . . . zhŏrzh zō-nā'.

Ohod, or . . . . ō-hōd'.

Ohud . . . . ō-hōōd'.

Oileus . . . . ō-ĭl'-ē-ŭs, ō-ĭ'-lūs.

Oise . . . . wäz.

Ojeda . . . . ō-ċhä'-dä.

Okefinokee . . . . . . ō''-kē-fĭ-nō'-kē.

Okhotsk Sea . . . . . ō-ċhōtsk', ō-hōtsk'.

Okinawa . . . . ō-kē-nä'-wä.

Oklahoma . . . . . . ŏk-lä-hō'-mä.

Olaf . . . . ō'-läf.

Olaus (St.) . . . . . . ō-lä'-ŭs.

Oldenbarneveldt, van . . vän ōl''-dĕn-bär'-nĕ-vĕlt.

Olifaunt . . . . ŏl'-ĭ-fȧnt.

Oliphant . . . . ŏl'-ĭ-fȧnt.

Olitzka . . . . ō'-lĭts-kä.

Oliva (Peace of) . . . . ō-lē'-fä.

Olivarez . . . . ō-lē-vä'-rĕth.

Olivia . . . . ō-lĭv'-ĭ-ä.

Ollivier, Émile . . . . ā-mēl' ō-lē-vē-ā'.

Olmütz	ŏl'-müt7.
Olympe	*Fr.* ō-lăṅp'.
Olympus	ō-lĭm'-pŭs.
Omaha	ō'-má-hä.
Oman	ō-män'.
Omar Khayyam, *see* Umar ⎱ Khaiyàm . . . . . . ⎰	ō'-mär khī-yäm'.
Omar Pasha, *see* Omer ⎱ Pasha . . . . ⎰	ō'-mär păsh-ô', pá-shä', päsh'-á.
Omega	ō'-mĕg-ä, ō-mĕg'-á.
Omer Pasha, *see* Omar ⎱ Pasha . . . . ⎰	ō-mēr pash-ô', pá-shä', päsh'-á.
Omeyyades, *see* Ommiads .	ō-mä'-yădz.
Ommaya	ŏm-mä'-yä.
Ommiads, *see* Omeyyades .	ō-mī'-ădz.
Omphale	ŏm'-fá-lē.
Omsk	ŏmsk.
Oñate	ōn-yä'-tä.
Onega (L.)	ō-nĕ'-gá. *Russ.* ō-nā'-gä.
Oneida	ō-nī'-dä.
Onesimus	ō-nĕs'-ĭ-mŭs.
Onesiphorus	ō-nē-sĭf'-ō-rŭs.
Ongaro, Dall'	däl ŏng'-gä-rō.
Onias . . . . . , . .	ō-nī'-ás.
Onondaga	ŏn-ŏn-dô'-gá.
Oodeypoor, *see* Udaipur .	ōō-dĭ-pōōr'.
Oonalaska, *see* Unalaska .	ōō-ná-lăs'-ká.
Ophelia	ō-fē'-lĭ-á, ō-fēl'-yá.
Ophir	ō'-fēr.
Ophiucus	ō-fī-yū'-kŭs, ŏf-ĭ-ū'-kŭs.
Opie	ō'-pī.
Opigena	ō-pĭj'-ē-ná. [tōō.
Oporto, *Port.*, o Porto .	ō-pōr'-tō. *Port.* ōōpōr'-
Ops . . . '	ŏps.
Oran	ō-rän'. *Fr.* ō-räṅ'.
Orcagna	ōr-kän'-yä.

Orel	ō-rĕl'.
Orellana	ō-rāl-yä'-nä.
Orense	ō-rĕn'-sā. [chĕ.
Orfeo ed Euridice . . .	ŏr-fā'-ō ĕd ā-o͡o-rē'-dē-
Origen, or	ŏr'-ĭ-jĕn.
Origenes	ō-rĭj'-ĕ-nēz.
Orinoco	ō-rĭ-nō'-kō.
Orion	ō-rĭ'-ŏn.
Orissa	ō-rĭs'-ä.
Orizaba	ō-rē-thä'-bä.
Orlando Furioso	ŏr-län'-dō fo͡o-rē-ō'-zō.
Orlando Innamorato . .	ŏr-län'-dō ēn-nä''-mō-
Orléanais, see Orléannais .	ôr-lā-ä-nā'. [rä'-tō.
Orleanists	ôr'-lē-án-ĭsts''.
Orléannais, see Orléanais .	ôr-lā-ä-nā'.
Orléans (Maid of) . . .	ôr'-lē-ánz. Fr. ôr-lā-äṅ'.
Orloff	ŏr-lŏf'.
Ormulum	ôr'-mū-lŭm.
Ormuzd	ôr'-mŭzd, ôr'-mo͡ozd.
Orne	ôrn.
Oronte	ō-rôṅt'.
Orontes	ō-rŏn'-tēz.
Orphée et Euridice . . .	ôr-fā' ā ē-rē-dēs'.
Orphéon	ôr-fā-ôṅ'.
Orpheus	ôr'-fē-ŭs, ôr'-fūs.
Orsay	ŏr-sā'.
Orsini	ŏr-sē'-nē.
Orsino	ôr-sē'-nō. It. ŏr-sē-nō.
Örsted, see Oersted . . .	ĕr'-stĕd.
Ortega	ōr-tā'-gä.
Orthez, see D'Orthez .	ōr-tĕss', ŏr-täz'.
Oruba	ō-ro͡o'-bä.
Orvieto	ōr-vē̤-ā'-tō.
Osage	ō-sāj', ō'-sāj. Fr. ō-zäzh'.
Osaka, see Ozaka	ō-sä'-kä.
Osbaldistone	ŏs-bôl'-dĭs-tŭn.

Osceola . . . . ŏs-ē-ō'-lä.

Osiris . . . . ō-sĭ'-rĭs.

Osman Digna . . . . . ŏs'-măn dĭg'-nä.

Osmanli . . . . ŏs-măn'-lĭ.

Osnabrück . . . . . . ŏs'-nä-brük.

Ospedale degli Innocenti . { ōs-pā-dä'-lĕ dāl'-yŏ ĕn-
                            { nō-chĕn'-tē.

Osrick . . . . ŏz'-rĭk.

Ossian . . . . ŏsh'-ȧn, ŏsh'-ē-ȧn.

Ossoli . . . . ŏs'-sō-lē.

Ostade . . . . ŏs'-tä-dĕ.

Ostend . . . . ŏs-tĕnd'.

Osterode (in Harz) . . . ŏs'-tĕ-rō''-dŭ.

Österreich, see Oesterreich ĕs'-tĕr-rĭċh.

Ostrogoths . . . . . . ŏs'-trō-gŏths.

Otaheite, or Otaheiti . . ō-tä-hē'-tē.

Othello . . . . ō-thĕl'-ō.

Othman . . . . ŏth-män'.

Otho . . . . ō'-thō.

Otranto . . . . ō-trän'-tō.

Otricoli . . . . ō-trē'-kō-lē.

Ottawa (Canada) . . . . ŏt'-ȧ-wä.

Ottawa (Ohio) . . . . . ŏt'-ȧ-wā.

Ottilie . . . . ŏt'-tēl-yŭ.

Otto . . . . ŏt'-tō.

Ottokar, see Odoacer . . ŏt'-tō-kär.

Oude, see Oudh, Audh . . owd.

Oudenaarde, or Oudenarde, } ow'-dĕn-är''-dĕ.
  see Audenarde . . . . }

Oudh, see Oude, Audh . . owd.

Oudinot . . . . ōō-dĕ-nō'.

Ouida . . . . ōō-ē'-dä, wē'-dä.

Ouse . . . . ōōz.

Outram . . . . ōō'-trȧm.

Ovalle (Alfonso) de . . . dā ō-väl'-yā.

Overijssel, or Overyssel . ō'-vĕr-ĭs''-sĕl.

Ovid	ŏv′-ĭd.
Oviedo	ō-vē-ā′-dō.
Owhyhee, *or* Owyhee . .	ō-wī′-hē.
Oxenstiern, *or*	ŏks′-ĕn-stērn.
Oxenstierna, *or* Oxen-	ŏks′-ĕn-shâr′′-nä.
stjerna, *Sw.*	
Oxon	ŏks′-ŭn.
Oxonian	ŏks-ō′-nĭ-ạn.
Oyama	ō-yä′-mä.
Oyer	ō′-yĕr.
Ozaka, *see* Osaka	ō-zä′-kä.

P

Paardeberg	pär′-dĕ-bĕrċh.
Pablo	*Sp.* päb′-lō.
Pabna	päb′-nä.
Pacchiarotto	päk′′-kē-är-ŏt′-tō.
Pacha, *see* Pasha	päsh-ŏ′, pȧ-shä′, päsh′-ȧ.
Pacheco	pä-chā′-kō.
Pachmann	päċh′-män.
Pachuca	pä-chōō′-kä.
Pactolus	păk-tō′-lŭs.
Padan-aram	pā-dȧn-âr′-ȧm.
Paderewski	pä-dā-rĕv′-skē.
Padilla, Juan Lopez de . .	ċhōō-ạn′ lō′-päth dä pä-
Padishah	pä-dē-shä′. [dēl′-yä.
Padoue, *Fr.*, *or*	pä-dōō′.
Padova, *It.*, *or*	pä′-dō-vä.
Padua	păd′-yū-ȧ.
Paedobaptist, *see* Pedobap-	pē-dō-băp′-tĭst.
tist	
Paesiello, *see* Paisiello . .	pä′′-ä-zē-ĕl′-lō.
Paestum	pĕs′-tŭm.
Paez	pä-ĕth′.

Paganini	{ på-gá-nĭn′-i.
	{ *It.* pä-gä-nē′-nē.
Paget	păj′-ĕt. *Fr.* pä-zhä′.
Pago-Pago, *see* Pango-Pango	pän′-gō-pän′-gō.
Pailleron	pä-yē-rôṅ′.
Paisiello, *see* Paesiello . .	pä″-ē-zē-ĕl′-lō.
Paiwar, *see* Peiwar . . .	pī-wär′.
Paix des Dames	pä dä däm′.
Pajou	pä-zhōō′.
Pakhoi, *see* Peihai . . .	päk-hoi′.
Palaemon	pá-lē′-mŏn, pă-lē′-mŏn.
Palaeologus	pā-lē-ŏl′-ō-gŭs.
Palais Bourbon	pä-lä′ bōōr-bôṅ′.
Palais de Justice	pä-lä′ dē zhüs-tēs′.
Palais du Trocadéro . . .	pä-lä′ dü trō-kä-dä-rō′.
Palais Royal	pä-lä′ rwä-yäl′.
Palamedes	păl-ā-mē′-dēz.
Palamon and Arcite . . .	păl′-á-mŏn and är′-sīt.
Palaos	pä-lä-ōs′.
Palatinate	pă-lăt′-ĭ-nāt.
Palatine	păl′-á-tīn, păl′-á-tĭn.
Palatinus	păl-ā-tī′-nŭs.
Palau, *see* Pellew, Pelew .	pä-low′.
Paláwan	pä-lä′-wän.
Palazzo Borghese	pä-lät′-sō bōr-gä′-zĕ.
Palazzo della Cancelleria .	{ pä-lät′-sō dĕl′-lä kän″-
	{ chĕl-lä-rē′-ä.
Palazzo Doria	pä-lät′-sō dō′-rĭ-ä.
Palazzo Farnese	*It.* pä-lät′-sō fär-nä′-zĕ.
Palazzo Pandolfini . . .	pä-lät′-sō pän-dōl-fē′-nē.
Palazzo Pitti	pä-lät′-sō pĭt′-tē.
Palazzo Pubblico	pä-lät′-sō pōōb′-lē-kō.
Palazzo Reale	pä-lät′-sō rä-ä′-lĕ.
Palazzo Vecchio	pä-lät′-sō vĕk′-kē-ō.
Palencia	pä-lān′-thē-ä.
Palenque	pä-lān′-kä.

Paleologus	pā-lē-ŏl'-ō-gŭs. [mō.
Palermo	pà-lĕr'-mō. *It.* pä-lĕr'-
Palestine	păl'-ĕs-tīn.
Palestrina	pä-lĕs-trē'-nä.
Palfrey	pôl'-frĭ.
Palgrave	pôl'-grāv.
Pali, *see* Pallee . . .	pä'-lē, pā'-lĭ.
Palikao	pä-lē-kä'-ō.
Palissy	păl'-ĭs-ĭ. *Fr.* pä-lē-sē'.
Palitana	pä-lē-tä'-nä.
Palladio	päl-lä'-dē-ō.
Pallee, *see* Pali . . .	pä'-lē.
Pall Mall	pĕl mĕl.
Palma Giovine . . .	päl'-mä jō'-vē-nĕ.
Palma Vecchio	päl'-mä vĕk'-kē-ō.
Palmerston	päm'-ĕr-stŭn.
Palmyra	păl-mĭ'-rȧ.
Palo Alto	pä'-lō äl'-tō.
Palos	pä-lōs', pä'-lōs.
Pameer, *see* Pamir . . .	pä-mēr'.
Pamela	pà-mē'-là, păm'-ĕ-là.
Pamir, *see* Pameer . . .	pä-mēr'.
Pampanga	päm-pän'-gä.
Pampeluna, *or*	päm-pä-lōō'-nä.
Pampelune, *Fr., or* . . .	pŏńp-lün'.
Pamplona	päm-plō'-nä.
Panama	păn-à-mä'. *Sp.* pä-nä-mä'.
Panathenæa	păn''-ăth-ē-nē'-à.
Panay	pä-nä'-ē.
Panch Mahalz	pánch mà-hälz'.
Pandæan, *see* Pandean .	păn-dē'-àn.
Pandarus	păn'-dà-rŭs.
Pandean, *see* Pandæan . .	păn-dē'-àn.
Pando	pän'-dō.
Pandoor, *see* Pandour . .	păn-dōōr', păn'-dōōr.
Pandora	păn-dō'-rä.

Pandour, *see* Pandoor . .	păn-dōōr', păn'-dōōr.
Pangaul	păng-găl'-ue.
Pangasinan	pän''-gä-sē-nän'.
Pango-Pango, *see* Pago-Pago	pän'-gō-pän'-gō.
Panizzi	pä-nēt'-sē.
Panjab, *see* Punjab, Penjab	pŭn-jäb'.
Panna, *see* Punnah . . .	pŭn'-ä.
Panslavic	păn-släv'-ĭk.
Pantagruel	{ păn-tăg'-rōō-ĕl. { *Fr.* pän-tä-grü-ĕl'.
Pantalon, *or*	păn'-tȧ-lŏn.
Pantalone	pän-tä-lō'-nĕ.
Pantheon	păn'-thē-ŏn, păn-thē'-ŏn
Panthéon	*Fr.* pän-tā-ôn'.
Panurge	păn-ērj'. *Fr.* pä-nürzh'.
Panza, Sancho	{ săn'-kō păn'-zä. { *Sp.* sän'-chō pän'-thä.
Paola (Fra.)	pä'-ō-lä.
Paoli, di	dē pä'-ō-lē.
Paolo Veronese . . .	pä'-ō-lō vā-rō-nā'-zĕ.
Pao-ting, *see* Pauting . .	pä-ō-tĭng'.
Paphian	pā'-fĭ-ȧn.
Paphos	pā'-fŏs.
Papin	pä-păn'.
Pappenheim	päp'-ĕn-hīm.
Papua	păp'-ōō-ȧ, pä'-pōō-ȧ.
Pará	pä-rä'.
Paracali, *see* Parakale . .	pä-rä-kä'-lē. [sŭs.
Paracelsus	păr-ȧ-sĕl'-sŭs, păr-ä-sĕl'-
Paraclet	*Fr.* pä-rä-klä'.
Paraclete	păr'-ȧ-klēt.
Paradiso	pä-rä-dē'-zō.
Paragoa	pä-rä-gō'-ä.
Paragua	pä-rä'-gwä. [păr'-ȧ-gwī.
Paraguay, *or*	păr-ȧ-gwī, pä-rä-gwā',
Paraguaya, *Sp. and Port.*	păr-ä-gwī'-ä.

Parahiba, *or* Parahyba	nä-rä-ê'-bä.
Parakale, *see* Paracali	pä-rä-kä'-lä.
Paramaribo	păr-à-măr'-ĭ-bŏ.
Paran	pā'-rȧn.
Paraná	pä-rä-nä'.
Parañaque	pär-än-yä'-kā.
Parcae	pär'-sē.
Parc-aux-Cerfs	pär-kō-sâr'.
Paré	pä-rā'.
Paredes	pä-rā'-dĕs.
Parepa-Rosa	pä-rā'-pä-rō'-zä.
Paria	pä-rē-ä', pä'-rē-ä.
Parian	pā'-rĭ-ȧn.
Paris	păr'-ĭs. *Fr.* păr-ē'.
Paris, Comte de	kŏṅt dŭ păr-ē.
Parisian	pă-rīz'-ĭ-ȧn, pā-rīzh'-ȧn.
Parmegiano, *see* Parmigiano	pär-mā-jä'-nō.
Parmenides	pär-mĕn'-ĭ-dēz.
Parmesan	pär-mē-zăn'.
Parmigiano, *see* Parmegiano	pär-mē-jä'-nō.
Parnassian	pär-năs'-ĭ-ȧn.
Parnassus	pär-năs'-ŭs.
Parnell	pär'-nĕl.
Parolles	pä-rŏl'-ĕs.
Paros	pā'-rŏs.
Parrhasius	pä-rā'-shĭ-ŭs.
Parsee, *or* Parsi	pär'-sē.
Parsifal, *or* Parsival, *see* Ger. Parzival	pär'-sē-fäl.
Partabgarh, *see* Pertabgurh	pŭr-täb-gŭr'.
Parthenope	pär-thĕn'-ō-pē.
Parthenopean	pär-thĕn''-ō-pē'-ȧn.
Parzival, *see* Parsifal	pärt'-sē-fäl.
Pascal	păs'-kăl. *Fr.* päs-käl'.
Pasha, *see* Pacha	păsh-ȯ', pȧ-shä', päsh'-ȧ.

Pasig . . . . pä-sĕg'.
Pasini . . . . pä-zē'-nē.
Pasiphaë . . . . . . pā-sĭf'-ā-ē.
Pasquier . . . . päs-kē̤-ā'.
Passarowitz . . . . . päs-sä'-rō-vĭts.
Passau . . . . păs'-sow.
Passy . . . . pä-sē'.
Pasteur . . . . päs-tēr'.
Patchogue . . . . . . păt-chōg', păt-chŏg'.
Pater Patriae . . . . . pā'-tēr pā'-trĭ-ē.
Patiala . . . . pŭt-ē-ä'-lä.
Patna . . . . păt'-nä.
Paton . . . . pāt'-n.
Patrae, or . . . . . . pā'-trē.
Patras . . . . pä-träs'.   [klŭs.
Patroclus . . . . . pā - trō'- klŭs,   pă-trō'-
Patti (Adelina) . . . . păt'-ē.
Paty de Clam, du . . . . dü pä-tē' dŭ kläm.
Pau . . . . pō.
Pauer . . . . pow'-ĕr.
Paul . . . . pôl. *Fr.* pōl. *Ger.* powl.
Paulina . . . . pô-lē'-nȧ, pô-lī'-nä.
Pauline, *adj.* . . . . . pô'-lĭn, pô'-lĭn.
Pauline, *n.* . . . . . . pôl-lēn'. *Fr.* pō-lēn'.
Paulo, *see* Polo . . . . pō'-lō.
Pauncefote . . . . . . pôns'-fŭt.
Paur . . . . powr.
Pausanias . . . . . . pô-sā'-nĭ-ȧs.
Pausilipo, *see* Posilipo . . pow-zē-lē'-pō.
Pauting, see Paoting . . pä̤-ō̤-tĭng'.
Pavia . . . . pä-vē'-ä.
Pavlovsk . . . . päv-lŏvsk'.
Pawnee . . . . pô'-nē.
Paz, La . . . . *loc.* lä päz'. *Sp.* lä päth.
Pazzi . . . . pät'-sē.
Peary (Robert E.) . . . pē'-rĭ.

Pecci, Gioachimo . . . . . jō ä ḳō' mō pĕch'-ī.

Pe-chi-li, see Petchili . . pĕ-chē-lē'.

Pedobaptist, see Paedobap- ⎫
tist . . . . ⎬ pē-dō-băp'-tĭst.
                           ⎭

Pedro . . . . pē'-drō. *Sp.* pā'-drō.

Pegasean, Pegasian . . . pē-gā'-sĭ-àn.

Pegasus . . . . pĕg'-à-sŭs, pĕg'-ā-sŭs.

Pegu . . . . pē-gōō', pĕ-gōō'.

Peihai, see Peihoi, Pakhoi pī-hī'.

Pei-ho . . . . pā-hō'. *pop.* pī-hō'.

Peihoi, see Peihai, Pakhoi pī-hoi'.

Peiræus, see Piræus . . . pī-rē'-ŭs.

Peirithous, see Pirithous . pī-rĭth'-ō-ŭs.

Peishwa, see Peshwa . . pĕsh'-wä.

Peiwar, see Paiwar . . . pī-wär'.

Peixoto . . . . pā-shō'-tōō.

Pekin (Ill.) . . . . . . pē'-kĭn.

Pekin, or . . . . pē-kĭn'.

Peking (China) . . . pē-kĭng'.

Pelagians . . . . . . pē-lā'-jĭ-ánz.

Pelagius . . . . pē-lā'-jĭ-ŭs.

Pelasgi . . . . pē-lăs'-jĭ.

Pelayo . . . . pā-lä'-yō.

Pele, or . . . . pē'-lē.

Pelee, or . . . . pē'-lē.

Pelée, Pointe . . . . . pwănt pĕ-lā'.

Peleus . . . . pē'-lē-ŭs, pē'-lūs.

Pelew, see Pellew, Palau . pĕ-lōō'.

Pelion . . . . pē'-lĭ-ŏn.

Pélissier . . . . pā-lēs-ē-ā'.

Pelleas . . . . pĕl'-ē-ăs.

Pellew, see Pelew, Palau . pĕ-lōō'.

Pellico, Silvio . . . . . sēl'-vē-ō pĕl'-lē-kō.

Pellieux (Gen.), Le . . . lē pĕl-ē-ē'.

Pelopid . . . . pĕl'-ō-pĭd.

Pelopidas . . . . pĕ-lŏp'-ĭ-dăs.

Peloponnesian	{ pĕl″-ō-pŏn-nē′-shĭ-àn, pĕl″-ō-pŏn-nē′-shàn.
Peloponnesus	pĕl″-ō-pŏn-ē′-sŭs.
Pelops	pē′-lŏps.
Pemigewasset	pĕm″-ĭj-ē-wŏs′-ĭt.
Peñas	pĕn′-yäs.
Penates	pē-nā′-tēz.
Penelope	pē-nĕl′-ō-pē.
Peniel	pĕ-nī′-ĕl.
Penjab, see Panjab, Punjab	pĕn-jäb′.
Penrith	pĕn′-rĭth.
Penryn	pĕn-rĭn′.
Penseroso, Il	ĭl pĕn-sĕ-rō′-sō.
Pensiero, Il	ēl pän-sē-ā′-rō.
Pensieroso, Il	ēl pän-sē-ā-rō′-zō.
Pentateuch	pĕn′-tá-tūk, pĕn′-tā-tūk.
Pentecost	pĕn′-tē-kŏst, pĕn′-tē-
Pentelic	pĕn-tĕl′-ĭk. [kōst.
Pentelican	pĕn-tĕl′-ĭ-cán.
Pentheus	pĕn′-thē-ŭs, pĕn′-thūs.
Penuel	pĕ-nū′-ĕl.
Penza	pĕn′-zä.
Penzance	pĕn-zäns′.
Pepe	pā′-pĕ.
Pepin	pĕp′-ĭn. Fr. pā-păṅ′.
Pepys	pēps, pĕps, pĭps, pĕp′-ĭs.
Pera	pā′-rä.
Perak	pā-räk′.
Perceval, Percival . . .	pĕr′-sĕ-vàl.
Percheron	pĕr-shĕ-rôṅ′.
Perdiccas	pĕr-dĭk′-ăs.
Perdita	pĕr′-dĭ-tä.
Père Goriot	pàr gō-rē-yō′.
Père Lachaise	pàr lä-shāz′.
Perez (Antonio)	pā′-räth.
Pergamos	pĕr′-gá-mŏs.

Pergamum . . . . . . pĕr'-gȧ-mŭm.
Pergolese, or . . . . . pĕr-gō-lā'-zĕ.
Pergolesi . . . . pĕr-gō-lā'-zē.
Peri . . . . pē'-rĭ.
Peri (It. composer) . . . pā'-rē.
Periander . . . . . . pĕr-ĭ-ăn'-dĕr.
Pericles . . . . pĕr'-ĭ-klēz.
Périer, Casimir . . . . käz-ē-mēr' pā-rḛ-ā'.
Périgord . . . . pā-rē-gōr'.
Périgueux . . . . . . pā-rē-gē'.
Periœci . . . . pĕr-ĭ-ē'-sĭ.
Perizzites . . . . . . pĕr'-ĭ-zīts.
Pernambuco . . . . . { pĕr-nȧm-bū'-kō, pĕr-näm-bōō'-kō. *Port.* pĕr-näṅ-bōō'-kōō.
Perowne . . . . pĕ-rown'.
Perpignan . . . . . . pĕr-pēn-yäṅ'.
Persephone . . . . . . pĕr-sĕf'-ō-nē.
Perseus . . . . pĕr'-sē-ŭs, pĕr'-sūs. [zhȧ.
Persia . . . . pĕr'-shĭ-ȧ, pĕr'-shȧ, pĕr'-
Persian . . . . pĕr'-shȧn, pĕr'-zhȧn.
Pertabgurh, see Partabgarh pĕr-täb-gŭr'.
Peru, or . . . . pĕ-rōō'.
Perú, Sp. . . . . pā-rōō'.
Perugia . . . . pā-rōō'-jä.
Perugino . . . . pā-rōō-jē'-nō. [sĕ.
Peruzzi, Baldassare . . . bäl-däs-sä'-rä pā-rōōt'-
Pesaro . . . . pā'-zä-rō.
Pescadores . . . . . . pĕs-kä-dō'-rĕs.
Pescara . . . . pĕs-kä'-rä.
Peschiera . . . . . . pĕs-kḛ-ā'-rä.
Peshawar, or Peshawur . pĕsh-ow'-ĕr.
Peshwa, see Peishwa . . pĕsh'-wä.
Pestalozzi . . . . . . pĕs-tä-lŏt'-sē.
Pesth . . . . pĕst. *Hung.* pĕsht.
Petchili, see Pe-chi-li . . pĕ-chŏ-lē'.

Petchora	pĕt-chō′-rä, pĕt′-chō-rä.
Pethion, *or* Petion . . .	pā-tē-ŏṅ′.
Petit André	pĕ-tē′ täṅ-drā′.
Petŏfi	pĕ′-tē-fī.
Petrarca, *It.*, *or*	pā-trär′-kä.
Petrarch	pē′-trärk.
Petrine	pē′-trīn, pē′-trĭn′.
Petruccio	pā-trŏŏch′-ō.
Petruchio	{ pē-trū′- chĭ - ō. *It.* pā-trŏŏ′-kē-ō.
Petschnikoff	pĕtsh′-nē-kŏf.
Peyrebrune	pâr-brün′.
Pfalz	pfälts.
Phæacians	fē-ā′-shĭ-ȧnz.
Phædo, *or*	fē′-dō.
Phædon	fē′-dŏn.
Phædra	fē′-drä.
Phædrus	fē′-drŭs.
Phaethon	fā′-ĕ-thŏn.
Phanariot	fă-năr′-ĭ-ŏt.
Pharaoh	fā′-rō, fā′-rā-ō.
Pharos	fā′-rŏs, fä′-rŏs.
Pharsalus	fär-sā′-lŭs.
Phèdre	fādr.
Phenice	fē-nī′-sē.
Phenicia, *see* Phœnicia . .	fē-nĭsh′-ĭ-ȧ.
Phidias	fĭd′-ĭ-ȧs.
Philemon	fĭ-lē′-mŏn, fī-lē′-mŏn.
Philinte	fē-lăṅt′.
Philippe Égalité	fē-lēp′ ā-găl-ē-tā′.
Philippi	fĭ-lĭp′-ī.
Philippians	fĭ-lĭp′-ĭ-ȧnz.
Philippine (Is.) *or* . . .	fĭl′-ĭp-ĭn. *pop.* fĭl′-ĭ-pīn.
Philippines	{ fĭl′-ĭp - ĭnz. *pop.* fĭl′-ĭ-pīnz.
Philistine	fĭl-ĭs′-tĭn, fĭl′-ĭs-tĭn.

Philo Judæus . . . . . fī'-lō jōō-dē'-ŭs.
Philomel . . . . fĭl'-ō-mĕl.
Philomela . . . . . . fĭl-ō-mē'-lä.
Phlegethon . . . . . . flĕj'-ĕ-thŏn, flĕj'-ē-thŏn.
Phlegyas . . . . flē'-jĭ-às.
Phocæa . . . . fō-sē'-à.
Phocian . . . . fō'-shĭ-àn.
Phocion . . . . fō'-shĭ-ŏn.
Phocis . . . . fō'-sĭs.
Phœbus . . . . fē'-bŭs.
Phœnicia, see Phenicia . . fē-nĭsh'-ĭ-à.
Phrygia . . . . frĭj'-ĭ-à.
Phryne . . . . frī'-nē.
Phthiotis . . . . thĭ-ō'-tĭs.
Piacenza . . . . pē-ä-chĕn'-zä.
Piauhí, or Piauhy . . . pē-ow-ē'.
Piave . . . . pē-ä'-vĕ.   [kä.
Piazza del Gran Duca, or . pē-ät'-sä dĕl grän dōō'-
Piazza della Signoria . . { pē-ät'-sä dĕl'-lä sēn-yō-
                      {   rē'-ä.
Piazza del Popolo . . . pē-ät'-sä dĕl pō'-pō-lō.
Piazza di Spagna . . . . pē-ät'-sä dē spän'-yä.
Picardy . . . . pĭk'-är-dĭ.
Piccini . . . . pē-chē'-nē.
Picciola . . . . pē'-chō-lä.
Piccolomini . . . . . . pĭk-ō-lō'-mē-nē.   [grü'.
Pichegru . . . . pēsh-grōō'.   Fr.   pēsh-
Pichincha . . . . . . pē-chēn'-chä.   [dō-lä.
Pico della Mirandola . . pē'-kō dĕl'-lä mē-rän'-
Pico, Giovanni . . . . . jō-vän'-nē pē'-kō.
Picot . . . . pē-kō'.
Picquard . . . . pē-kär'.
Picquigny . . . . . . pē-kēn-yē'.
Piedmont, see Plémont, }
Piemonte . . . . . . } pēd'-mŏnt.
Piedres (R.) . . . . . . pē-ä'-drās.

Piémont, *Fr.*, *see* Piedmont   pē-ā-môṅ′.

Piemonte, *It.*, *see* Piedmont   pē-ā-mōn′-tĕ.

Pierre . . . .   pē-âr′.

Pierrefonds . . . . .   pē-âr-fôṅ′.

Pierrette . . . . . .   pē-âr-ĕt′.

Pierrot . . . . . .   pē-ĕr-rō′.

Pietà . . . .   pē-ā-tä′.

Pietermaritzburg . . . .   pē-tĕr-mär′-ĭts-bŭrċh.

Pietro . . . .   pē-ā′-trō.

Pilate . . . .   *Bib.* pī′-lăt.   *Fr.* pē-lät′.

Pilatus (Mt.) . . . . .   pī-lā′-tŭs.   *It.* pē-lä′-tŏŏs.

Pilatus, Pontius . . . .   pŏn′-shĭ-ŭs pī-lā′-tŭs.

Piloty . . . .   pē-lō′-tē, pē′-lō-tē.

Pilpay . . . .   pĭl′-pī.

Pinacotheca . . . . .   pĭn″-á-kō-thē′-ká.

Pinacothek . . . . .   { pĭn′-á-kō-thĕk″.
                          { *Ger.* pē″-nä-kō-tāk′.

Pinar del Rio . . . .   pē-när′ dĕl rē′-ō.   [hĭl.

Pincian Hill . . . . .   pĭn′-shĭ-án, pĭn′-chán

Pincio, Monte . . . . .   mōn′-tĕ pēn′-chō.

Pindaric . . . . . .   pĭn-dăr′-ĭk.

Pindarus . . . . . .   pĭn′-dā-rŭs.

Pines, *see* Pinos, Isla de .   pīnz.

Pinos, Isla de, *see* Pines .   ēs′-lä dä pē′-nōs.

Pinta, La . . . . . .   lä pēn′-tä.

Pinto, Aníbal . . . . .   ä-nē′-bäl pēn′-tō.

Pinturicchio . . . . .   pēn-tŏŏ-rēk′-kē-ō.

Pinzon . . . .   *Sp.* pēn-thōn′.

Piombo . . . .   pē-ŏm′-bō.

Piotrkow . . . . . .   pē-yŏtr′-kŏv.

Piozzi . . . .   pĭ-ŏz′-ĭ.   *It.* pē-ŏt′-sē.

Pippa . . . .   pĭp′-pä.

Piqua . . . . . . *   pĭk′-wä, pĭk′-wā.

Piræeus, *or* . . . . . .   pī-rē′-yūs.

Piræus, *see* Peiræus . . .   pī-rē′-ŭs.

Pirithous, *see* Peirithous .   pī-rĭth′-ō-ŭs.

Pisa	pī'-sà. *It.* pē'-zä.
Pisano, Niccolò	nē-kō-lō' pē-zä'-nō.
Piscataqua	pĭs-kăt'-à-kwä.
Pisces	pĭs'-ēz.
Pisgah	pĭz'-gä.
Pisistratidæ, *or*	pĭs-ĭs-trăt'-ĭ-dē.
Pisistratids	pĭs-ĭs'-trà-tĭds.
Pisistratus	pĭ-sĭs'-trà-tŭs, pĭ-sĭs'- trā-tŭs.
Pistoia, *or* Pistoja . . .	pĭs-tō'-yä.
Pitcairn (I.)	pĭt'-kârn, pĭt-kârn'.
Pithom	pī'-thŏm.
Pittacus	pĭt'-à-kŭs.
Pitti	pĭt'-tē.
Pizarro	pĭ-zä'-rō. *Sp.* pē-thär'-rō.
Place de la Bastille . . .	pläs dŭ lä bäs-tē'-yŭ.
Place de la Concorde . .	pläs dŭ lä kôn-kōrd'.
Place du Carrousel . . .	pläs dü kä-rōō-zĕl'.
Place Vendôme	pläs vŏn-dōm'.
Plaideurs, Les	lä plā-dĕr'.
Planche	pläṅsh.
Planché	pläṅ-shā'.
Planchette	pläṅ-shĕt'.
Plançon, Pol	pōl pläṅ-sôṅ'.
Plantagenet	plăn-tăj'-ĕ-nĕt.
Plantin, Musée	mü-zā' pläṅ-tăṅ'.
Plassey, *or* Plassi . . .	pläs'-sĭ.
Plata, Rio de la, *see* Plate	rē'-ō dä lä plä'-tä.
Platæa, *or*	plă-tē'-à, plā-tē'-à.
Platææ	plă-tē'-ē.
Plate (R.), *see* Rio de la Plata	plāt, plät.
Platine	plä'-tĭn.
Plato	plā'-tō.
Platonic	plā-tŏn'-ĭk.
Plautus	plô'-tŭs.

Pléiade, La	lä plä-văd'.
Pleiades, or	plī'-à-dēz.
Pleiads	plī'-ădz.
Plessis-les-Tours . .	plĕ-sē'-lä-tōōr'.
Pleyel	plī'-ĕl.
Pliny	plĭn'-ĭ.
Plockhorst	plŏk'-hŏrst.
Ploërmel	plō-ĕr-mĕl'.
Plombières	plôṅ-bē-âr'.
Plotinus	plō-tī'-nŭs.
Pluto	plū'-tō.
Pluton	Fr. plü-tôṅ'.
Plutus	plū'-tŭs.
Pluviose	plü-vē-yōz'.
Pnyx	nĭks.
Pocono	pō'-cō̆-nō.
Poděbrad, or Podiebrad .	pŏd'-yĕ-bräd.
Podolia	pō-dō'-lĭ-à.
Podolsk	pō-dōlsk'.
Poictiers, see Poitiers .	poi-tērz'. Fr. pwä-tē̱-ā'.
Pointe Pelée, or . . .	Fr. pwăṅt pĕ-lā'.
(Point) Pelee, or Pele .	pē'-lē.
Poissy	pwä-sē'.
Poitevin	pwät-văṅ'.
Poitiers, see Poictiers .	poi-tērz'. Fr. pwä-tē̱-ā'.
Poitou	pwä-tōō'.
Polaris	pō-lā'-rĭs.
Polavieja, Camilo . . .	kä-mē'-lō pō''-lä-vē̱-āċh'-ä.
Polignac	pō-lēn-yäk'.
Polillo	pō-lēl'-yō.
Politian	pō-lĭsh'-ĭ-àn.
Polixenes	pŏ-lĭks'-ĕ-nēz.
Poliziano, It.	pō-lēd-zē-ä'-nō.
Polk	pōlk.
Pollaiuolo, or Pollajuolo	pŏl''-lä-yōō̲-ō'-lō.
Polo, see Paulo	pō'-lō.

Polonius	pō-lō'-nĭ-ŭs.
Poltava, *see* Pultowa . .	pōl-tä'-vä.
Polybius	pŏ-lĭb'-ĭ-ŭs.
Polycletus, *or*	pŏl-ĭ-klē'-tŭs.
Polyclitus	pŏl-ĭ-klī'-tŭs.
Polycrates	pŏ-lĭk'-rȧ-tēz, pŏ-lĭk'-
Polyeucte	pō-lē-ēkt'. [rȧ-tēz.
Polygnotus	pŏl-ĭg-nō'-tŭs.
Polyhymnia, *or*	pŏl-ĭ-hĭm'-nĭ-ȧ.
Polymnia	pō-lĭm'-nĭ-ȧ.
Polynesia	pŏl-ĭ-nē'-shĭ-ȧ.
Polyphemus	pŏl-ĭ-fē'-mŭs.
Pomerania	pŏm-ĕr-ā'-nĭ-ȧ.
Pomfret, *see* Pontefract .	pŏm'-frĕt.
Pomœrium	pō-mē'-rĭ-ŭm.
Pomona	pō-mō'-nȧ.
Pompadour, de	{ dŭ pŏm'-pȧ-dōōr. *Fr.* { dŭ pôṅ'-pä-dōōr'.
Pompeia	pŏm-pē'-yȧ. [pē'-yĭ.
Pompeii	pŏm-pā'-yē. *Lat.* pŏm-
Pompeius	pŏm-pē'-yŭs.
Ponape	pō'-nä-pā.
Ponce	pŏn'-sē. *Sp.* pōn'-thä.
Ponce de Leon	{ pŏns dŭ lē'-ŏn. *Sp.* pōn'- { thä dā lā-ōn'.
Pondicherri, *or* . . . . } Pondicherry, *or* . . . . }	pŏn-dĭ-shĕr'-ĭ.
Pondichéry, *Fr.*	pôṅ-dē-shä-rē'.
Pondoland	pŏn'-dō-lănd.
Poniatowski	pō-nē-ä-tŏv'-skē.
Pontchartrain	{ pŏn-chär-trān'. *Fr.* pôṅ- { shär-trăṅ'. [frĕt.
Pontefract, *see* Pomfret .	pŏn'-tĭ-frăkt. *pop.* pŏm'-
Ponte Vecchio	pŏn'-tĕ vĕk'-kē-ō.
Pontevedra	pŏn-tā-vä'-drä.
Pontine	pŏn'-tĭn, pŏn'-tīn.

Pontius	pŏn'-shĭ-ŭs.
Pont Neuf	pŏn nĕf.
Pont-Noyelles	pôn'-nwä-yĕl'.
Poo Choo, *see* Pou Tchou, Pu Chu	pōō chōō'.
Poona, *or* Poonah . . .	pōō'-nä.
Pooree, *see* Puri . . .	pōō-rē'.
Pooshkin, *see* Pouschkin, Puschkin	pŏŏsh'-kĭn, pōōsh'-kĭn.
Popocatepetl	pō-pō''-kä-tā-pĕt'-l, pō-pō'-kä-tā-pĕt''-l.
Poppæa Sabina . . .	pŏp-pē'-ä sä-bī'-nä.
Pordenone	pōr-dä-nō'-nĕ.
Pornic	pōr-nĕk'.
Porpora	pōr'-pō-rä.
Porsena, *or*	pôr'-sĕ-nå.
Porsenna	pôr-sĕn'-nå.
Port Arthur	pōrt är'-thĕr.
Port-au-Prince	pōrt'-ō-prĭns'. *Fr.* pōr-tō-prăns'.
Porteous	pōr'-tē-ŭs.
Porte St.-Antoine . . .	pōrt săn-tŏn-twăn'.
Porte St.-Denis . . .	pōrt săn-dĕ-nē'.
Porte St.-Martin . . .	pōrt săn-mär-tăn'.
Porthos	pōr-tōs'.
Portia	pōr'-shĭ-å, pôr'-shĭ-å.
Portici	pōr'-tē-chē.
Porto Bello, *see* Puerto Bello	pōr'-tō bĕl'-lō. *Port.* pōr'-tōō bāl'-yō.
Porto Rico, *see* Puerto Rico	pōr'-tō rē'-kō.
Port Saïd	pōrt sä-ēd'. *pop.* sād.
Portugal	pōrt'-yū-gål. *Port.* pōr-tōō-gäl'. [*or* gĕs.
Portuguese	pōrt-yū-gēz', pōr'-tū-gēz,
Poseidon, *or* Posidon . .	pō-sī'-dŏn.
Posilipo, *see* Pausilipo . .	pō-zē-lē'-pō.

Posthumus, Leonatus . . } lē - ō - nā'- tŭs pŏst'- hū-
mŭs, pŏs'-tū-mŭs.

Potchefstrom . . . . . pŏ'-chĕf-strŏm.

Potemkin . . . . . . { pŏ-tĕm'-kĭn, *Russ.* pŏt-
yŏm'-kĭn.

Potgieter . . . . pŏt'-gē-tĕr.

Potocka . . . . pŏ-tŏt'-skä.

Potocki . . . . pŏ-tŏt'-skē.

Potomac . . . . pō-tō'-mȧk.

Potosí . . . . pō-tō'-sē. *Sp.* pō-tō-sē'.

Potsdam . . . . pŏts'-dȧm. *Ger.* pŏts'-

Poughkeepsie . . . . . pō-kĭp'-sĭ. [dȧm.

Pourbus . . . . pōōr'-bŭs.

Pourceaugnac, de . . . . dŭ pōōr-sōn-yäk'.

Pourtalès . . . . pōōr-tä-lĕs'.

Pouschkin, *or* Pouchekine, }
see Pushkin, Pooshkin, }- pōōsh'-kĭn, pōōsh'-kĭn.
Puschkin . . . . . . }

Poussin . . . . pōō-săṅ'.

Pou Tchou, *see* Poo Choo, } pōō chōō'.
Pu Chu . . . . . . }

Powhatan . . . . . . pō-ăt-än', pow-hăt-än'.

Pozzuoli, *see* Puteoli . . pŏt-sōō-ō'-lē.

Prado . . . . prä'-dō.

Præmunire (Statute of) . prē-mū-nī'-rĕ.

Præterita . . . . . . prē-tĕr-i'-tä.

Prag . . . . präg.

Prague . . . . präg. *Fr.* präg.

Prairial . . . . prä-rē-ăl'.

Prairie du Chien . . . { prä'-rē dū shēn.
Fr. prä-rē' dü shē-ĕṅ'.

Prakrit . . . . prä'-krĭt, präk'-rĭt.

Prater . . . . prä'-tĕr.

Praxiteles . . . . . . präks-ĭt'-ĕ-lēz.

Pré aux Clercs (Le) . . . prä ō klâr.

Précieuses Ridicules . . . prä-sē-ēz' rē-dē-kül'.

Proci010	{ prĕs-ĭ-ō'-sä.
	{ *Ger.* prät-sē-ō'-zä.
Predis, Ambrogio de . . .	äm-brō'-jō dä prä'-dēs.
Prelude (The)	prē'-lūd, prĕl'-ūd.
Presbyterian	{ prĕz-bĭ-tē'-rĭ-ăn, prĕs-
	{ bĭ-tē'-rĭ-ăn.
Presidio	prä-sē'-dē-ō.
Pressensé	prĕs-sŏn-sä'.
Pretoria	prē-tō'-rĭ-ä.
Prévost-Paradol	prä-vō'-pä-rä-dŏl'.
Priam	prī'-ăm.
Priapus	prī-ā'-pŭs.
Priene	prī-ē'-nē.
Prieska	prēs'-kä.
Prigioni, Le Mie	lä mē'-ĕ prē-jō'-nē.
Prim (General)	prēm.
Prince	*Fr.* prăṅs.
Princesse de Clèves . . .	prăṅ-sĕs' dŭ kläv.
Princesse Lointaine, La .	lä prăṅ-sĕs' lwăṅ-tän'.
Principe	prēn'-chē-pĕ.
Principessa	prēn-chē-pĕs'-sä.
Prinz	prĭnts.
Prinzessin	prĭnts-ĕs'-ĭn.
Priscian	prĭsh'-ĭ-ạn.
Procne, *see* Progné . . .	prŏk'-nē.
Procris	prŏk'-rĭs.
Procrustean	prō-krŭs'-tē-ạn.
Proculeius	prō-kū-lē'-ŭs.
Procyon	prō'-sĭ-ŏn, prŏs'-ĭ-ŏn.
Profeta, Il, *see* Prophète, Le	ēl prō-fā'-tä.
Profillet	prō-fē-yā'.
Progné, *see* Procne . . .	prŏg-nā'.
Promessi Sposi, I	ē prō-mĕs'-sē spō'-zē.
Promethean	prō-mē'-thē-ạn. [thūs.
Prometheus	prō-mē'-thē-ŭs, prō-mē'-
Prophète, Le, *see* Profeta, Il	lĕ prō-fāt'.

Propylæa	prŏp-ĭ-lē'-ä. [pĭ'-nä.
Proserpina	prō-sĕr'-pĭ-nȧ, prŏs-ĕr-
Proserpine	{ prŏs'- ĕr-pĭn, prŏs'- ĕr- pĭn.
Protean	prō'-tē-ȧn, prō-tē'-ȧn.
Protesilaus	prō-tĕs''-ĭ-lā'-ŭs.
Protestancy	prŏt'-ĕs-tȧn-sĭ.
Protestant	prŏt'-ĕs-tȧnt.
Proteus	prō'-tē-ŭs, prō'-tūs.
Proudhon	prōō-dôṅ'.
Provençal	{ prō-vĕn'-sȧl. { *Fr.* prō-vŏṅ-sȧl'.
Provence	prō-vŏṅs'.
Prudhomme	prü-dŏm'.
Prud'hon (Pierre Paul) .	prü-dôṅ'.
Prussia	prŭsh'-ȧ, prōōsh'-ĭ-ȧ.
Prussian	{ prŭsh'-ȧn, prŭsh'-ĭ-ȧn, { prōōsh'-ĭ-ȧn.
Prytaneum	prĭt-ā-nē'-ŭm.
Psalms	sämz.
Psammetichus	sȧ-mĕt'-ĭ-kŭs.
Pskoff	pskŏf.
Psyche	sī'-kē.
Ptah	ptä.
Ptolemaic	tŏl-ē-mā'-ĭk.
Ptolemais	tŏl-ē-mā'-ĭs.
Ptolemy	tŏl'-ē-mĭ.
Puccio	pŏŏch'-ō.
Pucelle, La	lä pü-sĕl'.
Pu Chu, *see* Poo Choo, Pou Tchou	} pōō chōō'.
Puebla	pōō-ĕb'-lä. [blō.
Pueblo	pōō-ĕb'-lō. *Sp.* pōō-ā'-
Puerto, El	äl pōō-âr'-tō.
Puerto Bello, *see* Porto Bello	{ pōō-âr'-tō bĕl'-lō. *Sp.* { pōō-âr'-tō bāl'-yō.

Puerto Cabello	{ pōọ̱-âr'- tō kȧ-běl' - lō. Sp. pōọ̱-är'-tō kȧ-bāl'- yō.
Puerto de Santa Maria . .	{ pōọ̱-âr'-tō dā sän'-tä mä-rē'-ä.
Puerto d'España	pōọ̱-âr'-tō dā spän'-yä.
Puerto Plata	pōọ̱-âr'-tō plä'-tä.
Puerto Princesa	pōọ̱-âr'-tō prēn-thā'-sä.
Puerto Príncipe	pōọ̱-âr'-tō prēn'-thē-pä.
Puerto Real	pōọ̱ r'-tō rä-äl'.
Puerto Rico, see Porto Rico	pōọ̱-âr'-tō rē'-kō.
Puget (Pierre)	pü-zhā'.
Puget (Sound)	pū'-jĕt.
Puglia	pōōl'-yä.
Pugno	pōōn'-yō.
Pulci	pōōl'-chē.
Pulcinella, or	pōōl-chē-nĕl'-lä.
Pulcinello	pōōl-chē-nĕl'-lō.
Pulkowa	pōōl'-kō-vä.
Pultava, see Poltava, or .	pōōl-tä'-vä.
Pultowa	pōōl-tō'-vä.
Pultusk	pōōl'-tŏŏsk, pōōl'-tōōsk.
Punchinello	pŭn-chĭ-nĕl'-ō.
Punjab, see Panjab, Penjab	pŭn-jäb'.
Punjaub	pŭn-jôb'.
Punnah, see Panna . . .	pŭn'-ä.
Punta Gorda	pōōn'-tä gōr'-dä.
Puntilla	pōōn-tēl'-yä.
Purana	pōō-rä'-nȧ.
Purcell	pŭr'-sĕl.
Purgatorio	pōōr-gä-tō'-rē-ō.
Puri, see Pooree	pōō-rē'.
Purim	pōō'-rĭm. [zē-ä.
Puritani di Scozia, I . . .	ē pōō-rē-tä'-nē dē skōd'-
Purneah, or	pĕr'-nĕ-ä.
Purniah	pĕr'-nĭ-ä.

Pusey . . . . pū'-zĭ.
Puseyism . . . . pū'-zĭ-ĭzm.
Pushkin, *see* Pouschkin, } pōōsh'-kĭn.
Pooshkin . . . . . . }
Puteoli, *see* Pozzuoli . . pū-tē'-ō-lĭ.
Puvis de Chavannes . . . pü-vēs' dĕ shä-vän'.
Puy-de-Dôme . . . . . pṳ̈-ē'-dŭ-dōm'.
Pylades . . . . pĭl'-à-dēz.
Pyramus . . . . pĭr'-á-mŭs.
Pyrenean . . . . pĭr-ē-nē'-àn.
Pyrenees, *or* . . . . . . pĭr'-ē-nēz.
Pyrénées, *Fr.* . . . . . pē-rā-nā'.
Pyrrhus . . . . pĭr'-ŭs.
Pythagoras . . . . . . pĭth-ăg'-ō-răs.
Pythagorean . . . . . { pĭth''-ā-gō'-rē-àn, pĭth''-
à-gō-rē'-àn.
Pythia . . . . pĭth'-ĭ-à.
Pythian . . . . pĭth'-ĭ-àn.
Python . . . . pī'-thŏn.
Pythoness . . . . . . pĭth'-ŏn-ĕs.

Q

Quadragesima . . . . . kwäd-rä-jĕs'-ĭ-mä.
Quai d'Anjou . . . . . kā dän-zhōō'.
Quai d'Orsay . . . . . kā dôr-sä'.
Quangsi, *see* Kwangsi . . kwäng-sē'.
Quangtong, *see* Kwangtung kwäng-tōōng'.
Quanza, *see* Coanza, Kuanza kwän'-zä.
Quasimodo . . . . . . { kwä-sĭ-mō'-dō.
Fr. kä-zē-mō-dō'.
Quathlamba, *see* Kath- } kwät-läm'-bä.
lamba . . . . . . }
Quatre-Bras . . . . . kă'-tr-brä'.
Quatre-Vingt-Treize . . . kă'-tr-văn-trĕz'.

Quebec	kwē-bĕk'. *Fr.* kˌẽˌlˌĕk'
Queenston	kwēnz'-tŭn.
Queenstown	kwēnz'-town.
Queiros, *see* Quiros, de . .	dä kā-ē-rŏs'.
Quelpaerd, *or*	kwĕl'-pärd.
Quelpart, *or* Quelpaert . .	kwĕl'-pärt.
Quentin Durward . . .	kwĕn'-tĭn dẽr'-wärd.
Quercia, della	dĕl'-lä kwĕr'-chä.
Querétaro	kā-rā'-tä-rō.
Querimba	kā-rēm'-bä.
Quérouaille (Louise Renée de) *see* Kéroualle . . .	kā-rŏō-ä'-yŭ.
Quesada, Ximenez de . .	zĭ-mē'-nēz, *Sp.* 'hē-mā'-nāth dä kā-sä'-dä.
Quesnay	kā-nā'.
Quesnel	kā-nĕl'.
Quevedo y Villegas . . .	kā-bā'-dō ē vēl-yā'-gäs.
Quiberon	kē-brôṅ'.
Quijote, Don, *see* Quixote .	dŏn kē-'hō'-tā.
Quilimane, *see* Kilimane .	kē-lē-mä'-nä.
Quincy (Mass.)	kwĭn'-zĭ.
Quinet	kē-nā'.
Quiniluban	kē-nē-lŏō-bän'.
Quinquagesima	kwĭn-kwȧ-jĕs'-ĭ-mȧ.
Quintas da Recreo . . .	kēn'-täs dä rā-krā'-ō.
Quintilian	kwĭn-tĭl'-ĭ-ăn.
Quirinal, *or*	kwĭr'-ĭ-năl.
Quirinalis, Mons, *Lat.* . .	mŏnz kwĭr-ĭ-nā'-lĭs.
Quirites	kwĭ-rī'-tēz.
Quiros, de, *see* Queiros . .	dä kē'-rŏs.
Quito	kē'-tō.
Qui tollis	kwī tŏl'-ĭs.
Quixote, Don, *see* Quijote, Don	*Eng.* dŏn kwĭks'-ōt. *Sp.* dŏn kē-'hō'-tā.
Quogue	kwōg, kwŏg.
Quoniam	kwō'-nĭ-ăm.

R

Raamah	rā'-á-mä.
Rabelais	răb-ĕ-lā'.
Rabelaisian	răb-ĕ-lā'-zĭ-án.
Rabutin, Bussy	büs-sē' rä-bü-tăṅ'.
Raca	rā'-ká.
Rachel	rā'-chĕl. *Fr.* rä-shĕl'.
Racine	ră-sēn'. *Fr.* rä-sēn'.
Radack, *or* Radak . . .	rä'-däk.
Radetzki, *or* Radetzky . .	rä-dĕt'-skē.
Radom	rä'-dōm.
Raffaelle, *or*	räf-fä-ĕl'
Raffaello, *see* Raphael . .	räf-fä-ĕl'-lō.
Ragatz, *or* Ragaz	rä'-gäts.
Rages	rā'-jēz.
Ragnar Lodbrok	räg'-när lōd'-brōk.
Ragnarök	räg'-nä-rĕk'.
Ragon, Félix	fä-lēks' rä-gôṅ'.
Ragusa	rä-gōō'-zä.
Rahab	rā'-hăb.
Rahway	rô'-wā.
Rai Bareli, *see* Roy Bareilly	rī bä-rā'-lē.
Raimondi, Marcantonio .	{ märk-än-tō'-nē-ō rä-ē-mōn'-dē.
Rainer	rī'-nĕr.
Rainier (Mount)	rā'-nēr.
Raipur, *or* Raipoor . . .	rī-pōōr'.
Rais, de, *or*	dŭ räs.
Raiz, *see* Retz	räz.
Rajah, *or* Raja	rä'-jä.
Rajeshaye, *see* Rajshahi .	rä-jĕ-shä'-ē.
Rajpeepla	räj-pē'-plä.
Rajpoor	räj-pōōr'.
Rajpootana, *see* Rajputana	räj-pōō-tä'-nä.

Rajpoots, see Rajputs   răj-pōōtn'.
Rajputana, see Rajpootana   räj-pōō-tä'-nä.
Rajputs, see Rajpoots . .   räj-pōōts'.
Rajshahi, see Rajeshaye .   räj-shä'-hē.
Rákóczy . . . .   rä'-kōt-sē.
Rákos . . . .   rä'-kōsh.
Raleigh . . . . . .   rô'-lĬ, răl'-Ĭ.
Ralick, Ralik . . . . .   rä'-lĬk.
Rama . . . .   rā'-mȧ, rä'-mȧ.
Ramah . . . .   rā'-mä.
Ramapo . . . .   răm'-ȧ-pō, răm-ȧ-pō'.
Ramayana . . . . .   rä-mä'-yä-nä, răm'-ä-
Rambaud . . . . . .   räṅ-bō'.   [yä''-nä.
Rambouillet, de . . . .   dŭ räṅ-bōō-yä'.
Rameau . . . .   rä-mō'.
Ramée, Pierre de la . . .   pē-ȧr' dŭ lä rä-mä'.
Ramenghi . . . . . .   rä-mĕng'-gē.
Rameses, see Ramses . .   { răm'-ē-sēz,   ră-mē'-sēz,   răm'-ĕ-sēz,
Ramillies . . . . . .   răm'-Ĭl-ēz. *Fr.* rä-mē-yē'.
Ramiro . . . .   rä-mē'-rō.
Rammohun Roy . . . .   räm-mō-hŭn' roi.
Rampur . . . .   räm-pōōr'.
Ramses, see Rameses . .   răm'-sēz.
Ramus . . . .   rä-müs'.
Rancé . . . .   räṅ-sä'.
Rangoon, see Rangun . .   räṅ-gōōn'.
Rangpur, see Rungpoor .   rŭng-pōōr'.
Rangun, see Rangoon . .   räṅ-gōōn'.
Ranke, von . . . . . .   fōn räng'-kŭ.
Ranz des Vaches . . . .   räṅ dā väsh.
Raoul . . . .   rä-ōōl'.   [ĕl.
Raphael, see Raffaelle .   răf'-ā-ĕl, rä'-fä-ĕl, rā'-fä-
Raphaelesque . . . . .   răf''-ā-ĕl-ĕsk'.
Raphaelite . . . . . .   răf'-ā-ĕl-īt''.
Raphaelitism . . . . .   răf'-ā-ĕl-ī-tĬzm''.

Rapidan	răp-ĭ-dăn'.
Ras-el-Abiad	räs-ĕl-ä'-bē-äd.
Rasselas	răs'-ĕ-lăs.
Rata, *see* Rota	rä'-tä.
Ratisbon	răt'-ĭs-bŏn.
Ratlam, *see* Rutlam . . .	rŭt'-lăm.
Ratnagiri, *see* Rutnagherry	rŭt-nȧ-gē'-rē.
Rauch	rowċh.
Ravaillac	rä-vä-yäk'.
Ravenna . . . . . ▫ . . .	{ rȧ-vĕn'-ä. *It.* rä-vĕn'-nä.
Rawal Pindi, *or* Rawul Pindee	rô'-ŭl pĭn'-dē.
Rayo . . . . . ▫ . . .	rä'-yō.
Ré, Ile de, *see* Rhé . . .	ēl dŭ rä.
Reading	rĕd'-ĭng.
Réaumur, de	dŭ rä-ō-mür'.
Récamier	rā-kä-mē̤-ā̤'.
Rechab	rē'-kăb.
Rechabites	rĕk'-ȧ-bīts, rē'-kăb-īts.
Recife	rĕ-sē'-fĕ.
Reclus	rĕ-klü'.
Recollet	rĕk'-ŏl-lĕt.
Reddersburg	rĕd'-dĕrs-bŭrċh.
Redriff	rĕd'-rĭf.
Regensburg	rā'-gĕns-bōōrċh.
Reggio	rĕd'-jō.
Regillus (L.)	rĕ-jĭl'-ŭs.
Regnard	rĕ-när'.
Regnault	rĕ-nō'.
Régnier	rā-nē̤-ā̤'.
Regulus	rĕg'-ū-lŭs.
Rehan (Ada)	rē'-ȧn.
Rehoboam	rē-hō-bō'-ȧm.
Rehoboth . . . . . ▪ .	rĕ-hō'-bŏth.
Reichardt . . . . . ▪ .	rīċh'-ärt.

Reichenbach	rī'-ċhĕn-bäċh.
Reichsrath	rīċhs'-rät.
Reichstadt	rīċh'-stät.
Reichstag	rīċhs'-täċh.
Reikiavik, *see* Reykjavik .	rī'-kĭ-à-vĭk.
Reims, *see* Rheims . . .	rēmz. *Fr.* răns.
Reina Mercedes	rā-ē'-nä mâr-thā'-dās.
Reine de Saba, La . . .	lä rĕn dŭ sä-bä'.
Reine Margot, La	lä rĕn mär-gō'.
Reinhold	rīn'-hōlt.
Réjane	rā-zhăn'.
Religio Medici	rē-lĭj'-ĭ-ō mĕd'-ĭ-sī.
Rembrandt, *or* . . .	rĕm'-brănt.
Rembrandt van Rijn, *or* Ryn	} rĕm'-brănt văn rīn.
Remedios	rā-mā'-dē-ōs.
Remedius, *or*	rĕ-mē'-dĭ-ŭs.
Remi, *or*	rĕ-mē'.
Remigius	rĕ-mĭj'-ĭ-ŭs.
Rémusat, de	dŭ rā-mü-zä'.
Renaissance	rĕ-nā-säns', rĕ-nā'-sàns.
Renan	{ *Anglicized*, rē-nän', rē'-nän. *Fr.* rĕ-näṅ'.
Renard, *see* Reynard . .	*Fr.* rĕ-när'.
Renaud	rĕ-nō'.
René, Renée	rĕ-nā'.
Renfrew	rĕn'-frōō.
Reni, Guido	gwē'-dō rā'-nē.
Rennes	rĕn.
Renouvier	rĕ-nōō-vē̤-ā'.
Rensselaer	rĕn'-sē-lĕr.
Repnin, Nikolai	nē'-kō-lä̤-ē̤ rĕp-nēn'.
Resaca de Guerrero . . .	rā-sä'-kä dä gā-rā'-rō.
Resaca de la Palma . . .	rā-sä'-kä dä lä päl'-mä.
Reshid Pasha	{ rĕ-shēd' păsh-ô', pá-shä', pä'-shá.

Restigouche	rĕs-tē-gōōsh′.
Reszke, de	dŭ rĕsh′-kĕ.
Retté, Adolphe	ä-dōlf′ rĕt-tā′.
Retz, *see* Rais, Raiz . . .	räs.
Reuchlin	′roĭĉh′-lĭn.
Reunion, Ile de la . . .	{ rē-ūn′-yŭn.
	{ *Fr.* ēl dŭ lä rā-ü-nē-ôṅ′.
Reuss	rois.
Reuter	roi′-tĕr.
Reutlingen	roit′-lĭng-ĕn.
Reval, *or*	rĕv′-äl.
Revel	rĕv′-ĕl.
Revue des Deux Mondes .	rĕ-vü′ dā dĕ mōṅd.
Rewa, *or* Rewah	rā′-wä.
Reykjavik, *see* Reikiavik .	rī′-kĭ-ȧ-vĭk.
Reynard, *see* Renard . .	{ rĕn′-ȧrd, rā′-närd, rĕn′-
	{ ärd. *Fr.* rĕ-när′.
Reynier	rā-nē-ā′.
Reynolds	rĕn′-ŏldz.
Rezonville	rĕ-zôṅ-vēl′.
Rhadamanthine, Rhada-	} răd-ȧ-măn′-thĭn, -tĭn.
mantin . . . . }	
Rhadamanthus	răd-ȧ-măn′-thŭs.
Rhé, Ile du, *see* Ré . . .	ēl dŭ rā.
Rhea	rē′-ä.
Rheims, *see* Reims . .	rĕmz. *Fr.* răṅs.
Rheinberger	rĭn′-bĕr-gĕr.
Rheingold, Das	däs rĭn′-gŏlt.
Rhenish	rĕn′-ĭsh.
Rhodes	rōdz.
Rhodesia	rōd′-zhĭ-ȧ, rō-dē′-sĭ-ȧ.
Rhodope	rŏd′-ō-pē.
Rhys	rēs.
Rialto	rē-äl′-tō.
Riazan, *see* Ryazan . . .	rē-ä-zän′.
Ribault, *or* Ribaut . . .	rē-bō′.

Ribera	rū bā' rä.
Ribot	rē-bō'.
Ricardo	rĭ-kär'-dō, rē-kär'-dō.
Ricci	rēt'-chē.
Ricciarelli	rēch-är-ĕl'-lē.
Riccio (David), *see* Rizzio .	rēt'-chō.
Richelieu, de	{ dŭ rĭsh-ĕ-lū'. *Fr.* dŭ rēsh-ŭ-lē-ē'.
Richepin	rēsh-păṅ'.
Richier	rē-shē-ā'.
Richter	rĭċh'-tĕr.
Ricimer	rĭs'-ĭ-mẽr.
Rictus, Jehan	zhäṅ rĭk-tüs'.
Ridel	rē'-dĕl.
Riedesel (Gen.), von . . .	fŏn rēd'-ā''-zĕl.
Riego y Nuñez	rē-ā'-gō ē nōōn'-yĕth.
Rienzi, Cola di, *or* . . .	kō'-lä dē rē-ĕnd'-zē.
Rienzo	rē-ĕnd'-zō.
Riesen-Gebirge	rē'-zĕn-gā-bērg'-ŭ.
Riet (R.)	rēt.
Riga	rē'-gä.
Rigaud	rē-gō'.
Rigault	rē-gō'.
Righi, *or* Rigi	rē'-gĭ.
Rigoletto	rē-gō-lĕt'-tō.
Rigsdag	rĭgs'-dăg.
Rigveda	rĭg-vā'-dä.
Riis	rēs.
Rijks (Museum)	rīks.
Rijksdag	rīks-däċh.
Rimbault	răṅ-bō'.
Rimini	rē'-mē-nē.
Rimsky-Korsakov . . .	rĭm''-skĭ-kōr'-sä-kŏf.
Rinaldo ed Armida . . .	rē-näl'-dō äd är-mē'-dä.
Ring der Nibelungen, Der .	{ dâr rĭng dĕr nē' - bĕ- lōōng''-ĕn.

Rio Bravo del Norte, *see* } rē'-ō brä'-vō dĕl nōr'-tä.
Rio Grande del Norte   . }

Rio de Janeiro . . . . . { *pop.* re'-ō já-nēr'-ō, já-
                         { nĭ'-rō.   *Sp.* rē'-ō dā
                         { zhä-nā'-rō, zhä-nā'-ē-rō.

Rio de la Plata, *see* Plate . rē'-ō dā lä plä'-tä.

Rio Grande . . . . . . { rĭ'-ō grănd.
                       { *Sp.* rē'-ō grän'-dā.

Rio Grande de Cagayan . { rē'-ō grän'-dā dā kä-gä-
                        { yän'.

Rio Grande de la Pampanga { rē'-ō grän'-dā dā lä päm-
                          { pän'-gä.

Rio Grande del Norte, *see* } rē'-ō grän'-dā dĕl nōr'-tä.
Rio Bravo del Norte . . }

Rio Grande de Santiago { rē'-ō grän'-dā dā sän-
                       { tē-ä'-gō.   [tĕ.

Rio Grande do Norte . . rē'-ō grän'-dā dōō nōr'-

Rio Grande do Sul . . . rē'-ō grän'-dā dōō sōōl.

Rio Negro . . . . . { *Sp.* rē'-ō nā'-grō.
                    { *Port.* rē-ōō nā'-grōō.

Rio Negro, São José do . . { sowñ zhō-zā' dōō rē'-ōō
                           { nā'-grōō.

Ripon . . . . rĭp'-ŭn.
Ristori . . . . . . rē-stō'-rē.
Riviera . . . . . . rē-vē-ā'-rä.
Rivière, Duc de . . . dük dŭ rē-vē-âr'.
Rivinus . . . . . . rē-vē'-nŭs.
Rivoli, Rue de . . . . rü dŭ rē-vō-lē'.
Rizzio, *see* Riccio . . . . rĭt'-sē-ō, rēt'-sē-ō.
Roanoke . . . . . . rō-á-nōk'.
Roatan, *see* Ruatan . . rō-ä-tän'.
Robbia, Luca della . . lōō'-kä dĕl'-lä rŏb'-bē-ä.
Robert-Fleury . . . . rō-bâr'- flēr-ē'.

Robert Guiscard . . . { rŏb'-ĕrt gēs-kär'.
                      { *Fr.* rō-bâr'.

Robert le Diable . . . . rō-bâr' lĕ dē-ä'-bl.

Robespierre, de   { dŭ rō'-bĕs-pēr
                    { Fr. dŭ rŏbs-pĕ-âr'.
Robsart (Amy) . . . . rŏb'-särt.
Robusti, Jacopo . . . . yä-kō'-pō rō-bŏŏs'-tē.
Roch, Saint . . . . . . săṅ rōk.
Rochambeau, de . . . . dŭ rō-shäṅ-bō'.
Rochefort . . . . . . rŏsh-fōr'.
Rochefoucauld, La . . . lä rŏsh-fŏŏ-kō'.
Rochejacquelein, La . . . lä rŏsh-zhăk-lăṅ'.
Rochelle . . . . rō-shĕl'.
Rochet . . . . rō-shā'.
Rochus . . . . rō'-kŭs.
Rod, Édouard . . . . . ä-dŏŏ-är' rōd.
Rodenbach, Georges . . . zhŏrzh rō-dĕn-bäċh'.
Roderick, Dhu . . . . . rŏd'-ēr-ĭk dū.
Roderigo . . . . rŏd-ĕr-ē'-gō.
Rodin, Auguste . . . . ō-güst' rō-dăṅ'.   [bär'.
Rodrigo Diaz de Bivar . . rōd-rē'-gō dē'-äth dä bē-
Rodrigues, or . . . . . Fr. rōd-rēg'.
Rodriguez (I.) . . . . . rō-drē'-gĕs.
Rodriguez (José Joaquin) . rōd-rē'-gĕth.
Roelas, Juan de las . . . 'hŏŏ-än' dä läs rō-ā'-läs.
Roeselare, see Roulers, } rŏŏ-sĕ-lä'-rĕ.
  Rousselaere . . . . . }
Roeskilde, see Röskilde . rĕs'-kēl-dĕ.
Rofreit . . . . rōf'-rīt.
Rogero, see Ruggiero . . rō-jä'-rō.
Roget . . . . rō-zhā'.
Rohan, de . . . . . . dŭ rō-äṅ'.
Rohilcund, or Rohilkhand rō-hĭl-kŭnd'.
Rohtak . . . . rō-tŭk'.
Roi des Montagnes . . . rwä dā môṅ-tän'-yŭ.
Roi d'Yvetot, Le . . . . lĕ rwä dēv-tō'.
Roi s'Amuse, Le . . . . lĕ rwä sä-müz'.
Rois Fainéants, Les . . . lä rwä fā-nā-äṅ'.
Rojas-Zorilla, or Zorrilla . rŏ'-ċhäs-thōr-rēl'-yä.

Rokeby . . . . rōk'-bĭ.
Roland . . . . rō'-lánd. *Fr.* rō-läṅ'.
Roland, Chanson de . . . shäṅ-sôṅ' dŭ rō-läṅ'.
Roland de la Platière . . rō-läṅ' dŭ lä plä-tē-âr'.
Roland de Roncevaux . . rō-läṅ' dŭ rôṅs-vō'.
Roldan . . . . rōl-dän'.
Rolf . . . . rŏlf.
Rollin . . . . rŏl'-ĭn. *Fr.* rō-läṅ'.
Rollo . . . . rŏl'-ō.
Romagna. . . . . . . rō-män'-yä.
Romaic . . . . rō-mā'-ĭk.
Roman de la Rose . . . rō-mäṅ' dŭ lä rōz.
Roman de Rou . . . . rō-mäṅ'dŭ rōō.
Romanes . . . . rō-mä'-nēz.
Romano, Ezzelino da . . { ĕt-zā-lē'-nō dä rō-mä'-
                         { nō.
Romanof, *or* Romanoff . rō-mä'-nŏf.
Romany, *see* Rommany . rŏm'-á-nĭ.
Romero (Matias) . . . rō-mā'-rō.
Romilly . . . . rŏm'-ĭ-lĭ.
Rommany, *see* Romany . rŏm'-á-nĭ.
Romola . . . . rŏm'-ō-lá, rō-mō'-lá.
Roncesvalles, *or* . . . { rŏn-sē-väl'-lĕs.
                         { *Sp.* rōn-thĕs-väl'-yĕs.
Roncevaux . . . . . *Fr.* rôṅs-vō'.
Ronge . . . . rŏng'-ŭ.
Ronsard (Pierre de) . . . rôṅ-sär'.
Röntgen . . . . rĕnt'-gĕn.
Rooidam . . . . rō-ē-däm'.
Roosevelt . . . . . rōs'-vĕlt, rō'-sĕ-vĕlt.
Roquefort . . . . . . rŏk-fōr'.
Rosa, Salvator . . . . . säl-vä'-tōr rō'-zä.
Rosalind . . . . rŏz'-á-lĭnd.
Rosaline . . . . rŏz'-á-lĭn.
Rosamond, Rosamund . . rŏz'-á-mŭnd.
Rosbach, *see* Rossbach . rŏs'-bäċh.

Roscelin, *or* . . . . *Fr.* rŏs-ĕl-ăṅ'.

Roscellin, oı . . . . . . ı̆ŏs'-ĕl-ĭn.

Roscellinus, *see* Rucelinus rŏs-ĕ-lĭ'-nŭs.

Roscius . . . . rŏsh'-ï-ŭs.

Roscommon . . . . . . rŏs-kŏm'-ŭn.

Rosecrans . . . . . . rō'-zĕ-krănz.

Rosellini . . . . rō-zĕl-lē'-nē.

Rosenkranz . . . . . . rō'-zĕn-kränts.

Rosicrucian . . . . . . {rŏz-ĭ-krū'-shĭ-ạn, rōz-ĭ-
krō͞o'-shĭ-ạn.

Rosinante, *see* Rozinante rŏz-ĭ-năn'-tē.

Röskilde, *see* Roeskilde . rĕs'-kēl'-dĕ.

Rosny (Léon de) . . . . rō-nē'.

Rossbach, *see* Rosbach . . rŏs'-bäċh.

Rossellino . . . . . . rŏs-sĕl-lē'-nō.

Rossetti . . . . rŏs-sĕt'-tē.

Rossi . . . . rŏs'-sē.

Rossini . . . . rŏs-sē'-nē.

Rostand, Edmond . . . ĕd-môṅ' rŏs-täṅ'.

Rostock . . . . rŏs'-tŏk.

Rostoptchin . . . . . . {rŏs'-tŏp-chĭn, rŏs-tŏp-
chēn'.

Rota, *see* Rata . . . . . rō'-tä.

Rotherhithe . . . . . rŏṫh'-ĕr-hĭṫh.

Rothesay . . . . rŏth'-sā.

Rothschild . . . . . . {rŏths'-chīld, rōs'-child.
Ger. rōt'-shĭlt.

Rotrou . . . . rō-trō͞o'.

Rotterdam . . . . . . {rŏt'-ĕr-dăm.
D. rŏt-tĕr-dăm'.

Roubaix . . . . rō͞o-bā'.

Roubillac . . . . . . rō͞o-bē-yäk'.

Rouen . . . . rō͞o'-ĕn. *Fr.* rō͞o-äṅ'.

Rougé . . . . rō͞o-zhā'.

Rouget de Lisle, *or* l'Isle . rō͞o-zhā' dŭ lēl.

Rougon-Macquart, Les . . lä rō͞o-gôṅ'-mä-kär'.

Roulers,   *see*   Roeselare, ⎫
Rousselaere . . . . . ⎭ rōō-lā'.

Roumania, *see* Rumania .   rōō-mā'-nĭ-á.

Roumelia, *see* Rumelia . .   rōō-mē'-lĭ-á.

Rousseau . . . .   rōō-sō'.

Rousselaere, *see* Roeselare, ⎫
Roulers . . . . . . ⎭ rōōs-lär'.   [yôṅ'.

Roussillon . . . . . .   *Fr.* rōō-sē-yôṅ', rōō-sĕl-

Roustam, *see* Rustam . .   rōōs'-tám.   *Pers.* rōōs-

Rouxville . . . .   rōō-vēl'.   [tĕm.

Roveredo . . . .   rō-vĕ-rā'-dō.

Rovigo . . . .   rō-vē'-gō.

Rowe . . . .   rō.

Rowland . . . . . .   rō'-lánd.

Roxana, *or* . . . . . .   rŏks-ăn'-ä, rŏks-ā'-nä.

Roxane . . . .   *Fr.* rŏks-än'.

Roy, Rammohun . . . .   räm-mō-hŭn' roi.

Roy Bareilly, *see* Rai Bareli   roi bä-rā'-lē.

Royer-Collard . . . . .   rwä-yā'-kŏl-lär'.

Rozinante, *see* Rosinante .   rŏz-ĭ-năn'-tē.

Ruatan, *see* Roatan . . .   rōō-ä-tän'.

Rubaiyat (The) . . . .   rōō'-bī-yăt.

Rubens (Peter Paul) . .   rōō'-bĕnz.

Rübezahl . . . .   rü'-bĕ-tsäl.

Rubicon . . . .   rōō'-bĭ-kŏn.

Rubinstein (Anton) . . .   rōō'-bĭn-stīn.

Rucelinus, *see* Roscelin .   rōō-sĕ-lī'-nŭs.

Rucellai . . . .   rōō-chĕl-lä'-ē.

Rückert . . . .   rük'-ĕrt.

Rudesheim . . . . . .   rü'-dĕs-hīm.

Rüdiger . . . .   . .   rü'-dĭ-gĕr.

Rue de la Paix . . . .   rü dŭ lä pā.

Rue de Rivoli . . . . .   rü dŭ rē-vō-lē'.

Ruell . . . .   rü-ā'-yŭ.

Rue St.-Antoine . . . .   rü säṅ-täṅ-twän'.

Rue St.-Denis . . . . .   rü säṅ-dĕ-nē'.

Rue St.-Honoré . . . . rü săṅ-tō-nō-rā'.

Rufinel . . . . ˌöől-fē'-nĕ.

Rufinus . . . . rōō-fī'-nŭs.

Rug . . . . rōōg.

Rügen . . . . rü'-gĕn.

Rugglero, see Rogero . . rōŏd-jā'-rō.

Ruisdaal, or Ruisdael, see ⎫ rois'-däl.
Ruysdael . . . . . . ⎭

Ruk (I.) . . . . rōōk.

Rum (I.) . . . . rŭm.

Rumania, see Roumania . rōō-mā'-nĭ-á.

Rumelia, see Roumelia . rōō-mē'-lĭ-á.

Runeberg . . . . . . rōō'-nĕ-bĕrċh.

Rungpoor, see Rangpur . rŭng-pōōr'.

Runjeet Singh . . . . . rŭn-jēt' sĭngh.

Runnemede, see Runni- ⎫ rŭn'-ĕ-mēd.
mede . . . . ⎭

Runnimede, or Runny- ⎫ rŭn'-ĭ-mēd.
mede, see Runnemede . ⎭

Rupert . . . . rōō'-pĕrt.

Ruprecht . . . . rōō'-prĕċht.

Rurik . . . . rōō'-rĭk.

Rus . . . . rŭs.

Ruscuk, see Rustchuk . . rōōs-chōōk'.

Russia . . . . rŭsh'-ĭ-á, rōŏsh'-ĭ-á.

Russian . . . . rŭsh'-ĭ-ạn, rōŏsh'-ĭ-ạn.

Rustam, see Roustam and ⎫ rōŏs'-tảm. Pers. rōŏs'-
Rustum . . . . . . ⎭ tăm'.

Rustchuk, see Ruscuk . . rōōs-chōōk'.

Rustenburg . . . . . . rōŏs'-tĕn-bōōrċh.

Rustum, see Roustam, Rus- ⎫ rōōs'-tŭm.
tam . . . . ⎭

Rutherglen . . . . . . rŭth'-ĕr-glĕn, rŭg'-lĕn.

Ruthven (Raid of) . . . rŭth'-vĕn. loc. rĭv'-ĕn.

Rutlam, see Ratlam . . . rŭt'-lảm.

Rütli, see Grütli . . . . rüt'-lĭ.

Rutnagherry, *see* Ratnagiri   rŭt-nȧ-gĕr'-ĭ,
Ruy Blas . . . .   rü-ē' bläs.
Ruy Diaz . . . .   rōō'-ē dē'-äth.
Ruyghur . . . .   rī-gŭr'.
Ruysdael, *see* Ruisdaal, }   rois'-däl.
  Ruisdael . . . . . }
Ruyter . . . .   rī'-tĕr. *D.* roi'-tĕr.
Ryazan, *see* Riazan . . .   rē-ä-zän'.
Rydal . . . .   rī'-dȧl.
Ryswick, *or* . . . . . .   rĭz'-wĭk.
Ryswijk . . . .   *D.* rīs'-vĭk.

S

Saadi, *see* Sadi . . . . .   sä'-dē, să-dē'.
Saale . . . .   zä'-lŭ.
Saalfeld . . . .   zäl'-fĕlt.
Saarbrück, *or* . . . . .   zär'-brük.
Saarbrücken, *see* Sarrebruck   zär'-brük-ĕn.
Saardam, *see* Zaarrdam .   sär-dăm'.
Saavedra (Cervantes) . .   sä-ä-vä'-drä.
Saba, *see* Sabea . . . .   sä'-bä.
Saba (I.) . . . .   sä'-bä.
Sabana Grande . . . .   sä-bä'-nä grän'-dä.
Sabaoth . . . .   săb'-ä-ŏth, sä-bä'-ŏth.
Sabbatic . . . .   săb-ăt'-ĭk.
Sabea, *see* Saba . . . .   să-bē'-ä.
Sabeans . . . .   sä-bē'-ȧnz.
Sabine (Cross Roads) . .   să-bēn'.
Sabine (Mts.) . . . . .   sä'-bīn.
Sabine (Sir Edward) . .   săb'-ĭn.
Sabinella . . . .   sä-bē-nĕl'-lä.
Sabines . . . .   săb'-īnz, sä'-bīnz.
Sabini . . . .   să-bī'-nĭ.
Sabrina . . . .   să-brī'-nȧ, sä-brī'-nȧ.

15

Sacheverell . . . . săᴋ ᴀhŏv′ ŏ rŏl.

Sachs (Hans) . . . . . zäks.

Sachsen . . . . zäk′-zĕn.

Sachsen - Altenburg, *see* } zäk′-zĕn-äl′-tĕn-bōōrċh.
Saxe-Altenburg . . . . }

Sachsen-Coburg-Gotha, *see* } zäk′ - zĕn - kō′ - bōōrċh -
Saxe-Coburg-Gotha . . } gō′-tä.

Sachsen - Meiningen, *see* } zäk′-zĕn-mī′-nĭng-ĕn.
Saxe-Meiningen . . . }

Sachsenspiegel . . . . . zäk′-zĕn-spē″-gĕl.

Sachsen-Weimar-Eisenach, } zäk′ - zĕn-vī′-mär-ī′-zĕ-
see Saxe-Weimar-Eise- } näċh.
nach . . . . }

Sacile . . . . sä-chē′-lĕ.

Saco (R.) . . . . sᴏ̂′-kō.

Saco (José Antonio) . . . sä′-kō.

Sadducees . . . . . . săd′-yū-sēz.

Sadi, *see* Saadi . . . . sä-dē′.

Sadi-Carnot . . . . . . să-dē′-kär-nō′.

Sadowa . . . . sä-dō′-vä, sä′-dō-vä.

Saenz Peña . . . . . . sä′-änth pän′-yä.

Safed . . . . sä′-fĕd, sä-fĕd′.

Safed Koh, *see* Suffeed Koh sä′-fĕd kō.

Safll, *see* Sufi, Sofi . . . säf′-ĭ.

Sagan . . . . zä′-gän *Fr.* zä-gäṅ′.

Sagar, *see* Saugor, Saugur sä-gŭr′.

Sagasta (Praxedes Mateo) . sä-gäs′-tä.

Sage, Le, *see* Lesage . . . lĕ säzh′.

Saghalien, *or* Saghalin . . sä-gä-lē′-ĕn, sä-gä-lēn′.

Sagittarius . . . . . . săj-ĭ-tā′-rĭ-ŭs.

Sagua La Grande . . . . sä′-gwä lä grän′-dä.

Saguenay . . . . . . săg-ĕ-nā′, sä-gĕn-ā′.

Sahara, *see* Zahara, Sahra, } să-hä′-rä, sä′-hȧ-rä.
Sahhra . . . . }

Saharanpur, *see* Seharun- } sȧ-här-ȧn-pōōr′.
poor . . . . }

Sahhra, *see* Sahara, Zahara   sä′-hrä.

Sahib . . . .   sä′-hĭb.

Sahra, *see* Sahara, Zahara   sä′-hrä.

Said (Port) . . . . .   sä-ēd′. *pop.* säd.

Saida . . . .   sī′-dä.

Said Pasha . . . . .   { sä-ēd′, *pop.* säd, päsh-ô′, pá-shä′, päsh′-à.

Saigon . . . .   sī-gōn′. *Fr.* sī-gôṅ′.

Saigo Takamori . . .   sī′-gō tä-kä-mō′-rē.

Saikio . . . .   sī-kē′-ō.

St. Albans . . . . .   sänt, sĕnt ôl′-bànz.

St.-Amand, *or* . . . .   säṅ-tä-mäṅ′.

St.-Amand-Montrond . .   säṅ-tä-mäṅ′-môṅ-rôṅ′.

St.-Antoine, Faubourg . .   fō-bōōr′ säṅ-täṅ-twäṅ′.

Saint-Arnaud . . . .   säṅ-tär-nō′.

St. Augustine . . . .   { sänt, sĕnt ô-gŭs′-tĭn, ô′-gŭs-tīn.

St. Augustine (City) . . .   sänt, sĕnt ô′-gŭs-tēn.

St. Barthélemy . . . .   *Fr.* säṅ bär-tāl-mē′.

St. Bernard . . . . .   { sänt, sĕnt bĕr-närd′, bĕr′- närd. *Fr.* säṅ bĕr-när′.

St. Bernard de Menthon .   { säṅ bĕr-när′ dŭ môṅ- tôṅ′.

St. Cecilia, *see* Santa Cecilia   sänt sē-sīl′-ĭ-à.

St. Chad . . . .   sänt, sĕnt chăd.

St. Clair . . . .   { sänt, sĕnt klâr. *Eng.* sĭng′-klâr.

St. Cloud . . . .   { sänt, sĕnt klowd′. *Fr.* säṅ klōō′.

St. Croix, *see* Santa Cruz .   sänt kroi′.

St. Cyr . . . .   säṅ sēr′.

St. Denis . . . .   { sänt, sĕnt dĕn′-ĭs. *Fr.* säṅ dĕn-ē′.

Sainte-Aldegonde . . . .   säṅt-äl-dē-gôṅd′.

Sainte-Beuve . . . . .   säṅt-bĕv′.

Sainte-Chapelle . . . .   säṅt-shä-pĕl′.

Sainte-Croix, *see* Santa Cruz	săṅt-krwä'.
Ste. Geneviève	săṅt zhĕn-vē̤-ĕv'.
Sainte-Gudule	săṅt gü-dül'.
Sainte Lucie	săṅt lü-sē'.
Sainte Pélagie	săṅt pā-lä-zhē'.
Saintes	săṅt.
St.-Étienne	săṅ-tā-tē̤-ĕn'.
St. Eustache	săṅ tēs-täsh'.
St. Eustatius	sānt, sĕnt ū-stā'-shĭ-ŭs.
Saint-Évremond	săṅ-tāvr-môṅ'.
St. Francis Xavier . . .	{ sānt, sĕnt frăn'-sĭs zăv'- ĕ̤-ĕr. *Sp.* ċhä-bē-âr'. *Fr.* ksä-vē̤-ā'. }
St. Gall, *see* Sankt Gallen	sānt gôl. *Fr.* săṅ-gäl'.
Saint-Gaudens	{ sānt, sĕnt-gô'-dĕnz. *Fr.* săṅ-gō-dŏṅ'. }
Saint-Germain	săṅ-zhĕr-măṅ'.
St.-Germain-des-Prés . .	săṅ-zhĕr-măṅ'-dā-prā'.
St. Germain l'Auxerrois .	săṅ-zhĕr-măṅ' lōks-ĕr-
St. Gothard	*Fr.* săṅ gō-tär'. [wä'.
St. Gotthard	{ sānt, sĕnt gŏth'-ärd. *Ger.* sänkt gŏt'-härt. }
St. Helena (Mother of Con- stantine)	} sānt hĕl'-ē-nà.
St. Helena (I.)	sānt hĕ-lē'-nä.
Saint-Hilaire, Barthélemy	bär-tāl-mē' săṅ-tē-lâr'.
Saint-Hilaire, Geoffroy . .	zhō-frwä' săṅ-tē-lâr'.
Saintine	săṅ-tēn'. [tēv'.
Saint-Ives, *see* St. Yves . .	sānt, sĕnt īvz. *Fr.* săṅ-
St. Jean d' Acre	săṅ zhäṅ dä'-kr.
St.-Jean d'Angély	săṅ zhäṅ' däṅ-zhā-lē'.
St. John	{ sānt, sĕnt jŏn'. *Eng.* *sometimes* sĭn' jŏn. }
Saint-Just	săṅ zhüst'.
St. Leger	{ sānt, sĕnt lĕj'-ĕr. *Eng* *sometimes* sĭl'-ĭn-jĕr. }

St.-Leu . . . . săn-lĕ′.

St. Louis . . . . . . { sānt, sĕnt lōō′-ĭs, lōō′-ĭ.
{ *Fr.* săn lōō-ē′.

St. Lucia (I.) *see* Santa } sānt, sĕnt lōō′-shĭ-à.
Lucia . . . . . . }

St. Malo . . . . . . { *pop.* sānt măl′-ō.
{ *Fr.* săn mä-lō′.

Saint-Mars . . . . . . săn-mär′.

St. Martin . . . . . { sānt, sĕnt mär′-tĭn.
{ *Fr.* săn-mär-tăn′.

St. Michael . . . . . sānt, sĕnt mī′-kĕl.

St. Michel . . . . . săn mē-shĕl′.

St. Nicolas . . . . . *Fr.* săn nē-kō-lä′.

St. Olaus . . . . . . sānt, sĕnt ō-lā′-ŭs.

St. Omer . . . . . . săn tō-mâr′.

Saintonge . . . . . săn-tônzh′.

St. Ouen . . . . . . săn tōō-ŏn′. [dä.

St. Paul de Loanda . . . sānt, sĕnt pôl dĕ lō-än′-

St. Pierre, de . . . . . dŭ săn pḛ̄-âr′. [pḛ̄-âr′.

St. Pierre, Bernardin de . bĕr-när-dăn′ dĕ săn

St. Pol-de-Léon . . . . săn pōl-dŭ-lā-ôn′.

Saint-Preux . . . . . săn-prĕ′.

St. Quentin . . . . . { sānt kwĕn′-tĭn.
{ *Fr.* săn kŏn-tăn′.

St. Roch . . . . . . săn rōk.

St. Roque, *see* Sāo Roque, } sānt, sĕnt rōk.
see San Roque . . . . }

Saint-Saëns . . . . . săn-sän′.

St. Sebastian, *see* San Se- } sānt, sĕnt sĕ-băs′-tḛ̄-àn.
bastian . . . . . . }

St. Simon, de . . . . . { dŭ sānt, sĕnt sī′-mŏn.
{ *Fr.* dŭ săn sē-môn′.

St. Sulpice . . . . . săn sŭl-pēs′. [pôl.

St. Vincent de Paul . . . { sānt, sĕnt vĭn′-sĕnt dŭ
{ *Fr.* săn văn-sän′ dŭ pōl.

Saint Yves, *see* St. Ives . . săn tēv′.

Saïs . . . . sä'-ĭs
Saisiaz, La . . . . . . lä sā-zē-äs'.
Sakai . . . . sä'-kī.
Sakatal . . . . . . sä-kä-täl'.
Sala (G. A.) . . . . . sä'-lä, sä'-lá.
Saladin, see Salah-ed-Din . säl'-á-dĭn.
Salado de Tarifa . . . . sä-lä'-dō dä tä-rē'-fä.
Salah-ed-Din, see Saladin . *Arab.* sä'-lä-ĕd-dēn'.
Salamanca . . . . . . { säl-á-män'-kà.
                   { *Sp.* sä-lä-män'-kä.
Salamis . . . . . . säl'-á-mĭs.
Salammbô . . . . . sä-läm-bō'.
Salanio, *or* . . . . . sá-lä'-nĭ-ō, sä-lä'-nē-ō.
Salarino . . . . . . sä-lá-rē'-nō, sä-lä-rē'-nō.
Saldanha . . . . . . säl-dän'-yä.
Salerno . . . . . . sá-lěr'-nō. *It.* sä-lěr'-nō.
Sales (Francis of) . . . . sälz. *Fr.* säl.
Saléza . . . . sä-lä'-zä.
Salian . . . . sā'-lĭ-án.
Salic . . . . säl'-ĭk.
Salignac . . . . . . sä-lēn-yäk'.
Salisbury . . . . . sôlz'-bŭ-rĭ.
Salle, De la . . . . . dŭ lä säl'.
Salmon (Falls) . . . . säm'-ŭn.
Salm-Salm . . . . . zälm-zälm.
Salome . . . . . . sá-lō'-mĕ, sä-lō'-mē.
Salon (The) . . . . . sä-lôn'.
Salonica . . . . . . säl-ō-nē'-kà.
Saloniki . . . . . . sä-lō-nē'-kē.
Salpêtrière, La . . . . . lä säl-pā-trē̩-âr'.
Salta . . . . säl'-tä.
Saltikoff, see Soltikoff . . säl'-tē-kŏf.
Salvador . . . . . . säl-vä-dōr'.
Salvator Rosa . . . . säl-vä'-tōr rō'-zä.
Salvini . . . . säl-vē'-nē.
Salzburg . . . . . . zälts'-bōōrċh.

Salzkammergut . . . . zältz'-käm-ĕr-gōōt.
Samoin, Albert . . . äl-bâr' sä-măṅ'.
Samaná, Santa Barbara de sän'-tä bär'-bä-rä da sa-
Samar . . . . sä-mär'.   [mä-nä'.
Samara (City) . . . . . *Russ.* sä-mä-rä'.
Samarang . . . . . . sä-mä-räng'.
Samarcand, *or* Samarkand säm-är-känd'.
Samaveda . . . . . . sä-mä-vā'-dä.
Sambalpur, *see* Sumbulpur sŭm-bŭl-pōōr'.
Sambre (R.) . . . . . . sŏṅ'-br.
Samminiato, *see* San Min- } säm''-mĭn-ĭ-ä'-tō.
    iato . . . . }
Samoa . . . . sä-mō'-à.
Samoan (Is.) . . . . . sä-mō'-àn, sä-mō'-än.
Samos . . . . sā'-mŏs.
Samoset . . . . săm'-ō-sĕt.
Samothrace . . . . . . { săm'-ō-thrās.
                        { *Gr.* săm-ō-thrā'-sē.
Samson et Dalila . . . . sän-sôṅ' nä dä-lē-lä'.
San Ambrogio . . . . . sän äm-brō'-jō.
San Antonio (City) . . . sän ăn-tō'-nĭ-ō.
San Antonio (Cape) . . . sän än-tō'-nē-ō.
Sanballat . . . . . . sän-băl'-àt.
Sancho Panza . . . . . { săng'-kō păn'-zä.
                        { *Sp.* sän'-chō pän'-thä.
San Clemente . . . . . sän klā-mĕn'-tĕ.
San Cristobal . . . . . sän krēs-tō'-bäl.
Sand, George . . . . . jôrj sänd. *Fr.* zhŏrzh
Sandalphon . . . . . . sän-däl'-fŏn.   [sänd.
Sandeau . . . . sän-dō'.
Sandherr . . . . sän-dâr'.
San Diego . . . . . . sän dē-ā'-gō.
San Domingo, *see* Santo } sän dō-mēng'-gō.
    Domingo . . . . . . }
Sandoval . . . . sän-dō'-bäl.
Sandringham . . . . . săndʹ-rĭng-àm.

Sandys (Edwin)	săn'-dĭs, săndz.
San Fernando	săn fẽr-nan'-dŏ.
Sangallo	săng-gäl'-lō.
Sangar (Strait)	săn-gär'.
San Giorgio	săn jŏr'-jō.
Sangir (Is.)	săng-gẽr'.
Sangpo, see Sanpu . . .	săng-pō'.
Sangrado (Doctor) . . .	săn-grä'-dō.
Sanhedrim, or	săn'-hē-drĭm.
Sanhedrin	săn'-hē-drĭn.
San Jacinto	{ săn já-sĭn'-tō. { *Sp.* săn ċhä-thēn'-tō.
San Joaquin	săn ċhō-ä-kēn'.
San José	săn ċhŏ-sā'.
San José de Buenavista .	{ săn ċhŏ-sā' dä bōō-ä-nä- { vēs'-tä.
San Juan	săn ċhōō-än'. [tä.
San Juan Bautista . . .	săn ċhōō-än' bä-ōō-tēs'-
San Juan de Puerto Rico .	{ săn ċhōō-än' dä pōō- { ẽr'-tō rē'-kō.
San Juan de Ulloa . . .	săn ċhōō-än' ŏŏl-yō'-ä.
Sankt Gallen, see Saint Gall	sänkt gäl'-lĕn.
Sankt Goar	sänkt gō'-är.
Sankt Gotthard	sänkt gŏt'-härt.
Sankt Jakob	sänkt yä'-kŏp.
Sankt Moritz	sänkt mō'-rĭts.
San Luis de Apra	săn lōō-ēs' dä ä'-prä.
San Luis Potosí	săn lōō-ēs' pō-tō-sĕ'.
San Marco	săn mär'-kō.
San Marino	săn mä-rē'-nō.
San Martin	săn mär-tēn'.
San Miguel	săn mē-gĕl'.
San Miniato, see Sammin-	{ săn mē-nē-ä'-tō, mĭn-ĭ-
iato	{ ä'-tō.
San Onofrio	săn ō-nō'-frē-ō. [lē.
San Pietro in Vincoli . .	săn pē-ä'-trō ēn vēn'-kō-

Sanpu, *see* Sangpo . . . . sän-poo'.

San Remo . . . . . . sän rā'-mō.

San Roque, *see* St. Roque, } sän rō'-kā.
São Roque . . . . .

Sanscrit, *see* Sanskrit . . săn'-skrĭt.

San Sebastian, *see* Saint } sän sā-bäs''-tē-än'.
Sebastian, ...

Sans Gêne, Madame . . . mä-dăm' säṅ zhän.

Sanskrit, *see* Sanscrit . . săn'-skrĭt.

Sansovino . . . . . . sän-sō-vē'-nō.

Sans Souci . . . . . . *Fr.* sŏṅ soo-sē'.

San Stefano . . . . . . sän stĕf'-ä-nō.

Santa Ana . . . . . . sän'-tä ä'-nä.

Santa Cecilia, *see* St. Cecilia sän'-tä chä-chēl'-ē-ä.

Santa Croce sull' Arno . . sän'-tä krō'-chĕ sŏol är'-

Santa Cruz, *see* Sainte Croix săn'-tä krooz.   [nō.

Santa Cruz (Andres) . . sän'-tä krooth'.

Santa Cruz de la Palma . { sän'-tä krooth' dā lä
päl'-mä.

Santa Cruz de la Sierra . { sän'-tä krooth' dā lä
sē-ĕr'-rä.

Santa Cruz de Santiago . { sän'-tä krooth' dā sän-
tē-ä'-gō.

Santa Cruz de Tenerife . { sän'-tä krooth' dā tä-
nä-rē'-fä.

Santa Fé . . . . sän'-tä fā.

Santal Parganas . . . . sän-täl' pär-gŭn'-ás.

Santa Lucia, *see* St. Lucia { *It.* sän'-tä loo-chē'-ä.
Sp. sän'-tä loo-thē'-ä.

Santa Luzia . . . . . . sän'-tä loo-zē'-ä.

Santa Maria, La . . . . lä sän'-tä mä-rē'-ä.

Santa Maria degli Angeli . { sän'-tä mä-rē'-ä dāl'-yē
än'-jä-lē.   [mē'-nĕ.

Santa Maria del Carmine . sän'-tä mä-rē'-ä dĕl kär-

Santa Maria del Popolo . { sän'-tä mä-rē'-ä dĕl pō'-
pō-lō.

Santa Maria in Ara Cooli . { sän'-tä mä-rē'-ä ā' rá sē'-lĭ.

Santa Maria in Cosmedin . { sän'-tä mä-rē'-ä ĭn kŏs'-mĕ-dĭn.

Santa Maria Maggiore . . { sän'-tä mä-rē'-ä mäd-jō'-rĕ.

Santa Maria Novella . . . { sän'-tä mä-rē'-ä nō-vĕl'-lä.

Santa Maria sopra Minerva { sän'-tä mä-rē'-ä sō'-prä mē-nĕr'-vä.

Santander . . . . . . { sän-tăn-dâr'. *Sp.* sän-tän-dār'.

Sant' Angelo . . . . . *It.* sänt än'-jā-lō.

Santarem . . . . sän-tä-răń', sän-tä-rĕń'.

Santi, Raphael, *see* Raphael and Sanzio . . . } rä'-fä-ĕl sän'-tē.

Santiago . . . . { sän-tē-ä'-gō. *Sp.* sän-tē-ä'-gō.

Santiago de Chile . . . . sän-tē-ä'-gō dā chē'-lā.

Santiago de Compostela, *or* { sän-tē-ä'-gō · dā kōm-pōs-tā'-lä.

Santiago de Compostella . { sän-tē-ä'-gō dā kōm-pōs-tĕl'-ä.

Santiago de Cuba . . . . { sän-tē-ä'-gō dā kōō'-bä. *Eng.* kū'-bä.

Santiago de la Vegas . . { sän-tē-ä'-gō dā läs vā'-gäs.

Santiago del Estero . . . sän-tē-ä'-gō dĕl ĕs-tā'-rō.

Santillana . . . . . . sän-tēl-yä'-nä.

Santo Domingo, *see* San Domingo . . . . . } sän'-tō dō-mĭng'-gō, *Sp.* sän'-tō dō-mēng'-gō.

Santo Espíritu . . . . . sän'-tō ĕs-pē'-rē-tōō.

Santoveneo . . . . . . sän''-tō-vä-nā'-ō.

San Yuste . . . . . . sän yōōs'-tä.

Sanzio, Raphael, *see* Raphael and Santi . . . } rä'-fä-ĕl sänd'-zē-ō.

São Antão	sän än-tän'.
São José do Rio Negro . .	{ sän zhō-zä' dōō rē'-ōō nä'-grōō.
Saona	sä-ō'-nä.
Saône	sōn.
Saône-et-Loire	sōn-ä-lwär'.　　　[dä.
São Paulo de Loanda . .	sän pow'-lōō dĕ lō-än'-
São Roque, see Saint Roque	sän rō'-kä.
Sapho	sä-fō'.
Sapor, see Shapur and } Shahpoor . . . . . . }	sā'-pŏr.
Sapphic	săf'-ĭk.
Sapphira	să-fī'-rȧ.
Sappho	săf'-ō.
Saracen	săr'-ȧ-sĕn.
Saracenic	săr-ȧ-sĕn'-ĭk.
Saragossa, see Sp. Zaragoza	săr-ȧ-gŏs'-ȧ.
Saran, see Sarun	sä-rŭn'.　　　[kōō̤-ĕs.
Sarasate y Navascues . .	sä-rä-sä'-tā　ē　nä-väs'-
Saratoff	sä-rä'-tŏf.
Sarawak	sä-rä-wäk', să-rȧ-wăk'.
Sarcey, Francisque . . .	frän-sēsk' sär-sā'.
Sardanapalus	sär''-dä-nä-pä'-lŭs.
Sardou	sär-dōō'.
Sarpedon	sär-pē'-dŏn.
Sarpi	sär'-pē.
Sarrebruck, see Saarbrück	sär-brük'.
Sartain	sär-tän'.
Sarto	sär'-tō.
Sartoris	sär-tō'-rĭs.
Sartor Resartus	sär'-tôr rē-sär'-tŭs.
Sarum	sâr'-ŭm.
Sarun, see Saran	sä-rŭn'.
Saskatchewan	săs-kăch'-ĕ-wȧn.
Saskia	säs'-kē-ä.
Sassari	säs'-sä-rē.

Sassenach	săs' ĕ năŏh.
Sassoferrato	säs''-sō-fĕr-rä'-tō.
Satara, *see* Sattara	sä-tä'-rä.
Satire Ménippée, *see* Satyre Ménippée	} sä-tēr' mā-nē-pā'.
Satolli	sä-tŏl'-lē.
Satsuma	săt-sū'-má, săt-sōō'-mä
Sattara, *see* Satara	sä-tä'-rä.
Saturnalia	săt-ēr-nā'-lĭ-ä.
Satyre Ménippée, *see* Satire Ménippée	} sä-tēr' mā-nē-pā'.
Saugor, *or*	sô-gōr'.
Saugur, *see* Sagar	sô-gŭr'.
Sault Sainte Marie	{ sōō sänt mā'-rĭ. *Fr.* sō sänt mä-rē'.
Saumarez, *see* Sausmarez	sō-mä-rā'.
Saumur	sō-mür'.
Sausmarez, *see* Saumarez	sō-mä-rā'.
Sauternes	sō-târn'.
Savaii, *see* Sawaii	sä-vī'-ē.
Savana la Mar	*Sp.* sä-bä'-nä lä mär.
Savary	sä-vä-rē'.
Savigny	sä-vēn-yē'.
Savile	săv'-ĭl.
Savoie	sä-vwä'.
Savoja	sä-vō'-yä.
Savonarola	sä''-vō-nä-rō'-lä.
Savoy	să-voi'.
Savoyard	să-voi'-ärd.
Sawaii, *see* Savaii	sä-wī'-ē.
Sawantwari	sä-wŭnt-wä'-rē.
Saxe (Marshal de)	săks.
Saxe-Altenburg, *see* Sachsen-Altenburg	} săks-äl'-tĕn-bĕrg.
Saxe - Coburg - Gotha, *see* Sachsen-Coburg-Gotha	} săks-kō'-bĕrg-gō'-tà.

Saxe-Lauenburg	săks-low′-ĕn-boŏrċh.
Saxe-Meiningen, *see* Sach-sen-Meiningen	săks-mī′-nĭng-ĕn.
Saxe-Weimar-Eisenach, *see* Sachsen - Weimar - Eisenach	săks-vī′-mär-ī′-zĕ-näċh.
Say, Léon	lā-ôṅ′ sā.
Say (Viscount), *or* Saye	sā.
Scæan (Gate)	sē′-ȧn.
Scaevola, Mutius	mū′-shĭ-ŭs sĕv′-ō-lȧ.
Scafell, *see* Scawfell . . .	skä-fĕl′.
Scala, La	lä skä′-lä.
Scala Santa	skä′-lä sän′-tä.
Scaliger	skăl′-ĭ-jêr.
Scamander	skä-măn′-dĕr.
Scanderbeg, *see* Skanderbeg	skăn′-dĕr-bĕg.
Scapin	skä′-pĭn. *Fr.* skä-păṅ′.
Scapino	*It.* skä-pē′-nō.
Scaramouche	{ skăr′-ȧ-mowch. *Fr.* skä-rä-moōsh′.
Scarborough	skär′-bŭ-rŭ.
Scaria (Emil)	skä′-rē-ä.
Scarlatti	skär-lät′-tē.
Scarron	skä-rôṅ′.
Scawfell, *see* Scafell . .	skô-fĕll′.
Sceaux	sō.
Schadow	shä′-dō.
Schaffhausen	{ shäf-how′-zĕn, shäf-how-zĕn.
Scharwenka (Philipp) . .	shär-vĕng′-kä.
Schaumburg-Lippe . . .	showm′-boōrċh-lĭp′-pŭ.
Schedone	skä-dō′-nä.
Scheele (C. W.)	shēl. *Sw.* shĭl′-ĕ.
Scheherezade, *see* Sheherezade	{ shä-hä″-rä-zä′-dä, shĕ-hē′-rä-zād.
Scheideck, *or* Scheidegg .	shī′-dĕk.

Schelde, or . . . . schĕl'-dĕ.

Scheldt . . . . skĕlt. *pop.* shĕlt.

Schelling, von . . . . . fŏn shĕl'-lĭng.

Schenck . . . . skĕnk.

Schenectady . . . . . . skĕn-ĕk'-tȧ-dĭ.

Schérer . . . . shā-râr'.

Scheurer-Kestner . . . . shĕr-âr'-kĕst-nâr'.

Scheveningen . . . . . schā'-vĕn-ĭng-ĕn.

Schiedam . . . . { skē-dăm', skē'-dăm. { *D.* schē-dăm'.

Schiehallion . . . . . . shē-hăl'-yŭn.

Schiller, von . . . . . fŏn shĭl'-lĕr.

Schipka (Pass), *see* Shipka shĭp'-kä.

Schlegel, von . . . . . fŏn shlā'-gĕl.

Schlei, *see* Schley . . . shlī.

Schleiermacher . . . . shlī'-ĕr-mäċh''-ĕr.

Schlemihl, Peter . . . . *Ger.* pā'-tĕr shlā'-mēl.

Schleswig, *see* Sleswick, Slesvig . . . . . . } shlāz'-vĭg, shlĕs'-vĭg.

Schleswig-Holstein . . . shlĕs'-vĭg-hōl'-stīn.

Schley, *see* Schlei, Sley (Prussia) . . . . . . } shlī.

Schley (Winfield Scott) . . shlī.

Schliemann . . . . . . shlē'-män.

Schlüter . . . . shlü'-tĕr.

Schmalkalden, *see* Smal- kald, Smalcald . . . . } shmäl'-käl-dĕn.

Schnorr von Karolsfeld . shnôr fŏn kär'-ōls-fĕlt.

Schoeffer, *see* Schöffer . shĕf'-fĕr. [shĕl'-ċhĕr.

Schoelcher (Victor) . . . *Fr.* skĕl-shâr'. *Ger.*

Schöffer, *see* Schoeffer . shĕf'-fĕr.

Schoharie . . . . . . skō-hăr'-ĭ.

Schomberg, von . . . . { fŏn shŏm'-bĕrg. { *Fr.* shôn-bâr'.

Schömberg . . . . . . shĕm'-bĕrċh.

Schönbrunn . . . . . . shĕn'-brŏŏn.

Schönefeld	shö' nŭ fölt
Schongauer (Martin) . .	shōn'-gow-ĕr.
Schönhausen	shĕn'-how-zĕn.
Schopenhauer	shō'-pĕn-how"-ĕr.
Schouler	skōō'-lĕr.
Schouvaloff, see Shuvaloff .	shōō-vä'-lŏf.
Schreiner (Olive)	shrī'-nĕr.
Schreyer	shrī'-ĕr.
Schröder	shrē'-dĕr.
Schröder-Devrient . . .	shrē'-dĕr-dĕv-rē-ǒṅ'.
Schubert	shōō'-bĕrt.
Schumann	shōō'-män.
Schumann-Heink	shōō'-män-hīnk'.
Schurz	shŏŏrts.
Schuyler	skī'-lĕr.
Schuylkill	skōōl'-kĭl.
Schwanthaler	shvän'-täl-ĕr.
Schwartzkoppen	shvärts'-kŏp-pĕn.
Schwarzenberg	shvärt'-zĕn-bĕrċh.
Schwarzwald	shvärts'-vält.
Schwerin	shvä-rēn'.
Schwob (Marcel)	shvŏb.
Schwyz	shvĭts.
Scilly (Is.)	sĭl'-ĭ.
Scinde, see Sind	sīnd.
Scio, see Chios	sī'-ō, shē'-ō.
Scipio	sĭp'-ĭ-ō.
Scituate	sĭt'-yū-āt.
Sclav	skläv, sklăv.
Scone	skōōn, skōn.
Scopas	skō'-pàs.
Scorpio	skôr'-pĭ-ō.
Scotti	skŏt'-tē.
Scribe, Eugène	ē-zhän' skrēb.
Scriblerus	skrĭb-lē'-rŭs.
Scudéri, or Scudéry . . .	skü-dä-rē'.

Scuola di San Rocco . . . skōō-ō'-lä de san rōk'-

Scurcolla, *or* . . . . . skōōr-kŏl'-lä. [kŏ.

Scurcula, *or* . . . . . skōōr-kōō'-lä.

Scurgola, *see* Scurcolla . . skōōr-gō'-lä

Scutari . . . . skōō'-tä-rē.

Scylla . . . . sĭl'-ä.

Sealkote, *see* Sialkot . . sē-äl-kōt'.

Seattle. . . . . sē-ăt'-l.

Sebastian . . . . . . { sē-băs'-tĭ_ản. *Sp.* sä-
                       { bäs''-tē-än'.

Sebastiano del Piombo . . { sä - bäs - tē_ä' - nō dĕl
                          { pē_ŏm'-bō. [tō'-pōl.

Sebastopol, *see* Sevastopol . sē-băs'-tō-pōl, sĕb-äs-

Secchi (Angelo) . . . . sĕk'-ē.

Sechuen, *see* Szechuen, Se } sä-chōō-ĕn'.
Tchuen. . . . . . . }

Sedalia . . . . sĕ-dā'-lĭ-ä.

Sedan . . . . sē-dăn'. *Fr.* sĕ-dän'

Sedgemoor . . . . . . sĕj'-mōōr.

Sedlitz, *see* Seidlitz . . . sĕd'-lĭts.

Seeland . . . . sē'-länd.

Seetapoor, *see* Sitapur . . sē-tä-pōōr'.

Segan-fu, *see* Singan Fu, } sē-gän'-fōō.
Sian-fu . . . . }

Sego, *see* Segu . . . . . sä'-gō. [vē-ä.

Segovia . . . . sĕ-gō'-vĭ-ä. *Sp.* sä-gō'-

Segu, *see* Sego . . . . . sä'-gōō.

Ségur, de . . . . dŭ sä-gür'.

Seharunpoor, *see* Saharan- } sĕ-här-ŭn-pōōr'.
pur . . . . }

Seidl, Anton . . . . . . än'-tōn zī'-dl.

Seidlitz, *see* Sedlitz . . . zĭd'-lĭts.

Seine (R.) . . . . . . sän. *Fr.* sĕn.

Seine-et-Marne . . . . . sĕn'-ä-märn'.

Seine-et-Oise . . . . . sĕn'-ä-wäz'.

Seine-Inférieure . . . . sĕn'-ăn-fä-rē-ĕr'.

Sejanus . . . . sĕ-jā'-nŭs, sē-jā'-nŭs.
Sekiang, see Sikiang . . . sē-kē-äng'.
Seleucidae, or . . . . . sĕ-lū'-sĭ-dē.
Seleucids . . . . sē-lū'-sĭdz.
Seleucus . . . . sē-lū'-kŭs.
Selim . . . . sē'-lĭm, sĕ-lēm'
Seljuks . . . . sĕl-jōōks'.
Selous . . . . sē'-lŭs.
Sembrich . . . . zĕm'-brĭċh.
Semele . . . . sĕm'-ĕ-lē.
Semering, see Semmering . zĕm'-ĕr-ĭng.
Semiramide . . . . . . sā-mē-rä'-mĭ-dĕ. [mĭs.
Semiramis . . . . . . sĕ-mĭr'-à-mĭs, sē-mĭr'-ā-
Semites . . . . sĕm'-īts.
Semmering, see Semering . zĕm'-ĕr-ĭng.
Semonides, see Simonides . sĕ-mŏn'-ĭ-dēz.
Sempach . . . . zĕm'-päċh.
Sempione, It. for Simplon sĕm-pē-ō'-nĕ.
Senancour . . . . . . sĕ-näṅ-kōōr'.
Sendai . . . . sĕn-dī'.
Seneca . . . . sĕn'-ĕ-kä, sĕn'-ē-kà.
Seneffe . . . . sē-nĕf'.   [sĕn'-ē-gàl.
Senegal . . . . n. sĕn-ē-gôl'. adj. and n.
Sénégal . . . . Fr. sā-nā-gäl'.
Senegambia . . . . . . sĕn-ĕ-găm'-bĭ-à.
Senekal . . . . sĕn-ĕ-kăl'.
Senigallia, see Sinigaglia . sā-nē-gäl'-lē-ä.
Senlac . . . . sĕn'-lăk.
Sennaar, see Sennar . . . sĕn-när'.   [rĭb.
Sennacherif . . . . . sĕ-năk'-ĕ-rĭb, sĕn-à-kē'-
Sennar, see Sennaar . . . sĕ-när'.
Señor . . . . sān-yōr'.
Señora . . . . sān-yō'-rä.
Sens . . . . sŏṅs.
Seonee, or Seoni . . . . sē-ō'-nē.
Seoul, see Seul . . . . . sĕ-ōōl'.

16

Sepoy, *see* Spahi	sĕ-pô'-ē. *pop.* sē'-poi.
Septuagesima	sĕp'-tū-à-jĕs'-i-mà.
Septuagint	sĕp'-tū-à-jĭnt".
Seraglio	sĕ-räl'-yō.
Serapeion, *or*	sĕr-à-pē'-ŏn.
Serapeium, *or* **Serapeum** .	sĕr-à-pē'-ŭm.
Séraphita	sā-rä-fē-tä'.
Serapion, *see* Serapeion . .	sĕr-à-pē'-ŏn.
Serapis . :	sĕ-rā'-pĭs, sē-rā'-pĭs.
Sergius	sēr'-jĭ-ŭs.
Serinagur, *see* Srinagar .	sĕr"-ĭ-nà-gōōr'.
Seringapatam, *see* Sriranga- patam	sē-rĭng"-gā-pā-tăm'.
Serpukhoff	sĕr-pōō-ċhŏf'. [gāth.
Serrano y Dominguez . .	sĕr-rä'-nō ē dō-mēn'-
Servetus	sĕr-vē'-tŭs.
Servius Tullius	sēr'-vĭ-ŭs tŭl'-ĭ-ŭs.
Sesostris	sē-sŏs'-trĭs.
Se Tchuen, *see* Se Chuen, Szechuen	sā chōō-ĕn'.
Setebos	sĕt'-ĕ-bŏs.
Seul, *see* Seoul . . .	sĕ-ōōl'.
Sevastopol, *see* Sebastopol .	sē-văs'-tō-pŏl. *Russ.* sā-väs-tō'-pŏl.
Severus (Lucius Septimius)	sĕ-vē'-rŭs, sē-vē'-rŭs.
Sevier	sĕ-vēr'.
Sévigné, de	dŭ sā-vēn-yā'.
Sevilla, *Sp.*	sā-vēl'-yä.
Séville, *Fr.*	sā-vēl'.
Seville	sĕv'-ĭl, sē-vĭl'.
Sèvres	sâvr.
Sexagesima	sĕks-à-jĕs'-ĭ-mà.
Seychelles	sā-shĕl'.
Seydlitz	zīd'-lĭts.
Sfakus, *or*	sfä'-kŭs.
Sfax	sfäks.

Sforza	sfōrd'-zä.
Sganarelle	sgä-nä-rĕl'.
'S Gravenhaage, see The Hague	s-grä-vĕn-hä'-ċhĕ.
Shadrach	shā'-drăk.
Shafalus	shăf'-à-lŭs.
Shah	shä.
Shahabad	shä-hä-bäd'.
Shah Jahan, or Jehan	shä yà-hän', or yĕ-hän'.
Shah Jehanpoor	shä yĕ-hän-pōōr'.
Shahpoor, see Sapor, and Shapur	shä-pōōr'.
Shakuntala	shă-kōōn'-tă-lä.
Shalmaneser	shăl-mà-nē'-zĕr.
Shanghai	shăng-hī', shăng-hä'-ĭ.
Shanking	shän-kĭng'.
Shansi	shän-sē'.
Shantow, see Swatow	shän-tow'.
Shan-tung	shän-tōōng'.
Shapur, see Sapor, Shahpoor	shä-pōōr'.
Sharezer	shă-rē'-zĕr.
Sharon	shâr'-ŏn.
Shawangunk	shŏng'-gŭm.
Shebat	shē-băt'.
Sheboygan	shĕ-boi'-gàn.
Shechem, see Sichem	shē'-kĕm.
Shechemite	shē'-kĕm-īt.
Shechinah, see Shekinah	shē-kī'-nä.
Sheemogga, see Shimoga	shē-mŏg'-gä.
Sheeraz, see Shiraz	shē'-räz.
Sheherezade, see Scheherezade	shä-hä"-rä-zä'-dä, shĕ-hē'-rä-zäd.
Sheik, or Sheikh	shēk, shäk.
Shekinah, or Shechinah	shĕ-kī'-nä.
Shelley	shĕl'-ĭ.
Shenandoah	shĕn-ăn-dō'-à.

Shen-si, Shen-See . . . . shĕn-sē'.
Sheol . . . . shē'-ōl.
Sheriffmuir . . . . . . shĕr-ĭf-mūr'.
Shiites. . . . . shē'-īts.
Shikarpur . . . . . . shĭk-är-pōōr'.
Shikoku, see Sikoku . . . shē-kŏ'-kōō.
Shillaber . . . . shĭl'-á-bĕr.
Shimoga, see Sheemogga . shē-mō'-gä.
Shimonoseki, see Simonoseki shĭm-ō-nō-sĕk'-ē.
Shinar. . . . . shī'-när.
Shingking . . . . . . shĭng-kĭng'.
Shinto. . . . . shĭn'-tō.
Shintoism . . . . . . shĭn'-tō-ĭzm.
Shipka, see Schipka (Pass) shĭp'-kä.
Shiraz, see Sheeraz . . . shē'-räz.
Shiré . . . . shē'-rā.
Shirvan . . . . shĭr-vän'.
Shiva, see Siva . . . . . shĭ'-vá.
Shogun . . . . shō-gōōn'.
Sholapur . . . . shō-lä-pōōr'.
Shoshone . . . . shō-shō'-nē, shō-shō-nē'.
Shrewsbury . . . . . . shrūz'-bĕr-ĭ.
Shuntien-fu . . . . . . shōōn'-tē-ĕn'-fōō'.
Shushan . . . . shōō'-shän.
Shuvaloff, see Schouvaloff . shōō-vä'-lŏf.
Shylock . . . . shī'-lŏk.
Sialkot, see Sealkote . . sē-äl-kōt'.
Siam . . . . sī-ăm', sē-äm'.
Siamese . * . . . . . sī-á-mēz', sī-á-mēs'.
Sian-fu, see Singan-fu, Se-⎫ sē-än'-fōō.
gan-fu . . . . . . ⎭   ['skŏn'-sĕt.
Siasconset . . . . . . sī - ăs - kŏn' - sĕt. pop.
Sibola, see Cibola . . . . sē'-bō-lä.
Siboney . . . . . ⁎ . sē-bō-nā'-ē.
Sibuyan . . . . sē-bōō-yän'.
Sibyl . . . . sĭb'-ĭl.

Sichem, *see* Shechem *and* } nī'-kŏm.
Sychem . . . . . . }

Sickingen, von . . . . . fŏn zĭk'-ĭng-ĕn.

Sicyon . . . . sĭsh'-ĭ-ŏn.

Siddhârta, *or* . . . . sĭd-här'-tä.

Siddhartha . . . . . sĭ-dhär'-thä.

Sidon, *see* Zidon . . . sī'-dŏn.

Siegfried, *see* Sigfrid . sēg'-frēd. *Ger.* zēg'-frēt.

Siena, *see* Sienna . . . sē-ĕn'-nä.

Sienese . . . . . . sē-ĕn-ēz', sē-ĕn-ĕs'.

Sienkiewicz . . . . . sē-ĕn-kĕ-ĕ'-vĭch.

Sienna, *see* Siena . . . sē-ĕn'-ä. [nĕs.

Sierra de los Ladrones . . sē-ĕr'-rä dä lōs lä-drō'-

Sierra Leone . . . . . { sē-ĕr'-rä lē-ō'-nē. *loc.*
lē-ōn'. *Sp.* sē-ĕr'-rä
lä-ō'-nä.

Sierra Madre . . . . . sē-ĕr'-rä mä'-drä.

Sierra Maestra . . . . sē-ĕr'-rä mä-äs'-trä.

Sierra Morena . . . . sē-ĕr'-rä mō-rā'-nä.

Sierra Nevada . . . . . { sē-ĕr'-rä nĕ-vä'-dä.
Sp. sē-ĕr'-rä nā-vä'-dä.

Sieyès . . . . sē-yĕs', sē-ĕs', sē-ā-yĕs'.

Sigel, Franz . . . . . { fräntz sē'-gĕl. *Ger.* zē'-
gĕl.

Sigfrid, *see* Siegfried . . sēg'-frēd. *Ger.* zēg'-frēt.

Sigismund (Emperor), *see* } sĭj'-ĭs-mŭnd. *Ger.* zē'-
Sigmund . . . . . } gĭs-mōŏnt.

Sigmaringen . . . . . zēg'-mä-rĭng''-ĕn.

Sigmund, *see* Sigismund . sĭg'-mŭnd. *Ger.* zēg'-

Signora . . . . sēn-yō'-rä. [mōŏnt.

Signorelli . . . . . . sēn-yō-rĕl'-lē.

Signoria . . . . sēn-yō-rē'-ä.

Signory . . . . sēn'-yō-rĭ.

Sigourney . . . . . . sĭg'-ĕr-nĭ.

Sigurd . . . . zē'-gōŏrd. *Fr.* sē-gür'.

Sikhs . . . . sēks.

Sikiang, *see* Sehiang . . . sē-kē-äng'.

Sikoku, *see* Shikoku . . . sē-kō'-kōō.

Silenus . . . . sī-lē'-nŭs.

Silesia . . . . sĭl-ē'-shĭ-à.

Silhet, *see* Sylhet . . . . sĭl-hĕt'.

Siloah, *or* . . . . . . sĭ-lō'-ä.

Siloam . . . . sĭ-lō'-ám, sĭl-ō'-ăm.

Silva . . . . sēl'-vä.

Silvanus . . . . . . sĭl-vā'-nŭs.

Silvester . . . . . . sēl-vĕs'-tr.

Silvio Pellico . . . . sēl'-vē-ō pĕl'-lē-kō.

Simancas . . . . . . sē-män'-käs.

Simbirsk . . . . . . sĭm-bērsk'.

Simeon Stylites . . . . sĭm'-ē-ŏn stī-lī'-tēz.

Simla . . . . sĭm'-là.

Simois . . . . sĭm'-ō-ĭs.

Simon de Montfort . . . { sī'-mŏn dŭ mŏnt'-fōrt. / *Fr.* sē-môṅ' dŭ môṅ-fŏr'.

Simon, Jules . . . . . zhül sē-môṅ'.

Simonides, *see* Semonides . sĭ-mŏn'-ĭ-dēz.

Simonoseki, *see* Shimonoseki . . . . } sĭm-ō-nō-sĕk'-ē.

Simplon, *see* Sempione . . sĭm'-plŏn. *Fr.* săṅ-plôṅ'.

Sinai (Mount) . . . . . sī'-nā, sī'-nā-ĭ, sī'-nī.

Sinaitic (Peninsula) . . . sĭ-nā-ĭt'-ĭk.   [klâr.

Sinclair . . . . sĭn-klâr'.   *Eng.* sĭng'-

Sind, *or* Sinde, *or* Sindh, *see* Scinde . . . . . . } sĭnd.

Singan-fu, *see* Sian-fu, Segan-fu . . . . . . } sēn-gän'-fōō.

Singapore . . . . . . sĭng-gà-pōr', sĭn'-gà-pōr.

Sinigaglia, *see* Senigallia . sē-nē-gäl'-yä.

Sinope, *or* . . . . . . sĭ-nō'-pē.

Sinub, *Turk.* . . . . . sē-nōōb'.

Sion, *see* Zion . . . . . sī'-ŏn.

Sioux . . . . sōō.

Siraj-ud Daula, *see* Surajah Dowlah . . . . . . } sē-räj'-ōōd-dow'-lä.

Sirdar . . . . sĕr-där'.

Sirius . . . . sĭr'-ĭ-ŭs.

Sirsa . . . . sĕr'-sä.

Sisera . . . . sĭs'-ĕ-rä.

Sismondi, de . . . . . { dŭ sĭs-mŏn'-dĭ. *Fr.* dŭ sēs-môû-dē'.

Sistine, *see* Sixtine . . . sĭs'-tĭn.

Sisyphus . . . . sĭs'-ĭ-fŭs.

Sitapur, *see* Seetapoor . . sē-tà-pōōr'.

Siut, *see* Assiut, Asyoot . sē-ōōt'.

Siva, *see* Shiva . . . . . sē'-và.

Sivan . . . . sĭv'-àn.

Siward . . . . sē'-wärd.

Siwash . . . . sē-väsh'.

Six, Jan . . . . yăn sēks.

Sixtine (Chapel), *see* Sistine sĭks'-tĭn. [räk'.

Skager-Rack . . . . . skäg'-ĕr-räk', skäg'-ĕr-

Skaguay . . . . skäg'-wā.

Skanderbeg, *see* Scanderbeg skăn'-dĕr-bĕg.

Skaneateles (L.) . . . . skăn-ē-ăt'-lĕs.

Skeat . . . . skēt.

Skiddaw . . . . skĭd'-dô.

Skierniewice . . . . . skē-ĕr''-nē-ĕ-vēt'-sĕ.

Skobeleff . . . . skō'-bĕ-lĕf.

Skrzynecki, Jan Boncza . { yăn bŏn'-tsä skrĭzh'-nĕt-skĭ.

Skupshtina . . . . . . skōōpsh'-tĭ-nä.

Slav, *or* Slave . . . . . släv, slăv.

Slavonic . . . . slä-vŏn'-ĭk.

Slesvig (Dan.), *see* Schleswig . . . . } slĕs'-vĭg.

Sleswick, *see* Schleswig . slĕs'-wĭk.

Sley, *see* Schlei . . . . . slī.

Slidell . . . . slĭ-dĕl'.

Slovak . . . . slō-văk'
Slovene . . . . slō-vēn'.
Sluis, *or* Sluys . . . . . slois.
Smalcald, *or* Smalkald, *see*⎰ smăl'-kăld.
 Schmalkalden . . . .⎱
Smalcaldic . . . . . . smăl-kăl'-dĭk.
Smaldeel . . . . smălt'-āl.
Smectymnuus . . . . . smĕk-tĭm'-nū-ŭs.
Smetana . . . . smĕ'-tä-nä.
Smillie . . . . smĭ'-lĭ.
Smith Cay . . . . . . smĭth kä'-ē.
Smolensk . . . . smō-lĕnsk'.
Sneyders, *see* Snyders . . snĭ'-dĕrs.
Snorre, Snorri, *or* . . . . ⎰ snŏr'-rä, snŏr'-rē, *or*
 Snorro Sturleson . . . ⎱ snŏr'-rō stōōr'-lä-sŏn.
Snyders, *see* Sneyders . . snĭ'-dĕrs.
Snyman (Gen.). . . . . snĭ'-măn.
Sobieski . . . . sō-bē-ĕs'-kē.
Sobranje . . . . sō-brän'-yĕ.
Socapa, La . . . . . . lä sō-kä'-pä.
Socinian . . . . sō-sĭn'-ĭ-án.
Socinus . . . . sō-sĭ'-nŭs.
Socrates . . . . sŏk'-rá-tēz.
Södermanland . . . . . sē'-dĕr-män-länt".
Sodom . . . . sŏd'-ŏm.
Sodoma, *or* . . . . . . sō-dō'-mä.
Sodona . . . . sō-dō'-nä.
Soerabaya, *see* Surabaya . sōō-rä-bĭ'-ä.
Sofala . . . . sō-fä'-lä.
Sofi, *or* Sophi, *see* Sufi, Saffi sō'-fĭ.
Sofia, *see* Sophia . . . . sō-fē'-ä.
Soho (Square) . . . . . sō'-hō.
Sohrab, *see* Suhrab . . . ⎰ *mod. Pers.* sōō-hrŏb'.
 ⎱ *Arab.* sŏ-hrŏb'.
Soignies . . . . swän-yē'.
Soissons . . . . swä-sôn'.

Sokoto	sō-kō'-tō.
Solace (The)	sŏl'-ăs.
Solario (Antonio)	sō-lä'-rē-ō.
Soldau	zōl'-dow.
Solebay	sōl'-bā.
Solferino	sŏl-fä-rē'-nō.
Solinus	sō-lī'-nŭs.
Soltikoff, see Saltikoff . .	sŏl'-tē-kŏf.
Solyman, see Suleiman . .	sŏl'-ĭ-mȧn.
Somaj	sō-mäj'.
Somaliland	sō-mä'-lē-länd.
Sombor, see Zombor . . .	sŏm'-bŏr.
Sombrero	sōm-brä'-rō.
Somme (R.)	sŏm.
Sömmering	zĕm'-mĕr-ĭng. [nä'-tä.
Sonata Appassionata . .	sō-nä'-tä äp-päs''-sē-ō-
Sonata Tragica . . .	sō-nä'-tä trä'-jē-kä.
Sonderbund	zŏn'-dĕr-bŏŏnt.
Sonnambula, La	lä sŏn-näm'-bŏŏ-lä.
Sontag	sŏn'-tăg. Ger. zŏn'-täċh.
Soochow, see Su-chau . .	sōō'-chow'.
Soodan, see Sudan, Soudan	sōō-dän'.
Soodra, see Sudra	sōō'-drä.
Sooloo, see Sulu, Joló . .	sōō-lōō'.
Sopater	sŏp'-ä-tĕr, sō'-pȧ-tĕr.
Sophia, see Sofia	sō-fī'-ä. mosque, sō-fē'-ä.
Sophia Dorothea	sō-fī'-ä dŏr-ō-thē'-ä.
Sophrosyne	sō-frŏs'-ĭn-ē.
Sorbonne, La	lä sŏr-bŏn'.
Sorel	sō-rĕl'.
Soria	sō'-rē-ä.
Soriano	sō-rē-ä'-nō.
Sosigenes	sō-sĭj'-ē-nēz.
Soubise	sōō-bēz'.
Soudan, see Sudan . . .	sōō-dän'.
Soudanese, see Sudanese .	sōō-dän-ēz', sōō-dăn-ēs'.

Soufflot . . . . sōō-flō'.

Soulé . . . . sōō-lā'.

Soult . . . . sōōlt.

Sousa . . . . sōō'-zȧ.

Southey . . . . sow'-thĭ, sŭth'-ĭ.

Southampton (City) . . . { sowth-hămp'-tŏn, *or* sŭth-hămp'-tŏn.

Southampton (Earl of) . . { sŭth-ămp'-tŏn, *or* sŭth-hămp'-tŏn.

Southwark . . . . . . sŭth'-ērk.

Souvaroff, *see* Suvaroff, Su- } sōō-vä'-rŏf.
waroff . . . .

Souvestre, Émile . . . . ä-mēl' sōō-vĕs'-tr.

Souvigny . . . . sōō-vēn-yē'.

Spagnoletto . . . . . . spän-yō-lĕt'-tō.

Spahee, *or* . . . . . . spä'-ē, spä'-hē.

Spahi, *see* Sepoy . . . . spä'-hĭ.

Spalato, *or* . . . . . . spä-lä'-tō.

Spalatro . . . . spä-lä'-trō.

Spallanzani . . . . . . späl-länd-zä'-nē.

Spartacus . . . . . . spär'-tȧ-kŭs.

Speichern, *see* Spicheren . spī'-ċhĕrn.

Speier, *see* Speyer, Spire . spīr, spī'-ĕr.

Speranski, *or* Speransky . spä-rän'-skē.

Spetzia, *see* Spezia . . . spĕt'-zē-ä.

Speyer, *see* Speier, Spires . spī'-ĕr, spīr.

Speyerbach . . . . . . spī'-ĕr-bäċh.

Spezia, *or* Spezzia, *see* Spet- } spĕt'-zē-ä.
zia . . . .

Spica . . . . spī'-kä.

Spicheren, *see* Speichern . spē'-ċhĕr-ĕn.

Spielhagen . . . . . . spēl'-hä-gĕn.

Spinola, de . . . . . . dä spē'-nō-lä.

Spinoza . . . . spē-nō'-zä.

Spion Kop . . . . . . spē'-ŏn kŏp.

Spire, *see* Speier, Speyer . spēr.

Spires, see Speyer, Spire .	spīrz.
Spiridion	spĭ-rĭd'-ĭ-ŏn.
Spitalfields	spĭt'-ȧl-fēldz.
Spluga, or	splōō'-gä.
Splügen	splü'-gĕn.
Spohr (Louis)	spōr.
Spokan, or	spō-kăn'.
Spokane	spō-kān'.
Spoleto	spō-lā'-tō.
Spontini	spŏn-tē'-nē.
Sporades	spŏr'-ā-dēz.
Spree	sprā.
Spurgeon	spŭr'-jŭn.
Spurzheim	spōōrts'-hīm.
Spuyten Duyvil . . .	spī'-tĕn dī'-vĭl.
Spytfontein	spĭt'-fŏn-tīn.
Squarcione	skwär-chō'-nä.
Srinagar, see Serinagur .	srĭ-nȧ-gär'.
Srirangapatam, see Seringa-patam	srĭ-răng''-gȧ-pá-tăm'.
Staal, de	dŭ stäl. [mä'-tĕr.
Stabat Mater	stā'-băt mä'-tĕr, stä'-bät
Stadtlohn	stät-lōn'.
Stael-Holstein	{stä'-ĕl-hŏl'-stīn. Fr. {stä-ĕl'-ōl-stăn'.
Stagira	stā-jī'-rá.
Stagirite	stăj'-ĭ-rīt.
Stagirus	stā-jī'-rŭs.
Stamboul	stäm-bōōl'.
Stambuloff	stäm-bōō'-lŏf.
Stanhope	stăn'-ŏp.
Stanislas, see Stanislaus .	stăn'-ĭs-lȧs. [ȧkē.
Stanislas Lesczinski . .	stăn'-ĭs-lȧs lĕsh-chĭn'-
Stanislaus, see Stanislas .	stăn-ĭs-lā'-ŭs.
Stanislaus (R.) . . .	stăn'-ĭs-low.
Stanze	ständ'-zĕ.

Starhemberg	stä′-rĕm-bĕrċh.
Staubbach	stowb′-bäċh.
Stavanger	stä-väng′-gĕr.
Stavropol	stäv′-rō-pŏl.
Steen, Jan	yăn stān.
Steenkerke, or . . .	stān′-kĕrk-ĕ.
Steenkerken	stān′-kĕrk-ĕn.
Stefanie (L.)	stĕ-fä-nē′.
Stein, von	fŏn stīn.
Steinau	stĭ′-now.
Steinitz	stīn′-ĭts.
Steinmetz	stīn′-mĕts.
Steinwehr	stīn′-vär.
Stendhal, De	dŭ stŏn-däl′.
Stéphanie	stä-fä-nē′.
Stephano	⎰ Tempest, stĕf′-ā-nō. ⎱ Merchant of Venice, stĕf- ⎰ ä′-nō.
Stephen Báthori . . .	stē′-vĕn bä′-tō-rē.
Stepniak	stĕp′-nē-ạk.
Sterkstroom	stĕrk′-strōm.
Stettin	stĕt-ēn′.
Steuben	stū′-bĕn. Ger. stoi′-bĕn.
Steyn	stīn.
Steyne	stīn.
Stiberdigebit	stĭ′-bĕr-dĭ-jĕb″-ĭt.
Stigand	stĭg′-ạnd.
Stilicho	stĭl′-ĭ-kō.
Stilliano	stēl-ē-ä′-nō.
Stockholm	stŏk′-hōlm.
Stoke Poges	stōk pō′-jĕs.
Stolzenfels	stŏlt′-zĕn-fĕlz.
Stormberg	stŏrm′-bĕrċh.
Stor-thing	stōr′-tĭng.
Stötteritz	stĕt′-tĕ-rĭts.
Stour	stōōr.

Strabo . . . . strā'-bō.
Strakosch . . . . . strä'-kŏsh.
Stralsund . . . . . sträl'-sŏŏnd.
Strasbourg . . . . . *Fr.* sträs-bŏŏr'.
Strasburg, *or* . . . . sträs'-bĕrg.
Strassburg . . . . . *Ger.* sträs'-bŏŏrċh.
Stratford-on-Avon . . . străt'-fōrd-ŏn-ā'-vŏn.
Strauss . . . . strows.
Strelitz . . . . . . *Ger.* strā'-lĭts.
Strelitzes . . . . . . strĕl'-ĭts-ĕz.
Strephon . . . . . . strĕf'-ŏn.
Stromboli . . . . . strŏm'-bō-lē.
Strophades . . . . . strŏf'-à-dēz.
Strozzi . . . . . . strŏt'-zē.
Struve . . . . strŏŏ'-vŭ.
Sturm und Drang . . . . stŏŏrm ŏŏnt dräng.
Stuttgart . . . . . . stŏŏt'-gärt.
Stuyvesant . . . . . stī'-vĕ-sănt.
Stygian . . . . . . stĭj'-ĭ-àn.
Stylites . . . . . . stī-lī'-tēz.
Styx . . . . stĭks.
Suabia, *see* Swabia . . . swā'-bĭ-à.
Suabian, *see* Swabian . . swā'-bĭ-àn.
Subiaco . . . . . . sŏŏ-bē-ä'-kō.
Subig (Bay) . . . . sŏŏ-bēg'.
Sublime Porte . . . . sŭb-lĭm' pōrt.
Su-chau, *or* Suchow, *see* } sŏŏ'-chow'.
Soochow . . . . . }
Suchet . . . . sü-shā'.
Sucre, de . . . . . . dä sŏŏ'-krä.
Sudan, *see* Soudan, Soodan sŏŏ-dän'.
Sudanese, *see* Soudanese . sŏŏ-dän-ēz', sŏŏ-dän-ēs'.
Sudermann . . . . . zŏŏ'-dĕr-män.
Sudra, *see* Soodra . . . sŏŏ'-drä.   [sü.
Sue, Eugène . . . . . yū'-jēn sū. *Fr.* ĕ-zhän'
Suetonius . . . . . . swē-tō'-nĭ-ŭs.

Suez . . . . sŏō'-ĕz, sōō-ĕz'.

Suffed Koh, see Safed Koh　sŭf'-ĕd kŏ.

Suffren de Saint-Tropez . . { süf-frŏǹ' dǔ săṅ trō-pā' / süf-frĕn' dǔ săṅ-trō- pĕss'.

Sufi, see Saffi, Sofi . . . sŏō'-fĭ.

Suhrab, see Sohrab . . . { mod. Pers. sōō-hrôb'. / Arab. sŏ-hrôb'.

Sul, Rio Grande do . . . rē'-ō grän'-dā dōō sōōl.

Suleiman (Mosque of), see } Solyman . . . . . . } sōō-lā-män'.

Sully . . . . sŭl'-ĭ.　Fr. sü-lē'.

Sully-Prudhomme . . . sü-lē'-prü-dŏ̄m'.

Sultanpur . . . . . sŭl-tăn-pōōr'.

Sulu, see Sooloo, Joló . . sōō-lōō'.

Suluk . . . . sōō-lōōk'.

Sumag . . . . sōō-mäg'.

Sumatra . . . . . . sōō-mä'-trä.

Sumbulpur, see Sambalpur　sŭm-bŭl-pōōr'.

Sundi . . . . sōōn'-dē.

Suppé, von . . . . . . fŏn zŏŏp'-pā.

Surabaya, see Soerabaya . sōō-rä-bĭ'-ä.

Surajah Dowlah, see Siraj- } ud-Daula . . . . . } sōō-rä'-jä dow'-lä.

Surat . . . . sōō-rät'.

Surinam . . . . . . sōō-rĭ-näm'.

Susa . . . . sōō'-sà.　It. sōō'-zä.

Sutlej . . . . sŭt'-lĕj.

Suvaroff, or . . . . . . sōō-vä'-rŏf.

Suvoroff, see Souvaroff . . sōō-vō'-rŏf.

Suwalki . . . . . . sōō-väl'-kē.

Suwanee, or Suwannee . . sū-wŏ'-nē.

Suwaroff, or . . . . . sōō-vä'-rŏf.

Suwarrow, see Suvaroff . sōō-vä'-rŏv.

Swabia, see Suabia . . . swā'-bĭ-à.

Swabian, see Suabian . . swā'-bĭ-àn.

Swansea . . . . swŏn'-sē.

Swartow, *or* . . . . . swär-tow'.

Swatow, *see* Shantow . . swä-tow'.

Swaziland . . . . . . swä'-zē-länd.

Swedenborg . . . . . . { swē' - dĕn - bôrg.   *Sw.*
{   svĭd'-ĕn-bōrg.

Swedenborgian . . . . swē-dĕn-bôr'-jĭ-àn.

Swegen, *or* . . . . . . svä'-gĕn.

Swein, *or* . . . . . . swān.

Sweyn . . . . swān.

Sybaris . . . . . . sĭb'-à-rĭs, sĭb'-ā-rĭs.

Sybarite . . . . . . sĭb'-à-rīt.

Sybel, von . . . . . . fŏn zē'-bĕl.

Sychar . . . . sī'-kär.

Sychem, *see* Sichem, She- } sī'-kĕm.
chem . . . . }

Sycorax . . . . . . sĭk'-ō-räks.

Sylhet, *see* Silhet . . . . sĭl-hĕt'.

Sylva, Carmen . . . . . kär'-mĕn sĭl'-vä.

Sylvester . . . . . . sĭl-vĕs'-tĕr.

Symonds . . . . . . sĭm'-ŭndz, sī'-mŭndz.

Symons . . . . . . sĭm'-ŭnz, sī'-mŭnz.

Symplegades . . . . sĭm-plĕg'-à-dēz.

Synod . . . . sĭn'-ŏd.

Synope . . . . . . sī-nō'-pē.

Syracuse . . . . . . sĭr'-à-kūs, sĭr'-à-kūz.

Syrinx . . . . sī'-rĭngks.

Szechuen, *see* Sechuen, Se } sä-choō-ĕn'.
Tchuen . . . . . . }

Szegedin . . . . . . sĕg'-ĕd-ēn.

Sziget . . . . sĭg'-ĕt.

T

Taaffe, von . . . . . . fōn tä'-fŭ.
Tabago, *see* Tobago . . . tä-bä'-gō.   [kō.
Tabasco . . . . tȧ-bȧs'-kō. *Sp.* tä-bäs'-
Tablas. . . . . tä'-bläs.
Tabor . . . . *Mt.* tä'-bŏr. *Boh.* tä'-bŏr.
Tacna . . . . *pop.* tȧk'-nȧ, tȧk'-nä.
Taddeo . . . . täd-dä'-ō.
Tadema, Alma- . . . . äl'-mä-tä'-dĕ-mä.
Tadmir . . . . täd-mēr'.
Tadmor . . . . tȧd'-môr.
Taeping, *see* Tai-ping . . tī-pĭng'.
Tafna . . . . täf'-nä.
Tagal, *see* Tegal . . . . tä-gäl'. *D.* tä-ċhäl'.
Tagala . . . . tä-gä'-lä.   [rŏg'.
Taganrog. . . . . . . *pop.* tȧg-ȧn-rŏg', tä-gän-
Tagliacozzo . . . . . täl-yä-kōt'-zō.
Tagliamento . . . . täl-yä-mĕn'-tō.
Taglioni (Filippo) . . . täl-yō'-nē.
Tagus, *see Sp.* Tajo, *Port.* } tä'-gŭs.
  Tejo . . . . }
Tahamis . . . . tä-ä'-mēs.
Tahiti . . . . tä-hē'-tē.
Tahitian . . . . tä-hē'-tĭ-ȧn.
Tahlequah . . . . . tä-lĕ-kwä'.
Tai, *see* Thai, *or* T'hai . . tī.
Tai-chau . . . . . . tī'-chow'.
Taillebourg . . . . . tä-yŭ-bōōr'.
Taillefer . . . . . . tä-yŭ-fâr'.
Taine . . . . tān.
Tai-ping, *see* Taeping . . tī'-pĭng'.
Taiwan . . . . . . tī-wän'.
Tai-yuan . . . . . . tī-wän'.
Taj-e-mah (The) . . . . täzh'-ĕ-mä'.

Taj Mahal, *or* Mehal . . täzh mä-häl', *or* mĕ-häl'.
Tajo, *Sp. for* Tagus . . . tä'-ċhō.
Tajurrah . . . . tä-jōō'-rä.
Takala, *see* Tekele . . . tä-kä'-lä.
Takao, *or* Takow . . . . tä-kä'-ō, tä-kow'.
Taku . . . . tä'-kōō.
Talaut (Is.) . . . . . . tä-lowt'.   [nä.
Talavera de la Reina . . tä-lä-vä'-rä dä lä rä-ē'-
Talbot . . . . tôl'-bŭt.
Talca . . . . täl'-kä.
Talfourd . . . . tôl'-fŭrd.
Taliaferro . . . . . . tŏl'-ĭ-vĕr.
Ta Lien Wan, *or* Talien-wan tä'-lēn'-wän'.
Taliesin . . . . täl'-ĭ-sĭn.
Tallard . . . . tä-lär'.
Talleyrand-Périgord . . . { tăl'-ĭ-rănd.   *Fr.* täl-ā-
                          { rȧṅ'-pā-rē-gōr'.
Tallien . . . . tä-lē̤-ȧṅ'.
Talma . . . . tăl'-má, täl-mä'.
Talmud . . . . tăl'-mŭd.
Talmudic . . . . tăl-mŭd'-ĭk.
Talmudist . . . . . . tăl'-mŭd-ĭst.
Tamanieb . . . . . . tä-mä-nē-ĕb'.
Tamar . . . . tä'-mär.
Tamaulipas . . . . . . tä-mow-lē'-päs.
Tamboff . . . . täm-bŏf'.
Tamburlaine, *or* Tamber- } tăm-bĕr-lān'.
lane . . . . }
Tamerlane, *see* Timur-Leng tăm-ĕr-lān'.
Tamils . . . . tăm'-ĭlz, tä-mēlz'.
Tammuz . . . . tăm'-ŭz.   [pē'-kō.
Tampico . . . . tăm-pē'-kō.   *Sp.* täm-
Tamsui . . . . täm-sōō'-ē.
Tanagra . . . . tăn'-ȧ-grä.
Tanais . . . . tăn'-ā-ĭs, tä'-nä-ĭs.
Tananerivo . . . . . . tä-nä''-nä-rē'-vō.

Tancred	tănɡ' krŏd, tăn' krŏd,
Tancrède .	tän-krād'.
Tancredi .	tän-krä'-dē.
Taney (Robert)	tô'-nĭ.
Tanganyika (L.)	tän-gän-yē'-kä.
Tanger, *Fr.*, or .	tän-zhä'.
Tanger, *Ger.*, *see* Tangier .	täng'-ĕr.
Tangerine	tăn-jĕ-rēn'.
Tangier, *or*	tăn-jēr', tän-jēr'.
Tangiers, *or* .	tăn-jērz', tän-jērz'.
Tanja, *Native* .	tän'-jä.
Tanjore	tăn-jōr'.
Tan Kweilin	tän'-kwä'-lēn'.
Tannhäuser .	tän'-hoi-zĕr.
Tantalus .	tăn'-tá-lŭs.
Tao .	tä'-ō. [tow'-ĭzm.
Taoism	tä'-ō-ĭzm, tä'-ō-ĭzm,
Taparelli, Massimo	mäs'-sē-mō tä-pä-rĕl'-lē.
Tapia .	tä'-pē-ä.
Tapti (R.)	tăp'-tē.
Taranto	tä-rän'-tō.
Tarapacá .	{ *pop.* tă-rá-păk'-à. *Sp.* tä''-rä-pä-kä'.
Tarascon .	tä-räs-kôn'.
Tarbes .	tärb.
Tárlac, *or* Tarlac .	tär'-läk.
Tarn	tärn.
Tarn-et-Garonne .	tärn'-ā-gä-rŏn'.
Tarnovo, *see* Tirnova	tär'-nō-vō.
Tarpeia	tär-pē'-yä.
Tarpeian	tär-pē'-yán.
Tarquin	tär'-kwĭn.
Tarquinio	tär-kwē'-nē-ō.
Tarragona	tär-rä-gō'-nä.
Tartar, *see* Tatar .	tär'-tär.
Tartarean	tär-tä'-rē-án.

Tartarin . . . . tär-tä-răṅ'.

Tartarus . . . . tär'-tä-rŭs.

Tartufe, or Tartuffe . . . tär'-tŭf. Fr. tär-tüf'.

Tashkend, or Taschkend . täsh-kĕnd'.

Tasmania . . . . . . tăz-mā'-nĭ-à. [täs'-sō.

Tasso, Torquato . . . . tōr-kwä'-tō tăs'-ō. It.

Tatar, see Tartar . . . '. tä'-tär.

Taubert . . . . tow'-bĕrt. [nĭts.

Tauchnitz . . . . . . towk'-nĭts. Ger. towch'-

Taughannock . . . . . tô-găn'-ŏk.

Tauler . . . . tow'-lĕr.

Taunton . . . . tänt'-ŏn.

Taunus . . . . tow'-nōōs.

Tauric . . . . tô'-rĭk.

Taurida . . . . tow'-rē-dä.

Taurus (Mt.) . . . . . tô'-rŭs.

Tavannes . . . . tä-vän'.

Tavoy . . . . tä-voi'.

Tayabas . . . . tī-ä'-bäs.

Taygetus . . . . tă-ĭj'-ĕ-tŭs.

Taytay . . . . tä'-ē-tä'-ē.

Tchad (L.), see Chad, Tsad chäd.

Tchaikowsky . . . . . chī-kŏv'-skĭ.

Tchernaya . . . . . . chär'-nĭ-ä.

Tchernigoff . . . . . . chĕr-nē-gŏf'.

Tchernyshevsky . . . . chĕr-nē-shĕf'-skē.

Tchu . . . . chōō.

Tchukchis . . . . . . chōōk'-chēz.

Tean, see Teian . . . . tē'-án.

Tebeth . . . . tĕ-bĕt'.

Teck . . . . tĕk.

Tecumseh . . . . . . tē-kŭm'-sĕ.

Te Deum . . . . tē dē'-ŭm.

Tegal, see Tagal . . . . tĕ-gäl'.

Tegea . . . . tē'-jē-ä.

Tegetthoff . . . . . . tā'-gĕt-hŏf.

Tegnér	tĕng-nầ̇'
Teheran, *or*	tĕh-ĕ-rän'.
Tehran	tĕh-rän'.
Tehri	tĕh-rē'.
Tehuantepec	tä-wän''-tä-pĕk'.
Teian, *see* Tean . . .	tē'-ȧn.
Te Igitur	tē ĭj'-ĭ-tĕr.
Teignmouth	tān'-mŭth.
Tejo, *Port. for* Tagus . .	tä'-zhōō.
Tekele, *see* Takala . .	tä-kä'-lĕ.
Telamon	tĕl'-ä-mŏn.
Tel, *or* Tell El Kebir . .	tĕl ĕl kĕb-ēr'.
Telemachus	tĕ-lĕm'-ȧ-kŭs.
Télémaque	tä-lä-mäk'.
Tellez	tĕl'-yĕth.
Teman	tē'-măn.
Tembuland	tĕm'-bōō-lănd.
Téméraire	tä-mä-râr'.
Temesvár	tĕm'-ĕsh-vär.
Tempe	tĕm'-pä, tĕm'-pē.
Tenasserim	tĕn-ăs'-ēr-ĭm.
Tencin	tŏṅ-săṅ'.
Tenebræ	tĕn'-ē-brē.
Tenedos	tĕn'-ē-dŏs.
Tenerife, *or*	tä-nä-rē'-fä.
Teneriffa, *or*	tä-nä-rēf'-fä.
Teneriffe	tĕn-ēr-ĭf'.
Teniers (David) . . .	tĕn'-yĕrz. *Fr.* tĕ-nē̦-âr'.
Teocalli	tē-ō-käl'-ē.
Tepic	tä-pēk'.
Teplitz, *see* Töplitz . . .	tĕp'-lĭts.
Terburg	tĕr'-bŭrċh.
Terceira	tĕr-sä'-rä.
Terek	tĕr-ĕk'. [nä.
Ternina, Fräulein Milka .	froi'-lĭn mēl'-kä tĕr-nē'-
Terpsichore	tĕrp-sĭk'-ō-rē.

Terpsichorean . . . . . tĕrp″-sĭ-kō-rē′-ȧn.

Terracina . . . . . . tĕr-rä-chē′-nä.

Terra del Fuego, *see* Tierra
del Fuego . . . . . } tĕr′-rä dĕl fū-ē′-gō.

Terre, La . . . . lä târ.

Terre Haute . . . . . tĕr′-ĕ hōt.   *Fr.* târ-ōt′.

Tertullian . . . . . . tĕr-tŭl′-ē-ȧn.

Teruel . . . . tä-rōō-ĕl′.

Tesla . . . . tĕz′-lä.

Tête-Noire . . . . . . tät-nwär′.

Tethys . . . . tē′-thĭs.

Tetuan . . . . tĕt-ōō-än′.

Teufelsdröckh, Herr . . hĕr toi′-fĕlz-drēk.

Teuton . . . . tū′-tŏn.

Teutonic . . . . tū-tŏn′-ĭk.

Teviot . . . . tĭv′-ĭ-ŏt, tē′-vĭ-ŏt.

Tewfik Pasha . . . . . { tū′-fĭk păsh-ô′, pȧ-shä′,
                        påsh′-ȧ.

Texcoco, *or* . . . . . tās-kō′-kō.

Tezcuco . . . . tās-kōō′-kō.

Thaba N'Chu, *or* Thaba }
Ntschu, *or* Thabanchu . } tä′-bänts-chōō.

Thaddeus . . . . . . thăd′-ē-ŭs, thăd-ē′-ŭs.

Thai, *see* T'hi, Tai . . . tī.

Thais . . . . thā′-ĭs.

Thaisa . . . . thā′-ĭs-ä.

Thalberg . . . . täl′-bĕrch.

Thales . . . . thā′-lēz.

Thalia . . . . thā-lī′-ȧ.

Thames, *Am.* . . . . . thāmz.

Thames, *Eng.* . . . . . tĕmz.

Thanatopsis . . . . . thăn-ȧ-tŏp′-sĭs.

Theætetus . . . . . . thē-ē-tē′-tŭs.

Théâtre Comique . . . tä-ätr′ kō-mēk′.

Théâtre Français, Le . . lĕ tä-ätr′ fräṅ-sä′.

Théâtre Italien . . . . tä-ätr′ ĕ-tä-lē-äṅ′.

Thebaid (The)	thē'-hā-ĭd, thē-hā'-ĭd
Thébaide, La	lä tä-bä-ēd'.
Thebais	thē-bā'-ĭs, thĕb'-ā-ĭs.
The Hague, see Den Haag, } La Haye, S'Graven Haage }	thē hāg.
Theiss, see Tisza, Hung. .	tīs.
Thekla	tĕk'-lä.
Themis	thē'-mĭs.
Themistocles	thē-mĭs'-tō-klēz.
Theobald (Lewis)	thē'-ō-bôld, tĭb'-ăld.
Theocritean	thē-ŏk''-rĭ-tē'-án.
Theocritus	thē-ŏk'-rĭ-tŭs.
Theodoric	thē-ŏd'-ō-rĭk.
Theodorus	thē-ō-dō'-rŭs.
Theodosia	thē-ō-dō'-sĭ-á, -shĭ-á.
Theodosius	{ thē-ō-dō'-sĭ-ŭs, thē-ō- dō'-shĭ-ŭs.
Theodota	thē-ŏd'-ō-tá.
Theodotus	thē-ŏd'-ō-tŭs.
Theophilus	thē-ŏf'-ĭl-ŭs.
Theotocupuli	tä-ō''-tō-kōō-pōō'-lē.
Theresa	tĕ-rē'-sä. Ger. tä-rā'-zä.
Thermidor	{ thĕr-mĭ-dôr'. Fr. tĕr- mē-dōr'.
Thermopylæ	thĕr-mŏp'-ĭ-lē.
Thersites	thĕr-sī'-tēz.
Theseion	thē-sē'-ŏn.
Theseum	thē-sē'-ŭm.
Theseus	thē'-sūs, thē'-sē-ŭs.
Thessalonica	thĕs''-sá-lō-nī'-kà.
Thetis	thē'-tĭs.
Theuriet	tĕr-ē-ā'.
T'hi, see Tai, Thai . . .	tī.
Thibaut	tē-bō'.
Thibet, see Tibet	tĭb'-ĕt, tĭ-bĕt'.
Thierri, or Thierry . . .	tĭ-ĕr'-ĭ. Fr. tē-âr-rē'.

Thierry, Amédée	ä-mä-dä′ tē-ȧr-rē′.
Thiers	tē-ȧr′.
Thing	*Dan.* tĭng.
Thisbe	thĭz′-bē.
Thogji Chumo (L.) . . .	thŏg′-jē chōō′-mō.
Tholuck	tō′-lŭk. *Ger.* tō′-lŏŏk.
Thomas, Ambroise . . .	äṅ-brwäz′ tō-mä′.
Thopas (Sir)	thō′-pȧs.
Thor	thôr, tôr.
Thoreau	thō′-rō, thō-rō′.
Thorvaldsen, *or often* Thor- ⎫	tōr′-väld-zĕn.
waldsen . . . . . ⎭	tôr′-wôld-sĕn.
Thoth	tōt, thŏth.
Thou	*Fr.* tōō.
Thouars	tōō-är′.
Thrace	thrās. *class.* thrā′-sē.
Thracian	thrā′-shĭ-ȧn.
Thrasybulus	thrăs-ĭ-bū′-lŭs.
Thrasymenes	thrā-sĭm′-ē-nēz.
Thrasymenus	thrā-sĭ-mē′-nŭs.
Throndhjem, *see* Trondhjem	trŏnd′-yĕm.
Thucydides	thū-sĭd′-ĭ-dēz.
Thugut	tōō′-gōōt.
Thule	thū′-lē.
Thun (L.)	tōōn.
Thurgau, *or*	tōōr′-gow.
Thurgovie, *Fr.*	tür-gō-vē′.
Thüringen	*Ger.* tü′-rĭng-ĕn.
Thuringia	thū-rĭn′-jĭ-ȧ.
Thuringian	thū-rĭn′-jĭ-ȧn.
Thurn	tōōrn.
Thursby	thĕrz′-bĭ.
Thyrsis	thĕr′-sĭs.
Tibet, *see* Thibet	tĭb′-ĕt, tĭ-bĕt′.
Tibullus	tĭ-bŭl′-ŭs.
Tiburzio	tē-bōōrt′-zē-ō.

Ticao	tē-kä′-ō.
Tichborne	tĭch′-bŭrn, tĭch′-bŭn.
Ticino	tē-chē′-nō.
Ticinus (R.)	tĭ-sī′-nŭs.
Ticinus	tĭs′-ĭn-ŭs, tĭ-sī′-nŭs.
Tieck	tēk.
Tien-Tsin, or Tientsin . .	tē-ĕn′-tsēn.
Tiepolo	tē-ā′-pō-lō.
Tierra del Fuego, see Terra del Fuego	tē-ĕr′-rä dĕl fwā′-gō.
Tiers État	tērz ā-tä′, tē-âr′-zā-tä′.
Tietjens, see Titiens . . .	tēt′-yĕns.
Tiflis	tĭf-lēs′.
Tighe (Mary)	tī.
Tiglath-Pileser	tĭg′-lăth-pĭl-ē′-zĕr.
Tigris	tī′-grĭs.
Tilghman	tĭl′-maṅ.
Tillemont	tē-yŭ-môṅ′.
Tilly	tĭl′-ĭ.
Tilsit	tĭl′-sĭt.
Timæus	tī-mē′-ŭs.
Timbuctoo, or Timbuktu .	tĭm-bŭk′-tōō.
Timon	tī′-mŏn.
Timor	tē-mōr′.
Timotheus	tĭ-mō′-thē-ŭs.
Timour, or Timur, or . .	tē-mōōr′.
Timur Bey, or	tē-mōōr′ bā.
Timur-Leng, see Tamerlane	tē-mōōr′-lĕng.
Tinavelly, see Tinnevelli .	tĭn-å-vĕl′-ĭ.
Tindale, see Tyndale . .	tĭn′-dål.
Ting-hae, or Ting-hai . .	tĭng-hī′.
Tinnevelli, see Tinavelly .	tĭn-ĕ-vĕl′-ĭ.
Tino (Gen.)	tē′-nō.
Tintagel	tĭn-tăj′-ĕl.
Tintern	tĭn′-tĕrn.

Tintoret, *or* . . . . . . tĭn'-tō-rĕt. [rĕt'-ō.

Tintoretto, Il . . . . Il tĭn tō rĕt' ō, tōn tō

Tioomen, *or* Tioumen, *see* ⎱ tē-ōō-mĕn'.
Tiumen, Tyumen . . . ⎰

Tipitapa (R.) . . . . . tē-pē-tä'-pä.

Tipperah . . . . tĭp'-ĕ-rä.

Tipperary . . . . . . tĭp-ĕ-rā'-rĭ.

Tippoo Sahib, *see* Tipu Saib tĭp-ōō' sä'-hĭb.

Tippoo Tib, *or* . . . . . tĭp-ōō' tĭb.

Tippoo Tip . . . . . . tĭp-ōō' tĭp.

Tipu Saib, *see* Tippoo Sahib tĭp-ōō' sä'-ĭb.

Tirhakah . . . . tĕr'-há-kä.

Tirhoot . . . . tĭr-hōōt'.

Tirnova, *see* Tarnovo . . tĕr'-nō-vä.

Tischendorf, von . . . . fŏn tĭsh'-ĕn-dôrf.

Tishri . . . . tĭsh'-rĭ.

Tisiphone . . . . . . tĭ-sĭf'-ō-nē.

Tissot . . . . tē-sō'.

Tisza, *see* Theiss . . . tĭs'-ä.

Titania . . . . tĭ-tā'-nĭ-á.

Titian, *see* Tiziano . . tĭsh'-án, tĭsh'-ē-án.

Titicaca (L.) . . . . tĭt-ē-kä'-kä. [yĕnz.

Titiens, *see* Tietjens . . tēt'-yĕns. *pop.* tĭsh'-

Tito Melema . . . . tē'-tō mä-lā'-mä.

Titurel . . . . . . tĭt'-ū-rĕl.

Tityrus . . . . . . tĭt'-ĭ-rŭs.

Tiumen, *see* Tioomen, Tyu- ⎱ tē-ōō-mĕn'.
men . . . . ⎰

Tivoli (Italy) . . . . tē'-vō-lē.

Tivoli (New York) . . tĭv'-ō-lĭ, tĭv-ō'-lē.

Tiziano Vecelli, *It.* . . . tēt-sē-ä'-nō vä-chĕl'-lē.

Tobago, *see* Tabago . . tō-bā'-gō, tō-bä'-gō.

Tobias . . . . tō-bī'-ás.

Tobit . . . . tō'-bĭt.

Tobolsk . . . . . . tō-bŏlsk'. [vēl'

Tocqueville, de . . . . . dŭ tŏk'-vĭl. *Fr.* dŭ tŏk-

Togoland . . . . tō'-gō-lănd.

Toison d'Or, La . . . . lä twä-zôṅ' dōr.

Tokaj, or Tokay . . . . tō-kä'. *Hung.* tō'-koi.

Tokio, Tokyo . . . . . tō'-kē̤-ō. *pop.* tō-kī'-ō.

Tolbooth . . . . tōl'-bōōth.

Toledo . . . . tō-lē'-dō. *Sp.* tō-lä'-dō.

Tolentino . . . . tō-lĕn-tē'-nō.

Tolstoy . . . . tŏl'-stoi.

Tommaseo . . . . . . tŏm-mä-sä'-ō.

Tomsk . . . . tŏmsk.

Tonga (Is.) . . . . . . tŏng'-gä.

Tongaland, *see* Tongoland tŏng'-gä-lănd.

Tong Chow, *see* Tung-chau tŏng-chow'.

Tongking, *see* Tungking, ⎫ tŏng-kĭng'.
   Tonquin . . . . . . ⎭

Tongoland, *see* Tongaland tŏng'-gō-lănd.

Tonkin, *see* Tonquin . . tŏn-kēn'.

Tonnay-Charente . . . tŏn-nä'-shä-rŏṅt'.

Tonquin, *see* Tonkin . . tŏn-kēn'.

Tonquin, *Fr.,* *see* Tongking tôṅ-kăṅ'.

Tonstall, *see* Tunstall . . tŭn'-stál.

Toorkistan, *see* Turkestan tōōr-kĭs-tän'.

Topeka . . . . tō-pē'-ká.

Topete (Admiral) . . . tō-pā'-tā.

Töplitz, *see* Teplitz . . . tĕp'-lĭts.

Toral . . . . tō-räl'.

Torcello . . . . tŏr-chĕl'-lō.

Tordesilhas, *Port.,* or . . tōr-dä-sēl'-yäs.

Tordesillas, *Sp.* . . . . tōr-dä-sēl'-yäs.

Torgau . . . . tŏr'-gow.

Torino, *see* Turin . . . *It.* tō-rē'-nō.

Torquato Tasso . . . tōr-kwä'-tō täs'-sō.

Torquay . . . . tôr-kē'.

Torquemada . . . . . tōr-kä-mä'-dä.

Torregiano, *see* Torrigiano tŏr-rä-jä'-nō.

Torres Vedras . . . . . tŏr'-rĕs vä'-dräs.

Torricelli	{ tŏr-rĭ-sĕl'-lĭ. *It.* tŏr-rē-chĕl'-lē.
Torricellian	{ tŏr-ĭ-sĕl'-ĭ-ȧn, tŏr-rĭ-chĕl'-ĭ-ȧn.
Torrigiano, *see* Torregiano	tŏr-rē-jä'-nō.
Torso Belvedere	tôr'-sō bĕl-vĕ-dēr'.
Tortola	tôr-tō'-lä.
Tortuga	tŏr-tōō'-gä.
Tortugas	tôr-tōō'-gäz.
Tosca, La	lä tŏs'-kä.
Toscanelli	tŏs-kä-nĕl'-lē.
Tostig	tŏs'-tĭg.
Totila, *or*	tŏt'-ĭ-lä.
Totilas	tŏt'-ĭ-lȧs.
Toulmin	tōl'-mĭn.
Toulmouche	tōōl-mōōsh'.
Toulon	tōō'-lŏn. *Fr.* tōō-lôṅ'.
Toulouse	tōō-lōōz'.
Touraine	tōō-rān'.
Tourcoing	tōōr-kwăṅ'.
Tour d'Auvergne . . .	tōōr dō-vârn'-yŭ.
Tour de Nesle	tōōr dŭ nāl.
Tourgee	tōōr-zhā'.
Tourgueneff, *or* Tourgué-nief, *see* Turgenieff . .	} tōōr'-gĕn-yĕf.
Tournai, *or* Tournay . .	tōōr-nā'.
Tourneur	tĕr'-nĕr, tōōr-nĕr'.
Tours	tōōr.
Tourville	tōōr-vĕl'.
Toussaint Louverture, *or* L'Ouverture	} tōō-săṅ' lōō-vĕr-tür'.
Toxophilus	tŏks-ŏf'-ĭ-lŭs.
Trachonitis	trăk-ō-nĭ'-tĭs.
Trafalgar (Battle of) . .	trăf-ăl-gär', trȧ-făl'-gär.
Trafalgar (Square) . . .	trȧ-făl'-gär.
Transbaikalia	trăns-bī-kä'-lĭ-ȧ.

Transkei	trăns-kē'.
Transvaal	trăns-väl'.
Trapani	trä'-pä-nē.
Trapezunt, *see* Trebizond .	trăp-ĕ-zo͞ont'.
Trasimenus (L.)	träs-ĭ-mē'-nŭs.
Tras-os-Montes, *see* Traz-os-Montes . . . . . . }	träs'-ōs-mŏn'-tĕs.
Trastevere	träs-tā'-vā-rĕ.
Trauttmansdorff	trowt'-mäns-dŏrf.
Travailleurs de la Mer . .	trä-vī-yĕr' dŭ lä mâr.
Travancore	trăv-án-kōr'.
Traviata, La	lä trä-vē-ä'-tä.
Traz-os-Montes, *see* Tras-os-Montes . . . . . . }	träz'-ōs-mŏn'-tĕs.
Trebbia	trĕb'-ē-ä.
Trebizond, *see* Trapezunt .	trĕb-ĭ-zŏnd'.
Tregelles	trĕ-gĕl'-ĭs.
Trek	trĕk.
Trelawney	trē-lô'-nĭ. [trĕm'-ŏnt.
Tremont	trĕ - mŏnt', trē - mŏnt',
Trench	trĕnsh.
Trenck, von	fŏn trĕngk.
Trevannion	trē-văn'-yŭn.
Trevelyan	trĕ-vĕl'-yán.
Trevena	trĕ-vē'-nä.
Treves	trēvz.
Trèves	trāv.
Trevi (Fountain of) . . .	trā'-vē.
Trevisa	trĕ-vē'-sä.
Treviso	trā-vē'-zō.
Trianon, Grand	grän trē-ä-nôṅ'.
Trianon, Petit	pẹ̆-t̬ē' trē-ä-nôṅ'.
Trichinopoli	trĭch''-ĭn-ŏp'-ō-lĭ.
Tricoteuses, Les	lä trē-kō-tĕz'.
Tricoupis, *see* Trikoupis .	trē-ko͞o'-pĭs.
Trier, *Ger.*	trēr.

Triest, *or*	trē-ĕst'.
Trieste	trē-ĕst'. *It.* trē-ĕs'-tā.
Trifanum	trī-fā'-nŭm.
Trikala, *or* Trikkala . .	trē'-kä-lä.
Trikoupis, *see* Tricoupis .	trē-kōō'-pĭs.
Trimalchio	trĭ-măl'-kĭ-ō. [däd'.
Trinidad	trĭn-ĭ-däd'. *Sp.* trē-nē-
Trinkitat.	trĭng-kĭ-tät'.
Tripoli	trĭp'-ō-lĭ.
Tripolitan	trĭ-pŏl'-ĭ-tàn.
Trisagion	trĭ-sā'-gĭ-ŏn.
Tristan und Isolde . . .	trĭs-tän' ŏŏnt ē-zŏl'-dŭ.
Triton	trī'-tŏn.
Triumvirate.	trī-ŭm'-vĭ-rāt.
Trivulzio	trē-vŏŏl'-dzē-ō.
Trocadero	trō-kä-dā'-rō.
Trocadéro	*Fr.* trō-kä-dā-rō'.
Trochu	trō-shü'.
Troilus	trō'-ĭl-ŭs.
Troilus and Cressida . .	trō'-ĭl-ŭs and krĕs'-ĭ-dá.
Trois Échelles	trwä zā-shĕl'.
Trois Mousquetaires . . .	trwä mōōs-kĕ-târ'.
Trollope	trŏl'-ŭp.
Trondhjem, *see* Thrond-hjem	trŏnd'-yĕm.
Trosachs, *or* Trossachs . .	trŏs'-äks.
Troubadours	trōō-bä-dŏŏrz'.
Trouvères	trōō-vârs'.
Trouville	trōō-vēl'.
Trovatore, Il	ēl trō-vä-tō'-rĕ.
Troyes	trwä.
Troyes, Chrestien de . . .	krā-tē-ĕn' dŭ trwä.
Troyon	trwä-yôṅ'.
Trujillo, *or* Truxillo . . .	trōō-ċhēl'-yō.
Tsad (L.), *see* Chad, Tchad, Tschad	tsäd.

Tsarevna, *see* Czarevna	tsär-ĕv′-nä.
Tsarina, *see* Czarina	tsär-ē′-nä.
Tsaritsin	tsär-ēt′-sēn.
Tsaritza	tsär-ĭt′-zä.
Tsarovitch, *see* Czarevitch	tsär′-ŏ-vĭch.
Tsarowitz, *see* Czarowitz	tsär′-ō-vĭts.
Tsarskoi Selo	tsär-skō′-ĭ sä′-lō.
Tschad, *see* Chad, Tchad, Tsad	chäd.
Tschaikovsky	tshī-kŏf′-skĭ.
Tsech, *see* Czech	chĕk.
Tseng	tsĕng.
Tsimshian, *or* Tsimsian	tsĭm-shē-än′.
Tsi-nan	tsē-nän′.
Tsing	tsēng.
Tsugaru Strait	tsōō-gä′-rōō strāt.
Tsushima (Is.)	tsōō-shē′-mä.
Tübingen	tü′-bĭng-ĕn.
Tuesday	tūz′-dā.
Tugela (R.)	tōō-gä′-lä.
Tugendbund	tōō′-gĕnt-bŏŏnt.
Tuh Chau	tōō′ chow′.
Tuileries	twē′-lĕ-rĭz. *Fr.* twēl-rē′.
Tula	tōō′-lä.
Tulle	tül.
Tullia	tŭl′-ĭ-à.
Tully-Veolan	tŭl′-ĭ-vē-ō′-län.
Tuncha	tŭn-chä′.
Tung-chau, *see* Tong Chow	tōōng-chow′.
Tungking, *see* Tongking	tōōng-kĭng′.
Tunis	tū′-nĭs.
Tunisie, *Fr.*	tü-nē-zē′.
Tunstall, *see* Tonstall	tŭn′-stàl.
Turcaret	tür-kä-rä′.
Turcoman, *see* Turkoman	tĕr′-kō-màn, tōōr-kō-män′.

Turenne, de	dŭ tū-rĕn'. *Fr.* dŭ tü-
Turgai, *or*	tōōr-gī'. [rĕn'.
Turgansk	tōōr-gänsk'.
Turgenieff, *see* Tourgueneff	tōōr'-gĕn-yĕf.
Turgot	tür-gō'.
Turin, *It.* Torino	tū'-rĭn, tū-rĭn'.
Turkestan, *or*	tōōr-kĕs-tän'.
Turkistan, *see* Toorkistan .	tōōr-kĭs-tän'. [män'.
Turkoman, *see* Turcoman .	tĕr'-kō-màn, tōōr-kō-
Turquino	tōōr-kē'-nō.
Tuskeegee	tŭs-kē'-gē.
Tussaud's	tü-sōz'.
Tutuila	tōō-tōō-e'-lä.
Tver	tvâr.
Twickenham	twĭk'-ĕn-àm.
Tybalt	tĭb'-àlt.
Tyburn	tī'-bĕrn.
Tychicus	tĭk'-ĭ-kŭs.
Tycoon	tī-kōōn'.
Tyndale, *see* Tindale . .	tĭn'-dàl.
Tynemouth	tīn'-mŭth, tĭn'-mŭth.
Typhon	tī'-fŏn, tī'-fŏn. [rōl'.
Tyrol	tĭr'-ŏl, tĭ-rōl'. *Ger.* tē-
Tyrolean	tĭr-ō'-lē-àn.
Tyrone	tĭ-rōn'.
Tyrrhene	tĭr'-ēn.
Tyrrhenian	tĭ-rē'-nĭ-àn.
Tyrtaean	tĭr-tē'-àn.
Tyrtaeus	tĭr-tē'-ŭs.
Tyrwhitt	tĕr'-ĭt.
Tyumen, *see* Tioomen, Tiu- men . . . . }	tē-ōō-mĕn'.
Tzigane, La	lä tsē-gän'.
Tzigany	tsĭg'-à-nĭ.

U

Uarda	ōō-är'-dä.
Ubangi	ōō-bäng'-gĕ.
Ubiquitarian	ū-bĭk''-wĭ-tā'-rĭ-ȧn.
Uccello	ōō-chĕl'-lō.
Uchatius	ōō-ċhä'-tĭ-ŏŏs.
Uclés	ōō-klās'.
Udaipur, see Oodeypoor .	ōō-dī-pōōr'.
Udall (Nicholas)	yōō'-dȧl.
Udine	ōō'-dē-nĕ.
Ufa	ōō'-fä.
Uffizzi	ōō-fēt'-sē.
Uganda	ōō-gän'-dä.
Uggione, see Oggione . .	ōōj-jō'-nĕ.
Ugolino della Gherardesca	{ ōō-gō-lē'-nō dĕl'-lä gä- rär-dĕs'-kä.
Uhland	ōō'-länt.
Uhlans, see Ulans	ōō'-länz.
Uhrich	Fr. ü-rēk'. Ger. ōō'-rĭċh.
Uitenhage	oi-tĕn-hä'-ċhĕ.
Uitlander	oit'-lăn-dĕr.
Ujiji	ōō-jē'-jē.
Ukerewe	ōō-kĕ-rē'-wĕ.
Ukraine	{ yū'-krān, ōō-krān', ū'- krä-ĭn.
Ulalume	ōō-lä-lōō'-mĭ.
Ulans, see Uhlans . . .	ōō'-länz.
Ulfilas, see Ulphilas . . .	ŭl'-fĭ-lȧs.
Ulleswater	ŭlz'-wô-tĕr.
Ulloa	ŏŏl-yō'-ä.
Ulm	ŏŏlm.
Ulphilas, see Ulfilas . . .	ŭl'-fĭ-lȧs.
Ulpian	ŭl'-pĭ-ȧn.
Ulpianus	ŭl-pĭ-ā'-nŭs.

Ulrica	ŭl'-rĭ-kȧ. *It.* ŏŏl-rē'-kä.
Ulrich	ŏŏl'-rĭċh.
Ulrici	ŏŏl-rēt'-sē.
Ulrike Eleonore	ŏŏl-rē'-kŭ ĕl"-ĕ-ō-nō'-rŭ.
Ultima Thule	ŭl'-tĭm-ȧ thū'-lē.
Ulundi	ōō-lōōn'-dē.
Ulungu, *see* Urungu . . .	ōō-lōōng'-gōō.
Ulwar, *see* Alwar . . .	ŭl'-wär.
Umar Khaiyàm, *see* Omar Khayyam	ōō'-mär kĭ-yäm'.
Umkomanzi	ŭm-kō-män'-sē.
Umritsir, *see* Amritsar . .	ŭm-rĭt'-sĕr.
Unalaska, *see* Oonalaska .	ōō'-nȧ-lăs'-kȧ, yū-nȧ-lăs'-kȧ.
Unao	ōō'-nȧ-ō. [rä.
Un Ballo in Maschera . .	ōōn bäl'-lō ēn mäs'-kä-
Uncas	ŭng'-kȧs.
Undine	ŭn-dēn'. *Ger.* ŏŏn-dē'-nŭ.
Unitarian	yū-nĭ-tā'-rĭ-ȧn.
Unter den Linden	ŏŏn'-tĕr dän lĭn'-dĕn.
Unterwalden	ŏŏn'-tĕr-väl"-dĕn.
Unyoro, *see* Nyoro . . .	ōō-nyō'-rō.
Upanishads	ōō-pȧ-nĭ-shădz'.
Upernavik, Upernivik . .	ōō-pĕr'-nȧ-vĭk.
Upolu (I.)	ōō-pō-lōō'.
Upsal	ŭp'-săl.
Upsala	ŭp-sä'-lä.
Ural	ōō'-rȧl, yū'-rȧl.
Urania	yū-rā'-nĭ-ȧ.
Uranus	yū'-rȧ-nŭs.
Urban	ŭr'-bȧn.
Urbano, Pietro	pē-ä'-trō ōōr-bä'-nō.
Urbanus	ŭr-bā'-nŭs.
Urbino	ōōr-bē'-nō.
Urfé, Honoré d'	ō-nō-rā' dür-fā'.
Uri	ōō'-rĭ.

Uriah . . . . ū-rī′-ä.
Uriel . . . . yū′-ı̆-l̇.
Urraca . . . . ŏŏr-rä′-kä.
Ursa Minor . . . . ẽr′-så mī′-nŭr.
Ursula . . . . ŭr′-sū-lá.
Ursule Mirouët . . . . ür-sül′ mē-rōō-ā′.
Ursulines . . . . ŭr′-sū-lĭnz, ŭr′-sū-lĭnz.
Uruguay . . . . { yū′-rōō-gwā. *Sp.* ōō-
                        { rōō-gwī′.
Urundi . . . . ōō-rōōn′-dē.
Urungu, *see* Ulungu . . . ōō-rōōng′-gōō.
Ushant . . . . ŭsh′-ȧnt.
Usuramo . . . . ōō-sōō-rä′-mō.
Utah . . . . yū′-tä, yū′-tô.
Ute . . . . yūt.
Utopian . . . . yū-tō′-pĭ-ȧn.
Utraquist . . . . yū′-trȧ-kwĭst.
Utrecht . . . . yū-trĕkt. *D.* ü′-trĕċht.
Uvaroff . . . . ōō-vä′-rŏf.
Uzés . . . . ü-zās′.
Uzziah . . . . ŭz-zī′-ä.
Uzziel . . . . ŭz-zī′-ĕl, ŭz′-zĭ-ĕl.

V

Vaal (R.) . . . . väl.
Vaca, Cabeza, *or* Cabeça de kä-bā′-thä dā vä′-kä.
Vaccai, *or* Vaccaj . . . . väk-kä′-ē.
Vacuna . . . . vä-kū′-nä.
Vaga . . . . vä′-gä.
Vailima . . . . vī-lä′-mĕ.
Vaillant . . . . vä-yäṅ′.
Valais . . . . vä-lä′.
Val d'Arno . . . . väl där′-nō.
Valdenses, *see* Waldenses . väl-dĕn′-sēz.

Valdensian, *see* Waldensian väl-děn'-sĭ-án.
Valdés . . . . *Sp.* bäl-däs'.
Valdivia . . . . väl-dē'-vē-ä.
Valée . . . . vä-lā'.
Valence . . . . *Fr.* vä-lŏn̄s'. [lěn'-thē-ä.
Valencia . . . . vă-lěn'-shĭ-ạ. *Sp.* vä-
Valenciennes . . . . . { vă"-lŏn-sĭ-ěnz', *or* vä"-
                         { lěn-sĭ-ěnz'. *Fr.* vä-
Valens . . . . vä'-lěnz. [lŏn-sē̶-ěn'.
Valentine . . . . . . văl'-ěn-tīn.
Valentinian . . . . . väl-ěn-tĭn'-ĭ-án.
Valentinois . . . . . väl-ŏn̄-tē-nwä'.
Valera . . . . *Sp.* bä-lā'-rä.
Valère . . . . vä-lâr'.
Valeria . . . . vă-lē'-rĭ-ạ.
Val-es-Dunes . . . . väl-ā-dün'.
Valhalla . . . . văl-hăl'-ạ.
Valjean, Jean . . . . zhän̄ väl-zhän̄'.
Valkyrie . . . . väl-kē-rē'.
Valladolid . . . . . . { väl-lá-dō-lĭd'. *Sp.* bäl-
                         { yä-dō-lēd'.
Vallandigham . . . . văl-lăn'-dĭ-gám.
Vallière, La . . . . . lä vä-lē̶-âr'.
Vallombrosa . . . . väl-lŏ̃m-brō'-zä.
Valmy . . . . väl-mē'.
Valois . . . . väl-wä'.
Valparaiso . . . . . { väl-pà-rī'-zō, väl-pä-rī'-
                        { zō. *Sp.* bäl-pä-rä'̶-ē-sō.
Valtellina, *or* . . . . väl-těl-lē'-nä.
Val Tellina, *or* . . . . väl těl-lē'-nä.
Valtelline . . . . . . väl-těl-lēn'.
Vámbéry . . . . väm'-bā-rē.
Van . . . . vän.
Van Artevelde . . . . vän är'-tě-věl-dě.
Vanbrugh . . . . . . văn-brōō'.
Vandalic . . . . văn-dăl'-ĭk.

Vandamme	vän-däm'.
Van der Meulen	văn dĕr mē'-lĕn.
Vandyck, Vandyke . . .	văn-dīk'.
Van Eyck	văn īk'.
Van Hoeck	văn hōōk'.
Vanhomerigh, or	văn-ŭm'-ĕr-Ĭ.
Vanhomrigh	văn-ŭm'-rĭ.
Vanloo	Fr. vän-lō'.
Vannucchi	vän-nŏŏk'-kē.
Vannucci (Pietro) . . .	vän-nŏŏch'-ē.
Van Ostade	văn ŏs'-tä-dĕ.
Vanozza	vä-nǫt'-sä.
Van Schaick	văn skoik'.
Varanger Fjord, see Wa- ranger Fjord	vä-räng'-gĕr fē-ọrd'.
Varangians	vā-răn'-jĭ-ȧnz.
Varennes	vä-rĕn'.
Varicourt	vä-rē-kōōr'.
Vari, or Varj dei Porcari .	vä'-rē dä'-ē pōr-kä'-rē.
Varna	vär'-nä.
Varnhagen von Ense . .	värn'-hä-gĕn fǫn ĕn'-sŭ.
Varus	vā''-rŭs.
Varzin	vär'-tsīn.
Vasa	vä'-sä.
Vasari	vä-sä'-rē.
Vasco da Gama	väs'-kō dä gä'-mä.
Vashti	văsh'-tĭ.
Vasili	vä-sē'-lē.
Vasquez de Coronado, see Vazquez	Sp. bäs-kĕth' dä kō-rō- nä'-dō.
Vassy	vä-sē.
Vathek	văth'-ĕk.
Vatican	văt'-ĭ-kăn.
Vauban, de	dŭ vō-bäṅ'.
Vaucelles	vō-sĕl .
Vaucluse	vō-klüz'.

Vaucouleurs	vō-kōō-lĕr'.
Vaud, Pays de	pā-ē' dŭ vō'.
Vaudois	vō-dwä'.
Vaudreuil	vō-drē'-yŭ.
Vaughan	vôn, vō'-ȧn.
Vauvenargues	vōv-närg'.
Vaux	vôks. *Fr.* vō.
Vazquez de Coronado, *see* ⎰	*Sp.* bäth-kĕth' dä kō-rō-
Vasquez de Coronado . ⎱	nä'-dō.
Ve-Adar	vē'-ä-där.
Vecchio	vĕk'-ē-ō.
Vecellio	vä-chĕl'-ē-ō.
Veda	vä'-dȧ, vē'-dȧ.
Vedic	vä'-dĭk, vē'-dĭk.
Vega	vē'-gȧ. *Sp.* vä'-gä.
Vega Real	vä'-gä rä-äl'.
Vehmgerichte	fām'-gä-rĭch''-tŭ.
Veile	vī'-lĕ.
Veit	fīt.
Veitch (John)	vēch.
Velalcazar, *see* Benalcazar	bä-läl-kä'-thär.
Velasco	*Sp.* bä-läs'-kō.
Velasquez, *or*	*Sp.* bä-läs'-kĕth.
Velazquez	*Sp.* bä-läth'-kĕth.
Velletri	vĕl-lä'-trē.
Vendeans	vĕn-dē'-ȧnz.
Vendée, La	lä vŏn-dā'.
Vendémiaire	vŏn-dä-mē-ạr'. [däd'.
Vendidad	bĕn-dē-däd', vĕn-dē-
Vendôme, de	dŭ vôn-dōm'.
Venern (L.), *see* Wenern .	vä'-nĕrn.
Venetia	vĕ-nē'-shĭ-ȧ.
Venezia	vä-näd'-zē-ä.
Veneziano	vä-näd''-zē-ä'-nō.
Venezuela	⎰ vĕn-ĕz-wē'-lȧ. *Sp.* vä- ⎱ ĕth-wä'-lä.

Venlo, *or* Venloo	věn-lō'.
Ventersburg	fĕn'-tĕrs-bŭrċh.
Venters' Spruit	fĕn'-tĕrs sproit.
Ventose	vŏṅ-tōz'. [r̄ē.
Venus Anadyomene . . .	vē'-nŭs ăn''-à-dĭ-ŏm'-ĕ-
Venus Callipyge	vē'-nŭs kă-lĭp'-ĭ-jē.
Vera Cruz	{ vā'-rä krōōz, *commonly* věr'-à krōōz. *Sp.* vā'-
Veragua, *or*	vā-rä'-gwä. [rä krōōth'.
Veraguas	vā-rä'-gwäs.
Verazzano, *see* Verrazano .	vā-rät-sä'-nō.
Verboeckhoven	fĕr-bōōk'-hō-fĕn.
Vercelli	věr-chĕl'-lē.
Vercingetorix	věr-sĭn-jĕt'-ō-rĭks.
Verd (Cape), *or* Verde . .	vĕrd.
Verdi	vâr'-dē.
Verdun	věr-dŭṅ'.
Vereshagin, *or*	vē-rē-shä'-gĕn.
Verestchagin, Vassili . .	{ *Russ.* vä-sē'-lē vä''-rä- shä-gēn'.
Vergennes	věr-jĕnz'. *Fr.* věr-zhĕn'.
Vergil, *see* Virgil	věr'-jĭl.
Vergniaud	věrn-yē-ō'.
Verhaeren, Émile	ā-mēl' věr-hä'-rĕn.
Verlaine	věr-lān'.
Vermandois	věr-mŏṅ-dwä'.
Verne, Jules	zhül věrn.
Vernet	věr-nā'.
Verneuil	věr-nē'-yŭ.
Vernéville	věr-nā-vēl'.
Verocchio, *see* Verrocchio .	vā-rŏk'-kē-ō.
Verona	vā-rō'-nä.
Veronese (Paul)	vā-rō-nā'-zĕ.
Veronese (adj.)	věr-ō-nēz', věr-ō-nēs'.
Veronica	věr-ō-nĭ'-kà, vĕ-rŏn'-ĭ-
Verrazani, *see* Verrazzano .	věr-räd-zä'-nē. [kà.

Verrazano, or   vĕr-räd-zä'-nō,

Verrazzano . . . . . . vĕr-rät-sä'-nō.

Verrocchio, *see* Verocchio . vä-rŏk'-kē-ō.

Versailles . . . . . . vĕr-sālz'. *Fr.* vĕr-sä'-yŭ.

Vertumnus . . . . . . vĕr-tŭm'-nŭs.

Verulam (Lord) . . . . vĕr'-ōō-lăm.

Verus . . . . vē'-rŭs.

Verviers . . . . . . vĕr-vē͟-ā'.

Vervins . . . . . . vĕr-văṅ'.

Vesalius . . . . . . vĕ-sā'-lĭ-ŭs.

Vespasian . . . . . . vĕs-pā'-zhĭ-ạn. [chē.

Vespucci, Amerigo . . . ä-mä-rē'-gō vĕs-pŏŏt'-

Vespucius, Americus, *Lat.* ȧ-mĕ'-rĭ-kŭs vĕs-pū'-

Veszprém, *or* . . . . . vĕs'-präm. [shĭ-ŭs.

Veszprim . . . . . . vĕs'-prĭm.

Vet (R.) . . . . . . fĕt.

Vevay, *or* Vevey . . . . vĕv-ā'.

Via Æmilia . . . . . . vī'-ä ē-mĭl'-ĭ-ä. [äp'-pē-ä.

Via Appia . . . . . . vī'-ä äp'-pĭ-ä. *It.* vē'-ä

Via Aurelia . . . . . . vī'-ä ô-rē'-lĭ-ä.

Via Dolorosa . . . . . vī'-ä dŏl-ō-rō'-sä.

Via Mala . . . . . . vē'-ä mä'-lä.

Viardot-Garcia . . . . . vē͟-är-dō'-gär-thē'-ä.

Viareggio . . . . . . vē-ä-rĕd'-jō.

Via Salaria . . . . . . vī'-ä să-lā'-rĭ-ä.

Viatka, *see* Vyatka . . . vē-ät'-kä.

Viaud . . . . vē͟-ō'.

Via Valeria . . . . . . vī'-ä vă-lē'-rĭ-ä.

Vibert . . . . vē-bâr'.

Viborg, *see* Wiborg . . . vē'-bŏrg. [zä.

Vicenza . . . . vĕ-sĕn'-zä. *It.* vē-chĕn'-

Vichy . . . . { commonly, vĭsh'-ĭ. *Fr.*
                          {   vē-shē'.

Victor Amadeus . . . . vĭk'-tôr ăm-ȧ-dē'-ŭs.

Victor-Perrin . . . . . vēk-tōr'-pĕ-räṅ'.

Vidal (Pierre) . . . . . vē-däl'.

Vielé-Griffln . . . . . vē-lā'-grē-făṅ'.

Vienna . . . . vĭ-ĕn'-á.

Vieques . . . . vē-ā'-kās.

Viersen . . . . fēr'-sĕn.

Vierzehnheiligen . . . . fēr''-tsān-hī'-lĭg-ĕn.

Vieuxtemps . . . . . . vē‿ĕ̤-tŏṅ'.

Vigan . . . . vē-gän'.

Vigée-Lebrun . . . . . vē-zhā'-lĕ-brŭṅ'.

Vigero, (Marquis) di . . . dē vē-jā'-rō.

Vignola . . . . vēn-yō'-lä.

Vignon, Claude . . . . klōd vēn-yôṅ'.

Vigny, de . . . . . . dŭ vēn-yē'.

Vigo . . . . vē'-gō.

Viljoen . . . . fĭl-yōͬn'.

Villa Albani . . . . . vēl'-lä äl-bä'-nē.   [nē.

Villa Aldobrandini . . . vēl'-lä äl''-dō-brän-dē'-

Villa Borghese . . . . . vēl'-lä bōr-gā'-zĕ.

Villafranca, *It.*, *see* Ville- ⎫
franche . . . . . . ⎬ vēl-lä-fräng'-kä.

Villa Ludovisi . . . . . vēl'-lä lōō-dō-vē'-zē.

Villa Medici . . . . . . vēl'-lä mā'-dē-chē.

Villamil (Admiral) . . . vēl-yä-mēl'.

Villa Nazionale . . . . vēl'-lä nät''-zē-ō-nä'-lĕ.

Villani . . . . vēl-lä'-nē.

Villa Real . . . . . . vēl'-lä rā-äl'.

Villari . . . . vēl'-lä-rē.

Villars . . . . vē-lär'.

Villebois-Mareuil . . . . vēl-bwä'-mä-rē̃'-yŭ.

Villefranche, *see* Villa- ⎫
franca, *It.* . . . . . ⎬ vēl-fräṅsh'.

Villehardouin . . . . . vēl-är-dōō-ăṅ'.

Villemain . . . . . . vēl-măṅ'.

Villeroi . . . . vēl-rwä'.

Villers-Cotterets . . . . vē-lār'-kŏt-rā'.

Villiers . . . . vĭl'-yĕrz.

Villiers de l'Isle Adam . . vē-yä' dŭ lēl ä-däṅ'.

Villon	vēl-lôn'.
Vilna, *see* Wilna	vĭl'-nä.
Vimeure	vē-mēr'.
Vincennes	vĭn-sĕnz'. *Fr.* văn-sĕn'.
Vincent de Paul	{ vĭn'-sĕnt dŭ pôl'. *Fr.* { văn-sŏn' dŭ pōl'.
Vincentio	vĭn-sĕn'-shĭ-ō.
Vinci, da	{ dä vĭn'-chē, dä vĭn'-chĭ, { vēn'-chē.
Vingt Ans Après	văn tän zä-prä'.
Viola	vī'-ō-lä. *It.* vē-ō'-lä.
Viollet-le-Duc	vē-ō-lä' lĕ dük'.
Vionville	vē-ôn-vēl'.
Viotti	vē-ŏt'-tē.
Vira	vē'-rä.
Virchow	vĕr'-chow. *Ger.* fēr'-ċhō.
Virgil, *see* Vergil	vĕr'-jĭl.
Virginia	vĕr-jĭn'-ĭ-ạ̇.
Virginian	vĕr-jĭn'-ĭ-ạn.
Virginie	vĕr-zhē-nē'.
Virgo	vĕr'-gō.
Visayan	vē-sä'-yän.
Viscaya, *see* Vizcaya . .	*Sp.* bēs-kä'-yä.
Vischer, Peter	pä'-tĕr fĭsh'-ĕr.
Visconti	vĭs-kŏn'-tē.
Visigoths	vĭz'-ĭ-gŏths.
Vistula	vĭs'-tū-lä, vĭst'-yū-lä.
Vita Nuova	vē'-tä nōō-ō'-vä.
Vitebsk	vē-tĕbsk'.
Vitellius	vĭ-tĕl'-ĭ-ŭs.
Viterbo	vē-tĕr'-bō.
Viti Levu	vē'-tē lĕv'-ōō.
Vitoria, *or* Vittoria . . .	vē-tō'-rē-ȧ.
Vittoria Colonna	vē-tō'-rē-ä kō-lŏn'-nä.
Vizagapatam	vē-zä"-gȧ-pȧ-täm'.
Vizcaya, *see* Viscaya . . .	*Sp.* bīth-kä'-yä.

Vizier	vĭz'-yĕr, vĭz-ēr', vĭz'-yᵃr
Vladikavkaz	vlä''-dē-käv-käz'.
Vladimir, *see* Wladimir .	{ vlăd'-ē-mēr. *Russ. and Polish*, vlä-dē'-mĭr.
Vladislav, *see* Wladislaw .	vlä'-dĭs-läv.
Vladivostok	vlä''-dē-vŏs-tŏk'.
Vogelweide	fō'-gĕl-vī''-dŭ.
Vogesen, *see* Vosges . . .	vō-gä'-zĕn.
Vogler, Abbé, *or* Abt . .	äb-ā' (äpt) fō'-glĕr.
Vogüé	vō-gü-ā'.
Voiture	vwä-tür'.
Volapük	vō-lä-pük'.
Volga	vŏl'-gä.
Volksraad	fŏlks'-rät.
Vologda	vō-lŏg-dä'.
Volscian	vŏl'-shĭ-ạn.
Volsung	vŏl'-sŭng.
Volta	vŏl'-tä.
Voltaire	vŏl-târ'.
Voltas (Cape)	vŏl'-täs.
Volterra, da	dä vŏl-tĕr'-rä.
Voltigeurs	vŏl-tē-zhĕr'.
Vondel	vŏn'-dĕl.
Voortrekkers	fōr'-trĕk-ĕrs.
Vorarlberg	fōr'-ärl-bĕrĉh.
Voronetz, *or*	vō-rō'-nĕts.
Voronezh	vō-rō'-nĕzh.
Vosges, *see* Vogesen . . .	vōzh.
Vrede	frä'-dĕ.
Vryburg	vrī'-bŭrg. *D.* frī'-bŭrĉh.
Vryheid	*D.* frī'-hīt.
Vuelta Abajo	*Sp.* bōō-äl'-tä ä-bä'-ĉhō.
Vuelta Arriva	*Sp.* bōō-äl'-tä är-rē'-bä.
Vulgate	vŭl'-gāt.
Vyatka, *see* Viatka . . .	vē-ät'-kä.

W

Wacace	wä-shä'-shā.
Wace	wäs.
Wacht am Rhein, Die . .	dē väċht äm rĭn.
Wadai	wä-dĭ'.
Waddington	{ wŏd'-ĭng-tŭn. *Fr.* vä-dăṅ-tôṅ'.
Wadelai	wä-dĕ-lĭ'.
Wady-Halfa	wä'-dē-häl'-fä.
Wagner	wăg'-nĕr. *Ger.* väg'-nĕr.
Wagnerian	wăg-nē'-rĭ-án.
Wagram	vä'-gräm.
Wahabee	wä-hä'-bē.
Wahabis, *see* Wahhabees .	wä-hä'-bēz.
Wahaby	wä-hä'-bē.
Wahhabees, *see* Wahabis .	wä-hä'-bēz.
Wahlstatt (Battle of) . .	väl'-stät.
Wahnfried	vän'-frēt. [hĭt.
Wahrheit, Dichtung und .	dĭċh'-tŏong ŏont vär'-
Wahsatch	wô-säċh'.
Wailuku	wī-lōō'-kōō.
Wakkerstroom	väk'-ĕrs-strōm.
Walachia, *see* Wallachia .	wŏ-lä'-kĭ-á.
Walcheren	väl'-ċhĕr-ĕn.
Waldeck	wŏl'-dĕk. *Ger.* väl'-dĕk.
Waldemar	{ wŏl'-dĕ-mär. *Ger.* väl'-dĕ-mär.
Walden	wôl'-dĕn.
Waldenses, *see* Valdenses .	wäl-dĕn'-sēz.
Waldensian, *see* Valdensian	wäl-dĕn'-sĭ-án.
Waldersee	väl'-dĕr-zā.
Waldshut	välts'-hōōt.
Waldstätter, Die Vier . .	dē fēr vält'-stĕt-ĕr.
Waldstein	vält'-stīn.

Walewski	vä-lĕv'-skē.
Walhalla	väl-häl'-lä.
Walküre, Die	dē väl'-kü-rŭ.
Walkyrie	wäl-kĭr'-ĭ.
Wallachia, see Walachia .	wŏl-lä'-kĭ-à.
Wallenstein	{ wŏl'-ĕn-stīn. Ger. väl'- lĕn-stīn.
Waller	wŏl'-ẽr.
Wallis, Ger. for Valais . .	väl'-lĭs.
Walpurgis	väl-pōōr'-gēs.
Walsingham	wôl'-sĭng-àm.
Waltham (U. S.)	wäl'-thàm.
Waltham (Eng.)	wôlt'-hàm, wŏlt'-hàm.
Walther von der Vogelweide	{ väl'-tẽr fŏn dẽr fō'-gĕl- vī''-dŭ.
Wamba	wäm'-bä.
Wan-chow-fu	wän'-chow'-fōō'.
Waranger Fjord, see Var- anger Fjord	} vä-räng'-gẽr fē̩-ôrd'.
Warbeck	wôr'-bĕk.
Wartburg	värt'-bōōrċh.
Warwick	wŏr'-ĭk.
Warwickshire	wŏr'-ĭk-shĭr.
Wasulu	wä-sōō'-lōō. [lō'.
Waterloo	wô-tẽr-lōō'. D. vä-tẽr-
Watervliet	wô-tẽr-vlēt'.
Watteau	{ commonly, wŏt'-tō. Fr. vä-tō'.
Wauchope (Gen.) . . .	wô'-chŏp.
Waugh (Edwin)	wô.
Waukegan	wô-kē'-gàn.
Waukesha	wô'-kĕ-shô.
Wavre	vävr'.
Wawre	vä'-vrĕ.
Weald (The)	wēld.
Wealden	wēld'-n.

Weber, von	fŏn vā′-bĕr.
Weeninx	wā′-nĭnks.
Wei-ho	wā′-ē-hō.
Weimar	vī′-mär.
Weissenburg	vĭs′-sĕn-bōōrch.
Weissnicht-wo	vĭs′-nĭcht-vō.
Wellesley	wĕlz′-lĭ.
Wemyss (Castle) . . .	wēms, wē′-mĭs.
Wenceslaus	{ wĕn′-sĕs-lôs, wĕn′-sĕs-lás.
Wen-chau	wĕn-chow′.
Wenern, *see* Venern . . .	vā′-nĕrn.
Wenzel	vĕnt′-zĕl.
Wepener	vā′-pā-nĕr.
Werder, von	fŏn vĕr′-dĕr.
Werdt, *see* Werth . . .	vĕrt.
Werra	vĕr′-rä.
Werth, *see* Werdt . . .	vĕrt.
Werther	wĕr′-tĕr. *Ger.* vĕr′-tĕr.
Wesel	vā′-zĕl.
Weser	wē′-zĕr. *Ger.* vā′-zĕr.
Wesleyan	wĕs′-lĭ-àn.
Westmoreland	wĕst′-mŏr-lănd.
Westphalia	wĕst-fā′-lĭ-à.
Weyden, van der	vän dĕr vī′-dĕn.
Weyler	wā′-lĕr.
Weyman	wī′-màn.
Weymouth	wā′-mŭth.
Whewell	hū′-ĕl.
Whitefield, *or* Whitfield .	hwĭt′-fēld.
Whydah, *see* Widah . . .	hwĭd′-ä.
Wiborg, *see* Viborg . . .	vē′-bôrg.
Wickliffe, *see* Wyclif . .	wĭk′-lĭf.
Widah, *see* Whydah . . .	wĭd′-ä.
Widdin, *or* Widin . . .	vĭd′-ĭn.
Widukind, *see* Wittekind .	wĭd′-ōō-kĭnd.

Wied . . . . vēt.

Wieland . . . . wē'-länd. *Ger.* vē'-länt.

Wien . . . . vēn.   äv'-skĭ.

Wieniawski . . . . . vē-nē-ŏf'-skē, vē-yä-nē-

Wiertz . . . . vērts.

Wiesbaden . . . . . vēs'-bä-dĕn.

Wigan . . . . wĭg'-àn.

Wildenbruch . . . . vĭl'-dĕn-brōōċh.

Wilhelm . . . . vĭl'-hĕlm.

Wilhelmine . . . . . *Ger.* vĭl-hĕl-mē'-nŭ.

Wilhelmj . . . . . . vĭl-hĕl'-mĭ.   [yär''-ŭ.

Wilhelm Meister's Lehrjahre vĭl'-hĕlm mīs'-tĕrz' lâr'-

Wilkesbarre, *or* Wilkes-Barre . . . . . . } wĭlks'-băr-ĭ.

Willamette . . . . . . wel-ä'-mĕt.

Wilna, *see* Vilna . . . vĭl'-nä.

Wiltshire . . . . . . wĭlt'-shĭr.   [fĕn.

Wimpffen (de) . . . . . *Fr.* vän-fŏn'. *Ger.* vĭmp'-

Winburg . . . . vĭn'-bŭrċh.

Winckelmann . . . . { wĭngk'-ĕl-män. *Ger.* vĭngk'-ĕl-män.

Windischgrätz . . . . . vĭn'-dĭsh-gräts.

Windsor . . . . wĭnd'-zôr.

Winkelried, von . . . . { fŏn wĭng'-kĕl-rēd. *Ger.* vĭng'-kĕl-rĕt.

Winnepesaukee, *or* Winnipiseogee . . . . . } wĭn''-ē-pē-sô'-kē.

Witenagemot . . . . . wĭt'-ĕ-nä-gĕ-mōt''.

Wittekind, *see* Wittikind . wĭt'-ĕ-kĭnd.

Wittelsbach . . . . . vĭt'-tĕls-bäċh.

Wittenberg . . . . . { wĭt'-ĕn-bĕrg. *Ger.* vĭt'-tĕn-bĕrċh.

Wittgenstein . . . . . vĭt'-gĕn-stīn.

Wittikind, *see* Wittekind . wĭt'-ĭ-kĭnd.

Wittstock . . . . . . vĭt'-stŏck.

Wituland . . . . . . vē'-tōō-länd.

Witwaterstrand . . . . vĭt-vä'-tĕrs-rănd.

Wladimir, see Vladimir . { vlăd'-ē-mēr. *Russ.* vlä-
                           { dē'-mĭr.

Wladislaw, see Vladislav . vlä'-dĭs-läv.

Woden . . . . wō'-dĕn.

Woerth, see Wörth . . . vĕrt.

Wöhler . . . . vē'-lĕr.

Wohlgemuth . . . . . vōl'-gā-mo͞ot.

Wolf, von, see Wolff . . . *Ger.* vŏlf.

Wolfenbüttel . . . . . vŏlf'-ĕn-büt''-ĕl.

Wolff, see Wolf . . . . *Ger.* vŏlf.

Wolfgang . . . . . . vŏlf'-gäng.   [bäch.

Wolfram von Eschenbach . vŏlf'-räm fŏn ĕsh'-ĕn-

Wolgast . . . . vōl'-gäst.

Wolkonsky . . . . . . vŏl-kŏn'-skē.

Wollaston . . . . . . wo͝ol'-ăs-tŭn.

Wollstonecraft . . . . . wo͝ol'-stŭn-krăft.

Wolowski . . . . . . vŏ-lŏv'-skē.

Wolseley . . . . wo͝olz'-lĭ.

Wolsey . . . . wo͝ol'-zĭ.

Wolzogen . . . . . . vōl-tsō'-gĕn.

Woochang, see Wuchan . wo͞o-chăng'.

Woolwich . . . . . . wo͝ol'-ĭch, wo͝ol'-ĭj.

Worcester (Eng.) . . . . wo͝os'-tĕr, wo͞os'-tĕr.

Worcester (U. S.) . . . . wo͞os'-tĕr, wo͝os'-tĕr.

Worcestershire . . . . . wo͞os'- *or* wo͞os'-tĕr-shĭr.

Worms . . . . vŏrms.

Wörth, see Woerth . . . vĕrt.

Wouverman, *or* Wouwerman wow'-vĕr-măn.

Wouvermans . . . . . wow'-vĕr-mănz.   [ĕl.

Wrangel . . . . räng'-gĕl. *Ger.* vräng'-

Wrede . . . . vrā'-dĕ.

Wren . . . . rĕn.

Wriothesley . . . . . . rŏts'-lĭ, rŏt'-ĕs-lĭ.

Wuchan, see Woochang . wo͞o-chăn'.

Wun . . . . wo͞on.

Wundt . . . . vŏŏnt.

Wurmser . , , , , , , vŏŏrm′٭zĕr

Wurtemberg . . . . . vür′-tĕm-bĕrċh.

Würzburg . . . . . . vürts′-bŏŏrċh.

Wyandot, *or* Wyandotte . wī-ăn-dŏt′.

Wyborg, *see* Viborg . . . vē′-bôrg.

Wycherley . . . . . . wĭch′-ĕr-lĭ.

Wyclif, *or* Wycliffe, *see* } wĭk′-lĭf.
 Wickliffe . . . . . .

Wyoming . . . . . . wî-ō′-mĭng.

Wyss . . . . vĭs.

Wythe . . . . wĭth.

X

Xalapa, *see* Jalapa . . . ċhä-lä′-pä.

Xalisco, *see* Jalisco . . . ċhä-lēs′-kō.

Xanadu . . . . zăn-à-dŏŏ′.

Xanthippe, *see* Xantippe . zăn-thĭp′-ē.

Xanthippus . . . . . zăn-thĭp′-ŭs.

Xanthus . . . . zăn′-thŭs.

Xantippe, *see* Xanthippe . zăn-tĭp′-ē.

Xauxa, *see* Jauja . . . . ‘how′-ċhä.

Xaver . . . . ksä′-vĕr.

Xavier . . . . { zăv′-ĭ-ĕr. *Fr.* ksăv-ē-ā′.
 { *Sp.* ċhä-vē-âr′.

Xenia . . . . zē′-nĭ-à.

Xenocrates . . . . . . zĕn-ŏk′-rà-tēz.

Xenophon . . . . . . zĕn′-ō-fŏn.

Xeres, *see* Jeres, *or* . . . ‘hā′-rĕs.

Xerez, *see* Jerez . . . . ‘hā-rĕth′.

Xerez de la Frontera, *see* } ‘hā-rĕth′ dā lä frŏn-tā′-
 Jerez de la Frontera . . } rä.

Xerona, *see* Gerona, Jerona ‘hā-rō′-nä.

Xerxes . . . . zĕrk′-sēz.

Ximena, *see* Jimena . . . ċhē-měn'-ä.
Ximenez, *see* Jimenez . . { zǐm-ē'-něz. *Sp.* chē-
                        { měn'-āth.   [dä.
Ximenez de Quesada . . . ċhē-měn'-āth dā kā-sä'-
Xingú . . . . shēn-gōō'.
Xorullo, *see* Jorullo . . . ċhō-rōōl'-yō.
Xucar, *see* Jucar . . . . 'hōō'-cär.
Xury . . . . zū'-rǐ.

Y

Yafa, *see* Jaffa, Japho . . yä'-fä.
Yahoo . . . . yä-hōō'.
Yahveh . . . . yä-vä'.
Yaka . . . . yä'-kä.
Yakama, *or* . . . . . . yăk'-ä-má.
Yakima . . . . yăk'-ǐ-má.
Yakonan . . . . yă'-kō-năn.
Yakootsk, *see* Yakutsk, Ja- } yä-kōōtsk'.
  kutsk . . . . . . }
Yakub Khan . . . . . yä-kōōb' khän.
Yakutsk, *see* Yakootsk, Ja- } yä-kōōtsk'.
  kootsk . . . . . . }
Yalu . . . . yä-lōō'.
Yana . . . . yä'-nä.
Yang-chau . . . . . . yäng'-chow.
Yang-tse-Kiang, *or* . . . yäng"-tsē-kǐ-äng'.
Yang-tze . . . . yäng'-tsě.
Yanina, *see* Janina . . . yä'-nē-nä.
Yankton . . . . yăngk'-tŭn.
Yap, *see* Guap . . . . . yäp.
Yaqui . . . . yä'-kē.
Yare . . . . yâr.
Yarkand, *or* . . . . . . yär-känd'.
Yarkend . . . . yär-kěnd'.

19

Yarmouth	yär' müth.
Yaroslaff, *or*	yä-rō-släv'.
Yaroslavl, *see* Jaroslaff . .	yä-rō-slä'-vl.
Yarra-Yarra	yä'-rä-yä'-rä.
Yarriba, *see* Yoruba . . .	yä'-rē-bä.
Yauco	yä'-ōō-kō.
Yeats	yāts.
Yeddo, *see* Jeddo, *or* . .	yĕd'-dō.
Yedo	yĕd'-ō.
Yeisk, *see* Jeisk	yā'-Isk.
Yekaterinburg, *see* Ekater-inburg	yĕ-kä''-tĕ-rēn-bōōrg'.
Yekaterinodar	yĕ-kä''-tĕ-rē-nō-där'.
Yekaterinoslaff	yĕ-kä''-tĕ-rē-nō-släv'.
Yelisavetpol, *or* Yelizavetpol	yĕ-lē''-zä-vĕt-pŏl'-yĕ.
Yellala	yĕl-lä'-lä.
Yemen	yĕm'-ĕn.
Yenesei	yĕn-ē-sā'-ē.
Yenikale (Strait) . . .	yĕn-ē-kä'-lä.
Yeniseisk	yĕn-ē-sā'-Isk.
Yesso, *see* Jesso, *or* . . .	yĕs'-sō.
Yezo	yĕz'-ō, yā'-zō.
Yggdrasil, *see* Igdrasil . .	Ig'-drä-sIl.
Yguerne, *see* Igerna, Igerne	I-gĕrn'.
Y-lin	ē-lēn'.
Yoga	yō'-gà.
Yohchau	yō-chow'.
Yokohama	yō-kō-hä'-mä.
Yonge	yŭng.
Yonkers	yŏngk'-ērz.
Yonne	yŏn.
Yorick	yŏr'-Ik. [bōōrċh.
York von Wartenburg . .	yōrk fŏn vär'-tĕn-
Yoruba, *see* Yarriba . . .	yō'-rōō-bä.
Yosemite	yō-sĕm'-It-ē.
Youghal	yôl, yô'-hál.

Youghiogheny . . . . . yŏ-hŏ-gā'-nĭ.
Youmans . . . . yōō'-mánz.
Ypres . . . . ēpr.
Ypsilanti . . . . ĭp-sĭl-ăn'-tĭ.
Yriarte, see Iriarte . . . ē-rē-är'-tā.
Ysaye . . . . ĕ-zĭ'-yŭ.
Yseult, see Isolde, Iseult . ē-sēlt', ē-sōōlt'.
Ysoude, see Isoude . . . ē-sōōd'.
Yssel . . . . ĭ'-sĕl.
Yucatan . . . . yōō-kä-tän'.
Yuen . . . . yōō-ĕn'.
Yukon . . . . yōō'-kŏn.
Yungchau . . . . . . yōōng-chow'.
Yunnan-fu . . . . . . yŭn-nän'-fōō'.
Yuste . . . . yōōs'-tā.
Yvetot, Le Roi d' . . . . lĕ rwä dēv-tō'.

Z

Zaandam, see Saardam . . zän-dăm'.
Zaardam, see Saardam . . zär-dăm'.
Zab . . . . zäb.
Zabulon . . . . zăb'-yū-lŏn.   [tā'-käs.
Zacatecas . . . . tzä-kä-tā'-käs,   sä-kä-
Zacchaeus, or Zaccheus . zăk-ē'-ŭs.
Zachariah . . . . . . zăk-á-rī'-á.
Zadkiel . . . . zăd'-kĭ-ĕl.
Zadok . . . . zā'-dŏk.
Zahara, see Sahara, Sahhra zä-hä'-rä, zä'-há-rä.
Zahn . . . . tsän.
Zama . . . . zā'-má.
Zamacoïs . . . . thä-mä-kō'-ĭs.
Zambales . . . . { zäm-bä'-lĕs. Sp. thäm-
                        { bä'-lĕs.   [bē'-zĭ.
Zambesi . . . . zäm-bā'-zĕ, pop. zăm-

Zambezia	zăm-bē'-zhĭ-à.
Zamboanga	zăm-bo-ang'-gà.
Zamora	thä-mō'-rä.
Zampieri	dzäm-pē-ä'-rē.
Zand (R.)	zănt.
Zanguebar	zäng-gä-bär'.
Zankoff	zän'-kŏf.
Zanoni	ză-nō'-nĭ.
Zante	zän'-tĕ, zän'-tä.
Zanzibar	zän-zĭ-bär'.
Zaragoza, see Saragossa	thä-rä-gō'-thä.
Zarathushtra	ză-rà-thōōsh'-trá.
Zauberflöte, Die	dē tsow'-bĕr-flē''-tŭ.
Zaylah, see Zeila	zā'-lä.
Zealand, see Zeeland . .	zē'-lănd.
Zebedee	zĕb'-ĕ-dē.
Zebú, see Cebú	zē-bōō'. Sp. thä-bōō'.
Zebulon, or	zĕb'-ū-lŏn.
Zebulun	zĕb'-ū-lŭn.
Zechariah	zĕk-á-rī'-à.
Zedekiah	zĕd-ĕ-kī'-ä.
Zeeland, see Zealand . .	zā'-länt.
Zeila, see Zaylah	zā'-lä.
Zela	zē'-lä.
Zelaya	sä-lä'-yä.
Zenaida	zē-nä'-ĭ-dä.
Zeno	zē'-nō.
Zenobia	zĕ-nō'-bĭ-à.
Zenta	zĕn'-tä.
Zephaniah	zĕf-à-nī'-à.
Zephon	zē'-fŏn.
Zephyrus	zĕf'-ĭ-rŭs.
Zerafshan	zĕr-äf-shän'.
Zerin	zĕ-rēn'.
Zerlina	dzĕr-lē'-nà.
Zermatt	zĕr-mät', tsĕr-mät'.

Zerubbabel, *see* Zorobabel	zĕ-rŭb′-á-bĕl.
Zeus	zūs.
Zeuxis	zūk′-sĭs.
Zhitomir, *see* Jitomir . .	zhĭt-ōm′-ēr.
Zidon, *see* Sidon	zī′-dŏn.
Ziethen, *or* Zieten . . .	tsē′-tĕn.
Zimri	zĭm′-rī.
Zincali	zĭng′-kä-lē.
Zingara	dzēn-gä′-rä.
Zingarelli	dzēn-gä-rĕl′-lē.
Zion, *see* Sion	zī′-ŏn.
Zipporah	zĭp′-ō-rä.
Ziska, *or*	zĭs′-kä.
Zižka	zhĭzh′-kä.
Znaim	tsnīm.
Zobeidah, *or* Zobeide . .	zō-bā′-dä, zō-bī′-dä, zō-bī-dā.
Zola	zō′-lä. *Fr.* zō-lä′.
Zollverein	tsōl′-fā-rīn.
Zombor	zŏm′-bŏr.
Zophiei	zō′-fĭ-ĕl.
Zorilla, *see* Zorrilla . . .	thōr-rēl′-yä.
Zorn	tsôrn.
Zorndorf	tsôrn′-dôrf.
Zoroaster	zō-rō-ăs′-tĕr.
Zorobabel, *see* Zerubbabel	zō-rŏb′-ä-bĕl.
Zorrilla, *see* Zorilla . . .	thōr-rēl′-yä.
Zorrilla y Moral	thōr-ēl′-yä ē mō-räl′.
Zouave	zōō-äv′.
Zoutpansberg	zowt′-päns-bĕrċh.
Zschokke	tshŏk′-kŭ.
Zuccarelli	dzōŏk-kä-rĕl′-lē.
Zug	zōōg. *Ger.* tsōōċh. [zä.
Zuider Zee, *see* Zuyder Zee	zī′-dĕr zē. *D.* zoi′-dĕr
Zuinglius	zwĭng′-glĭ-ŭs.
Zukertort	tsōŏk′-ĕr-tōrt.

Zuleika	nū-lā'-kā
Zulu	zōō'-lōō.
Zululand	zōō'-lōō-länd.
Zumpt	tsōōmpt.
Zuñi	zōōn'-yē.
Zunz	tsōōnts.
Zurbaran	thōōr-bä-rän'.
Zurich, *or*	zōō'-rĭk.
Zürich, *Ger.*	tsü'-rĭch.
Zurlinden (Gen.) . . .	zür-lĭn-dĕn'.
Zütphen	züt'-fĕn. [zā.
Zuyder Zee, *see* Zuider Zee	zī'-dĕr zē. *D.* zoi'-dĕr
Zwartkopjesfontein . .	zvärt'-kŏp-yĕs-fŏn'-tin.
Zweibrücken	tsvī'-brük-ĕn.
Zwickau	tsvĭk'-ow.
Zwingle	zwĭng'-gl. [lē.
Zwingli	zwĭng'-glē. *Ger.* tsvĭng'-
Zwolle	zwŏl'-lĕ.

Printed in the United States
127725LV00004B/15/A